T0329463

James Monroe
Diplomatic Correspondence

JAMES MONROE
DIPLOMATIC CORRESPONDENCE
PARIS, 1794–1796

Edited and Annotation
by
Brett F. Woods, Ph.D.

Algora Publishing
New York

Library of Congress Cataloging-in-Publication Data

Names: Monroe, James, 1758-1831. | Woods, Brett F., editor.
Title: James Monroe : diplomatic correspondence, Paris, 1794–1796 / edited
  and annotation by Brett F. Woods.
Description: New York : Algora Publishing, [2021] | Includes
  bibliographical references and index. | Summary: "This is the first time
  an editor has focused principally on James Monroe's written
  communications while serving as President George Washington's minister
  to France, a delicate and grueling service. The letters will interest a
  general readership as well as students of military, diplomatic, or
  political history; explanatory notes place the letters in their
  particular historical, political, or conceptual context"— Provided by
  publisher.
Identifiers: LCCN 2021042633 (print) | LCCN 2021042634 (ebook) | ISBN
  9781628944525 (trade paperback) | ISBN 9781628944532 (hardback) | ISBN
  9781628944549 (pdf)
Subjects: LCSH: Monroe, James, 1758–1831— Correspondence. | Diplomatic and
  consular service, American— France. | Ambassadors— United
  States— Correspondence. | United States— Foreign
  relations— 1783–1815— Sources. | United States— Foreign
  relations— France. | France— Foreign relations— United States.
Classification: LCC E372.A4 2021 (print) | LCC E372.A4 (ebook) | DDC
  973.324— dc23
LC record available at https://lccn.loc.gov/2021042633
LC ebook record available at https://lccn.loc.gov/2021042634

TABLE OF CONTENTS

EDITOR'S NOTE

> Upon mature reflection, therefore, it appeared that I had but one alternative, which was to remain where I was, and proceed in the functions of my office, notwithstanding the embarrassments to which I might be personally subjected, or to retire, and in retiring, to do it tranquilly, without explaining my motives for it; or by explaining them, denounce the administration to the public....Besides, it seemed probable that my retreat at that moment, in either mode, might have some influence in inducing the French government to adopt a system of policy toward us, which it was equally my duty and my wish to prevent. I resolved, therefore, to stand firm at my post....

> - James Monroe[1]

James Monroe was born in Westmoreland County, Virginia, to Spence and Elizabeth Monroe, on April 28, 1758. Like George Washington, Thomas Jefferson, and James Madison, Monroe came from a slaveholding plantation family. Unlike them, his parents were not in Virginia's upper stratum. However, he had a prosperous uncle who made it possible for him to attend a leading preparatory academy. Monroe entered the College of William and Mary in 1774, but he became absorbed in the American Revolution and left in February 1776 to serve as a lieutenant in a Virginia regiment. In December of that year, Monroe took part in the Battle of Trenton, receiving a near-fatal wound while leading an advance party that silenced a battery of cannons threatening Washington's offensive. He was promoted to captain in recognition of his heroism and saw further combat in the Battles of Brandywine, Germantown, and Monmouth.

Monroe returned to Virginia to form a new regiment in 1778, but that proved not to be feasible. Making the best of his situation, he read law under

---

[1] Hamilton 1900, 476.

Thomas Jefferson and became the older man's friend and disciple. Jefferson introduced Monroe to James Madison, with whom he formed a more tenuous bond. Monroe's long political career began with his election to the Virginia legislature in 1782. The following year, he was named to the Congress of the Confederation, the successor body to the Continental Congress. He served for three years, taking a particular interest in the development of the area between the Allegheny Mountains and the Mississippi River. In 1790, the Virginia legislature appointed Monroe to the U.S. Senate. He became that body's leading Republican, joining with his House counterpart, James Madison, in opposition to Alexander Hamilton's financial program.[2]

In 1794, President Washington named Monroe minister to France. In assigning a prominent Republican to the post, Washington sought to address French concerns that the United States was siding against France in its war with Great Britain. Shortly after arriving in Paris, Monroe gave a speech to a French governmental body in which he spoke of the parallels between the American and French revolutions, declaring that the two nations were united in their respect for "the equal and unalienable rights of men."[3] To be sure, Monroe's tenure in France was far from easy. Revolutionary France was an unstable place and the new minister had to tread carefully. His mission was to uphold President Washington's policy of strict neutrality toward Britain and France while still assuring the French that America was not favoring Britain. This task became harder when France learned that the United States had signed a new accord, the Jay Treaty, with Great Britain. When France asked Monroe to spell out its details, Monroe found himself unable to comply: Jay had refused to send him a copy of the document. Although Monroe told the French that the treaty did not alter their agreements, the French were convinced that the United States now favored Britain. Washington came to believe that Monroe had been excessively outspoken in support of revolutionary France and, in the end, U.S. domestic politics doomed Monroe's tenure in Paris. The Federalists blamed Monroe for deteriorating relations with France, and Washington recalled him.[4]

I have long believed that the most comprehensive portrait of the founding fathers can be seen in their personal letters and journal entries. James Monroe is no exception, and those he wrote during his time as minister to France, through many of the more critical episodes in both American and French history, are of singular importance. This is particularly true when one

---

[2] Greenstein 2009, 276.
[3] Ibid.
[4] Preston 2020.

reviews them in their entirety, as opposed to selected excerpts that, if indeed they have been reprinted at all, have been available only in part, reduced to quotes that, in many instances, have been repeatedly cited as the foundation for a particular interpretation of events or conclusion of fact. Accordingly, in this selection of a comparatively few letters from the voluminous body of Monroe correspondence that has been preserved, my intention is twofold: first, to add to the body of literature exploring early American consular history; and secondly, and perhaps more importantly, to provide an additional glimpse into the character and thought processes of Monroe the diplomat.

The source material for this compilation is primarily *The Writings of James Monroe 1794–1796*, vols. 2 and 3, edited by Stanislaus Murray Hamilton, which was published in 1899-1900 by G.P. Putnam's Sons. These volumes include Monroe's Paris correspondence, while my efforts have been directed to refining the presentation, addressing selected formatting and spelling issues, identifying the addressees, many of whom have been lost to history, and, where indicated, providing explanatory notes so as to assist the reader in placing the correspondence in its particular historical, political, or conceptual context. This methodology, I believe, serves to make the material more palatable to a general readership, as well as to students of military, diplomatic, or political history.

Any errors in selection, fact, transcription, and interpretation remain, of course, my responsibility.

Brett F. Woods, Ph.D.

INITIAL INSTRUCTIONS FROM THE SECRETARY OF STATE TO JAMES MONROE

Philadelphia, June 10, 1794

Col. James Monroe, Minister Plenipotentiary to the Republic of France:

You have been nominated as the successor of Mr. Gouverneur Morris, in the office of Minister Plenipotentiary of the United States of America to the Republic of France, from a confidence, that, while you keep steadily in view the necessity of rendering yourself acceptable to that government, you will maintain the self-respect due to our own. In doing the one and the other of these things, your own prudence and understanding must be the guides, after first possessing yourself of the real sentiments of the Executive relative to the French nation.

The President has been an early and decided friend of the French Revolution, and whatever reason there may have been, under our ignorance of facts and policy, to suspend an opinion upon some of its important transactions, yet is he immutable in his wishes for its accomplishment, incapable of assenting to the right of any foreign prince to meddle with its interior arrangements, and persuaded that success will attend their efforts, and particularly that union among themselves is an impregnable barrier against external assaults.

How the French Government, when it shall be no longer attacked by foreign arms, will ultimately settle, is a point not yet reduced to any absolutely certain expectation. The gradation of public opinion from the beginning of the new order of things to this day, and the fluctuation and mutual destruction of parties, forbid a minister of a foreign country to attach himself to any as such, and dictate to him not to incline to any set of men, farther than they appear to go with the sense of the nation.

2. When the Executive Provisory Council recalled Mr. Genet, they expressed a determination to render it a matter of eclat, as you have seen, and at the same time disavowed all his offensive acts. Nothing having been forwarded to us relative to Mr. Morris which requires a disavowal, you will, if you should be interrogated as to any particular feeling prevailing with the President upon the occasion, refer to the letter from the Secretary of State to Mr. Fauchet, as explanatory of the President's promptness to comply with their demand.[5]

3. From Mr. Genet and Mr. Fauchet we have uniformly learned that France did not desire us to depart from neutrality, and it would have been unwise to have asked us to do otherwise. For our ports are open to her prizes, while they are shut to those of Great Britain; and supplies of grain could not be forwarded to France with so much certainty, were we at war, as they can even now, notwithstanding the British instructions; and as they may be, if the demands to be made upon Great Britain should succeed. We have therefore pursued neutrality with faithfulness; we have paid more of our debt to France than was absolutely due, as the Secretary of the Treasury asserts; and we should have paid more, if the state of our affairs did not require us to be prepared with funds for the possible event of war. We mean to continue the same line of conduct in future; and, to remove all jealousy with respect to Mr. Jay's mission to London, you may say that he is positively forbidden to weaken the engagements between this country and France.

It is not improbable that you will be obliged to encounter, on this head, suspicions of various kinds. But you may declare the motives of that mission to be, to obtain immediate compensation for our plundered property, and restitution of the posts. You may intimate, by way of argument, but without ascribing it to the government, that if war should be necessary, the affections of the people of the United States towards it would be better secured by a manifestation that every step had been taken to avoid it, and that the British nation would be divided when they found that we had been forced into it. This may be briefly touched upon, as the path of prudence with respect to ourselves; and also with respect to France, since we are unable to give her aids of men or money. To this matter you cannot be too attentive, and you

---

[5] Jean Antoine Joseph Fauchet was the French minister to the United States. Succeeding Edmond Charles Genet in 1794, he would suffer under Genet's shadow. Fauchet was given a dual mission. He was directed to repair damages with the administration, while helping the French Party. While he would face resistance in the administration and commercial centers, the support among the common people was strong. (Dawson 2000, 12)

will be Amply justified in repelling with firmness any imputation of the most distant intention to sacrifice our connection with France to any connection with England. You may back your assertions by a late determination of the President to have it signified abroad, that he is averse to admit into his public room, which is free to all the world besides, any Frenchmen who are obnoxious to the French republic, although perhaps it may again happen sometimes, as many go thither whose names and characters are utterly unknown.

It is very probable that our country will become the asylum for most of the French who expatriate themselves from their native land. Our laws have never yet made a distinction of persons, nor is such a distinction very easy. Hence some of those, who are perhaps attainted in France, have thrown themselves upon the protection of the United States. This will not, as it surely ought not, to be misinterpreted into any estrangement from the French cause. You will explain this, whensoever it shall be necessary.

The stories of Genet, as to the royal medallions, &c., being exhibited in the President's room, and his giving private audiences to certain French emigres, are notoriously untrue; and if any insinuation should be made with regard to M. de la Fayette, so directly as indispensably to call for an answer, it may be affirmed, that notwithstanding the warmest friendship contracted between the President and him, in the most interesting scenes, notwithstanding the obligation of the United States to him, and the old pre-possessions in his favour, the efforts of the President in his behalf have never gone further than to express a wish to the authority which held him in confinement, that he should be liberated. But even thus much need not be said without the most invincible necessity; because, though what has been done is justified by every consideration, it is never well to give notice of it to those whose extreme sensibility may see impropriety where none exists.

4. If we may judge from what has been at different times uttered by Mr. Fauchet, he will represent the existence of two parties here irreconcilable to each other, one republican and friendly to the French Revolution; the other monarchical, aristocratic, Britannic, and Anti-Gallican; that a majority of the House of Representatives, the people, and the President, are in the first class, and a majority of the Senate in the second. If this intelligence should be used in order to inspire a distrust of our good will to France, you will industriously obviate such an effect; and, if a fair occasion should present itself, you may hint, that the most effectual means of obtaining from the United States what is desired by France, will be by a plain and candid application to the government, and not by those insidious operations on the people, which Genet endeavoured to carry on.

5. The information which we possess of France, before and in the early stages of the Revolution, must be considerably changed at this day. You will therefore transmit to us, as soon as possible, an account of the navy, the agriculture, and the commerce of France. It is desirable, too, to know upon what footing religion really stands. These, however, are general objects. But we are particularly concerned to understand the true state of the different sects of politics. Are there any of the old friends to the ancient regime remaining? Are any new friends created by the course of things? Are the Brissotines extinguished?[6] Are the Dantonists overwhelmed?[7] Is Robespierre's party firmly fixed? Is he capable, from talents and personal fortitude, to direct the storm?[8] Is his character free from imputation as to money? Is he friendly to the United States? How is the executive power administered now? What new accession of authority may have lately accrued to the Committee of Public Safety? What relation do the twelve Commissions of Administration, which have been lately established, bear to that committee? What is the true cause of the various changes which have lately taken place, by one party rising upon the ruins of another? What assurance can be had, that any party can so long maintain itself as to promise stability to the government? Are the people sincerely affectionate to their present government; or are they restrained by the terror of the revolutionary tribunal, or by the danger of having their country dismembered by the coalesced princes? What species of executive will probably be at last adopted? What characters bid fair to take the helm of affairs after the great destruction and banishment of able men? These, and many other questions of the same nature, ought to be solved, to enable us to see things in a true light. For, without doubting the solidity of the French cause, we ought not to be unprepared for any event. If, there-

---

[6] The war prone Brissotines believed a limited war would test the loyalty of Louis XVI and help consolidate the gains of the revolution. (Gardner 2002, 36)

[7] The Dantonists sought the overthrow of the Jacobin monopoly of power in France. (Thompson 1945, 500).

[8] Maximilien François Marie Isidore de Robespierre was a lawyer, deputy in the Estates General (and National Assembly), deputy in the National Convention, and member of the Committee of Public Safety. During one of the most dramatic and stormy debates imaginable in a parliamentary body, with the lives of the bitter antagonists literally at stake, the National Convention, by acclamation, ordered, even as he tried to speak, his arrest and removal from the floor of the Convention. When the Commune of Paris (the municipal authorities) ordered that no prison in Paris accept Robespierre and ordered several other members expelled at the same time, the National Convention, learning that Maximilien was free, voted to place him *dehors de loi* (execution without trial after identification). Robespierre was captured at the Hôtel de Ville by forces of the Convention at about 2:00 A.M. on the morning of 28 July, identified at a special session of the Revolutionary Tribunal, and executed at about 7:30 P.M. the same day. Thus ended the career of the man who probably best personifies the multifaceted character of the French Revolution from May 1789 until his death in July 1794. (Beach 1987, 908)

fore, any very momentous turn should arise in French affairs, upon which the conduct of our government may depend, you need not hesitate at the expense of an advice boat, if no other satisfactory opportunity should occur. But it is the wish of the President, that, at the end of every week, you commit to a letter the transactions of it, and embrace every proper conveyance, by duplicates, and in great cases even by triplicates.

6. Should you be interrogated about the Treaty of Commerce, you may reply that it has never been proposed to us by Mr. Fauchet. As to any thing else concerning it, you will express yourself not to be instructed, it being a subject to be negotiated with the government here.

7. In like manner, if a Treaty of Alliance, or the execution of the guarantee of the French Islands by force of arms, should be propounded, you will refer the Republic of France to this side of the water. In short, it is expected, with a sure reliance on your discretion, that you will not commit the United States by any specific declarations, except where you are particularly instructed, and except, too, in giving testimony of our attachment to their cause.

8. There is reason to believe that the embargo, when it was first laid, excited some uneasy sensations in the breast of the French minister. For it so happened, that, at the moment before its operation, pretty considerable shipments of flour were made to the British West Indies; and a snow [a two-masted sailing vessel] called La Camille, laden with flour for France, was arrested near Newcastle, on the Delaware, after she had quitted the port of Philadelphia. But you know enough of the history of this business to declare, that the embargo was levelled against Great Britain, and was made general, merely because, if it had been partial against her, it would have amounted to a cause of war; and, also, that it was not continued, merely because it was reputed to be injurious to France. My letters to Mr. Fauchet will explain the case of La Camille, and all his complaints about the embargo.

Should our embargo be brought up, the way will be easy for our complaint against the embargo of Bordeaux; at any rate, you will remonstrate against it, and urge satisfaction for the sufferers. You will receive all the papers which have come into the Department of State relative to these matters; and you will, besides, open a correspondence with the captains and persons interested at Bordeaux, in order to obtain more accurate information.

But you will go farther and insist upon compensation for the captures and spoliations of our property, and injuries to the persons of our citizens, by French cruisers. Mr. Fauchet has been applied to, and promises to co-operate for the obtaining of satisfaction. The dilatoriness with which business is transacted in France will, if not curtailed in the adjustment of these cases, produce infinite mischief to our merchants. This must be firmly represented to the French republic: and you may find a season for intimating how unfortunate it would be, if so respectable a body as that of our merchants should relax in their zeal for the French cause, from irritation at their losses. The papers on this head are a statement of French cases, Mr. Fauchet's letter to me, and the documents themselves.

9. You know the extreme distress in which the inhabitants of St. Domingo came hither after the disasters of the Cape. Private charity, and especially at Baltimore, most liberally contributed to their support. The Congress at length advanced 15,000 dollars, with a view of reimbursement from France. This subject has been broken to Mr. Fauchet here, and he appears to have been roused at the idea of supporting, by French money, French aristocrats and democrats indiscriminately. Both he and his nation ought to be satisfied, that in the cause of humanity, oppressed by poverty, political opinions have nothing to do: add to this, that none but the really indigent received a farthing. It was the duty of the French republic to relieve their colonists labouring under a penury so produced; and, as it would have been too late to wait for their approbation before the payments were decreed, it will not be deemed an offensive disposal of French money, that we now make a claim for repayment. If Mr. Fauchet has power upon the subject, an attempt will be made for a settlement with him here; but, that being very doubtful, it will forward the retribution by discussing it in Europe.

10. You will be also charged with the demands of several American citizens for bills of exchange drawn in the French West Indies on France. The report of a committee of them, Mr. Fauchet's letter, and the vouchers winch you will carry, leave no doubt of your success. But, if there should be any difficulty, do not fail to communicate it to the Secretary of State instantaneously. The sooner, therefore, the affair is entered upon, the better.

11. It is important that no public character of the United States should be in France, which is not acceptable. You will inquire into the consuls, and inform how they are approved, and whether they be deserving. Although the President will avoid as much as possible to appoint any obnoxious person consul, it may happen otherwise, and must be considered as accidental. Mr. Alexander Duvernah goes for Paris in the quality of Vice-Consul; and Mr. Fauchet said that he had nothing to object to him.

Consulates are established in every port of France, where they are conceived useful. But perhaps you may find it advisable to mark out some other places for such officers.

12. It is recommended that no business of consequence be carried on, verbally or in writing, but in your own language. The Minister of each nation has a right to use his national tongue; and few men can confide in their exact-

ness, when they do business in a foreign one. But great care is necessary in the choice of interpreters, when they are to be resorted to.

13. It is a practice of great utility to note down every conversation of consequence which you hold, immediately after retirement; and the Executive will expect to receive copies of what shall be thus written.

14. A communication with our other ministers in Europe, under proper caution, may be advantageous.

15. Let nothing depend upon verbal communications, which can be carried on in writing.

16. To conclude: You go. Sir, to France, to strengthen our friendship with that country, and you are well acquainted with the line of freedom and ease to which you may advance, without betraying the dignity of the United States. You will shew our confidence in the French Republic, without betraying the most remote mark of undue complaisance. You will let it be seen, that in case of war with any nation on earth, we shall consider France as our first and natural ally. You may dwell upon the sense which we entertain of past services, and for the more recent interposition in our behalf with the Dey of Algiers. Among the great events with which the world is now teeming, there may be an opening for France to become instrumental in securing to us the free navigation of the Mississippi. Spain may perhaps negotiate a peace, separate from Great Britain, with France. If she does, the Mississippi may be acquired through this channel, especially if you contrive to have our mediation in any manner solicited.

With every wish for your welfare, and an honourable issue to your ministry,

I am, Sir, Your most obedient Servant,
Edm. Randolph

SELECTED CORRESPONDENCE

1794

To Thomas Jefferson, Baltimore, June 17, 1794

Dear Sir,—The urgent pressure of the Executive for my immediate departure has deprived me of the pleasure of seeing you before I sailed. I sincerely regret this for many reasons, but we cannot control impossibilities. Will you forward me a cypher, and letters for your friends remaining in Paris to the care of Mr. R. as soon as possible.[9] They may probably reach Paris as soon as I shall. I beg you to add whatever occurs which may be useful where I am going to the cause in which I am engaged, or to myself in advocating it. Being well acquainted with the theatre on which I am to act it will be much in your power to give me hints of that kind which may be serviceable.

---

[9] Edmund Randolph. As Secretary of State (1794–1795), Randolph faced many of the same challenges that his predecessor, Thomas Jefferson, had attempted to address. Randolph managed the settlement of the Citizen Genêt Affair. He prompted a resumption of talks with Spain and assisted in the negotiations of the 1795 Treaty of San Lorenzo, which opened the Mississippi River to U.S. navigation and fixed the boundaries between Spanish possessions and the United States. Randolph attempted to continue Jefferson's efforts to maintain close relations with France and minimize Alexander Hamilton's influence over President Washington. However, Washington chose to endorse Jay's Treaty, an agreement that secured commercial ties with Great Britain. Randolph, along with the Senate, strongly objected to provisions that would disrupt the trade of neutral countries, particularly U.S. shipping to France. Political intrigue against Randolph ended his term as Secretary of State. Hoping to neutralize Randolph's opposition to the favorable Jay Treaty, the British Government provided his opponents in Washington's Cabinet with documents written by French Minister Jean Antoine Joseph Fauchet that had been intercepted by the British Navy. The documents were innocuous, yet Federalists in the Cabinet claimed they proved that Randolph had disclosed confidential information and solicited a bribe. Randolph was innocent, but his standing with Washington was permanently weakened. Randolph resigned in 1795. (Office of the Historian 2020)

As you will shortly see Mr. Madison who leaves this tomorrow or next day, I decline saying anything on the subject of the late proceedings in Phila. in either department of the government.[10] Indeed, you know so much of them already that I can add but little.

I shall place in the hands of James Maury of Liverpool a sum of money to answer my engagement to you.[11] I have written to Colo. Lewis and Mr. Divers to entreat them to value Theresa and her children and hope they will do it immediately.[12] Let your draft be about Sept. and payable at 60 days sight. Let it be accompanied with a letter of advice. The money shall certainly be deposited, unless you would prefer it in France of which you will advise me and draw on myself. I beg you not to omit this as the money will be idle in his hands in case you do not direct otherwise soon.

I shall confide to Mr. Madison yourself and Mr. Jones the fixing on a spot where my house shall be erected. The doubt will be between the hill to the left of the road as you approach towards Blenheim or the one where the barn stands. On which ever you place it I have given orders for an enclosure and the commencement of those improvements which are contemplated. Your advice on that head as well as the most suitable for the commencement of orchards of different kinds will be regarded.

We expect to embark tomorrow and to fall down the bay immediately. Accept my most affectionate wishes for your welfare and that of Mr. Randolph and your daughters and be pleased likewise to unite with them those of Mrs. Monroe. We contemplate a return in about 3. or 4. years at farthest, perhaps sooner. In the interim I wish every preparation for our final repose, I mean from active life, be in the farm adjoining yours. To this object my attention will be turned whilst abroad and I will endeavor to bring back what will contribute [to] its comforts. I wish you to command me in all respects wherein I can serve you. Perhaps you may wish things from the quarter I shall be in not obtainable so easily elsewhere.

I am Dear Sir with the sincerest regard

yr. affectionate friend & servt

Jas. Monroe

---

[10] Madison accompanied Monroe from Philadelphia to Baltimore. (Hamilton 1899, 9)

[11] James Maury, of Virginia, was Consul of the United States at Liverpool. Appointed by Washington, he acquired almost the grandeur of a mythical personage in the annals of the Consulate. (Heath and Barnes 1961, 105)

[12] To Monroe, slavery was a familiar practice. By the time he was born to Spence Monroe and Elizabeth Jones, the family owned 600 acres of land that his father farmed. His father's death in 1774 had left him in possession of slaves. Theresa appears to be one of these slaves. (Thomas Jefferson Foundation 2019)

To James Madison, Baltimore, June 17, 1794 [Power of Attorney]

Mr. Madison will be pleased to receive from Gen'l Wilkinson, or draw on him for the sum of three hundred dollars or thereabouts (due me by him) according as the Gen'l shall direct.[13] He will likewise receive whatever is obtained from Gen'l Bradley from the sale of our Vermont property, or otherwise from the sale or upon acc't of it.[14] He will likewise be pleased, in case he is applied to, to give advice as to the course to be taken for obtaining justice ag'nst J. Kortright and others under the will of L. Kortright (father of Mrs. M.) of New York and whatever he does in the above will be satisfactory & binding on me.[15]

Jas. Monroe.

To the President of the National Convention [Merlin de Douai], Paris, August 13, 1794

Citizen President,[16]—Having arrived here a few days past, commissioned by the President of the United States to represent those States in character of Minister Plenipotentiary with the French Republic, and not being acquainted with the competent department or forms of recognition prescribed by law, I have thought it expedient to make known my mission

---

[13] Major General James Wilkinson was a controversial figure. In time of war Wilkinson proved unfit for high military command. His ability was not pronounced in the conduct of active operations; it lay in a sort of practical diplomacy, often dubious in its ethics though usually acceptable in his time. His conclusions were not arrived at by the careful process of synthetic reasoning; they were based more frequently on a superficial examination of information that was easily available but not always true. On the other hand, as a clever politician he skillfully catered first to the Federalists, then to the Democratic-Republicans, convincing both of his friendship and ability to serve them. (Jacobs 1938, x-xi)

[14] Born in Connecticut, Stephen R. Bradley, a Jeffersonian Republican, served intermittently in the state militia and was aide-de-camp to General David Wooster at the Battle of Danbury when the general was killed in 1777. Bradley represented Westminster in the Vermont General Assembly and served on the 1789 commission that settled the boundary dispute between New York and Vermont. He became the first United States senator from Vermont and as the President pro tempore of the United States Senate. (Jefferson 1950, 298)

[15] Captain Lawrence Kortright, a British army officer, and Hannah Aspinwall were the parents of Monroe's wife, Elizabeth. (Watson 2000, 225)

[16] The selection of Merlin de Douai as head of the National Assembly's committee charged with drawing up such legislation was symptomatic. Merlin had made his reputation before the Revolution through his ingenuity in the defense of lords' claims against their peasants. Merlin, for example, gained legal recognition for one lord's right to enlarge the roads through the local communal lands and to compel nearby peasant communities to pay the wages of the road crews. (Markoff 1996, 533)

---

immediately to the Representatives of the people. They possess the power to affix the time and prescribe the mode by which I shall be recognized as the representative of their ally and sister Republic; and they will likewise have the goodness in case such department now exists, to cause the same to be designated to me that I may immediately present myself before it to be recognized in the character I bear. I make this communication with the greater pleasure, because it affords me an opportunity of testifying to the Representatives of the Free Citizens of France, not only my own attachment to the cause of liberty, but of assuring them at the same time and in the most decided manner of the deep concern which the Government & people of America take in the liberty, prosperity, and happiness of the French nation.

With sentiments of the highest respect,

Jas. Monroe[17]

Address to the National Convention, Paris, August 14, 1794

Citizens, President and Representatives of the French People:[18]—My admission into this Assembly, in the presence of the French Nation (for all the citizens of France are represented here) to be recognized as the Representative of the American Republic, impresses me with a degree of sensibility which I cannot express. I consider it as a new proof of that friendship and regard which the French Nation has always shewn to their ally, the United States of America.

Republics should approach near to each other. In many respects they all have the same interest. But this is more especially the case with the American and French Republics; their governments are similar; they both cherish the same principles and rest on the same basis, the equal and unalienable rights of men. The recollection too of common dangers and difficulties will increase their harmony, and cement their union. America had her day of oppression, difficulty and war, but her sons were virtuous and brave and the storm which

---

[17] As soon as this letter was read in the National Convention, it was decreed that it should be inserted in its process both verbally and in the bulletin of correspondence, and that a copy of it, with one of the letters of credence which accompanied it, should be sent to the committee of public safety, with instructions to report thereon during the present sitting; and afterwards, upon the report of the committee, the Convention decreed as follows: Art. I. The Minister Plenipotentiary of the United States shall be introduced into the bosom of the Convention, tomorrow at two o'clock p.m. He shall then explain the object of his mission; and after which the President shall salute him fraternally, in testimony of the friendship which unites the American and French people. Art. II. The President of the Convention shall write a letter to the President of the United States and transmit to him the process verbal of this sitting. (Hamilton 1899, 11-12)

[18] This was subsequently the subject of severe criticism by the Administration at home when Monroe was charged with having exceeded his instructions. (Hamilton 1899, 13)

long clouded her political horizon has passed and left them in the enjoyment of peace, liberty and independence. France our ally and our friend and who aided in the contest, has now embarked in the same noble career; and I am happy to add that whilst the fortitude, magnanimity and heroic valor of her troops, command the admiration and applause of the astonished world, the wisdom and firmness of her councils unite equally in securing the happiest result.

America is not an unfeeling spectator of your affairs in the present crisis. I lay before you in the declarations of every department of our Government, declarations which are founded in the affection of the citizens at large, the most decided proof of her sincere attachment to the liberty, prosperity and happiness of the French Republic. Each branch of Congress, according to the course of proceedings there, has requested the president to make this known to you in its behalf; and in fulfilling the desires of those branches I am instructed to declare to you that he has expressed his own.

In discharging the duties of the office which I am now called on to execute, I promise myself the highest satisfaction; because I well know that whilst I pursue the dictates of my own heart in wishing the liberty and happiness of the French nation, and which I most sincerely do, I speak the sentiments of my own Country; and that by doing everything in my power to preserve and perpetuate the harmony so happily subsisting at present between the two Republics, I shall promote the interest of both. To this great object therefore all my efforts will be directed.

If I shall be so fortunate as to succeed in such manner as to merit the approbation of both Republics I shall deem it the happiest event of my life, and return hereafter with a consolation, which those who mean well and have served the cause of liberty alone can feel.[19]

To the Secretary of State [Edmund Randolph], Paris, August 15, 1794

Sir,—On the 31th ultimo I arrived at Havre, and on the second instant at this place. Mr. Morris was, upon my arrival, from town, but he came in as soon as advised of it.[20] By him I was presented to the commissary of foreign

[19] Although Monroe, as minister to France, told the French National Convention that republics should approach near to each other, the Federalists countered with the argument that American commerce could hardly expect to flourish without the friendship of Britain, the dominant power on the seas. Since Britain and France were at war, the Americans could not have it both ways. This would emerge as a matter of continuing concern in the months to come. (Brown 1954, 90)

[20] Monroe arrived in France a mere five days after the execution of French leader Maximilien Robespierre, the major architect of the Terror. In this letter it is clear that he held few

affairs, who assured me that, as soon as the form of my reception should be settled, he would apprize me of it, but that this would unavoidably create a delay of some days, as well from the present derangement of their affairs on account of the late commotion of Robespierre, as from the necessity of making some general regulation in that respect, it being the first instance in which a minister had been addressed to the Republic. I assured him I should wait with pleasure the convenience of those whom it concerned, since which I have not seen him, but hear that the subject is under consideration of the committee of public safety and will probably be concluded in a day or two.

I heard at Havre of the crimes and execution of Robespierre, St. Just, Couthon and others of that party, and should have written you on the subject from that port, but that I knew I could only give the current report, varying, perhaps, in every seaport town, and which might reach you before my letter. I hastened, therefore, to Paris, in the hope of acquiring there immediately more correct information of facts, as well as of the causes which gave birth to them; but even yet, I suspect, I am on the surface only, for it will take some time to become well acquainted with the true state of things on a theatre so extensive and important.

That Robespierre and his associates merited their fate, is a position to which every one assents. It was proclaimed by the countenances and voices of all whom I met and conversed with from Havre to Paris. In the latter place,

---

illusions with respect to the death of Robespierre and his supporters. Robespierre had for the past year ruled France with an iron fist. The Thermidorian Reaction, a revolt against the Jacobins, executed Robespierre on 28 July, though only after his Reign of Terror had sent thousands to the guillotine. Monroe felt no sympathy for "The Incorruptible" as Robespierre's adherents had nicknamed him. He told Secretary of State Edmund Randolph that Robespierre bore sole responsibility for the recent bloodshed in France. Robespierre, in Monroe's estimation, "amassed in his hands all the powers of the government." Before his fall he stood nearly "omnipotent" within the Committee of Public Safety, which then ruled France. Most importantly, it was Robespierre's "spirit" that had directed "the unceasing operation of the guillotine" that horrified so many Americans. To be sure, Monroe knew his audience well. Americans strongly distrusted executive tyranny, and he assured them that none of antiquity's great tyrants could match Robespierre, whose "acts of cruelty and oppression are perhaps without parallel in the annals of history." Monroe focused so exclusively on this "bloody and merciless tyrant" in order to defend the French Revolution from attack by its enemies in America. He told Randolph that Robespierre "aimed at despotic powers" and ultimately hoped to "establish himself on the throne of the Capets." He depicted Robespierre as a power hungry aspiring monarch entirely antithetical to true republicanism. Such imagery innately resonated with Americans. Doubtless, Monroe aimed to evoke memories of George III or even thoughts of Julius Caesar and the fall of the Roman Republic. A single tyrant could easily and most plausibly assume blame for the Revolution's descent into brutality. (Poston 2016). Most succinctly, in this, his first letter to the Secretary of State, Monroe seems to intimate his optimism that wisdom and moderation were winning the day over the violence of the Robespierrean regime and that the Revolution was drawing to a happy close. (Hazen 1897, 126).

where the oppression was heaviest, the people seem to be relieved from a burden which had become insupportable. It is generally agreed that, from the period of Danton's fall, Robespierre had amassed in his own hands all the powers of the government and controlled every department in all its operations. It was his spirit which ruled the committee of public safety, the Convention, and the revolutionary tribunal. The Convention was soon found, after the abrogation of the constitution to be too unwieldy, and slow in its deliberations, to direct the great and complicated mass of executive business; this had given birth to two committees, the one of salut publique, the other of sureté generale, into whose hands the whole was deposited. To the former was assigned the management of foreign affairs, the direction of the armies, &c. to the latter, the interior administration, and they were respectively enjoined to render an account monthly of their transactions to the Convention. It was intended that those committees should be independent of each other, and both under the immediate control of the Convention; but by the distribution of their powers, this design was defeated, for such an ascendancy was thereby given to the committee of public safety, that the other became its instrument, acting only under its authority. The principal members of the Convention were placed in these committees, and Robespierre, who was by far the most influential one, was assigned to the committee of public safety. It soon happened in the course of the administration, from the very extensive patronage, comparative weight of character, and immense power that this committee gained likewise an entire ascendancy in the Convention and controlled all its measures. Nor was the organization of the evolutionary tribunal more favorable to the independence of that branch, and of course to public and personal liberty. It was equally dependent on, and the creature of, this committee. Robespierre therefore had become omnipotent. It was his spirit which dictated every movement, and particularly the unceasing operation of the guillotine. Nor did a more bloody and merciless tyrant ever wield the rod of power. His acts of cruelty and oppression are perhaps without parallel in the annals of history. It is generally conceded, that for some months before his fall the list of prisoners was shewn him every evening, by the President of the revolutionary tribunal, and that he marked those who were to be the victims of the succeeding day, and which was invariably executed. Many whole families, those under the age of sixteen excepted, were cut off upon the imputation of conspiracies, &c. but for the sole reason that some members had been more friendly to Brissot, Danton, &c. or had expressed a jealousy of his powers. His oppression had, in fact, gained to such a height, that a convulsion became unavoidable. The circumstances which immediately preceded and brought on the crisis are differently recounted. Some make him the active party and believed that he had arranged with the commune and the guards of the city, the plan of a general massacre of his enemies in the Convention. But I am of opinion, that these projects, for they were certainly contemplated, proceeded from despair, and were adopted at the moment only, as the means of defence. The time and manner of the explosion which was in the Convention support this idea. It had been intimated some days before by him or St. Just, that other conspiracies threatened the safety of the Republic and which ought to be laid open. The communication was given in such a manner as to satisfy the audience, that he meant Tallien and some other members of the house. And, in the moment of the explosion, St. Just had commenced a development of this pretended conspiracy, leading to a denunciation of these members. If the power of Robespierre remained, it was well known, that death and denunciation were hand in hand. To repel it by a counter one was the only remaining hope. It could, in no event, produce a worse effect. Tallien therefore rose and interrupted St. Just, demanding: "How long shall we be abused with denunciations of pretended conspiracies. 'Tis time to draw the veil from perfidy so flagrant." St. Just was silenced and driven from the tribune. Robespierre ascended and made many efforts to speak in vain. The whole Convention rose and cried out with one voice, "Down with the tyrant." He stood like one amazed and stupefied, staring at the Convention with a countenance equally bespeaking indignation and terror; deprived of the power of utterance, but yet afraid to descend. As soon as the convention saw its strength, he was arrested and sent a prisoner to the committee of public safety; but by this time, his immediate coadjutors had taken the alarm, and were endeavoring to excite commotions in the city in his behalf. Henriot, the commander of the guard, with a few followers, pursued and rescued him from the committee. He then took his station with the commune, heretofore the theatre of his power, and began to harangue the people, and with some effect; whilst Henriot, in the character of general was busied in assembling the guards in the place before the Hall of the Convention, with intention to fire on it. There was at this moment an awful pause in the affairs of the Republic. Everything was suspended, and the public mind greatly alarmed and agitated. The situation of the Convention was truly interesting. They knew that all the appointments were conferred by Robespierre, that he had been long deemed a patriot, and still possessed, by means of affection or terror, a wonderful influence over the citizens at large; and more immediately in their presence, they saw Henriot at the head of a respectable force menacing an attack. But that body was not unmindful of its dignity or its duty upon that great occasion. On the contrary, it displayed a degree of fortitude and magnanimity, worthy of those who aspire to the exalted character of defenders of their country. It calmly entered upon the subject of defence, declared Robespierre, St. Just, Couthon, Henriot, and the commune without the protection of the law, appointed a commandant of the guard, and sent deputies to the sections to admonish them of their danger, and warn them to stand at their posts in defence of their country. A moment's reflection settled the public mind. The people beheld on the one side, the Convention labouring to save the Republic, and on the other, Robespierre and his associates in open rebellion. Hesitation was at an end. The citizens rallied immediately to the standard of their sections, and Robespierre and his associates were taken at the same time to prison, and on the next day to execution, amidst the rejoicing and acclamations of the people.

Many believe that Robespierre aimed at a despotic power, and sought to establish himself upon the throne of the Capets,[21] in the character of protector, or some such character; and, in pursuit of this idea, say, that he counted upon the support of the armies, and particularly the army of the North, and had otherwise arranged things in such order as to favour the project. What his views of ambition and carnage were, I know not. That they had been great was certain; but that he had concerted any plan of permanent establishment for himself, or been promised such support, even where his influence was greatest, cannot be true, nor is it warranted by circumstances. If he was not promised the support, it is not probable he had such a scheme; and that it was not promised, must be obvious to those who take into view all the circumstances which merit consideration. It will be observed, by those who wish to form a just estimate of the future course and fortune of this revolution, that from its commencement, to the present time, no person ever raised himself to power but by the proof he had furnished of his attachment to the cause, by his efforts to promote it; and that from the moment doubts were entertained of the solidity and purity of his principles, did his influence begin to decline in equal degree. This was seen in the instances of La Fayette, Dumourier, Brissot, Danton, and finally, Robespierre himself; two of whom, though popular generals, were abandoned by the armies they commanded; the former compelled to seek refuge in a foreign country, and the latter in the camp of the enemy; and the others, tho' eminent in the civil department, were, upon like charges, condemned by the public voice to the same fate. In fact, the current of sentiment and principle has been such, that no character or circumstance has been able to obstruct its course; on the contrary,

---

[21] Hugh Capet founded the dynasty in 987. It was among the largest and oldest royal houses in Europe and one or another of its branches was to reign uninterruptedly until 1792. This Capetian line would have good claims to the crown of France, by hereditary succession, if the Republic were to be changed again into a monarchy. (Davis 1919, 41)

it has swept everything before it. Can it be presumed then, and especially at this moment, when the ardour of the nation, in flamed by conquest, is at the height, that any respectable number of citizens, of any description, would turn aside from the great object of the revolution, to countenance, in any individual, schemes of usurpation and tyranny? Did not the late event, even in Paris, disprove it where Robespierre had most influence. There was no opposing force but what depended on public opinion, and everything tended to favour his views.

From due consideration of all circumstances, I am led to ascribe the sanguinary course of Robespierre's proceedings to a different cause. I consider the contest between him and Danton as a contest for power between rivals having the same political objects in view. The former was jealous of the latter; and having gained the ascendancy, and the defective organization of the Government permitting it, by means of his influence in the judiciary, he cut him off. But the arrestation and condemnation were regular, according to the forms prescribed by law, and were, on that account, submitted to. The public, however, saw into the oppression, and disapproved of it; for, at the moment when Danton was led to execution, there was a general gloom upon the countenances of the citizens. They all attended at the place, in hope of hearing the explanation: they heard none and retired dissatisfied. Robespierre saw this, and in it the foreboding of his own ruin. From that moment he saw nothing but conspiracies, assassinations, and the like. He was surrounded by informers and had spies and emissaries in every quarter. By means of severity, he sought his safety, and therefore struck at all his enemies in the hope of extirpating them. But it happened in this as it always happens in like cases, every new execution increased them tenfold. It progressed thus till it could be no longer borne and terminated as I have already stated.

It may be asked: Is there any reason to hope that the vicious operation of the guillotine will be hereafter suspended? May not factions rise again, contend with and destroy each other as heretofore? To this I can only answer, that the like is not apprehended here, at least to the same extent; that the country from Havre to Paris, and Paris itself, appears to enjoy perfect tranquility; that the same order is said to prevail in the armies, who have addressed the Convention, applauding its conduct, and rejoicing at the downfall of the late conspirators. Some circumstances, it is true; have been seen indicating a suspicion that all Robespierre's associates had not suffered the fate they merited and ought not to escape; but latterly this has abated, though it is possible it may revive again. In general, it may be remarked that, until peace and a well organized Government shall be established, no sure calculation can be formed of what may happen in this respect. I am happy, however, to observe, that the subject of reform in the committees and revolutionary tribunals (and which was taken up immediately after the late commotion subsided) is now under discussion, and that the propositions which are depending are calculated to preserve, as far as possible, the control of the Convention over the former, and promote the independence, and otherwise improve the organization, of the latter.

But are not the people oppressed with taxes, worn out by continual draughts to reinforce the armies? Do they discover no symptoms of increasing discontent with the reigning Government, and of a desire to relapse again under their former tyranny? What will become of the army at the end of the war? Will it retire in peace, and enjoy in tranquility that liberty it has so nobly contended for; or will it not rather turn its victorious arms against the bosom of its country? These are great and important questions, and to which my short residence here will not permit me to give satisfactory answers. Hereafter I shall be able to give you better information in these respects. At present I can only observe that I have neither seen nor heard of any symptom of discontent showing itself among the people at large. The oppression of Robespierre had indeed created an uneasiness, but which disappeared with the cause. I never saw in the countenances of men more apparent content with the lot they enjoy, than has been shown everywhere since my arrival. In the course of the last year the Convention recommended it to the people, as the surest means of support for their armies, to increase the sphere of cultivation, and from what I can learn, there never was more land under cultivation, nor was the country ever blessed with a more productive harvest. Many fathers of families, and a great proportion of the young men, are sent to the frontiers, and it was feared it would be difficult to reap and secure it; but the women, the boys, and the girls, even to tender age, have supplied their places...I saw this with amazement upon my route from Havre to this place and am told it is generally the case. The victories of their armies are celebrated with joy and festivity in every quarter, and scarcely a day has latterly passed without witnessing a deputation to the Convention, and often from the poorest citizens, to throw into its coffers some voluntary contribution for the support of the war. These are not symptoms of disgust with the reigning Government, and of a desire to change it!

With respect to the present disposition of the army, or what it may be at the end of the war, I can say less, as I have not seen it. At present the best understanding subsists between it and the Convention. It is possible that, in the course of service, if the war should last long, many of its members may acquire habits unfriendly to retirement; but in an army composed of the yeomanry of the country, as this is, that sentiment will be less apt to gain ground than in any other. Besides, is it not presumable, that the spirit which has raised and influenced this, will continue to produce some effect, even in its final disposition? If, however, there should still remain a considerable force on foot, which could not be prevailed on to retire; fond of conquest, of rapine, and of plunder; can it be supposed that its parent country will furnish the only and most grateful theatre to act on? Will no other portion of Europe present before it a more productive field, whereon to gratify ambition, avarice, or revenge? There must always remain in the breasts of the soldiers some sentiment in favor of their relatives; and the fortunes of the wealthy will be pretty well broken and dissipated here by the course of the revolution. The example of the Roman empire is always before those whose apprehensions are greatest upon this head: they see there nothing but kindred armies fighting against each other, and tearing the commonwealth in pieces, but they make no allowance for the great difference in the state of things. The armies of the empire were raised in the conquered provinces and composed of foreigners. They, therefore, had no attachment to Rome. The state of the country and the spirit of the age are likewise different. The dissensions of Rome were the convulsions of a corrupt and worn out monarchy, verging rapidly to a decline. But here the case is different; the armies are otherwise composed, and the spirit of the age, that of a rational and philosophical reform, seeking to establish the public liberty, and sweeping before it old and corrupt institutions which were no longer tolerable.

I have thus gone into this interesting subject from a desire to give the best view in my power of the late commotions and present state of the internal affairs of this country, because I well know its importance to my own. It will be my object to improve my knowledge of it, and keep you correctly informed in every particular, and as regularly as opportunities offer.

With respect to the state of the war, I can only say, in general, that the armies of France have prevailed over the combined forces everywhere. The commencement of the campaign was favorable to them; but the action which took place in July, near Charleroy, on the plains of Fleurus, between Cobourg, at the head of about one hundred thousand men, and Jourdan, with an inferior force; and which terminated, after the severest conflict and great slaughter on both sides, in favor of the French arms, has evidently given them the superiority ever since. This was certainly one of the most important and bloody actions which has been fought in the course of the present war. Cobourg, unwilling to retire before the republican troops, had gathered together all his forces, with design to hazard a general action, and in the hope of regaining Charleroy. He attacked them at every point, about five in the morning, formed in the field, and ready to receive him. Three times he drove them back within their entrenchments, reluctant to yield the day: but they sallied out a fourth time, with still greater impetuosity, shouting through all their ranks, "we will retreat no more!" and singing the Marseillaise hymn, and other patriotic songs, advanced with an ardor which was irresistible: The attack succeeded. Cobourg, with his routed army, fled before them, leaving on the field, according to the French accounts, about ten thousand slain. The French, it is supposed, lost about fifteen thousand men. They have taken, in the course of the present campaign, Ostend, Mons, Tournay, Namur, Tirlemont; Landrecy, Anyers, Ghent, Charleroy, Brussels, Quesnoy, Louvain, Liege, Nieuport, Cadsandt, (at the mouth of the Scheldt) with some other places lying in that quarter. Cobourg at present occupies the ground in the neighborhood of Maestricht, and endeavors to cover the frontier of Holland. It is, however, daily expected another action will take place, which may settle the fate of the Low Countries. Condé and Valenciennes, you observe, are left in the rear; they are yet possessed by the combined forces, but are invested, and it is thought will soon fall.

Their success in Spain has likewise been great. They are in possession, at present, of the whole of the province of Guypuscoa, Bilboa excepted. Many prisoners and immense parks of artillery have been taken from the Spaniards. The detail I cannot give you with any kind of accuracy, but will endeavor to comprise it in my next.

There has been but one sea action, and which was between the French and English fleets, in the course of the present summer. The French had twenty-six ships, and the English twenty-eight. The English, having the wind, bore down on the French, and separated seven ships from their main force. Of these they took six and sunk the other. It is said there never was a more bloody, or better fought action on both sides. It lasted three days. On the fourth, the British filed off with the ships they had taken and sailed into port. The French, having offered to renew the combat, likewise retired afterwards to Brest, whither they conducted the merchantmen convoyed from America; and which was the object of the contest, safe.

I shall write you again in a few days, and I hope to inform you of my reception. For the present, therefore, I shall conclude, with assurances of the great respect and esteem with which I am, &c.

Jas. Monroe

To the Commissary of Foreign Relations, Paris, August 22, 1794

Citizen:—I was favoured yesterday with yours of that date, informing me that the Committee of Public Safety had authorized you, in the name of the Republic, to appropriate a house for my use, as minister of their ally, the United States of America, and in such a part of the city as I should designate. I received this communication with peculiar satisfaction, because I consider it a proof of the sincere regard which the Committee entertain for their ally, whose servant I am. Upon this occasion I am not permitted to indulge, in any respect, my own opinion or feelings. The Constitution of my country, an extract from which is hereto annexed, has prescribed a line of conduct for me, which it is my duty to follow.[22]

The Committee of Public Safety and you, citizen, respect too highly the fundamental laws of your own country, not to approve my reason for declining the kind offer you have made me. I shall however immediately communicate it to my government, and doubt not, it will produce there the good effect it merits.

To the Secretary of State [Edmund Randolph], Paris, August 25, 1794

Sir,—In my last of the 15th., instant, I mentioned to you that I had been presented to the Commissary of foreign affairs, for reception, and was assured he would lay the copy of my credentials, which I left with him, before the committee of public safety, under whom he acted, and to whom it more particularly belonged to appoint the time and regulate the mode.[23] After this I waited eight or ten days without progressing an iota; and as I heard

---

[22] Monroe also provided the following excerpt from the United States Constitution: "No title of nobility shall be granted by the United States, and no person holding any office of profit or trust, under them, shall without the consent of Congress, accept of any present, emolument, office, or title of any kind whatsoever, from any King, Prince or Foreign State." (Hamilton 1898, 286)

[23] At the time of this letter, Monroe was seeing a shift in French political circles as the "Thermidorian Reaction" against Jacobinism set in. During 1794–1795 its leaders dismantled the Terror, manned the committees with their own men, jailed or executed more terrorist leaders, repealed the Terror's more egalitarian laws, and lifted those decrees that regulated the economy, including the Law of the Maximum. It further limited the authority of the Committee of Public Safety to matters of war and foreign policy. It closed the Jacobin Club and dissolved most of the capital's forty-eight surveillance committees. It revoked the Law of 22 Prairial, released over 3,500 prisoners in Paris alone, and in August 1794 allowed only six executions in the capital. (There were forty during the rest of 1794.) They annulled the extraordinary powers of the Revolutionary Tribunal and put moderates on the bench. It ordered the arrest of the infamous prosecutor Fouquier Tinville, who was ultimately guillotined, and replaced the slogan "terror is the order of the day" with "justice is the order of the day." Monroe's optimism is clearly reflected in

---

that a minister of Geneva had been here about six weeks before me, and had not yet been received, I was fearful I might remain as long, and perhaps much longer in the same situation. It was obvious that the public boards had been so much shocked by the late disaster, that from a variety of considerations, some public and others personal, they could scarcely move forward upon any subject. At the same time, I had reason to believe it was the general desire that I should be received as soon as possible, and with every demonstration of respect for the country I represented. Upon the most mature consideration, therefore, I thought it incumbent on me to make an effort to break through these difficulties and expedite my reception. The Convention, I knew, possessed the sovereign authority of the nation; and I presumed, that by addressing myself to that body, and especially in the present state of things, I should not only avoid the censure of any subordinate department, but perhaps relieve it from an unpleasant dilemma, and at the same time, make an experiment of the real disposition of this country towards my own. The latter consideration I deemed of some importance, as it would ascertain to me a fact which might have influence on my conduct on other occasions. I therefore addressed a letter to the President of the Convention, of which the enclosed No. 1, is a copy, and was happy to find it well received; for it was immediately taken, by a member present, to the committee of public safety, by whom a report was made in two hours afterwards to the Convention, and a decree adopted by the latter body, of which No. 2 is a copy, for my reception by the Convention itself at two the following day. I deemed it my duty to avail myself of this opportunity to dissipate, if possible, by the documents in my possession, impressions which had been made and are still making, of the unfriendly disposition of the American government towards the liberty and happiness of the French nation. At the same time, therefore, that I presented my credentials, I laid before the Convention the declarations of the Senate and House of Representatives, as conveyed to me by the President, through the Secretary of State, with an assurance that I was authorised to declare, that the President was actuated by similar sentiments. The communication was received in a manner very interesting, and which furnished at the same time, the strongest proofs of the affection entertained by the French nation for the United States of America. The enclosed No. 3 is a copy of my address to the Convention and of the President's answer. Every department has since shewn the strongest disposition to prove its attachment to their ally, by embracing every opportunity which the slightest incident has offered. A few stores brought for the accommodation of my family, in the ship in which

his statement to Randolph, "A perfect tranquility too continues to reign throughout the Republic." (Connelly and Hembree 1993, 116-117)

I sailed, were arrested at Havre because no declaration was rendered of them by the Captain. This was casually heard of by the Committee of public safety, and, without any intimation from me, by their order, restored. But being desirous more formally to certify their regard, the Commissary of foreign affairs announced to me yesterday, that he was instructed, in the name of the Republic, to appropriate a house for my use, as minister of the United States, of such accommodations and in such part of the city as I would designate. The enclosed No. 4 is a copy of his letter and of my reply. These latter acts, it is true, may be deemed in some measure, acts of ceremony. So far, however, as they furnish any indication of the disposition of this country towards our own, it is a favorable one.

I found here many of my countrymen, captains of vessels, who were taken at sea and brought in, in derogation of the treaty.[24] I intend immediately to make an effort to have that decree rescinded, and compensation rendered for the injury sustained. I have written to Mr. Fenwick who is best acquainted with the affair of the Bordeaux embargo, to request his attendance here, or to forward such documents as will enable me to pursue, with suitable information, the interest of those who were affected by it.[25] And I shall likewise bring forward at the same time, the claims of others of our citizens for supplies rendered to the government of St. Domingo.

The position of the armies is nearly the same as when I wrote you last. No action has been fought, nor any other material change taken place since.

A perfect tranquility too continues to reign throughout the Republic. The execution of Robespierre and his associates has produced the same effect everywhere. Every person seems to be freed from an oppression which was really destructive and terrible, and the more so, because it was sanctified by the authority of the people and covered with the mask of patriotism. It is, however, said, that others who have been equally guilty (for Robespierre who was a small and timid man, could not make the majority of the Committee vote against their own opinions) will probably yet be brought to justice. Of this I shall be able to give you better information in my next.

---

[24] This is arguably the modest beginning of what would become the French Spoliation Claims. This was a set of claims of citizens of the United States against their own government for rights surrendered under the treaty of 1800. The other set of claims was for outrages committed later by France which she agreed to pay for under a treaty in 1803. The former claims were not paid until ninety years and more had elapsed. The latter claims were not pressed because of France's misfortunes, until another treaty in 1831 provided for their payment. (Adams 1924, 110)

[25] Joseph Fenwick was the American consul at Bordeaux. William Lee, a political diarist of the period, later wrote that Fenwick had made a considerable fortune while consul, but that, as he was an American, he should not be taxed to support French military campaigns. (Lee 1958, 265)

The reform which I suggested in my last, contemplated in the organization of the committees and revolutionary tribunal, is now completed or nearly so. I will enclose you copies of the decrees in my next. A great number of prisoners have been discharged, who were confined here, and in other parts of the Republic, in consequence of a decree, that those should be liberated who were committed upon suspicion only. It was, however, greatly unfortunate, that Robespierre was not cut off a month sooner; for it is most certain, that his last days were stained with some of the most innocent blood of the Republic.

The Vice Consul has not yet arrived, and, to be candid, I doubt when he does, whether he will be received or not.[26] A native of this country, is at the present moment, unable to render any service to our own, although he may have always resided here, and his political principles been unquestionable. But one who has been absent, is considered, if not an emigrant, at best indifferent, and perhaps unfriendly, to the revolution, and therefore, odious. If this gentleman has arrived, I think it probable he is confined at the port where he landed. I deem this unfortunate, for there is much business which properly belongs to the Consular department here; as all the commercial affairs of the Republic are transacted here.

I have reason to believe that Laforest and Petri are displeased, and that a frigate is dispatched to announce it with you, and that Leblanc and Fauchet, the former for British connection the latter as followers of the fortunes of Robespierre.[27]

With great esteem, I am, dear Sir, Very respectfully your very Humble Servant,

Jas. Monroe

To James Madison, Paris, September 2, 1794

Dear Sir,—Tomorrow will make one month since our arrival here, and such have been my engagements that altho. I resolved that I would begin a letter to you every succeeding day yet when the day arrived it was not in power heretofore. You will readily conceive that the variety of the objects to which I have been forced to attend, many of which requiring the utmost effort of my judgment, all delicate and interesting and you will readily admit

[26] Alexander Duvernay was nominated vice-consul for Paris, June 7, 1794. (Hamilton 1899, 36)
[27] When a commission of four was appointed in 1793 to represent the interests of the French republic in the United States, Claude Fauchet was appointed minister; Antoine de Laforest, consul general; Pierre Leblanc, the legation's secretary; and Jean Baptiste Petry, consul for the port of Philadelphia. (Mitchell 1916, 222)

my embarrassment when you know that I have not had a single person (Mr. Skipwith[28] excepted and who is new in this line) with whom I could confidentially confer. I wished not to write you a superficial letter, but whether I shall be forced to hurry this is what I cannot at present determine. Between Baltimore and Paris we were 45 days. The passage was free from storms and between the soundings of each coast short, being only 29 days. We enjoyed our health; none were sick except Joseph a few days, & myself an hour or two. Mrs. M. and the child escaped it altogether. We landed at Havre and left it for this the day after, whither we arrived in three days being the 3. of August. We are yet at lodgings but expect to be fixed in Mr. M's house, which I took, in less than a week. I found Mr. Morris from town but he came in, in two or three days after my arrival.

About a week before my arrival Robespierre had been executed with St Just, Couthon and others so that the scene upon which I had to commence was a troubled one.[29] The publick councils were yet somewhat agitated but tranquillity and joy upon acc' of that event reigned everywhere else. The whole community seemed to be liberated from the most pestilent scourge that ever harassed a country. I found I had better look on for some days, merely to inform myself of the course to be taken to obtaining recognition.

I found myself under difficulties from the commencement. The fall of Robespierre had thrown a cloud over all whom it was supposed he had any connection with or in whose appointment he had been in any wise instru-

---

[28] Fulwar Skipwith, a relative of Thomas Jefferson, had been appointed to the American consulship in Martinique in June 1790. Antoine de Laforest, the French consul in New York, immediately challenged the action on the ground that the appointment contradicted French commercial regulations, a view expanded by the indignation of the French Foreign Office into the general proposition that no nation ever allows foreign trade with colonies. Despite the bluster of the French, Jefferson (then Secretary of State) called upon the consular convention of 1788 for his authority and refused to recall Skipwith. Ultimately the French government permitted Skipwith to remain in the colony, provided he carry no official title as such. They could be "commercial agents." (Kaplan 1967, 46)

[29] As the conspiracy to overthrow Robespierre began to develop both in the Convention and in the Committee of Public Safety itself, Robespierre's enemies engineered an arrest decree. Georges Auguste Couthon's demand to be included was immediately granted, and he was imprisoned at the De la Bourbe prison. Released by the sympathetic municipal government, he returned home, but later that night he joined Robespierre at the Hôtel de Ville and was there when the troops sent to arrest them arrived. Along with Robespierre, he was guillotined on July 28, 1794. (Scott and Rothaus, v.1, 1985, 274) Louis Antoine Leon de Saint Just was deputy to the National Convention. Another supporter of Robespierre, Saint Just enjoys the reputation of a dynamic but icy figure. Detractors see him as a sinister terrorist devoted to the ruthless elimination of enemies of the republican regime. Admirers consider him a dedicated Revolutionary devoted to liberty and the welfare of the people. He was guillotined on January 21, 1793. (Scott and Rothaus, v.2, 1985, 868) Since Robespierre, Couthon, Saint Just and those accused with them had been declared outlaws, it was only necessary to have their identity verified before they could be executed.

mental. This included my fellow passenger so that it was not prudent to avail myself of his aid in presenting me or even making known my arrival to the Committee of public safety, and I was averse to taking the introduction of my predecessor for as good a reason. I did not know the ground upon which the Americans stood here, but suspected as the acquisition of wealth had been their object in coming, they must have attached themselves to some preceding party & worn out their reputations. Upon mature reflection therefore I resolved to await the arrival of my predecessor & present myself as a thing of course with him. I concluded it could do me no detriment as it was the official mode & more especially as he would have to file off at the moment I took my ground. This was done. He accompanied me to the office of foreign aff', notified his recall & my succession. I left with the commissary a copy of my credentials & requested my recognition from the competent department as soon as possible which was promised. But my difficulties did not end here. Eight or ten days elapsed and I was not accepted, nor had I heard a syllable from the Committee or seen a member. And upon enquiry I was informed that a minister from Geneva had been here 6 weeks before me and was not yet received. Still further to increase my embarrassments I likewise heard that the Commissary to whom I was presented being of Robespierre's party was out of favor, and that probably his letter covering my credentials had not been read by the Committee. I could not longer bear with this delay. I foresaw that the impression to be expected from the arrival of a new minister might be lost, and that by the trammel of forms and collision of parties I might while away my time here forever without effect. I was therefore resolved to place myself if possible above these difficulties, by addressing myself immediately to the Convention. I knew this would attract the publick attention and if my country had any weight here produce a proportional effect not only upon that body, but upon every subordinate department. The result was as I had expected; my letter being read in the Convention was well received; taken immediately to the Committee of Publick Safety, reported on in two hours afterwards by that body & a decree passed the same day for my admission on the next, at two in the afternoon. It was at the same time intimated by a special messenger from the President that he should be glad to have a copy of what I should say an hour or two before I was presented. I had of course but little time to prepare my address. I thought it expedient to make the occasion as useful as possible in drawing the two republicks more closely together by the ties of affection by shewing them the interest which every department of our government took in their success and prosperity. With this view I laid before the Convention with suitable solemnity the declarations of the Senate and H. of R., and added a similar one for the President. The effect surpassed my expectation. My reception occupied an hour and a half, of not merely interesting but distressing sensibility, for all who beheld it. It was with difficulty that I extricated myself from the House and Committee of Public Safety and indeed the crowd which surrounded it, after the business was over. The cordial declaration of America in favor of France and of the French Revolution (for although I have not mentioned the word revolution, after the example of both houses yet after the example of both and especially the H. of R. I have strongly implied it) in the view of all Europe and at a time when they were torn in sunder by parties, was a gratification which overpowered them.

I doubt not this measure will be scanned with unfriendly eyes by many in America. They will say that it was intended that these things should have been smuggled in secretly and as secretly deposited afterwards. But they are deceived if they suppose me capable of being the instrument of such purposes. On the contrary, I have endeavoured to take the opposite ground, with a view of producing the best effect here as well as there. And I am well satisfied that it has produced here a good effect. It is certain that we had lost in a great measure the confidence of the nation. Representations from all parties had agreed (and men of different characters...)[30]

To the Committee of Public Safety, Paris, September 3, 1794

Citizens,—There are some subjects to which I wish to call your attention and which I deem of equal importance to both Republics. They have grown out of the occurrences of the present war; have pressed particularly hard on the United States, and will I doubt not be immediately rectified in a manner becoming the French nation and of course satisfactory to us.[31]

The first respects the departure on the part of France from the 23d and 24th. articles of the treaty of commerce subsisting between the two Republics.

---

[30] The remaining pages of the letter are missing. (Hamilton 1899, 41)

[31] Seemingly in at least partial response to this letter, by the latter part of 1794 and the early months of 1795, the French government agreed to recognize the claims of American merchants for losses sustained by the Bordeaux embargo, to suspend restrictions against American commerce, to recognize the principle that "free ships make free goods," to honor the commercial agreements of the Treaty of 1778, and even to allow American ships to become the carriers of England and her allies in the war." "In short," Monroe later opined, "such was our situation with the French Republic, and with other powers, so far as depended on the French Republic, that there was but one point upon which we had cause to feel or express any solicitude, which was that it might not vary." (Brown 1954, 118)

The second the embargo of our vessels at Bordeaux and the injuries arising from it to those whom it concerns.

The third, respects the claims of some of our citizens for supplies furnished to the Government of S? Domingo, authenticated by Bills upon the Minister of the Republic in Philadelphia, by Bills upon France, and by Mandates and other instruments usual in such cases.

By the 23rd Article of the Treaty of Amity and Commerce it is stipulated that free ships shall make free goods, and that all goods shall be free except those which are termed contraband and that no dispute might arise as to contraband, all those which should be deemed such on the one hand, and which should be deemed free on the other are particularly specified in the 24th.

It is necessary for me, in bringing this subject to your view, briefly to observe, that these articles have been dispensed with on your part: that our vessels laden with merchandize, not only the property of your enemies, made free by these articles, but likewise our citizens, the latter of which was always free, have been brought into your ports, detained for a great length of time, their cargoes taken, and the captains and proprietors otherwise subjected to great embarrassments, losses and injuries. But I will not dwell upon this subject in this view, because I frankly own to you it is painful for me thus to contemplate it. I wish to reserve my free comments for the other side of the picture where I shall favorably explain the motives of the act, in communicating to my country what I hope you will enable me to communicate, the ready acquiescence with which the decree was rescinded.

It may be said that Great Britain has rendered us the same injury, and that when she shall change her conduct in that respect, France will likewise follow her example. But the case is widely different. Britain may dispute the law of nations, however clear its doctrine even with respect to contraband; but with France it is in both respects regulated by treaty. Besides we are allies, and what is more interesting, the friends of France. These considerations naturally inspire in the councils of the two countries, different sentiments in regard to us; and if Britain proves true to those which belong to her situation, shall we, on the other hand, find France reluctant to cherish such as are friendly to us, and correspondent with hers? Will she say that the injuries of Britain furnish a justificatory example for her to render us like injuries? Will our ally contend with that nation in rivalship, which shall harrass our commerce most and do us the greatest detriment? This is surely not a relation for the two Republics to bear towards each other. Other sentiments will I hope inspire their common councils; sentiments more congenial with their mutual interests and consonant to the dispositions of the citizens of both countries.

If the French Republic gained the smallest benefit from the regulation, there might be some motive for adhering to it. But this cannot, it is presumed, be the case. The most to be derived from it, is the occasional seizure of a straggling vessel destined for the ports of Spain and Portugal; for they are excluded from the ports of England, except under particular circumstances and which rarely happen. It must be obvious, if the price was higher here, this would be their destination; add to which the charges attending the seizure and conducting of vessels from their course, must be great, and will make it not only an uncertain but unprofitable mode of supply.

It may be apprehended that if this decree should be rescinded, it will open a door, through which, under the protection of our flag, the commerce of Britain may be carried on with advantage to her, and detriment to France. But a moment's reflection will demonstrate, that this apprehension cannot, in any degree, be well founded; for the navigation act of England, whose great principles have been wisely adopted here, forbids almost altogether any such commerce. By this act the manufactures of the metropolis cannot be carried to the colonies, nor can the productions of the colonies, nor the productions or manufactures of any other country, be carried in our bottoms to Great Britain. This restriction must in a great degree inhibit the use of our vessels in any but the direct trade between the two nations; for it is not probable that Great Britain will use the American vessels to export her cargoes to other countries, to any amount, if at all; since, not being able to return, they would generally be left there empty and idle. On the contrary we know that her practice, in such cases, has been not to countenance the navigation of any other country at the expense of her own; but to protect the latter by convoys. But if this were otherwise, it is to be presumed that the fortune of the present war, in the triumphant success of the French arms, will have decisively settled itself, before that could have produced any material defect.

It must be obvious that the conduct of Great Britain, and especially in regard to the articles of contraband, must depend in a great measure upon that of France in this particular. For if France decline to rescind this decree, Great Britain most probably will, unless indeed she should make a merit of receding at the expence of France; for if France should comply in the first instance, she will put Great Britain in an embarrassing dilemma; for, if she refuses afterwards, it will tend not only to cement our union with France, but combine all America in the condemnation of the conduct of Britain: And if they should then comply, to France will the credit be given of having forced her into it.

At the same time I express to you a desire that this decree be rescinded, and the parties heretofore affected by it compensated for the injuries they have received, I consider it likewise my duty to add some observations upon the state of our trade in general with the Republic. When an American vessel arrives in any port of France, it is immediately in the hands of the government. The Captain or Supercargo cannot sell the cargo to any other person, nor can he get more for it than the public agents will give, nor sail elsewhere without permission. Oftentimes it happens that great delays take place, from the necessity of communicating from the seaports with the metropolis, and other inconveniences detrimental to the parties. A regulation of this kind, in its fullest extent, must prove very injurious to both countries, and especially to France. Trade cannot exist under it. It will soon happen that not a single adventurer will seek the French ports: no merchant will enter them but by restraint. The consequence must be, that the commerce of America so extensive and productive, and especially in those articles in greatest demand here, will be either exterminated, thrown into other channels, or forced here by public funds, and under the direction of public agents: a resource which, however productive, should not be the sole one, for many reasons; but more especially because the produce of our country, having thus become the property of France, will be liable, by the law of nations, equally in yours and in our vessels, to seizure and condemnation by your enemies; and because if we succeed in securing the respect which is due to our flag by other nations, and which would enable our citizens in their own bottoms to supply in abundance your markets (and in which I trust we shall succeed) it would be of no use to you; and lastly, because the competition of private adventurers would thus be destroyed, a competition which, with suitable encouragement, would not only supply the defect of these agents and satisfy the demand of the market; but by making known constantly and regularly the prices in America, form a check on their conduct and furnish the best test of their integrity.

You will observe I do not complain that the public are the sole purchasers and regulate at pleasure what shall be exported, provided the vendors are paid for their cargoes in some commodity or specie, at their option; or that agents of the public are appointed in the United States, and as many as may be thought necessary, to purchase our productions on public account and send them here. These are subjects which the legislators of the Republic will regulate according as public exigencies may in their judgment require. What I wish is that the ports of France may be opened freely to the enterprizes of my countrymen, and which will be the case provided they be permited to leave them immediately if they do not like the market, and despatched without delay in case they do. To accomplish the first point a general order only will be requisite to the officers of the customs or other persons in authority in the several ports; and the latter, a regulation of the prices to be immediately given by these officers upon all occasions, when a vessel should arrive, and which might be furnished as often as any change should be deemed necessary. This would, I am satisfied, banish every cause of complaint, greatly increase the competition and of course the supply of the market, and at a much less expense.

Free ships which secures to the persons interested an indemnity for the delay and other injuries sustained; it only remains, therefore, to adjust the amount of the claims and pay the parties entitled to it.

The third which respects the claims for supplies rendered by our citizens to the government of St. Domingo, is likewise a matter of account, and which it is earnestly hoped will be immediately adjusted and paid. A person authorized will appear in support of the claims, with the evidence, before any board or tribunal which shall be appointed for that purpose.

I have to observe that I shall be happy to give every aid in my power to facilitate the adjustment and subsequent payment of these several classes of claims. So far as they are well founded I doubt not they will be allowed by the French Republic, and where this is not the case they will not be supported by me. Is the aggregate view they respect the great mass of American merchants. It is of importance for France to cultivate that interest, and the present is, for many reasons, a critical moment to make an impression on it. I hope, therefore, it will not be neglected.

It is my duty to observe to you that I am under no instruction to complain of, or request the repeal of, the decree authorizing a departure from the 23d. and 24th. articles of the Treaty of Amity and Commerce; on the contrary I well know that if, upon consideration, after the experiment made, you should be of opinion that it produces any solid benefit to the Republic, the American government and my countrymen in general will not only bear the departure with patience but with pleasure. It is from the confidence alone which I entertain that this departure cannot be materially beneficial to you, and that the repeal would produce the happiest effect, in removing every possible cause of uneasiness and concilliating still more and more toward each other the affections of the citizens of both Republics, and thereby cementing more closely their union, that I have taken the liberty, as connected with the other concerns, to bring the subject before you. To cement that union in other situations has long been the object of my efforts; for I have been well satisfied that the closer and more intimate it was, the happier it would be for both countries. America and France thus united, the one the greatest power in the

European World and the other rapidly repairing the wastes of war, and rising to the first rank in the scale of nations, both bounding by and measuring an immense space along the Atlantic, abundant in productions, suiting the demand of each other, and above all, both Republics, have nothing to fear from foreign danger, and everything to hope from the happiest and most beneficial domestic intercourse. By a generous and liberal policy, France has it at the present moment much in her power to promote this more intimate union, and in the hope she will avail herself of it I have thought proper thus to develope the subjects which I have submitted to your consideration.

Jas. Monroe

To Thomas Jefferson, Paris, September 7, 1794

Dear Sir,—I have been here rather more than a month and so much engaged with the duties which devolved on me immediately that I have not yet been able to send a single private letter to America. It happened that I took my station a few days after Robespierre had left his in the Convention by means of the guillotine, so that everything was in commotion, as was natural upon such an event; but it was the agitation of universal joy occasioned by a deliverance from a terrible oppression & which had pervaded every part of the Republick.32 After encountering some serious difficulties growing out of the existing state of things, I was presented to the Convention and recognized in the manner the enclosed paper will shew you. Many incidents have since turned up to shew the pleasure with which the organized departments and the people generally have received a mission immediately from our Republick to theirs, and I have every reason to believe that it will not only remove any previous existing solicitude, but tend to encrease permanently the harmony between the two countries.

After Robespierre's exit there seemed to be an end of divisions and altercations for some time in the Convention. Even those of his own party were most probably happy in the event, for in the progress of his power a connection with him had already been of little service, and it was to be apprehended

<hr>

32 Jefferson was aware of the fate of his unfortunate Girondist friends at the hands of demagogues like Robespierre, who had seized control of the Convention with the help of the Paris mobs. By suppressing the terrorists the Directory appeared to have saved the Revolution and to have provided safeguards in the Constitution of 1795 against future anarchy. In fact, Monroe was Jefferson's chief correspondent in France from 1794 to 1797, and he facilitated the transfer of his affections from the Girondists to the Directory by molding his impressions of events in Europe. The men who in turn influenced Monroe were moderate republicans, veterans for the most part of exile and imprisonment under the Terror, who could be excused for welcoming the arrival of a government that seemed to restrict liberties to limits the people could absorb. (Kaplan 1967, 78)

that it would prove of less hereafter. It was not only necessary to be devoted to him, but to be unpopular with the community also. The list of his oppressions and the acts of cruelty committed by means of his influence, in the Convention & in consequence the revolutionary tribunal, would amaze you. He was believed by the people at large to be the foe to Kings, nobles, Priests, etc., the friend of republican govt. regardless of mercy & in fact devoted to their cause. Under this impression he perpetrated acts, which without perceiving the cause, had gradually spread a gloom over the whole republick. But as soon as they saw him in opposition to the Convention, the cause was known, his atrocities were understood, and the people abandoned him with demonstrations of joy rarely seen.

But it seemed improbable he sho'd. have been able to carry every thing in the committee of p: safety & by means of it in the Convention &c. with out more associates than St. Just & Couthon, who were executed with him or rather this was the opinion of others, for I can readily conceive that a man may gain an influence in society powerful enough to control every one & every thing. As soon, therefore, as the preternatural calm subsided, which the liberation from him had universally created, a spirit of enquiry began to shew itself, as to other accomplices. It terminated in the denunciation of Barrere, Collot d' Herbois, & some others. The Convention gave a hearing to the charges, rejected them, & pass'd a censure upon the author as seeking to disturb the publick repose. Thus, therefore, that business rests, and I declare to you that I not only think hereafter they will be more free from parties of the turbulent kind heretofore known, but if they sho'd. not, that I am persuaded their revolution rests perfectly secure in the unanimity & affections of the people. Greater proofs of patriotism and personal sacrifice were never seen in any country than are daily shewn in this, and in acts of heroism they have thrown a shade over the ancient and modern world. The spirit of the combination is absolutely broken. In the neighbourhood of Charleroy a decisive action was fought in July between Jourdan &cob': & in which the former gained the victory with the loss of abt. 1500 men, & at the expense to the latter of abt. 10,000 slain on the field. This has eventually driven the troops of the combined powers to Mastrecht and the neighbourhood of the Rhine, & of course out of all their possessions, not only in France [including Conde & Valenciennes] but likewise their proper territory in the low countries. 'Tis thought they are abt. to hazard another great action, but they do it with hazard for they fight dispirited troops against those who are flushed with victory, superior numbers, & resolved to conquer, & sure in case of misfortune of immediate succour. If France succeeds and which I am led to believe from every thing I can hear & very dispassionately, the combination in the ordinary course of war will be at an end, and the several powers composing it entirely at the mercy of France, except the Islands in her neighbourhood whose safety will depend altogether on the superiority at sea, if preserved there. 'Tis said that these powers (the Islanders excepted & who probably prompted the others with a view of taking advantage in case of success) sounded this govt, last winter upon the subject of peace, but without effect: that on the contrary they were treated with the utmost contempt, and I have reason to believe they will never treat with them under the govts, at present existing in each, to press the war till no force shews itself against them & in case the people sho'd. rise in any one & organize themselves, treat such organiz'd body as the only legitimate gov't. & aid it in crushing the ancient one. If France succeeds in the battle contemplated this will soon be the state of things: indeed it must be so immediately after.

That Mr. Jay sho'd. easily obtain the object of his errand in Engl'd. will be readily inferred.[33] The successful battles of France have plead our cause with great effect in the councils of that humane Cabinet. He will however arrogate to himself much merit for address in negotiation, and the concession of the court will be a theme for high panegyric to many in our country. They will deem it a proof of that sincere attachment to us which has already been shewn in that quarter.

The spirit of liberty begins to shew itself in other regions. Geneva has undergone revolution; the people have taken the gov't, into their hands, apprehended the aristocrats, & executed seven of the most wicked. And in Poland under the direction of Kosciusko who acted with us in America, a formidable head has been raised against Prussia & Russia. I have hopes that our trade, by mere negotiation, will be plac'd on a very safe & good footing shortly: and that France will rescind the decree respecting the seizure of our vessels laden with provisions &c. as heretofore. Indeed I think she will go back to the ground of the commercial treaty. I have hinted the good effect such a measure wo'd. have in America, without positively requesting it to be done.[34]

---

[33] Hamilton notes that it is to be remembered that the report that Jay's negotiations contained stipulations unfriendly and injurious to the interests of the French nation did not reach Paris until December; and that Monroe's only understanding of the purpose of Jay's mission at this time was based on the language of Randolph's instructions. (Hamilton 1899, 53)

[34] Following the French Revolution, by the spring of the year 1792 the revolutionary movement had led to war with Austria and Prussia. By the winter of 1793, the invasion of the Netherlands and the execution of Louis XVI brought Great Britain into the struggle and transformed a purely Continental conflict into one which was waged also upon the sea, and inevitably affected the interests of the United States. As to the merits of the struggle American opinion was deeply divided; men like Alexander Hamilton inevitably viewed the onward surge of the revolutionary movement with a deep distrust;

It is to be remembered that the report that Jay's negotiations contained stipulations unfriendly and injurious to the interests of the French nation did not reach Paris until December; and that Monroe's only understanding of the purpose of Jay's mission at this time was based on the language of Randolph's instructions.

I rely upon yr. self & Mr. Jones in planning the many little tho' very important matters for me, abt. my farm. Such as fixing the place for my house orchards & the like.[35] It will not be very long before we join you; we are all well. Mrs. M. is with her child a pupil to a professor in the French language. They desire to be affectionately remembered to yr. self & family taking it for granted you have Mrs. Randolph & both yr. daughters with you. I am, Dear Sir, Yr. affectionate friend & servant,

Jas. Monroe

To the President of the National Convention, Paris, September 9, 1794

Citizen,—The Convention having decreed, that the flag of the American and French Republics should be united together and suspended in its own hall, in testimony of eternal union and friendship between the two people; I have thought I could not better evince the impression this act has made

---

men like Jefferson and Madison, on the other hand, naturally sympathized with the French republicans and viewed with optimism the overthrow of the French monarchy and the birth pangs of the young French republic. In circumstances such as these, it was the obvious dictate of prudence that the United States should pursue the course of neutrality. George Washington, "of all American public men the most invariably judicious," as William Edward Hartpole Lecky once put it, had clearly perceived, even before the actual outbreak of war, that neutrality in any European war should be the keystone of American policy. As early as 1790, when the international situation appeared threatening, he had written in this strain to Lafayette. In the fall of 1792, when the cabinet had under discussion the possibility of a rupture with Spain, and the ebullient Hamilton had brought forward, as he had two years earlier, the idea of an alliance with Great Britain, the President had declared that "the remedy would be worse than the disease." And on March 23, 1793, in a private letter written after news of the British declaration of war on France, Washington again indicated his hope that the United States would be able to hold aloof from the conflict. Washington's consistent position, backed as it was by a united cabinet, only served to further alienate him from Monroe who continued to support the French perspective. (Perkins 1954, 12-13)

[35] When his father Spence died in 1774, Monroe, his sister, and two younger brothers were placed under the guardianship of his uncle, Judge Joseph Jones of King George County. Jones, who was then childless, took an active interest in his nephew, and it was with Jones's encouragement that Monroe entered William and Mary College in 1774. (Ammon 2001, 3)

---

on my mind, or the grateful sense of my constituents, than by presenting in their behalf, that of the United States to the representatives of the French people. Having caused it, therefore, to be executed, according to the modes prescribed by a late act of Congress, I now commit it to the care of Captain Barney, an officer of merit in our own revolution, and who will attend for the purpose of depositing it wherever you will be pleased to direct.[36] I pray you therefore to accept it, as a proof of the sensibility with which my country receives every act of friendship from our ally, and of the pleasure with which it cherishes every incident which tends to cement and consolidate the union between the two nations.

To the Secretary of State [Edmund Randolph], Paris, September 15, 1794

Sir,—As soon as I could command a moments leisure, I applied myself to the immediate duties of my station. I found many of my countrymen here laboring under embarrassments of a serious kind growing out of the war, and was soon furnished with like complaints from others in several of the seaports. Correct information upon every point was my first object, for unless I knew the nature & extent of the evil, I could not seek a remedy.[37] I encouraged therefore by my letters these representations, as the only means by which I could acquire it, nor was it difficult to be obtained, for the parties interested have been deeply affected and long delayed, to be remiss upon the present occasion. In the course of a few weeks, I believe most of the complaints which had been occasioned by the War, and especially where

---

[36] Joshua Barney, a French partisan, was a capable American naval officer. During the Revolutionary War, his capture of the British vessel *Monk*, a ship larger than his own, the *Hyder Ally*, in the presence of other British vessels, was considered one of the more noteworthy events of the naval war. (Headley 1848, 328)

[37] Here, Monroe provides additional evidence of a certain growth in his spirit of moderation when he mentions the case of Barrère, Collot d'Herbois and Billaud Varennes, who were denounced in the Convention as having been supporters and encouragers of Robespierre. The Convention, however, after having heard the long list of charges, dismissed them with disdain, and even censured the accuser, Lecointre de Versailles, as a disturber of the public peace. The attacking party were now alarmed for their own safety, thinking that the rejection of their motion showed the invincible strength of the faction they had tried to proscribe. But herein they showed themselves superficial observers of the trend of events and opinions. They did not perceive that there was a force in the Convention that was making for peace, that was determined to curb the passions of all violent factions. The accusers did not have a majority of the Convention. Neither did the accused, as was shown by their defeat shortly after in their effort to be re-elected to the Committee of Public Safety. "I have mentioned this incident," opined Monroe, "because I deem it an important one, in the character of the present moment; tending to prove the certainty with which the Revolution progresses toward a happy close; since the preponderance of those councils which are equally distinguished for their wisdom, temperance and humanity, continues to increase." (Hazen 1897, 196-197)

the parties were present either in person or by attorney, were laid before me. By analysing them (including those which were committed to me from your department whilst in Philadelphia) I found they might be classed under the following heads.

1. Those who were injured by the embargo of Bordeaux.

2. Those who had claims upon the Republic for supplies rendered the government of St Domingo.

3. Those who had brought cargoes in for sale and were detained by delay of payment or some other cause.

4. Those who had been brought in by the Ships of the Republic in derogation of the treaty of amity and commerce and were subjected to like detention and delay.

5. Those who had been taken at sea or elsewhere and were confined in derogation of the treaty of amity and commerce or rights of citizenship in the United States.

Upon the two first heads, and indeed upon the two latter, so far as compensation to the injured parties was in question I had no difficulty how to act. Your instructions had fully marked the course to be taken. I therefore required that compensation be made as soon as possible, and upon just principles according to the contract where such was the case, and the fair estimated value where it was not. But the two latter involved in them something more than the mere adjustment of existing claims, and which closed the scene when that was made. They grew out of measures which if suffered to continue might create like injuries every week, & which would require a like interposition on my part. I therefore considered it my duty not only to require a full indemnity to the claimants, as in the other instances, but to mount to the source of the evil and seek a remedy commensurate therewith.

I found that the delays above spoken of did not proceed from interest or design on their part; from interest they could not for they not only disgusted and injured the claimants but likewise exposed the Government to considerable loss, upon account of demurrage. And if there was no motive of interest there could be none for design. They proceeded in fact from the system of trade adopted here by which the whole commerce of the country was taken into the hands of the republic itself. The regulation was such, that none but the officers of Government could purchase, nor could any contract be concluded and executed in any of the seaports, or elsewhere than in Paris. This threw every case into the hands of a board of commerce in this city, who were otherwise borne down with an immense weight of the most extensive and complicated duties. The defeat in our arrangements too, had increased the embarrassment; for as we had no Consul here every Captain or Supercargo became his own negotiator, and as they were generally ignorant of the City, the language and the prices last given, they were badly calculated for the purpose. Every new cargo formed a distinct negotiation, and as there was no system on the part of the vendors, who wished as was natural, to make the most of their voyage, they usually asked an extravagant price for it in the first instance. This occasioned a kind of traffic between the parties, and which frequently terminated in the disgust of both, and particularly of the vendors, who after they were wearied out with the clerks in the department, and whose duty it was to receive them, generally assigned the business over to some agent, and who as he was not cloathed with any public character, could neither be much respected by the French Government, nor possessed in any high degree of the confidence of his employers. Such was the state of our trade in the Republic, and such the cause of the delay. As soon therefore as I understood it I considered it my duty to bring the subject before the Government, and desire on its part a suitable remedy: and if the person lately appointed does not soon arrive, I shall deem it equally necessary to nominate someone as Consul provisionally, to take charge of the business on ours. And if he does arrive I am by no means certain it will remedy the difficulty, for reasons I shall hereafter explain.

I had more difficulty in determining how to act on the fourth point. I was not instructed to desire a repeal of the decree, and did not know but that it had been tolerated from the soundest motives of political expedience. This Republic had declined calling on us to execute the guarantee, from a spirit of magnanimity, and strong attachment to our welfare. This consideration entitled it to some attention in return. An attempt to press it within the pale of the stipulations contained in the 23d and 24th articles of the treaty of Amity and Commerce might give birth to sentiments of a different kind and create a disposition to call on us to execute that of the treaty of alliance. The subject was therefore of the utmost delicacy, and I saw that I could not enter on it without the greatest care. But yet I was pursuaded that France gained nothing by the departure, and had reason to believe if it were otherwise she would at the present time concede it for our accommodation: and I knew its importance to our commerce, and especially as it would deprive the Cabinet of St. James of the smallest pretext for continuing the violation on its part. Upon full consideration of all these circumstances the paper presented was drawn and I trust whatever may be its effect, it will have the approbation of the President, since it may prove a beneficial one, and has in no respect compromitted him. My note was presented a few days past, and I shall expect an answer as soon as circumstances will permit paying due regard to the immense weight of business before the department.

Upon the article of Citizenship I have as yet said nothing. I did not wish to complicate the subjects which I presented before them too much at any one time. It is however an important one, and shall be soon attended to, as shall likewise the claim for reimbursements of 50,000 dollars advanced to the French Emigrants from S' Domingo.

Nothing of great importance has lately taken place in the public councils. The remaining spirit of ancient parties has, it is true, occasionally shewn itself, but not with its former vigor, for it seems in a great measure to have withdrawn and to lurk in the bosoms of the more inveterate only. Happily a different spirit more congenial with the temper of the nation and which inclines to humanity, to peace and concord, seems to pervade the great mass of the convention. I think this latter will soon prevail so as not only to prevent, at least for the present further enormities, but to heal in some degree the wounds which have already been inflicted. Some latter circumstances authorise this expectation. Barrere, Collet d'Herbois, and Billaud Varenne of the Committee of Public Safety and several of the Committee of Surety general, were suspected by many of having countenanced and supported the measures of Robespierre, and it was apprehended that after the perfect and preternatural calm, which ensued his execution, should subside some discussion would take place on that subject. Accordingly they were lately denounced by Le Cointre of Versailles, who brought forward a long list of charges against them. But it was immediately seen that the party in favor of the denunciation though violent was weak. The convention heard the accusation with patience and rejected it with disdain, and Le Cointre himself was eventually censured as a disturber of the public repose. Many of this party were now in their turn alike agitated and alarmed because they thought they saw in the rejection of the motion the invincible strength of the other party and the certainty of their own fate. But they were superficial observers of the course of the present revolution, and of the theatre on which they acted. They did not perceive that there was a force in the Convention actuated by more humane and dignified principles, able to controul both, and render their extravagant and pernicious efforts abortive and harmless. This latter fact was farther demonstrated by an event which followed immediately after. Under the reorganization of the committee of public safety, it became necessary to re-elect its members; and if the influence of those lately denounced had preponderated, they would of course have been re-chosen. But the contrary was the case for they were every one rejected and others preferred in their stead. I have mentioned this incident because I deem it an important one in the character of the present moment, tending to prove the certainty with which the revolution progresses towards a happy close, since the preponderance of those Councils which are equally distinguished for their wisdom, temperance and humanity, continues to increase.

Nor is fortune less propitious to the affairs of this Republic in the field than in the Cabinet. Within a few days past Conde and Valenciennes have surrendered to its victorious arms. About 6,000 troops were taken in these garrisons and 1,100 emigrants and which latter were immediately put to the sword. The rigor with which the emigrants have been pursued continues nearly the same and seems still to be dictated equally by the sentiments of the public councils and the people at large: it will therefore not be easily or soon removed.

The surrender of these garrisons has relieved from a state of inactivity about 50,000 men who were immediately added to the armies upon the Meuse and on the frontier of Holland. These armies are at present of great strength and certainly upon the ordinary rules of calculation, not to be resisted by the force now embodied against them. In point of numbers they are by far superior and they possess the means by which this superiority may be increased at pleasure and to any amount. Their discipline too is exact, their spirits high and enterprize astonishingly great, whilst on the other side everything wears a more gloomy aspect. Their troops are dispirited and daily wasting away by the events of War and reinforcements have been for a long time past with difficulty obtained & seem now to be exhausted or at least at a stand. And to increase the embarrassments on their part 'tis said a dispute has taken place between Cobourg and York for the command, in case they should unite their forces: the latter having set up a claim in consequence of the great force, Prussians &c. in British pay.

Cobourg occupies at present a position near Maestricht, and York one in the neighbourhood of Bergen-op-Zoom. 'Tis thought the French will direct their principal force towards these posts, since their conquest will not only lay open the whole country to the Rhine, but likewise deprive Holland of its chief barrier. They are strong and well provided but deemed by no means impregnable to the ardor and enterprize of the French troops. 'Tis therefore probable some severe rencontre may take place in each quarter, for surely nothing but absolute despair will induce the combined forces to abandon them and which they must otherwise do, in case the French continue to exert themselves with their usual vigor.

You will observe I have adopted in my movements here the plan of conciliation, and that I have intimated in consideration of the alliance subsisting between the two Republics, the preference we have on that and other accounts, for France to any other country. I have done so not only in obedience to the dictates of my own judgment, but because I thought I thereby followed the spirit of your instructions, and because I well knew I could not otherwise count upon success in any thing I undertook. In the brilliant career of victory which now attends the arms of the Republic you will readily conceive that a cordial but dignified tone is better calculated to produce a happy effect, than one which was distant, formal, and merely diplomatic. And I was the more inclined to it from a belief that I saw in the temper of the nation a sincere disposition to accomodate us in all cases within its power, and to cultivate the most perfect harmony between the two countries. Whether this is real or fallacious, time, and a very short one, will now disclose, since I have presented before the Government proposi-tions which must eventually test it.

I have the honor to be with great respect and esteem,

Your most obedient servant, Jas. Monroe

To the Minister of the Republic of Geneva [M. Reybaz], Paris, September 15, 1794

Citizen Minister,—I have received, with great satisfaction, the account you have been pleased to render me of the generous impression which the suspension of the flags of the three Republics of America, France and Geneva, in the hall of the National Convention, has excited in the breasts of your countrymen. The standards of Republics should always be ranged together, and I am perfectly satisfied, that this event will be received with equal joy by the Government and Citizens of the United States, to whom I shall commu-nicate it. I beg of you, citizen minister, to be assured of the solicitude which the Government and People of America feel for the freedom, prosperity and happiness of the Republic of Geneva, and of the pleasure with which I shall at all times become the instrument of the most intimate and friendly commu-nications between them.[38]

To James Madison, Paris, September 20, 1794

Dear Sir,—Mr. Swan of Boston who has resided for some years past in this city in the character of a merchant & in which time he has been extensively engaged will present you this. He leaves this for the purpose of purchasing & shipping to this country the productions of ours & relies much on the

---

[38] Geneva's revolution followed that of France, her National Convention adopting, in 1794, a constitution that declared political equality to all the Genevese. In March 1798, Geneva elected to become a part of France and, in June, the French authorities entered the city. By the Treaty of Paris its independence was restored, and it became one of the Cantons of the Swiss Confederation. The first American treaty with the Swiss Confederation was effected in May 1847. (Hamilton 1899, 64)

advances to be made by our gov't for the means. He will I understand be sole agent in that line of this republick in America. He well knows y'r disposition on this head & will confer with you in regard to it. I beg you to be attentive to him as he has been very obliging to us here. I have written you very fully by the way of Bordeaux, and as Mr. S. proposes landing at Ch'stown shall have more early opportunities of apprizing you of those events of the present day which may escape him.[39]

We are well.

Very sincerely, I am y'r friend & serv't,

Jas. Monroe

To the Commissary of Foreign Relations [M. Buchat.], Paris, September 22, 1794

Citizen Commissary,—I have this moment received the enclosed memorial from the masters of two American vessels; the Mary, commanded by Henry Preble and the Severn, by Jared Goodrich, who were boarded at sea by the Proserpine, a frigate of the Republic, and all the passengers taken from the one vessel, and the other, with her cargo and passengers, brought into Brest where they are now detained. As these cases form like departures from the treaty of amity and commerce between the two Republics, and are in that respect, analogous with those complained of in my note lately presented to the committee of Public Safety, I have thought it my duty, as connected with that subject, to bring them immediately before the same department. Independently of the propriety of accommodating the principle to the wishes of my country and which I earnestly hope, for the common interests of both Republics, will be soon done, I presume the embarrassment of virtuous men, and good patriots, as is the case in the present instance, will be an additional motive for their immediate enlargement.[40]

[39] James Swan, a Boston expatriate speculator, was a significant claimant under the Convention of 1803, having no less than nine cases before the Board of Commissioners. They were rejected mainly on the ground of his being in partnership with foreigners and that he was an agent of the French government. He was regarded by Monroe as "the greatest scoundrel in Europe." (Hamilton 1899, 65; Brant, 1970, 332)

[40] The *Severn* from Bristol to New York, with emigrants for America on board, was captured September 1st, and sent into Brest, where the passengers were placed on board the prison ship *L'Orient*. The *Mary*, captured on August 18th, experienced the same treatment. These appear to have been among the first cases brought up as a result of the French Spoliation Claims. The case of the *Severn* subsequently appears on the Records of the Board of 1803, by which it was adjudicated. (Williams 2009, 324; Hamilton 1899, 66)

To the Commissary of Exterior Relations [M. Miot], Paris, September 1794

Citizen Commissary,—A short experience has already demonstrated the interest which my country has in the appointment of some person here known to your government and responsible to ours to take charge of the affairs of its citizens in the commercial line. This consideration has induced me to appoint Fulwar Skipwith[41] heretofore Secretary of Legation, to the office of Consul for the department of Paris, and who will take on himself and discharge the duties properly belonging thereto, until the sense of our government shall be known on the subject. I have therefore to request you will be so obliging as to cause this to be communicated to the several departments of your government, in such manner that he may be known and respected as such.

To the Commissary of Foreign Affairs [M. Buchat], Paris, September 1794

Citizen Commissary,42—My predecessor Mr. Morris, finding it impossible to procure a vessel to embark his baggage and sail for some weeks yet to come, wishes to employ that time in an excursion into Switzerland, and has requested me to obtain, for him, a passport for that purpose. The better, however, to explain to you his wishes, I have enclosed a copy of his letter to me on that subject. Perhaps, it may be more conformable to the course of proceedings in such cases, that it should be granted, in the present instance, by the Committee of public safety. But in either case, I presume it will be more agreeable to him, as it likewise would be to me, that their approbation of the measure should be previously obtained. I have, therefore, to request,

---

[41] Originally from Virginia, Fulwar Skipwith was Consul for the island of Martinique, June 4, 1790, until June 5, 1795, when he was nominated Consul General of the United States in France. On January 6, 1802, he was appointed Commercial Agent at Paris. On June 18, 1803, he was appointed by Monroe and Livingston to assist in the operations of the Board of Commissioners under the Convention with France of 1803. (Hamilton 1899, 67)

[42] While laboring to conciliate France and to obtain the other objects of his mission, Monroe seems to have feared that the worst possible scenarios might be continually based upon his actions by his political opponents. With this view he thought best to forestall any complaints from Gouverneur Morris by writing directly to the President of a misunderstanding that he had had with the American ex-minister. Gouverneur Morris, it seems, had applied for a passport to travel in Switzerland. Since practically all of his French connections and friends (the émigrés) were in Switzerland, the Committee of Public Safety, who were suspicious of his intentions, did not wish to grant this permission. Finally, Morris was compelled to accept the passport from his successor, Monroe, rather than from the Directory as he had wished. This incident illustrates the difficulties under which Monroe labored as the successor to a minister, Morris, whom he knew to be more in favor at home than himself. (Bond 1897, 75)

---

citizen, that you will be so obliging as to make known to that body his wishes, and obtain their sanction.

To Le Ray Du Chaumont, Paris, October 13, 1794

Sir,—I was lately advised by the Secretary of State, that the negotiation of a treaty with Algiers had been committed to Col. Humphreys, our Minister at Lisbon; and that of course every movement having that object in view, must be conducted under his care. Your agency if carried into effect, must of course be in that line. I give you this information that in case you wish to render your services in that respect to the United States, you may communicate the same to Colonel Humphreys; who will I doubt not, pay every attention to it that a sense of your merit and existing arrangements will allow of. I have also the pleasure to inform you, that the President has approved of the measures taken by Mr. Morris and of the confidence reposed in you by him, in relation to that object.43

To the Secretary of State [Edmund Randolph], Paris, Oct 16, 1794

Sir,—I gave you in my last a sketch of the embarrassments under which our commerce laboured in the ports of this Republic, and of my efforts to emancipate it, as shewn by my letter to the Committee of Public Safety, a copy of which was likewise forwarded. To this I have as yet received no answer although I have requested it more than once. To my applications, however, which were informal I was informally answered, that the subject was under consideration, and would be decided on as soon as possible.44

---

43 Jacques Donatien Leray de Chaumont was very wealthy French aristocrat and an early supporter of the American revolution. Upon Benjamin Franklin's arrival in Paris as one of the first commissioners to France, de Chaumont, then commissary of the French Ministry of Marine, allowed him to stay free of charge in the Hôtel Valentinois, a large estate with stately gardens at Passy, one mile from Paris and seven miles from Versailles. Named after a previous owner, the Duchesse de Valentinois, there were actually two houses on the property (which was considerable), one designated a "grand" hotel and the other a "petite" hotel, the larger being occupied by de Chaumont and his family and the other by the American commissioners. The house became the informal headquarters of the American delegation and served as a meeting place for the sympathizers as well as the representatives of the new American republic. De Chaumont continued his friendly relations with Monroe's predecessors Thomas Jefferson and Gouverneur Morris. (Langguth, 434; De Koven, 241-42).

44 As background to this lengthy letter, it is well to remember that European interference with American shipping and commerce was not new. Of course, the British did not stop maritime aggression. John Quincy Adams sarcastically wrote that British maritime policy was "comprised in one line of a popular song, Rule Britannia! Britannia Rule the waves!" However, the French combined political, diplomatic, and maritime aggression in a way that threatened America's rights of self-determination. Before Jay's Treaty, American

But as these propositions were of extensive import, and connected with the system of commerce and supply, which had been adopted here, 'tis probable I shall not be favoured with an answer until the subject is generally reviewed. Nor shall I be surprized to find extraordinary efforts to protract a decision, and even defeat the object in view. But as the opposition will not be warranted by the interest, so I am well satisfied it will not be supported by the sense of the French nation, when the object is well understood. To make it so will be the object of my future, and I trust not ineffectual endeavours.

You were, I doubt not, surprised to hear that the whole commerce of France, to the absolute exclusion of individuals, was carried on by the government itself. An institution of this kind would be deemed extraordinary, even in a small state; but when applied to the French Republic it must appear infinitely more so. Nor were the circumstances which gave birth to it, more a proof of the calamities with which the society was inwardly convulsed than of the zeal and energy with which it pursued its object. Through the channel of trade it was found, or suspected, that the principles of the revolution were chiefly impaired; that through it, not only the property of the emigrants and the wealth of the country were exported, but that foreign money was likewise thrown in, whereby the internal dissensions were fomented, and in other respects the intrigues of the coalesced powers promoted. For a considerable time it was believed that most of the evils to which France was a prey, proceeded from this source. Many remedies were in consequence applied, but still the disease continued. Finally an effort was made to eradicate the cause by exterminating private trade altogether, and taking the whole commerce of the country into the hands of the government. A decree to this effect accordingly passed on the day of October 1793, and which has since continued in force.

But now many circumstances incline to a change of this system. The act itself was considered as a consummation of those measures which completed the ruin of the Girondine party, whose principal leaders had already fallen under the guillotine. By it, the commercial interest, as distinct from the landed, and dividing in certain respects with opposite views, the councils of the country, was totally destroyed. All private mercantile intercourse with foreign nations was cut off, and so severe were the measures, and great the

shippers experienced trouble with France; and the consul in Paris, Fulwar Skipwith, had provided Monroe a list of 300 ships experiencing difficulties in French ports. These depredations, albeit modest compared to French action following Jay's Treaty, were the norm. The treaty, however, added to Europe's impending "commercial revolution...[one that threatened to be] as complete as the political revolution" the French had authored. This combination of events only hurt the French in the eyes of many of Washington's political elite. (Dawson 2000, 33)

odium on the mercantile character that none were pleased to have it attached to them. But when the apprehension of danger from that source was done away, the motive for the act itself was greatly diminished. Accordingly the public mind was soon seen vibrating back to its former station; and in which it was greatly aided by the fortune of the late dominant party, whose principal leaders had now likewise in their turn settled their account with the Republic at the receipt of the guillotine. Thus we find, and especially in great commotions, that extraordinary measures not only bear in general the strong character of their author, but frequently share his fate. The fall of the Brissotine party extirpated private trade; the fall of Robespierre's may probably soon restore it.

At present many symptoms indicate that a change is not distant, though none seem willing so prominently to take the lead, as to make themselves responsible for the consequences. The only active interest that I can perceive against it, consists of those who have managed the public trade and been entrusted with the public monies for that purpose. They readily foresee that a change will not only take from them the public cash but likewise lead to an adjustment of their accounts for past transactions. 'Tis however generally the fortune of an opposition of this kind, to precipitate the adoption of the measure it wishes to avert; for as every one suspects that its motive is not found, and which is proportionally increased by the degree of zeal shewn, so every one feels an interest in defeating it.

I have endeavoured in my propositions to confine them entirely to external objects, by suggesting such remedies as might be adopted without any interference with the interior general system of France. By so doing I hoped that the injuries of which we complain might be sooner redressed and not made dependant on the great events which happen here.

I soon found that the extraordinary expedient to which this Republic had had recourse, of excluding individuals from trade and conducting it themselves, would require in a great measure, a correspondent regulation on our part: For if the conduct of the public servants, on the one side, was not in some measure supervised, and which it could not be, but by public agents on the other, the impositions which might be practised on our improvident countrymen would be endless. In every contest between a public officer here, and the citizens of another country in the purchase of supplies for the Republic or execution of a contract, the bias of the government and of the people would be in favour of the former. The consulate, under the superintendance of the minister, forms their natural bulwark in the commercial line against impositions of every kind. Indeed it is the only one which can be provided for them. But to guard them against those proceeding from the source above described, it should be organized with peculiar care. I was sorry, therefore, upon inspecting into our establishment, to find that whatever might be its merits in other situations, it was by no means in general endowed with sufficient strength or vigour for the present crisis. American citizens alone can furnish an adequate protection to their countrymen. In the hands of a Frenchman or other foreigner, the consular functions lie dormant. In every litigated case the former shrinks into the citizen and trembles before the authority of his country; and the latter, especially if the subject of one of the coalesced powers, finds our commission only of sufficient force to exempt him from the decree which would otherwise doom him to a prison. I annex at the foot of this a list of our Consuls and Consular agents, with a note of those who have been actually under arrestation and confinement and by which you will be better enabled to comprehend the nature of these remarks.

My situation was, therefore, in every view, beyond measure an embarrassing one. But as there was no consul or agent of any kind or country here, where the whole business was concentred, and every transaction closed, it became on that account infinitely more so; for I was in consequence not only daily surrounded by many of my countrymen, complaining of delays and injuries and entreating my intercession for redress, but applied to by them from every quarter and upon every difficulty. I could not settle their accounts with the departments, nor could I interfere in any other respect in particular cases, where there were more of the same description. I could not even go through the forms in the offices where it was necessary to verify facts, and which if true furnished ground for complaint; nor could I demand redress of the government upon any supposititious case, and which every one must be until verified. I remained thus for some time in expectation of the arrival of M. Duvernat, although I was apprehensive such an event, in consequence of the general objection above stated, and the decree which applied particularly to his case, instead of affording relief would plunge me into a new embarrassment. But finding that he had not arrived, and that I could make no progress in the public business here, without the aid of a consul, I finally nominated my Secretary, Mr. Skipwith, provisionally Consul for this City, on the ___ day of ___, and notified it to this government, a copy of which and of the answer of the Commissary of Foreign Affairs I herewith enclose you. To him I have since assigned the interesting duty of developing and demonstrating the cause of these difficulties, by an appeal to authentic facts; and the better to enable him to perform this service, I have instructed our consuls and agents in the several ports to render him a statement of those within their particular jurisdictions. Thus enlightened he will make a report upon the whole subject to me and which I will immediately lay before the Committee of Public Safety, in illustration of my former comments, and with such others as may be found necessary.

At present I can say nothing decisively upon the subject of a general arrangement of the Consulate. What I have said may furnish some hints that may be useful. But I wish before any thing is definitively done in that respect to give you the result of my further remarks on it. Mr. Fenwick will be here in a few days, and from whom I doubt not I shall derive much useful information. In the interim Mr. Skipwith will perform the duties of the office in which I have placed him. But as he undertook it without the prospect of emolument in the official line (for in truth the duties required of him are not strictly consular, but novel and growing out of the emergence of the time) and more from a regard for the public interest, and to accommodate me than himself, although I was thereby deprived of his services in the immediate station in which he had accompanied me, yet I could not bereave him of the appointment I had personally conferred, nor divert from him the salary belonging to it. By permitting things to stand where they are for a few weeks longer, the public will derive no detriment, and I shall be able to acquire and give such information as will enable you to proceed with more propriety afterwards; a consideration which will enable me to bear the inconvenience to which I shall be personally subjected, with pleasure.

I found, upon my first arrival, that I should have much difficulty upon the subject of passports. The jealousy of this government was immediately discovered with respect to those who, being subjects of England, or any other of the coalesced powers, had passed over to America since our revolution, become citizens of some one of the States, and returned to their proper country, where they now resided. It was suggested to me by the Commissary of Foreign Affairs, that if these people were covered by my passports, I should immediately spread through France, in the armies, and in presence of the public councils, a host of spies who would report the circumstances of the country to their enemies. It was likewise urged that I had no right to do it; for although this description of persons had acquired for the time, the right of citizenship with us, yet they were more attached to other countries since they resided and had their property there. I was likewise told of instances wherein this privilege had been abused by such persons, two of whom were said to be confined at Dunkirk as spies. The subject was in point of principle difficult, and I was really embarrassed how to act in it so as to satisfy this government and do justice to the parties concerned; for if citizens of America it seemed difficult to distinguish between such and any other citizens. And yet the argument was equally strong on the other side; for if the subject of another power, it was equally difficult to distinguish between such and any other subject of the same power, where the right of expatriation is generally denied. But in point of expedience there was less difficulty in the case. Citizenship is in its nature a local privilege. It implies a right within the government conferring it. And if considerations of this kind are to be regarded, I can see no reason why it should not, in the present instance, be construed strictly: For if a temporary emigrant, after availing himself of this benefit for a few years, and for the purposes of trade, in our indulgent country, chuses to abandon us and return from whence he came, why should we follow him on this side of the Atlantic to support in his behalf a privilege which can now only be claimed at best for private and perhaps dishonourable purposes? Can any motive be urged of sufficient force to induce us to embark here in this kind of controversy at the hazard of our national character and the good will of the nation believing itself injured by it? Will the refusal to grant passports to such persons check emigration to our country? I am satisfied it will not, of the kind that merits encouragement; for it will rarely happen that a single member of that respectable list of philosophers, artists and yeomen who seek an asylum with us from the troubled governments on this side of the Atlantic will ever re-cross it. These observations apply only to those who settled with and abandoned us since the peace; for I consider those, be they of whatever country they may, and especially if of the British territory (who were of course, in the common character of British subjects, equally members of our revolution) who threw their fortunes into our scale, as being as much Americans as if they were born with us. After some discussion with the commissary on the subject, it terminated by an assurance on my part that I should be particularly cautious as to such characters and refuse my passports to all of that description (except in particular cases of hardship, and upon which he should be previously consulted) who were not actually resident within the United States. This arrangement was satisfactory to the government as you will perceive by the commissary's letters to me, copies of which are herewith transmitted. I shall, however, be happy to be instructed by you on that head.

The Councils of this Republic still continue to present to view an interesting, but by no means an alarming spectacle. Instances of animated debate, severe crimination and even of vehement denunciation, sometimes take place; but they have hitherto evaporated without producing any serious effect. It is obvious that what is called the mountain party is rapidly on the decline, and, equally so, that if the opposite one acts with wisdom and moderation, at the present crisis, it will not only complete its overthrow, but destroy the existence (if possible in Society) of all party whatever. The agitation which now occasionally shews itself, proceeds from the pressure of this latter party on the mountaineers, and who in their defence, sometimes make a kind of incursive or offensive warfare upon their enemy; for having since the fall of the Brissotines, wielded the councils of the nation, and been accustomed to a pretty liberal use of their authority over the remaining members of that party, they bear with pain, and not without apprehension of danger, their present decline.[45] The tone of the discussion, therefore, frequently exhibits to view the external of a violent controversy between two rival parties, nearly equally balanced, and which must terminate under the preponderance of either, in the extirpation of the other. But this I deem only the external aspect, and upon considerations, in my judgment the most solid. I have observed generally, that the first indications of warmth have proceeded from the weaker party, and from its less important members, who occasionally break through the restraint imposed on them by their leaders; (if, when a force is broken and routed, there can be any leader) and sally forth into extravagancies, which provoke resentment, where they should only endeavour to excite pity; and whilst a different conduct is observable by the leaders themselves; for neither Barrere, Billaud de Varennes, nor Collot d'Herbois, ever take part in these discussions, otherwise than to explain some severe personal attack, and to which they confine their comments strictly and with all suitable respect for their opponents. I observe it rarely happens that any very distinguished member in the preponderating party takes share in these discussions; though the field invites, and much might be said with truth and of course with effect. From these considerations I infer, not only that the party of the plain [affiliated with the Girondins] has already acquired the complete preponderancy; but also that its motive is

---

[45] The new National Convention, in reality, was no more united than the preceding assemblies. The Girondins and the Montagnards were political factions that emerged and solidified in 1792–93. But once the new deputies had formally declared the monarchy abolished and decreed that henceforth all public documents should be dated "Year I of the French Republic," agreement ended. A fierce, murderous struggle for political control then broke out between the Girondin deputies of the Right and the Montagnards on the Left. The Montagnards (literally the mountaineers, from the high tier of seats on which they sat) were the deputies who supported the policies of the Paris delegation, all of whom were members of the Jacobins. Although the Girondins were also once members of the Society, most of them had now been expelled. More to the point, personal rivalries entered into the fray. Leading Girondins, such as Brissot, Condorcet, Vergniaud, and Roland, feared and were jealous of Montagnard leaders, particularly of Danton. Brissot and Robespierre, who had clashed over foreign policy, were the bitterest of enemies. The morbidly suspicious Marat was hated by all the Girondins. Sharp disagreement over the role that Paris should play in the revolutionary movement also set the groups apart, but most of all they were divided by their divergent social views and conception of political tactics. Where the Girondins opposed governmental regulation of economic activities, the Montagnards, who were no less middle class in social origins and certainly as property-minded, realistically accepted the necessity of instituting controls at least for the duration. (Gershoy 1957, 56)

---

rather to save the Republic, than to persecute its enemies. There is, likewise something in the origin and spirit of these debates, which authorizes a belief they portend nothing alarming; for they generally proceed from a review of past enormities, which most deny, and few justify. But the scene through which they have past, cannot always be covered with a veil; on the contrary it frequently breaks in upon their discussions, and always excites, like the Ghost of Hamlet, whenever it appears, the horror of the innocent and the terror of the guilty spectators. The debates, therefore, which ensue, though violent, are more of the exculpatory than of the assailing and sanguinary kind. Each party endeavours to vindicate itself from the charges alledged against it; sometimes by absolute denial, and at others by a counter crimina-tion of its adversary. Hitherto the business has ended by a general reference of the depending motions to the committee of Public Safety solely; or to it, associated with the two other committees of general surety and legislation, and who have had sufficient wisdom, either to keep up the subject till it was forgotten, or to report such a general essay upon the state of affairs, the views of the coalesced powers, trade, finance and the like, as always to obscure, and sometimes to throw it entirely out of view.

By this, however, I do not wish to be understood as intimating, that in my opinion none of the members of the Convention will in future be cut off. On the contrary I think otherwise; for it cannot be possible that some of those who have perpetrated such enormities in their missions in the several parts of the Republic and particularly at Nantes, should escape the justice of their country.

In the movements of the present day, the Jacobin Society has, as hereto-fore, borne its part. The history of this Society, from its origin to the present time, is of importance to mankind and especially that portion upon which Providence has bestowed the blessing of free government. It furnishes a lesson equally instructive to public functionaries and to private citizens.[46]

---

[46] Monroe's history of the Jacobins arrived very seasonably for Washington in his denun-ciation of the "Democratic" societies in the United States. Randolph, in acknowledging it, wrote, "Your history of the Jacobin societies was so appropriate to the present times in our own country, that it was conceived proper to furnish the public with those useful lessons, and extracts were published, as from a letter of a gentleman in Paris to his friend in this city." Madison wrote to Monroe on March 11, 1795, "I have not yet rec'd a single line from you except yours of Sept. 2 long since acknowledged. Your last letters of the official kind were duplicates of October 16, Nov. 7 & 20. You will perceive in the news-papers that the parts of them relating to the Jacobin Societies have been extracted and printed. In New York they have been re published with your name prefixed. The question agitated in consequence of the President's denunciation of the Democratic Societies will account for this use of your observations. In New York where party contests are running high in the choice of a successor to Clinton who declines, I perceive the use of them is extended by adroit comments to that subject also. It is proper you should be apprised

I am not yet fully possessed of the details, although I have endeavoured to acquire them; but the outline I think I now understand. In its history, as in that of the revolution itself, there are obviously two great eras. The first commenced with the revolution and ended with the deposition of the King. The second fills the space between that event and the present day. The former of these is still further di visible into two parts, upon each of which distinct characters are marked. The first commenced with the revolution and ended with the constituent assembly, or adoption of the constitution. The second comprises the administration under the constitution. During the first of these, the Jacobin Society was composed of almost all the enemies to the ancient despotism; for in general those who were friends of the public liberty, and wished its establishment under any possible modification, became at this time members, and attended the debates of this Society. But with the adoption of the constitution many were satisfied and kept it. After this and during the second part of this era, it was composed only of the enemies to hereditary monarchy, comprising the members of the three succeeding parties, of Brissot, Danton, and Robespierre. During the whole of the first era, therefore, or until the deposition of the King, this society may be considered as the cradle of the revolution, for most certainly the Republic would not have been established without it. It was the organ of the public sentiment and, by means of discussion and free criticism upon men and measures, contributed greatly to forward that important event.

But from that period and through the whole of the second era, this Society has acted a different part and merited a different character. The clergy, the nobility and royalty were gone; the whole government was in the hands of the people, and its whole force exerted against the enemy. There was, in short, nothing existing in that line which merited reprehension, or with which the popular sentiment could take offence. But it had already gained a weight in the government, and which it had now neither sufficient virtue nor inclination to abandon. From this period, therefore, its movements were counted Revolutionary, and we behold the same Society which was hereto fore so formidable to the despotism, now brandishing the same weapon against the legitimate representation of the people.

Its subsequent story is neither complicated nor various. As the revolution was complete so far as depended on the interior order of things, it had no service of that kind to render, nor pretext to colour its movements. It was reduced to the alternative of either withdrawing from the stage, or taking part in the ordinary internal administration, and which it could not

of these circumstances that your own judgement may be the better exercised as to the latitude or reserve of your communications." (Hamilton 1899, 81)

do otherwise than becoming an instrument in the hands of some one of the parties against the other. This station, therefore, it at once occupied, and has since held it to the present time. It became the creature of Robespierre and under his direction the principal agent in all those atrocities which have stained this stage of the revolution. It was by means of this society that he succeeded in cutting off the members of the two succeeding parties of Brissot and Danton, and had finally well nigh ruined the Republic itself.

It is an interesting fact and very deserving of attention, that in the more early and latter stages of this society, the best men of France were seeking an admittance into it, but from very different motives. In the commencement and until the establishment of the Republic, it was resorted to by them for the purpose of promoting that great event. But in the latter stage and until the fall of Robespierre, it was resorted to by them merely as a shelter from danger. Virtue and talents, with every other great and noble endowment, were odious in the sight of that monster, and were of course the object of his persecution. Nor was any man of independent spirit, possessing them, secure from his wrath. The Jacobin Society could alone furnish any kind of protection, and to this circumstance it was owing that many deserving char-acters were seen there, apparently countenancing measures which in their souls they abhorred. It is therefore only justice that the present preponder-ating party in France, and the world at large, should now look with indul-gence, and indeed with forgive ness, upon the conduct of many of those who seemed at the time to abet his enormities. Unfortunately for them and for their country, their presence secured only a personal exemption from danger: the preponderating influence had long been in the hands of those of a different description.

In the last scene which was acted by Robespierre, and in which he placed himself at the Commune in open rebellion against the Convention, 'tis said that this Society arranged itself under his banner against that assembly. But after his fall, and which was instantaneous, it immediately endeavoured to repair the error of this step, by charging it upon some who were admitted to be bad members, and others who were said to have forced themselves, at that tumultuous moment, unlicensed into the society, and who were not members at all. It even went into high crimination of Robespierre himself. But the principles of the controversy were too deeply rooted in the minds of all to be so suddenly eradicated. It was obvious that a crisis had arrived which must eventually settle the point, whether the Convention or this Society should govern France, and equally so, that the public mind was, and perhaps long had been, decisively settled in favor of the former. As the catastrophe was approaching, this Society, as heretofore, used, at one time, an elevated or commanding tone, and at others, an humiliating one. But the Convention acted with equal dignity throughout. Whether it contemplated to strike at its existence, by an overt act, or to seek its overthrow by contrasting the wisdom, the justice and magnanimity of its own present conduct, with the past and recent enormities of this Society is uncertain. The leading members of the preponderating party seemed doubtful upon this point. But finally the rash and outrageous extremities of the Society, which was secretly exciting commotions through the country forced the convention into more decisive measures. By its order the Secretary of the Society at Paris was arrested, and all the deputies from those associated with it through France, and who had arrived to deliberate upon the state of their affairs, were driven from the city, under a decree which exempted none, not inhabitants of Paris, except our country men. Of all France, Marseilles was the only district, in which its efforts produced any effect. A small commotion, excited there, was immediately quelled by the ordinary police, and who after making an ex ample of the leaders, reported it to the Convention.

What further measures may be adopted by the Convention, in regard to this Society is uncertain. The subject is now under discussion, and, I shall, I presume, be able in my next to give you the result.

The same success continues to attend the arms of the Republic, and in every quarter. They have taken, since my last, in the north, Juliers, Aix-la-Chapelle, Cologne and Bois-le-duc, and in the south, Bellegarde, with immense stores of cannon, provision, &c. in each, and particularly in Juliers and Bois-le-duc, at both of which latter places, a general action was hazarded by the opposite generals, and in which they were routed with great loss. It is said, indeed, that the action which atchieved Juliers, was among the most important of the present campaign, since they consider it as deciding, eventually, the fate of Maestricht, Bergen-op-Zoom, and of Holland itself. Maestricht is now closely invested and must fall in the course of a few weeks, since the Austrian general has obviously abandoned it to its fate. Holland must fall immediately afterwards; for there is, in truth, nothing to prevent it. Indeed I think it probable they will previously detach twenty or thirty thousand men to take possession of it; for it is generally believed it may be easily accomplished.[47]

[47] In various notes, Monroe elects to include details of the ongoing French Revolutionary Wars, a series of sweeping military conflicts partly inspired by the ideology of the French Revolution. They were chiefly driven by geopolitical considerations and pitted France against Great Britain, Austria, Prussia, Russia, and several other monarchies. By autumn 1794, Prussian and Austrian forces had been driven from French territory, and the Low Countries were again secured against them. During the earlier part of 1795, the Basel treaties with Prussia, Spain, and Holland were generally advantageous to France, leaving Britain and Austria as her sole active enemies. Early in 1796, at the time of this letter, the

What effect these events may produce in England it is difficult for me to say. That Austria, Prussia and Spain have been for some time past wearied with the war, and have wished to withdraw from it is certain. That they will withdraw from it soon is more than probable, and upon the best terms they can get. England, therefore, will have to maintain the contest alone; for Holland will be conquered and subject to the will of the conquerors. This, however, is not the only danger which impends over her. Denmark and Sweden, offended at the unlawful restraints imposed by her on their trade, in the arbitrary rule of contraband, have for near three months past, united their fleet to the amount of about thirty sail, for the purpose of vindicating their rights; and Spain, equally unfriendly, and irritated with that power, has, I have reason to believe, serious thoughts, not only of abandoning the war but of acceding to this combination. The lapse of a few weeks, however, will, no doubt, unfold these subjects more fully to view.

I have the honor to be, dear Sir, with great respect and esteem,

Your most obedient and very humble servant,

Ja. Monroe

List of Consuls

Mr. Fenwick, Consul

Mr. Cathalan, V. Consul

Mr. Dobree, V. Consul, arrested but released.

Mr. Lamotte, V. Consul, arrested but released.

Mr. Coffyn, V. Consul, arrested but released.

Mr. Carpentier, Agent, arrested but released.

P.S. I likewise send you a copy of my application for the release of some persons, emigrating from England for America, taken in two of our vessels, and which I presume will experience the fate of the other question which depends on the Treaty.

To the Committee of Public Safety, Paris, October 18, 1794

Citizens,—Upon the several subjects on which I addressed you on the 17th. Fructidor (September 3rd) viz, the embargo of Bordeaux; the supplies rendered to the government of St Domingo, and the departure by France from the 23rd and 24th articles of the treaty of amity and commerce subsisting between the two Republics, I have but little to add at present. The two former were matters of account only, and could of course involve no topic

new regime of the Directory had launched attacks both on the Germanic and the Italian territories of the Hapsburg Empire. (Atkin, Biddiss and Tallett 2011, 161-162)

for discussion between the committees and myself. I had only to ask for such dispatch in the adjustment and payment, as the exigence of the parties and the circumstances of the Republic would admit of. Nor shall I add any thing upon the third point to change the principle upon which I rested it. The committee will therefore be pleased to decide upon each under the considerations which have already been urged.

I likewise stated in that note, generally the embarrassment under which our commerce laboured in the ports of the Republic. A general view was all I could then give: But the appointment of a consul for this city has since enabled me to obtain a more circumstantial and accurate statement on this head. This officer has already examined it with great attention and reported the result to me, a copy of which I now lay before you.[48] It presents to view a frightful picture of difficulties and losses, equally injurious to both countries, and which if suffered to continue, will unavoidably interrupt, for the time, the commercial intercourse between them. I trust, therefore, the causes will be immediately removed, and suitable remedies adopted; and in this I am the more confident, because those which would be deemed adequate will not, in any degree, interfere with the internal police or regulations of the country.

I also suggested in my former note, that however necessary it might be for France to avail herself of Agents in America at the present crisis, for the purchase and shipment of supplies thence here, it should not be relied on as a principal resource. The more attention I have since paid to this subject, the better satisfied I have been of the justice of that remark. I have therefore, thought it my duty to add some further observations on it, and which I now beg leave to submit to your consideration in the annexed paper. You will observe the consul has likewise comprised in his report the cases of many seamen and other persons, citizens of the United States, taken at sea or elsewhere, and who are now held as prisoners in confinement. I hope an order will be issued for their immediate enlargement; and as it is possible many others may be in like situation, that it may be made to comprehend all the citizens of the United States not charged with any criminal offence against the laws of France, and of which latter description I hope there are none. The committee will, I doubt not, designate such species of evidence necessary to establish the right of citizenship in doubtful cases, as it will be practicable for the parties to furnish. Permit me to request an early decision upon these subjects, that I may immediately communicate it to our government. The Congress will commence its session in a few weeks, and it is the duty of the

---

[48] This includes material from the previously mentioned report by Fulwar Skipwith which detailed the embarrassments and difficulties of American commerce in France. (Hamilton 1899, 88)

President to lay before that body, and at that time, the state of public affairs; comprising, as the most interesting particular, the conduct and disposition of other nations towards the United States. Information upon these points will of course be expected from me, and I should be mortified not to be able to give such as would be deemed satisfactory.

James Monroe

Supplemental Observations to the note of the 3d. of September, upon the American Commerce.

That France will have occasion, whatever may be the crop for the present year, for supplies of provision from foreign countries for the next, is certain. These must be obtained from the neutral countries, and chiefly from the United States of America. It is important for her to ascertain how they shall be obtained, and brought into her ports with greatest certainty and least expense. There are but two possible ways or modes by which these supplies or any others can be brought here, which are: First; by public exertion, or by agents in those countries, whose duty it is to purchase the articles in demand, and send them here on public account: And secondly; by the enter-prize of individuals. Both shall be partially examined.

First, as to the certainty; and which will depend upon prompt purchases, safe carriage and integrity of the agents.

As soon as agents arrive in America, it will be known to the commercial interest in every quarter. Whenever they appoint sub-agents, this will like-wise be known. When it is intended to make purchases and shipments, this will be known. The movement of vessels to take in cargoes will be observed. Immediately a combination will be formed among the merchants of the place, who will buy up the four, &c. with a view of taking an advantage of the emergence, and this will raise the price and create delay. A monopoly naturally revolts the society against it, and this will add a new stimulus to the otherwise sufficiently active one of private interest, to speculate and prey upon these agents, and of course upon the embarrassments of their country.

But the purchase is finally made and shipped for France; the ships are at sea; the property belongs to France, and the ships though American, give no protection, by the ancient law of nations, which is in force where not other-wise regulated by treaty, and of course with England. The cargo of every vessel which shall be taken will be condemned; and will not many be taken? The movements of this agency will be well known to the British administra-tion, and it will be employed to counteract it in the purchase and upon the sea. It will be apprised of the ports from whence shipments will be made, and have vessels of war stationed to seize them.

It is the nature of an agency to be at war with every other mode of supply. The amount of its profits will depend upon the exclusion of every other; for every cargo which shall arrive from another source, will take from it so much. It will, therefore, see with jealously the commencement of enterprises of this kind, and deem each in the degree a robbery of its own resources. It will fear that not only the amount of its profits will be diminished, but that the funds upon which they are to be made, will be exhausted. It will, therefore, discourage there enterprises, by hinting that the Republic does not want them; that it has no money to pay for them; that the captains and supercargoes are ill-treated in France by delay. It will be the interest of the agency to crush every other mode of supply, and it will accomplish it, unless the wisest precautions are used to prevent it.

These latter observations apply to the motive of interest only, supposing the agency disposed to discharge the trust as faithfully as it could, making, at the same time, the greatest profit for itself and which would generally be done. But let it be supposed that it was capable of defrauding the public as much as possible, without being detected. In that case it would have additional motives for discouraging private adventurers; because as these would flock to the market and bid one against the other, they would keep the price at its proper level, and thus check its conduct, for if it charged more than they (allowing for the difference of the Commission) it would of course be convicted of fraud, and if capable of fraud, other and numerous temptations to seduction might be counted. The chief agent would be known to the British administration. Suppose France in great distress for bread and without any other resource. The withholding it might bring on a crisis in her affairs, and which might terminate in an arrangement that would applaud the agent for his perfidy. Would he not be an object for the British administration to assail, and would it be proper that France and the French Revolution should be thus made dependent on agents in foreign countries.

As to the comparative expense there could be no question on that point. The commission itself would be no inconsiderable thing, in addition to which the freight will be increased; for if American vessels are employed, the owners will charge more on account of the hazard, than if there was none and which would be the case if the property was their own: Not to repeat the increased price which would be demanded by the agents in consequence of the combination among the merchants, to take advantage of circumstances which would be known to them; nor to suggest that, under any probable modification, it would be the interest of the agents to give the highest price possible.

Besides, funds must be raised somewhere to answer the drafts of these agents: Will it be in the seaports, in Paris, Hamburgh or some other neutral town? The former, as heretofore, will probably be in a great measure declined; and if the latter is adopted, how will they be raised there? By the exportations of the productions or other commodities of the country; incurring thereby the expense of double commissions, storage, the hazard of the sea and of the enemy, together with the further inconvenience of overstocking the market, and raising at the same time, such town to grandeur, by making it the entrepot of French provisions, whilst her own were impoverished.

Everything that has been said or can be said against a chief dependence on agencies, forms an argument in favour of encouraging the ordinary private trade by individuals and shews that the supply by that mode might be made more sure and cheap. If France would regulate things so that the parties bringing provisions into her ports were paid immediately and dispatched, she might command, if necessary, the whole produce of America. Nor would it be necessary that the payment be always in specie: On the contrary, return cargoes would more frequently be taken of productions, manufactures and of prize goods.

The above is a short sketch of the conveniences and inconveniences which attend the two modes of supply. The one which commences in a monopoly will be attended with all the inconveniences which belong to monopolies in general, greater expense, disgust to all parties affected by it, &c. &c. with others which are peculiar to it: For other monopolies of foreign trade, are confined to luxuries of little importance, and of countries whose citizens cannot send them to market; whereas the present one is a monopoly of the necessaries of life in great demand here; to be obtained from countries whose citizens can best supply them, and at a crisis of affairs when the failure may hazard everything valuable to France, and when of course it should be most avoided. Whilst on the other hand, the latter, which is a system of free trade, will not only be free from these objections, but enjoy some benefits which are peculiar to it. It will leave commerce in the hands of individuals and under the protection of the flags of both countries. If it was made known that France would protect the neutral commerce, the merchants would have a new encouragement to enterprize, and the neutral powers would be more decisive in vindicating their own rights. The French flag would be deemed the guardian of trade and the asserter of the freedom of the seas. The American merchants would behold it with pleasure, because they would find under its banner, not only the friendly welcome of their ally, but likewise a safety from the pirates of the ocean. If the demand in France was great, it would be known in the United States, whose merchants would immediately supply the demand. And if it was interrupted on the sea by the vessels of another power; what would be the obvious effect of such interruption? Might not France op pose it and conduct the vessels safe to her ports, and would it not rouse the nation injured to vindicate its rights and protect its own commerce?

Unhappily France has adopted a different policy towards us heretofore. Instead of encouraging individuals to supply her market, she has given them every possible discouragement which could be devised. Instead of protecting our commerce at sea and leaving us to seek reparation for the injuries which were rendered us by other powers, she has rendered us like injuries and thus embarrassed our councils. But it is not too late to change this system of policy. The Americans have lamented it not more on their own account than that of France. It has, as yet, left no unkind impression behind it, and if the necessary regulations are made, commerce will soon resume its ordinary course.

I do not by this object to the plan of supplying by agency altogether: On the contrary, I deem it necessary, because I think it proper for France to avail herself at the present crisis of every resource within her reach. I only wish that it be not relied on as the sole one, and which it will certainly be if the wisest measures are not adopted at home, to encourage the ordinary private trade, and to restrict and otherwise guard against any misconduct in the agency abroad.

Jas Monroe.

To the Committee of General Surety, Paris, November 1, 1794

Citizens,—In all cases where the citizens of the United States commit themselves to the jurisdiction of the French Republic, it is their duty to obey the law, in consideration of the protection which it gives, or otherwise submit to its penalty. This principle is unquestionable; it belongs to the nature of sovereignty, it can never be separated from it. All that my countrymen thus circumstanced have a right to claim of me as their representative, is to see that they have justice rendered them, according to the nature of the charge, and their offence, if they have committed any, by the tribunals whose duty it is to take cognizance of it.

I hope that few cases will ever happen where the conduct of an American citizen will become the subject of discussion here before a criminal tribunal. In those cases which may happen, if any do, I shall re pose entire confidence in the justice of the tribunal, being well satisfied, that if any bias existed in the bosom of the judge, it would be in favor of my countrymen. To hasten their trial before the judge, where one was deemed necessary is I am persuaded, the only point upon which I shall ever feel or express any solicitude.

I should not at the present crisis, call your attention to any case of the kind, if I were not impelled by considerations of peculiar weight. Considerations which I know you will respect; because every succeeding day more fully demonstrates how thoroughly the whole French nation is devoted to the cause which gave birth to them. The great efforts which it has already made and is now making in favor of the public liberty, sufficiently shows how highly it estimates that blessing, and gratitude to those who have served that cause is deemed by you inseparable from a veneration for the cause itself.

The citizens of the United States can never look back to the era of their own revolution, without remembering, with those of other distinguished Patriots, the name of Thomas Paine. The services which he rendered them in their struggle for liberty have made an impression of gratitude which will never be erased, whilst they continue to merit the character of a just and generous people. He is now in prison, languishing under a disease, and which must be increased by his confinement. Permit me then, to call your attention to his situation, and to require that you will hasten his trial in case there be any charge against him, and if there be none, that you will cause him to be set at liberty.[49]

Ja. Monroe.

To the Secretary of State {Edmund Randolph], Paris, November 7, 1794

Sir,—I have been favoured with yours of the 30th July, original and duplicate, and had the pleasure to receive them unopened.[50]

---

[49] Thomas Paine, author of *Common Sense*, had moved to Paris in September 1792. He had just been made a French citizen and elected to the Convention, but after being arrested in December 1793, he was incarcerated in the Luxembourg prison for almost a year. Paine was liberated by the Committee of General Surety as a result of Monroe's assertion of his American citizenship and demand for his release; but he had suffered an imprisonment of ten months and nine days before Monroe's intervention. (Vincent 2005, 69; Hamilton 1899, 98)

[50] His weariness aside, it seems clear that Monroe was well aware of the political tightrope he would be expected to walk while in Paris. Early in 1793 the French had sent Edmond Genêt to negotiate a new treaty with the United States aimed at political and commercial cooperation between the two countries that would go beyond the treaties of 1778. In disregard of President Washington's neutrality proclamation, Genêt's instructions authorized him to enlist the American people's support for the cause of the French Revolution and to issue military and naval commissions to Americans and others willing to fight for France. The French diplomat's arrogant and indiscreet conduct compelled Washington to request his recall, which brought the serious differences between the governments in Paris and Philadelphia into the open. If divergent policies drove the two

September and 16th. October, I informed you of the several subjects which I had brought before the Committee of public safety, as also of the ill-success which had attended my efforts to obtain an answer upon any one; and I am sorry to be under the necessity now to add, that although I have pressed a decision with the utmost possible zeal, yet I have not been able to accomplish the object.

Being wearied with the delay, I notified to the committee soon after the date of my last letter to you, that I should be glad to confer with them, or some few members on the subject; provided it com ported with their rules in such cases, and would otherwise be agreeable. The proposition was immediately assented to, and the evening of the same day appointed for the interview. I attended in their chamber; we had some discussion, and which ended in a request, on their part, that I would present in writing the sum of what I had said, or wished to say, either on the points depending, or any others I might find necessary to bring before them, and which I readily promised to do.

By this time I had obtained from Mr. Skipwith a comprehensive state-ment of the embarrassments at tending our trade here; as well those which proceeded from the cruizers of the Republic, and applied to what was destined or cleared out for foreign countries, as those which proceeded from the commercial system of France and applied to the direct commerce between the two Republics. As his report to me specified not only each particular cause of complaint but likewise furnished facts to support them, I thought it best to make that report the basis of this my second commu-nication on that head. I accordingly laid it before the committee with such comments as appeared to me suitable; and I now transmit to you a copy of it, that you may be apprized how fully the subject is before them. I was assured that it exhibited a picture which shocked them; for these evils, progressing with the course of their own affairs, were long accumulating, and had prob-ably attained a height of which they had no conception.

As I had reason to suspect, that the chief opposition proceeded from those who conducted the public trade, and who were attached to that mode,

---

governments increasingly apart, their respective choices of diplomats promoted further ill-feeling and suspicion. Gouverneur Morris, the "insolent and vile man" who repre-sented the United States in France, made no secret of his hostility toward republican France. According to Thomas Jefferson, Morris poisoned President Washington's mind with his prejudiced interpretations of events in France. In June 1792, for instance, Morris wrote to Jefferson: "The best picture I can give of the French nation is that of cattle before a thunderstorm. And as to the government, every member of it is engaged in the defense of himself or the attack of his neighbor." Genêt's fate in America finally afforded the Jacobin government of France the longed-for opportunity of requesting the recall from France of this "disdainful and aristocratic" American. (Blumenthal 1970, 12-13)

from motives not the most patriotic, I thought it better to examine the question; whether it were best for the Republic to encourage the competition of individuals in neutral countries, for the supply of its markets, or depend on agencies employed in or sent to countries for that purpose. This subject had been incidentally touched in my first note; but I thought some benefit might be derived from a more thorough development of it. With this view I sent in at the same time, the paper entitled "Supplemental observations on the American Commerce."

I felt extremely embarrassed how to touch again their infringement of the treaty of commerce; whether to call on them to execute it, or leave that question on the ground on which I had first placed it. You desired me in your last to contest with them the principle, but yet this did not amount to an instruction; nor even convey your idea, that it would be advisable to demand of them the execution of those articles. Upon full consideration therefore I concluded that it was the most safe and sound policy to leave this point where it was before, and in which I was the more confirmed by some circumstances that were afterwards disclosed. The day after this last communication was presented, I received a letter from the Committee assuring me, that the subject engrossed their entire attention, and that an answer should be given me as soon as possible; and a few days after this I was favoured with another, inviting me to a conference at 12, the next day. I attended and found only the three members of the diplomatic branch of the committee present, Merlin de Douay, Thuriot and Treilhard. Merlin commenced by observing that I had advised and pressed them to execute the 23rd and 24th articles of the treaty of amity and commerce: that they were pursuaded their compliance would be useful to us, but very detrimental to them. It would likewise be distressing for Frenchmen to see British goods protected by our flag, whilst it gave no protection to theirs; and after making other comments, he finally came to this point: "Do you insist upon our executing the treaty?" I replied, I had nothing new to add to what I had already said on that subject. Treilhard seemed surprised at the reply, and expressed a wish that I would declare myself frankly on the subject. I told him I was surprised at his remark, since I had not only declared myself frankly but liberally. We then passed from the point of demand to a more general discussion of the policy in France to execute the Treaty, and in which I urged, that if she considered her own interest only, she ought not to hesitate, since it gave her the command of neutral bottoms, and under the protection of their own flag, to supply her wants; with other considerations which had been before pressed in my notes that were before them. I was, however, brought back twice again to the question: "Do you insist upon or demand it?" I found that a positive and formal declaration on this point was the sole object of the interview; and as I perceived that something was intended to be founded on it, either now or hereafter, if given in the affirmative, I was the more resolved to avoid it, and to adhere to the ground I had already taken. I therefore repeated my declaration, and in the most explicit terms, that I was not instructed by the President to insist on it; that their compliance would certainly be highly beneficial to my country, but that in my observations I had considered the proposition merely in relation to France, and wished them to do the same, since I was satisfied that the true interest of France dictated the measure. They all expressed an attachment to us, spoke much of the difficulty of the situation, and of the peculiar delicacy in adapting, in the present state of the public mind, any measure which might be construed as eventually favouring England; and thus the conference ended.

In revolving the subject over since, I have been doubtful whether the solicitude shewn to draw from me a decisive answer to the question: "Whether I insisted, or demanded of them to execute the articles of the treaty," was merely intended as the basis of their own act, complying with it, and a justification for themselves in so doing, or as a ground to call on us hereafter, in the prosecution of the war against England, to fulfil the guarantee. I was, at the moment of the discussion in the committee, of the latter opinion; but I must confess, upon a more general view of all circumstances that have passed under my observation since my arrival, that I am at present inclined to be of the former. I rather think, as there is an opposition to the measure, and it would commence an important change in their system, and might also be construed into a partiality for England, (a nation by no means in favor here) that the dread of denunciation in the course of events suggested it. Be this as it may, I am perfectly satisfied it would be impolitic to demand it, since the refusal would weaken the connection between the two countries, and the compliance, upon that motive, might perhaps not only produce the same effect, but likewise excite a disposition to press us on other points, upon which it were better to avoid any discussion. I hope, however, soon to obtain an answer, and a favourable one. If the subject was before the Convention, in the same light it was before the Committee, I am convinced it would since have been the case: But it is difficult to get it there; for if I carried it there myself, it would be deemed a kind of denunciation of the committee. Yesterday there was a change of several of the members of that body, and which I deem, from my knowledge of those elected, favourable to our views. Be assured that I shall continue to press this business with all suitable energy; and in the mode that shall appear to me most eligible; and in the interim that I will do everything in my power to prevent abuses under the existing system.

Upon the subject of the fifteen thousand dollars, advanced for the emigrants from St. Domingo, I have made no formal demand, because I wished the other points, which were depending, settled first; from an apprehension that if they granted several little matters it would fortify them in a different position to reject those that were important. I have, however, conferred informally upon it, and have no doubt it will be peremptorily allowed. I think, therefore, this should be calculated on by the department of the treasury. I shall certainly bring it before them shortly, as I shall immediately the affair of the Consul in the Isle of France, upon which latter point, however, permit me respectfully to add, that the appointment of a person, not an American, perhaps an Englishman, to the office of Consul, has not only been the cause of the disrespect shewn to our authority, but even of the embarrassments to which our countrymen were exposed there.[51]

With respect to the business with Algiers, I have not known how to act. It will be difficult for France, in the present state of affairs, to support the measures of our resident in Portugal, or for them to concert any plan of co-operation. It seems, however, in every view, proper to rid ourselves of the person in Switzerland who I understand has been in readiness to prosecute the business for some time past. I have, in consequence, written him a letter in conformity to your idea, of which I inclose you a copy, and which I presume, he will consider as a respectful discharge." I am inclined to think France will co-operate with us upon this point, and if any plan can be adopted by which she may forward the measure of Colonel Humphreys, I will endeavour to avail him of it. But certainly if it is expected that her aid will be efficacious, or that she will embark with zeal in the business, the whole should be concerted and executed from this quarter. Perhaps as I have heard nothing from Colonel Humphreys, the business is now done, or he is pursuing it without calculating upon any aid from France. A letter which was presented me by Mr. Cathalan, our Consul at Marseilles (and who is now here, as are Mr. Fenwick, Dobrée and Coffyn, a son of Mr. Coffyn, Consul, and who came

---

[51] William McCarty was United States Consul in the Isle of France (Mauritius). He was in business there but also was an American citizen, born in Connecticut. The circumstances which gave rise to the Secretary of States' instructions to Monroe were serious and important. The strongest prejudices existed against American interests: merchantmen were seized, their cargoes confiscated, and the masters and seamen continually molested and imprisoned with no pretense of legal proceedings, and usually on the grounds that they were Englishmen or had English goods on board. In short it appeared that Americans were outrageously treated. The American flag was fired upon, and no attention paid to the representations of the American consul, whose stores were sealed up and keys seized. (Hamilton 1899, 104)

here to represent his father,) from Captain O'Brien, and which I now enclose, will shew you the state of the business in August last. Be assured I shall be happy to render my country any service in this distressing business, in my power, even by visiting Algiers if it were necessary.

I have enquired into the character of our Consuls at the several forts: I mean those who are French men; for Mr. Fenwick is well known, viz., La Motte at Havre; Dobrée at Santes: Coffyn at Dunkirk and Cathalan at Marseilles, and find them likewise all men of understanding and of excellent reputation, attached to our country and grateful for the confidence reposed in them. If displaced, it will subject them to some censure: I do not, therefore, wish it, though I most earnestly advise that in future none but Americans be appointed.

I was extremely concerned, upon my arrival here, to find that our countryman Mr. Paine, as likewise Madame La Fayette were in prison; the former of whom had been confined near nine months and the latter about two. I was immediately entreated by both to endeavour to obtain their enlargement. I assured them of the interest which America had in their welfare; of the regard entertained for them by the President, and of the pleasure with which I should embrace every opportunity to serve them; but observed at the same time that they must be sensible it would be difficult for me to take any step officially, in behalf of either, and altogether impossible in behalf of Madame La Fayette. This was admitted by her friend, who assured me, her only wish was that I would have her situation in view, and render her, informally, what services I might be able, without compromitting the credit of our government with this. I assured him she might confide in this with certainty, and further, that in case any extremity was threatened, that I would go beyond that line and do everything in my power, let the consequence be what it might to myself to save her; with this he was satisfied. She still continues confined, nor do I think it probable she will be soon released. I have assured her that I would supply her with money and with whatever she wanted; but as yet, none has been accepted, though I think she will soon be compelled to avail herself of this resource.

The case was different with Mr. Paine. He was actually a citizen of the United States, and of the United States only for the revolution, which parted us from Great Britain, broke the allegiance, which was before due to the crown, of all those who took our side. He was, of course, not a British subject, nor was he strictly a citizen of France; for he came by invitation, for the temporary purpose of assisting in the formation of their government only, and meant to withdraw to America when that should be completed: And what confirms this, is the act of convention itself arresting him, by which he is declared to be a foreigner. Mr. Paine pressed my interference. I told him I had hopes of getting him enlarged without it; but if I did interfere, it could only be by requesting that he be tried in case there was any charge against him, and liberated in case there was none. This was admitted. His correspondence with me is lengthy and interesting, and I may probably be able hereafter to send you a copy of it. After some time had elapsed without producing any change in his favour, as he was pressing and in ill health, I finally resolved to address the Committee of general surety in his behalf, resting my application on the above principle. My letter was delivered by my secretary, in the Committee to the President, who assured him he would Communicate its contents immediately to the Committee of public safety and give me an answer as soon as possible. The conference took place accordingly between the two Committees and as I presume, on that night, or the succeeding day; for on the morning of the day after, which was yesterday, I was presented by the Secretary of the Committee of general surety, with an order for his enlargement. I forwarded it immediately to the Luxembourg and had it carried into effect, and have the pleasure now to add that he is not only restored to the enjoyment of his liberty, but in good spirits. I send you a copy of my letter to the Committee of general surety, and of their reply.

Since my last the French have taken Coblentz, and some other post in its neighborhood; they have likewise taken Pampeluna, and broken the whole of the Spanish line through a considerable extent of country. About twenty standards, taken from the routed Spaniards, were presented to the Convention a few days past.

I likewise send in the enclosed papers, a decree respecting the Jacobins by which all correspondence between the different societies is prohibited, as likewise is the presenting a petition to the Convention in their character as such, with some other restraints I do not at present recollect.

With great respect and esteem, I am, Dear Sir, your most obedient & very Humble Servant, Jas Monroe.

To Colonel David Humphreys, Paris, November 11, 1794

Sir,[52]—I have lately received a letter from the Secretary of State, mentioning that the power to treat with the regency of Algiers was committed to you, and that the aid of this Republic, if attainable, must be thrown into that line. I was likewise apprised by Mr. Morris of some measures taken by him in concert with the government here, relative to that object, but which

---

[52] One of Washington's aides-de-camp during the American Revolution, Humphreys was the minister at Lisbon when commissioned, on March 21, 1793, as Commissioner Plenipotentiary to Algiers. (Hamilton 1899, 109)

were unconnected with you. As I have reason to think you possess powers flowing from the last session of Congress, I think it possible you have already progressed in the business, and therefore that the aid of this government will be useless. But if you have not how shall a cooperation be converted, supposing this government disposed to enter into it? Will it not be necessary for you to come into some part of France and depart thence with some agent from her? Your thoughts upon this head will be useful; but until I know the state of the business in your hands, it will be useless and improper for me to occupy the councils of this Republic on the subject. I therefore hope to hear from you on it as soon as possible.

To the Committee of Public Safety, Paris, November 12, 1794

Citizens,—I received some weeks past, a letter from Mr. Gardoqui, minister of the Spanish finances, inclosing one to my care for Mr. Otto, then in the department of foreign affairs, requesting me to present it to him.[53] As I did not wish to be the channel of communication from Mr. Gardoqui to any citizen of France, whatever might be its object, and whether of a private or public nature, I resolved, neither to deliver the letter, nor give an answer for the time, to that which was addressed to me. And I was the more inclined to this, from the persuasion that, if of a private nature, the delay could be of no great importance, and, if of a public one, and especially upon an interesting subject, that when it was found I attended only to the concerns of my own country, and did not chuse to interfere in those of Spain, that he would take some course more direct for the attainment of the object in view. As some weeks had now elapsed, I took it for granted, that this was the case. In this, however, I have been disappointed; for I was favored within a few days past with a second letter from Mr. Gardoqui, in which he enters more fully into the object of the first communication. Finding, therefore, that he still addressed himself to me, notwithstanding the discouragement already given, I deemed it necessary, not only to examine more attentively the object of this communication, but likewise to adopt, definitively, some plan in regard to it. Nor had I much difficulty in either respect; for when I recollected that he was a minister of Spain, and observed that his letters, as well as that to Mr. Otto,

---

[53] Louis Guillaume Otto, a diplomat, was the former French Charge d'Affaires in Washington. He had returned to France in late 1792 and shortly afterwards the Committee of Public Safety made him head of the first political division for foreign affairs. However, the fall of the Girondins in May 1793 led to Otto's dismissal and arrest. He then came close to being guillotined but survived and followed Emmanuel Joseph Sieyès to Berlin as secretary to the legation. He was posted there at the time of this letter. (Carriere 1960, 486; Hart 1901, 150)

and which I have since examined, as those to me, expressed only a wish to be admitted within the government of France, to attend some baths, I could not but conclude, that this was the ostensible motive whilst some other in reality existed. And in this I am the more confirmed from a recollection of the relation in which Mr. Gardoqui and myself formerly stood in America to each other, and which on account of my strong opposition in the Congress to his proposition for secluding the Mississippi, was not the most amicable one. From that consideration, I do not think he would solicit a correspondence with me for a trilling object.[54] What other then must be the motive? In my judgment there can be none other than the hope of thereby opening the door for the commencement of a negotiation for peace, and that the Spanish Court has availed itself of this mode of making that wish known to you.

Presuming then that this was in truth the object, it remained for me only to decide what course I should take in regard to Mr. Gardoqui's communications; nor could I hesitate long upon this point; for I well knew it was of importance to you to become acquainted with the disposition of other powers towards the French Republic. I have therefore deemed it consistent with the sincere friendship which the United States bears towards you, and the interest they take as your ally in whatever concerns your welfare, as well as with that candour which I mean to observe in all my transactions, to lay the letters before you; knowing their contents you will be enabled to determine how to act in regard to them. As it respects the United States whom I serve, or myself personally, it can be of no importance to me to be acquainted with the result; since I doubt not, that under the wise councils of the Republic, the revolution will progress to a happy close: But permit me to assure you, that if I can be of any service to the French Republic, in regard to the answer to be given to this communication, it will give me the highest satisfaction to render it.

---

[54] Under the Treaty of Paris, the Mississippi was recognized as the western boundary of the United States. It was open for navigation by Americans, and many in the western part of the Confederation depended on the waterway for economic survival. Then Spain closed the river to American navigation and sent Congress scrambling to resolve the crisis. Secretary for Foreign Affairs John Jay negotiated with the Spanish diplomat Don Diego de Gardoqui and was willing to give up Americans' navigation of the Mississippi River for a term of years if Spain would enter into a commercial treaty with the United States that would primarily benefit New England commercial interests. Jay made a formal proposal to Congress in May 1786. Giving up rights to the river was contrary to Jay's instructions from Congress, but many northerners were willing to accept such a compromise. Congress debated altering Jay's instructions, however, the treaty was opposed by Virginia leaders James Madison and James Monroe, who secured its rejection by the Continental Congress, thus spawning a future of continued friction between Monroe and Jay. (Watkins 2009)

To the President [George Washington], Paris, November 19, 1794

Dear Sir,—I had the pleasure some weeks past to receive your favor of the 25 of June and should have answered it sooner, had any safe private opportunity offered for Bordeaux, from whence vessels most frequently sail for America.55 I called the evening after its receipt on Mr. Morris & put your letter for him into his hands so that he rec'd it unopened. He left this about the beginning of Oct'r for Switzerland, from whence I understood he would probably proceed to Engld. His first intention was to have sailed from Havre to America, but this was afterwards declined and the latter rout preferred. As there was some delay in obtaining his passport & which gave him displeasure, and as I disliked from motives of delicacy to him to mention it in an official dispatch, I take the liberty to communicate it to you. Some weeks after my arrival, he intimated to me, that as it would take some time to pack up his baggage and he should in the interim be idle, he wished me to procure for him a passport from the Committee for the seat of John James Rosseau in Switzerland where he wo'd stay that time & return to take his departure. I did so. It was in reply suggested to me that he might choose his rout to leave France, but that they did not like to permit him to go into Switzerland, where the emigrants (his connections) were & return back into the Republick: that indeed they were surprised he had made such a request. I was asked would I take the measure on myself, and in case any censure attended it, be responsible to the publick opinion? To this I replied that I had shown Mr. Morris my letter submitting it to the Committee, and that it would be more agreeable to him as well as myself should it proceed from them. Thus the matter rested for some time; finally as Mr. Morris pressed for a passport and complained much of the delay, and which I knew proceeded solely from an objection to his return, a circumstance I did not wish to mention to him, I found it indispensably necessary to send Mr. Skipwith explicitly to ask whether he was anxious upon that point. He had suspected this difficulty before and immediately agreed to abandon the idea. The form of the passport

---

55 Monroe's relationship with Washington was awkward at best and his 1794 appointment as minister to France was tainted by political rationale. In assigning a prominent Republican to the post, Washington sought to address French concerns that the United States was siding against France in its war with Great Britain. Shortly after arriving in Paris, Monroe gave a speech to a French governmental body in which he spoke of the parallels between the American and French revolutions, declaring that the two nations were united in their respect for "the equal and unalienable rights of men." Washington came to believe that Monroe had been excessively outspoken in support of revolutionary France and recalled him. When he returned to the United States, Monroe published a lengthy treatise defending his actions in France, the facts of which were severely challenged by Washington. (Greenstein 2009, 276)

---

then became a question. It was notified to him that if he would take one from me, viséed by the Commissary of foreign aff'rs, what depended on them sho'd be performed immediately. But he wished one from the Committee or the gov't independently of me: the latter being the ordinary mode in the case of private citizens, merchants & others travelling thro' France. I was of opinion this sho'd be granted him & said so to the Commissary. I was equally so that the other mode sho'd have been quietly accepted by him, or in other words that neither party should have made an object of the mode. I think it was Mr. Morris's expectation I should demand a passport in the form desired by him & risque whatever consequences might result from it; he did not ask this of me but it was to be inferred from what I heard him say on the subject. I was, however, resolved to embark in no such discussion and especially upon a point so unimportant in itself. The passport was of course granted by me & certified by the Commissary in the usual course, and under whose protection he has safely passed beyond the bounds of the Republick. I do not know that this incident will ever reach you thro' any other channel but as it possibly may, I have thought proper to state it to you correctly & according to my own knowledge.

The successes of this Republick have been most astonishingly great in every quarter. In my letter to the Sec'y of State I have detailed the many victories gained and posts taken up to the 7th of this month: since which Mastricht has fall'n with ab't 300 cannon & 8 or 10,000 troops: for a considerable time past the combin'd powers have been able only to retard the progress of the French by defending posts; for ever since the battle of Fleury they have avoided, except where not to be avoided, a general action. And every post w'h the French have sat down before, has yielded sooner than was expected. At present there appears to be nothing to impede their march to Amsterdam if they incline & of which there can be no doubt. 'Tis said the Prince of Orange has requested of the States General to overflow the country, & which is opposed & will probably be rejected. If the people rise & change the gov't they will be treated with as a free people, and I am inclined to think no treaty will otherwise be made with them. In Spain their success has been equally great: great part of that country has been overrun and in truth it appears to me to be within their power, even to march to Madrid if it was their wish. 'Tis said that a treaty has already been made with Prussia, but this I do not credit, not because it is not attainable for I am convinc'd it is, but because I do not think the Committee wo'd form a treaty without some hint of it to the Convention, & indeed their approbation. Spain and Austria both want peace & will I doubt not soon make one: and that Engl'd likewise wants it there can be no doubt. In short it appears to me unquestionable that France can command a peace from every power & upon her own terms. Engl'd alone can at present hesitate or talk of terms, and this she is enabled to do only by her fleet which may secure her from invasion: but I am inclined to think a storm is gathering over her more dangerous than any she has yet known: for I have reason to believe that Denmark and Sweden are ready to fall on her, and that Spain will be compelled to purchase her peace with France by uniting in a similar operation. A curious incident relative to this latter power has lately come to my knowledge, and which from the delicacy of the subject—, I shall put in cypher to the Sec'y of State, by which you will perceive how critically we are circumstanced in respect to that power, if she sho'd close with France upon terms of neutrality, being at liberty to unite with England in case of such an event in hostility against us.

Every consideration of expedience invites us in my judgment to a close union with our ally: and believe me I have done all in my power to promote this object. But I have had to contend with many difficulties of a serious nature & which still embarrass me to a certain degree. These I cannot hazard otherwise than in cypher tho' I would with pleasure, did I know that my letter would reach you unopened, speak more confidentially than I can do in an official despatch. A new minister will leave this for America in a few days: I think the change a fortunate event, for I am persuaded the successor will see cause to doubt many of the communications heretofore given. I am told the successor is a cool, well-disposed & sensible man.[56] Within a few days past Nimeughen has also been taken, the hall of the Jacobin society shut up by the Convention, & two members appointed by the Committee by consent of the Convention, whose names & offices are unknown; some say the object is to treat with Prussia, Spain or the States Gen'l, or rather to accompany the army with power to treat with the people in case they rise; others say 'tis to treat with Denmark & Sweden, whose agents are said to be incog in town. Certain, however, it is the Committee asked for permission to appoint such persons under such circumstances & that it was granted.

---

[56] This was Jean Antoine Joseph Fauchet, as the new French government had decided to replace Edmond Charles Genêt. The Ministry of Foreign Affairs had taken him severely to task back in July, accusing him of trying to exercise proconsular powers and acting with "indiscrete enthusiasm." But now, faced with the pending American request for the envoy's recall, the ministry downplayed its recommendation to the Committee of Public Safety. In a half-hearted defense of the envoy, it suggested that "some opponents, more familiar with the true nature of the American people than Citizen Genêt, purposely surrounded him with a false popularity in order to make him appear disagreeable to the United States Government. This Minister was too enthusiastic, badly advised, and carried away by his reception...." The Committee of Public Safety, however, was not so lenient. Robespierre called Genêt a traitor, and in November named a commission of four, headed by Fauchet, to replace him in function (and arrest him in person) upon their arrival in the United States. (Brown 2005, 87)

I found myself plac'd here as you will readily conceive upon a theatre new & very difficult to act on. And what has encreased my embarrassment has been the ignorance of the disposition of Engld towards us as well as of the U. States towards her. I have also been destitute of all kind of council except Mr. Skipwith, & some is necessary in every situation. I have, however, acted as well as my judgment could dictate & I hope to y'rs & the satisfaction of my Country men in general.

With great respect & esteem I am, Dear Sir, y'r most obt. & very humble servant, Jas Monroe.

To the Secretary of State {Edmund Randolph], Paris, November 20, 1794

Sir,—I was favored about five weeks past with a letter from Mr. Gardoqui, minister of finance in Spain, inclosing one for Mr. Otto formerly in America, and at present Chief of a Bureau in the department of foreign affairs; mentioning the decline of his health, and requesting my cooperation with Mr. Otto, in soliciting of this government, permission for him to visit certain baths within the Republic. This application surprized me. The season I knew was too far advanced for him to derive any benefit from the waters, and I was not apprized that those suggested were better than others within his reach: Besides Mr. Gardoqui and myself were, in consequence of a collision on the much litigated question of the Mississippi, not on the best terms while in America; certainly not on such as to authorize an application of this kind to me. The disguise was therefore too thin to hide from me the true object; I immediately inferred that it was the body politic of Spain that was disordered, and not the animal one of Mr. Gardoqui. As I did not wish to become the instrument of Spain in this business, or incur the slightest suspicion of the kind, since I well knew it would benefit Spain at the expense of the United States, I declined delivering his letter to Mr. Otto, or answering, for the time, that of Mr. Gardoqui to me.[57]

About three weeks afterwards I received a second letter, which confirmed me in the opinion first taken up, that the object was to open the door, through me, to the commencement of a negotiation for peace. I found, therefore, that it became my duty to take some step in regard to this business, and was, in consequence, resolved to shape my course in such manner as to make the incident, if possible, productive of some good to the United States, if of none to Spain.

---

[57] For explanation, see note to Monroe's letter to the Committee of Public Safety, Paris, November 12, 1794.

When I reflected that we had interfering claims with Spain, as well in respect to boundaries as the Mississippi; and that we had a minister there negociating upon those points; that the negotiation was closed without a satisfactory adjustment, and that Spain was probably in concert with England, exciting the Indians against us, I was from these considerations inclined to deem this movement of Mr. Gardoqui an insidious one. I was the more so from the further consideration that he had made this application to me without the knowledge of Mr. Short; through whom it ought to have been made, had the proposition been a candid one, and founded on any claim of Spain upon the United States. I was therefore the more resolved to suffer myself to be restrained by no unnecessary and false motives of delicacy towards Mr. Gardoqui, in the manner in which I should treat the subject.[58]

I was persuaded that a peace between France and Spain, at the present moment, whilst our claims were unsettled, must be prejudicial to the United States. Such a peace would free Spain from a pressure which at present shakes her monarchy to the foundation. By continuing the war, it enables the United States in case they should take decisive measures to do what they please with that power. For it is not reasonable to suppose, when the French troops are over-running a great part of Spain, and her whole force is exerted for her protection at Rome, that she would be able to make a respectable opposition to any effort we might make on the other side the Atlantic. But a peace with France would remove such pressure, and leave the Spanish government at liberty to act with its whole force against us.

I was likewise persuaded it was the interest of France to have our accommodation in view, and to give her aid in forwarding our arrangement with Spain at the same time that she adjusted her own; for if she should close a peace with that power whereby she left it at liberty to act against us singly, or jointly with England, in case of a war with the latter, she would not only expose us to great unnecessary detriment, but likewise hazard time probability of being drawn into it again, in case it should take an adverse course in regard to us.

Upon full consideration of all these circumstances, I thought it best to lay the letters of Mr. Gardoqui before the Committee, with my free comments upon them. I did so and told them explicitly that, in my opinion, it was the wish of the Spanish court to commence a negotiation and that it had addressed itself through me, to inspire distrust in me by creating a belief that the United States were more friendly to Spain and Britain than to France. I explained full our situation with both powers, assuring them that we were

---

[58] Monroe's conduct in this was approved by the Administration as evincing his "judgment and assiduity." (Hamilton 1899, 119)

threatened with war from both. I also mentioned the indelicacy and artifice of Mr. Gardoqui, in applying to me without the knowledge of the minister at the court; which never existed to any great degree. I assured them at the same time, that if I could be of any service in forwarding their wishes in regard to peace, in the present or any other instance, it was the wish of the United States I should be, and would personally give me great pleasure to render it. I intimated also the danger which would attend a peace between the Republic and Spain, unless our differences should be compromised at the same time. The communication was well received, and the business terminated in an arrangement by which I was to answer Mr. Gardoqui's letters, declining any agency in the business myself; advising him, at the same time, to make his application directly (in case he continued indisposed) to the committee, and from whom I was persuaded, he would obtain a satisfactory answer. This was accordingly done in a letter which was forwarded about five days past.

In the close of this affair I was invited by the diplomatic members of the committee of public safety, to a conference upon a new topic. I was informed it was their intention to press the war against England in particular; but that they were distressed for funds, and was asked, could any aid be obtained from the United States? I told them I was satisfied if it was in their power, it would be rendered; that I possessed no power on the subject, and could only advise of the probability &c., that, with their permission, I would put on paper such ideas as occurred to me in respect to that point, and upon which I would more fully confer. This incident furnished me with a new opportunity of pressing more forcibly the propriety of their securing for us the points in discussion with England and Spain, at the time their own peace should be made with those powers. I send you a copy of the paper delivered to them today [See Sidebar] and to which I have as yet received no answer.

Whether France will make any arrangement upon this point with us, I cannot tell. When I mentioned in the committee the danger which menaced us, of a war with Britain and Spain, I asked what reliance we might have on France in such an event. I was answered they should consider ours as their own cause. No other arrangement can well be made than that of lending money to France, if in our power; it being understood that she will secure at the time of her own peace, the complete recognition of our rights from Britain and Spain, and which she may easily do in my judgment, and without prolonging the war a moment on that account.

On the other hand if the United States ever mean to assert those rights, the present is of all others, the most suitable moment. The Fortune of France has risen to the utmost height of splendor; whilst that of her enemies has declined to the lowest state of depression. Her armies are everywhere trium-

Observations Submitted to the Consideration of
the Diplomatic Members of the Committee of Public Safety

It is the wish of the French Republic to obtain by loan, a sum of money from the United States of America, to enable it to prosecute the war.

This is to be expected from three sources: the general government, the State governments and from individuals.

The French cause and the French nation are greatly regarded in America, and I am persuaded some money may be obtained, and perhaps a very respectable sum, from the three sources above mentioned. For this purpose the Minister should possess power to make loans from either of the above parties and to give such security as the Republic shall deem suitable.

The committee, however, should advert to the situation of the United States in regard to England and Spain. Both those countries have encroached upon our rights; the one holding the western posts, in violation of the treaty of peace of 1783, whereby she harrasses our frontiers, by means of the Indians; and the other by shutting the Mississippi and likewise exciting the Indians against us to the south: So that the United States are in a kind of hostility with both powers. There is likewise reason to believe that a Convention subsists between Britain and Spain, defensive and probably offensive against us, in support of their respective claims.

In this situation would it be proper for France to make peace with either of those powers, whilst our claims were unsettled with either, and whilst both encroach on our territory? Would it not leave those powers free to attack us united, and, in that situation would not France be forced again to embark in the war or tamely look on and see our dismemberment? Could the Republic in short deem its own peace secured or durable whilst these points remained unsettled between the United States and those powers and should it not therefore seek an adjustment of the whole at the same time?

I have suggested these considerations in the hope that the Committee will give the Minister about to depart for America, full power in relation thereto, and in the confidence that a satisfactory assurance on that head would greatly facilitate the object of the loan; for if the United States were assured that they would have no occasion for their own resources to support a war against those powers, it would of course be more in their power to lend them to the French Republic.

It must be obvious that France may not only secure these points for us and without any difficulty, but with Spain whatever else she pleased; for I am persuaded that the Spanish monarchy would even agree to open the islands to the world and perhaps even South America to end a war which endangers the crown itself. The mode would be by insinuating to both those powers, when France commenced her negotiation, that they must also adjust at the same time their differences with the United States.

The sum which might be raised in America from the different sources above mentioned, upon an assurance of this kind, would, in my judgment be considerable. In any event, however, I shall be happy to give the Minister about to depart every information and aid in my power, in forwarding the object in view.

I submit to you however whether it would not be proper to enable me in my letters on that subject, to declare what your sense is upon these points.

phant, whilst theirs are everywhere routed and broken. Spain makes no head against her; but in trying as already shewn, to steal a peace in obscurity. And Britain is perhaps in nearly as bad a situation. Maestricht has lately surrendered; whereby eight thousand troops were yielded with about three hundred pieces of cannon, two hundred and fifty-seven of which were brass; with other warlike stores and in great abundance. Nimeguen was likewise taken a few days afterwards, with considerable amount in stores; and, it is said, that commotions are taking place in five of the provinces, who have formally resolved to dismiss the Stadtholder; reform the government by the Republican standard, and ally with France. This must be felt in England and will probably excite disturbance there. In any event it will produce such effect, that if America strikes the blow her own interest dictates, and which every other consideration prompts, it must be decisive, and if not ruinous to the fortunes of that proud and insolent nation, it will certainly secure us the objects we have in view.

If I hear further from the committee about the proposition for a loan, &c., I will advise you of it by the French minister who leaves this in about five days. By the paper which I send you will understand how far the point has been discussed, of the propriety of France to support our claims against Britain and Spain; the opportunity for which was furnished by my friend Mr. Gardoqui, and you will soon be able to ascertain from the minister, what his powers on that head are.

Within a few days past, two deputies were appointed by the committee of public safety, by consent of the convention to some important trust, but whose names and office were unknown. It is supposed they are commissioned to treat on peace with some one of the powers, and which is most probable; but with which of the powers or whether this is the object are only matters of conjecture.

I apprized you in a late letter that I had written to Colonel Humphreys, and was endeavoring to concert with him, if possible, the mode by which the aid of this government, if disposed to grant it (and which I presume to be the case), may be given him in the negotiation with Algiers. As yet, I have not heard from him. As soon as I do, provided I find it necessary, I will apply for the support contemplated. Previous to this it will be improper. Touching this subject, I send you a proposition from the government of Malta, presented by its chargé d'affaires here, to be forwarded for your consideration. You will give me for that government such answer as shall be deemed suitable.

Within a few days past, the hall of the Jacobins was shut up by order of the Convention. That body was constantly at work to undermine and impair the regular and constituted authority of the government. Moderate measures to check its enormities were found only a stimulus to greater excesses. This last step was therefore taken, and there is reason to fear its dispersed members will still continue to provoke by some rash measure, the indignation of the Convention to such a height, as to bring upon them a degree of severity it were better to avoid. Within a few days past also, the commission to whom was referred the charge against Carrier, formerly representative at Nantes, has reported there was ground for accusation; and today, it is believed, the Convention will approve the report and consign him over to the Revolutionary tribunal, who will, with equal certainty and with the general plaudit of the nation doom him to the guillotine.[59]

With great respect and esteem, I am, Dear Sir, Sincerely Yours, Jas Monroe.

To the Chargé d'Affaires of Malta [Monsieur Cibon], Paris, November 22, 1794

Citizen,—I have received with great pleasure the considerations you were pleased to present to me; pointing out the mode by which the United States of America and the Isle of Malta may be serviceable to each other. It is the duty of nations to cultivate, by every means in their power, these relations subsisting between them, which admit of reciprocal good offices, and I am persuaded the United States will omit no opportunity which may occur to testify that disposition towards the Island of Malta.[60]

The Americans have, it is true, received already great injury from the Algerines, and it is their intention to adopt such measured as shall prevent the like in the future. The Island of Malta by its situation and maritime

---

[59] In the winter of 1794–95 perhaps the most forceful conception of the Terror was the image of "republican marriages" carried out by the Jacobin deputy Jean Baptiste Carrier in Nantes. According to testimony offered at his trial, men and women had been stripped naked, bound together, and forced into the Loire River to drown a cruel death. Prints circulated that emphasized the innocence and suffering of these stricken, youthful couples, whose nudity and innocence stood in stark contrast to the heartlessness of their executioners. Terrorists at Nantes were said to have taken a special oath to "renounce parenthood, fraternity, the tenderness of a father or son." (Desan 2004. 56)

[60] This letter is in response to a proposal put forth by the Chargé d'Affaires of Malta, Commander de Cibon, that put forth an alliance between the Order of Malta and the United States. Certainly, there was much to be gained by both governments. American ships, like those of other Christian nations, were then the prey of the Barbary pirates. Malta would have afforded them a base and place of safety, and perhaps active assistance against the pirates might have been given by the Knights of Malta. On the other hand, the foreign affairs of the Order were then in a precarious condition and distant America a place of refuge would have been of great worth. No record has been found of any instructions on the alliance ever having been sent to Monroe, and there the record ends. (Hume 1936, 222)

strength possess the means of yielding that protection, and your suggestion on that subject merits, in my opinion, the serious consideration of our
government, to whom I already transmitted it.

The United States possess at the present extensive and very valuable
territory. It is their intention to dispose of it by sale; by which however the
right soil only will be conveyed; the jurisdiction still remaining with them.
The government too of such territory is already prescribed: it must be elec-
tive or republican and forming a part of the existing national system. I have
thought proper to add this information that you may know the powers of
our government in relation to this object. Permit me to assure you, that as
soon as I shall be instructed thereon, I will immediately communicate the
same to you.[61]

Mr. Paine who is of my family desires to be re membered to you.[62] He will
be with you in the spring. Not being able to present Mr. Fauchet's draft here
for 3000 dol'rs on acc't of the depreciat'n I shall return it to Mr. Randolph &
subject it to Mr. Jones's order. Will you attend to this?

To the Secretary of State [Edmund Randolph], Paris, Decem-
ber 2, 1794

Sir,—I have at length obtained an answer from the Committee of Public
Safety, to the several propositions heretofore presented before it, in an arrêté
of the 15th. ultimo. By this arrêté the Commission of Marine is ordered to
adjust the amount due to such of our citizens as were injured by the Embargo
of Bordeaux, and likewise to such others as have claims for supplies rendered
to the Government of St. Domingo.[63] By it also many embarrassments which
impeded the direct trade between the two countries are removed: The arbitrary rule of contraband, which authorised the seizure of our vessels laden

---

[61] In fact, the Knights of Malta possessed considerable estates in Spain, Portugal, France,
Italy, and Germany conferred on them by pious Catholics to enable them to protect
Christians going to the holy places. The property of the Order was sufficient to maintain
a considerable naval force, but the Knights took no pains to form one; they had but two
or three old frigates and a few galleys, which went to give and receive entertainments in
the ports of Italy. (Hamilton 1899, 129)

[62] Thomas Paine was released from prison a result of Monroe's intervention and lived in
Monroe's residence from November 1794 to the spring of 1796. (Ammon 2001, 136, 137)

[63] Problems with trade continued to plague Monroe. American shipping to Bordeaux,
France, once minimal, increased dramatically after 1793, the year that marked the beginning of the French Wars. The conflicts compelled merchants to adopt new patterns of
trade, as the policies of the belligerent parties increasingly determined the evolution of
neutral shipping. Merchants on both sides of the Atlantic strove for closer connections
across political boundaries and tried to bypass the difficulties created by warfare and
develop strategies to minimize the impact of new risks. These merchants tended to rely
on personal acquaintances, and they traveled frequently across the Atlantic in order to
build and fortify relations of trust. (Marzagalli 2005, 811)

---

with provisions destined for other countries, is done away; and the stipulation of the Treaty of Commerce which gives free passage under our flag to the subjects of any of the powers at war with the Republic is likewise inforced. In short everything has been conceded that was desired, except the execution of that part of the Treaty which gave freedom to goods in ships that were so.

I have, in consequence, notified to the Commission of Marine that I had empowered Mr. Skipwith to take charge of these claims, and attend their adjustment on the part of our citizens, and I shall continue to give every aid in my power to obtain for them the justice to which they are entitled. In respect to the liquidation, unless indeed, some difficulty should arise, as to the mode of payment, whether in assignats or specie, I presume all difficulty, is at an end. But in regard to the payment, I think it probable, unless assignats are taken and which are now depreciated,[64] further delay will be desired, owing to the great expenditures of the government at this very important crisis of its affairs. Upon this, however, I shall be able to give you more correct information in my next.

If the treaty could have been carried into effect by general agreement, I should have deemed it a fortunate thing; because it would have secured our commerce hereafter from the possibility of vexation, and upon any pretext whatever by the French cruisers; and because it would have ranged the French Republic at an important period of its affairs on the side of a principle founded in benevolence and necessary to the freedom of the high seas. But as connected with other considerations more immediately applicable to ourselves and especially if the hope of forcing it upon other nations, as a law, is abandoned, I have deemed it of but little consequence. It certainly precludes the probability of our being called on hereafter to fulfil any stipulation whatever, and will of course gain us greater credit for any services we may render them, in case it should suit us to render them any. I am likewise persuaded, from the responsibility the arrêté imposes, and the increasing partiality pervading all France towards us and which is felt by the Americans and observed by the subjects of other neutral powers that the execution will not vary much from the import of the treaty itself; for I cannot think that many of our vessels will hereafter be brought in upon the suspicion of having enemy's goods on board.

I informed you some time since that I was persuaded if the subject was before the Convention it would readily be granted; and in this I have not only been since confirmed, but in the further belief that a majority of the several

[64] The assignats at this time was passed only for one-fifteenth of the real value. (Hamilton 1899, 141)

committees were favorable to the object. The dread however of denunciation in the course of events deterred them from adopting it. It was opposed as was likewise every other change by a party who would not fail to take advantage of it, should a favorable opportunity occur. The sordid spoilers of the public wealth never forgive those who detect and expose to view their iniquities. And this was the most vulnerable point upon which recrimination could hereafter act; for as it is contemplated when the other powers are withdrawn to prosecute the war against England with the collected force of the Republic, and this might be construed into a partiality for that nation, it was deemed too hazardous a measure in respect to the personal safety of the members, to be encountered. In this decision too it is probable they were the more confirmed by the necessity of cultivating Denmark and Sweden at the present moment, from whence great resources are drawn in support of the war; whose councils are wielded by Bernstorff, a man believed to be well disposed to a reform in the existing governments of Europe[65] and whose fleets are combined with no friendly disposition towards England. They would most probably have pressed to be put on the same footing, and the pressure could not easily have been resisted, after the example was given. As a proof, however, of the disposition of the Committee, upon the subject generally, I transmit to you a copy of a report drawn upon my notes by Merlin of Douai to whom they were referred and which was informally given me by its diplomatic members.[66]

I apprized you in my last of the 20th., instant of Mr. Gardoqui's attempt to obtain permission to attend certain baths within the Republic; ostensibly upon account of his ill health, but in my judgment to commence a negotiation for peace (a finesse too often practiced by a certain grade of politicians) and at the same time lessen any weight the United States might have upon that subject, in respect to their own affairs, by inspiring a distrust in me in the outset. I like wise stated to you in what manner I had acted upon that occasion, laying his original letters before the Committee, with my free and candid comments upon them. As also the further discussion which took place between the committee and myself in regard to Spain, and to which

---

[65] Monroe, in his *View*, indicates his uncertainty respecting this disposition on the part of Christian, Count of Bernstorff. As far as Denmark's neutrality was concerned, she adhered to that plan until the Emperor Paul's compact of 1801; but appears to have furnished France in the meantime with breadstuffs, the dearth of which in the latter country rendered them extremely valuable, besides the timber and hemp requisite for her navy. (Hamilton 1899, 143)

[66] This report may be found in full in the Official Record Book of Communications from James Monroe to the Secretary of State (France, No. 4. James Monroe, p. 148]. For the Arrêté by the Committee of Public Safety (Acts of Reparation in consequence of Monroe's Memoir of September 3d), see American State Papers, Foreign Relations, vol. i., p. 689. (Hamilton 1899, 144)

an incident of a different kind gave birth; in which I exposed as far as the nature of the case would admit of, the real situation of the United States with respect to Spain and Britain, menaced with war by both; shewing how France would be affected by that event and of course the part she should take in our affairs at the present moment. To that communication I have now nothing new to add, having since heard neither from Mr. Gardoqui on the subject of his proposition, nor the Committee upon that, or the one which afterwards occurred. I omitted, however, at that time, to transmit to you a copy of my letter accompanying Mr. Gardoqui's to the Committee, and which I now enclose for the purpose of presenting that business more fully before you.

I am convinced that this exposition of our situation with Britain and Spain, and to which the incident of Mr. Gardoqui furnished the first opening, has been useful: For before that exposition, I had reason to believe that it was not only unknown, but that a very erroneous opinion was entertained by many in the committee upon that subject. I thought I had felt the effect of that opinion, created no doubt in the manner you suggest; but as it was not communicated in a way to enable me to take official notice of it, I was embarrassed how to act or what measure to adopt in regard to it. For awhile as it was circulated only in private, I thought it best to counteract it, by making the necessary explanation only to those who mentioned it to me. Finally as I knew the campaign was progressing towards a close, and that the winter was the season for negotiation; and more especially as I feared its commencement with either of those powers, with such improper opinion of our situation with each, because I well knew they would improve it with great dexterity to their advantage, I deemed it my duty to make an extraordinary effort to remove it. With this view I appointed a rendezvous with the diplomatic members of the Committee, and which took place accordingly. I was resolved, however not to meet the imputation as a charge supposed to exist, or which I was bound to answer in case it did. A denial of a charge might beget a suspicion where there was none. I took different ground by informing the committee, that the war in which they were engaged, like all other wars, must have a termination: that most were concluded by the friendly mediation of third powers: That I was well convinced the United States would be happy to render the French Republic any service in their power, in that respect, to bring the present war to a happy close: That it was not their interest to interfere even by mediation, nor, in my judgment, would they, otherwise than at the instance and by the request of the French Republic, in the hope of promoting thereby the success of their revolution. I observed further that I wanted no answer to this, and had only given the information, that they might retain it in memory for the purpose of availing themselves of it hereafter, in case it should be found expedient. It was received respectfully but calmly. By one of the members it was observed: "That having beaten their enemies completely, it belonged to those enemies to determine whether they wished peace or not; and if they did, they would no doubt, be able to find a way whereby to make it known to the Republic." By another, I was asked: "Whether Mr. Jay was still in London and whether he intended to come over to Paris, as had been published in an English paper?" This was the very suspicion I wished to combat and remove; though indeed I did not expect it would have been avowed in so abrupt a manner. I replied I could not tell whether he had returned or not; but that it was impossible the paragraph in the English paper should be true, as he was sent to England upon an especial business only; to demand reparation for injuries, and to which his authority was strictly limited. I then repeated what I had before said of the friendly disposition of the United States towards the French Republic, in all cases, and of the pleasure with which they would, in my judgment, serve it upon the present one, if in their power. That I was persuaded they would listen to no proposition on the subject of mediation from any other power; for as it was a business which could not possibly benefit them, they would, of course, embark in it only upon account of their ally. I likewise added, that I knew nothing of the disposition of any power upon the subject of peace; but presumed the success of their arms had disposed them all well towards it; and thus I left them to reflect at leisure upon what I had said; in the belief however that the communication must produce a good effect. As this took place prior to the affair of Mr. Gardoqui, and which was more particularly detailed in my last, I have thought proper to communicate it to you, that you may be possessed of every, the minutest, circumstance relative to our affairs upon this very interesting theatre.[67]

---

[67] Monroe well realized that John Jay's treaty put his own mission in serious jeopardy. But Secretary of State Randolph told Monroe that he should assure the French that Jay received no authorization to make any agreement with the British Empire that imperiled America's relationship with France. Time and again Randolph assured Monroe that the goals of Jay's mission included only securing compensation for property lost during the Revolutionary War and the restoration of America's western frontier posts. Jay's mission, the administration insisted, did not signal a decision to forfeit the U.S. relationship with France in exchange for a closer connection to England. In his instructions, Randolph told Monroe to "remove all jealousy with respect to Mr. Jay's mission in London." He assured Monroe that Jay "is positively forbidden to weaken the engagements between this country and France." He also instructed Monroe to assure the French that Jay's mission only had the goals of obtaining "immediate compensation for our plundered property, and the restitution of the posts." Monroe dutifully conveyed "solemn declarations" to the French Committee of Public Safety to that effect. While this may have been strictly true, Randolph and the administration misled Monroe when it came to Jay's mission. Along with the goals Monroe understood, the administration had also authorized Jay to

If the subject of a loan is mentioned again here, or in America, that of securing for us the points in question, must likewise be; but as I have said every thing on that head that I can say, having only a right to conjecture, I am not anxious to revive it here. I am, however persuaded it will be revived with you; for so vast are their armies, and extensive their operations, that they must be distressed for money, and forced to gain it from whence they can. And I sincerely wish we may assist them, if possible, and which I presume it will be, especially if not comprised in the war, and which I think cannot be, although we should immediately wrest from Britain and Spain the rights they have usurped from us. The credit of the United States is such in Europe and America, and their means of reimbursement so unquestionable, especially in the particular of the Western Territory (an object viewed at present with great cupidity on this side the Atlantic) that I am persuaded the amount expected might be obtained by loan; and I am equally so that the people would cheerfully bear a tax, the product of which was to be applied in aid of the French Republic. Upon these topics, however, I have a right only to conjecture, and as such you will be pleased to consider what I have said.[68]

The day after my remarks upon the subject of a loan were handed in, I was favored with yours of the 25th. of September, and which I beg leave now to acknowledge. Finding that my idea of our situation with Britain and Spain was correct, I was extremely happy that I had given that representation of it. The motive for a strong union here, on our part, is the greater, and nothing tends so effectually to promote that object as the belief that we are not cordial with England. In consequence I waited on the Committee again, and told them I had received a dispatch from you since our last conference and that our dilemma with those two powers was even more critical than I had before intimated. Facts of this kind go further in removing doubts than any assurances I could otherwise give them. These discussions have enabled me to examine attentively whether it was their real wish that we should embark with them in the war, and I can assure you that whatever it may have been at any previous stage, upon which I can give no opinion, that at present I am persuaded they would rather we would not; from an idea it might diminish their supplies from America: But such is their disposition towards us that I am inclined to think, if the point depended on them they

negotiate a commercial treaty with the British. Monroe knew nothing of these instructions. The administration kept Monroe in the dark because only someone believed to be a friend to the Revolution could mollify both the French government and the growing pro-French faction in the United States. Furthermore, the administration needed to keep the French happy in the event that Jay failed to secure a treaty. (Poston 2012, 103-104)

[68] The sum that the French Republic wanted from the United States was about five million dollars, to be borrowed under the guarantee of the United States but secured by a mortgage of an adequate portion of their national domains. (Hamilton 1899, 148)

would leave us to act in that respect according to our wishes. And I am likewise persuaded, if we do embark in the war, that they will see us through it; and have some hope if we do not, and especially if we aid them in the article of money, that they will support, as far as they will be able, our demands upon Spain and England.

I intimated in my last that we could not have asked of fortune a more seasonable opportunity for possessing ourselves of those rights which have been so long usurped by Britain and Spain, and that if it was the sense of America ever to possess them, it should not be pretermitted.[69] Britain is certainly not in a condition to embark in a war against us, though we should dispossess her of Canada: She would of course be less apt to do it, if we only placed her troops beyond the lakes. Her own land force was scarcely felt in the present war against France: Nor has she been otherwise regarded than on account of her fleet and pecuniary resources by which she subsidized Prussia and other powers. But that force, small as it was, is greatly diminished, and the combination in which she has been associated appears, not only to be completely foiled, but in a great measure broken. The prospect now before her is that Prussia, Austria and all the other powers will extricate themselves from the war, upon the best terms they can and leave her singly to support it against France; and that the latter will be aided by Spain unless a particular combination against us should prevent it; and likewise by Denmark and Sweden, if not directly, yet in a manner to produce a serious effect. The preponderance of her fleet and the wanton and licentious use made of it, have excited the disgust of all nations against her; who would be pleased to see it reduced, and the present is considered as a favorable time to reduce it. She likewise knows or confidently believes that it is the intention of France to prosecute the war against her, for the purpose of breaking her maritime strength and ridding the ocean from such a tyranny. At home too she cannot be free from disquietude. The total failure of her operations in this quarter (what they are in the West Indies is better known to you) has excited some uneasiness in the public mind, and proportionately lessened the weight of the court. This was lately shewn in a prosecution against a Mr. Hardy, and in which the verdict was given for the defendant. And should the French take Holland (which nothing but an inundation already commenced can prevent, if even that can) this sensation will of course be increased. Thus circumstanced what have we to fear from her? Will she, in her decline, bring upon herself another enemy who can wound her so vitally; for let her merchants and politicians boast as they will of her resources, yet it is well known, if the American demand was cut off, upon which she thrives so much, that

---

[69] Written "taken advantage of" in the Record Book. (Hamilton 1899, 150)

it would greatly diminish her revenue and impair her strength. How is she enabled to support her engagements and carry on her operations, but by commerce? and lessened as this already is by the war, how could she sustain such a stroke at the present crisis? From her friendship we have nothing to hope: The order of the 6th. November was war in fact, and that has since been modified according to circumstances. Be assured she is infinitely less disposed for such an event at the present, than at any preceding period. On the contrary, if we only took possession of what we are entitled to, she will readily join with us in reprehending the conduct of her own officers for having transcended their orders.[70] With respect to Spain I have nothing new to add since my last, except that in two days' successive actions two complete victories were obtained over her troops by those of this Republic; unless, indeed, some ingenious sophist, jealous of the honour of Spain should contend, that as they were completely routed on the first, and maintained only a straggling battle on the second, it ought to be called but one. Certain it is that in the two days conflict, several thousands were slain and upwards of two thousand taken prisoners, with their camp on each day, and on one, tents for fifty thousand men.

I promised you, sometime since, my comments upon the subject of a Consular arrangement, for the ports of this Republic. The consuls have been here to confer with me upon the subject of trade, and I have obtained from them their ideas on that of the arrangement which I now enclose to you. I will add my own comments on it in my next, and will subjoin the names of some Americans now here, that may be deemed worthy of your attention. I think proper however now to mention that Mr. Skipwith will accept the office of Consul for this city, and that I think him worthy of it. He is in my opinion, a sensible man, of strict integrity, and well acquainted with the duties of the office. The duties of Consul here will be those of Consul General, and in strictness the Commission should be correspondent. They may, however, be performed under that of Consul only; for I presume those in the ports will respect him equally in either character.

I have the honor to be with great respect and esteem,

Your obedient Servant, Jas Monroe.

---

[70] It was Monroe's opinion that the United States should take a strong position with respect to England, which would not only have put it at ease permanently with France, lessening the impact of the misunderstandings that had previously occurred, but, by also obtaining her assistance against England, without any danger of war, and on America's own terms. Further, it could reduce the level of dialogue regarding the propriety of America repaying France any obligations owed her. (Hamilton 1899, 41)

To James Madison, Paris, Dec. 18, 1794

Dear Sir,—I enclose you three letters one for Mr. R. and the other two for whomever you may think it best to direct them.[71] You will in case they are delivered take a copy of one for y'rself, for I have not had time to write you nor indeed is it necessary on that subject as I send them open to y'r inspection. You will know whether there is any thing in the report & act accordingly either by presenting or suppressing all. I really wish mine to Mr. R. to be seen by the Pr:[72] if expedient to be delivered. As to the persons to whom to be addressed I leave it entirely to you (advising that you consult with no one on that point lest it be known they were not addressed by me) but am inclined to think that one sho'd be addressed to Langdon[73] & the other either to Burr,[74] Butler[75] or Ross.[76] As you will take a copy, you will be able to show it to our Virg'a friends and others as by my request & which will apologize for my not writing them. After all there is but one kind of policy which is safe, which is the honest policy. If it was intended to cultivate France by sending me here Jay sho'd not have been sent to Engl'd but if indeed it was intended to cultivate Engl'd it was wise to send some such person as myself here, for it was obvious that in proportion as we stood well with France sho'd we be respected by Engl'd. I have not time to write you further at present than to assure you that the aff'rs of the Republick are in every respect in the most flourishing condition. Wise, humane & just in its councils, & eminently successful in its armies, & also that we are well.

Affec'y I am y'r friend & serv't, Jas Monroe.

---

[71] See December 18, 1794, private letter to Edmund Randolph.

[72] President George Washington.

[73] A Revolutionary and Federal era leader, John Langdon was one of the first two senators from New Hampshire. Born in Portsmouth, he became a successful owner of seagoing merchant vessels, and he served as a member of the Continental Congress in 1775 and 1776. He was elected to the U.S. Senate from New Hampshire in 1788 (the first session under the federal Constitution) he served until 1801. (U.S. House of Representatives 2020)

[74] Aaron Burr was a senator from New York and a vice president of the United States. A former attorney general of New York and the commissioner of revolutionary claims, he was elected to the senate and served from 1791 to 1797. (U.S. Senate 2020)

[75] Pierce Butler, an Irishman, came to America in 1758 as an officer in the British Army; he resigned his commission prior to the Revolutionary War and settled in Charles Town, South Carolina. He was a delegate to the Continental Congress in 1787 and to the Federal Constitutional Convention in Philadelphia in 1787; he was a signer of the Constitution. He was elected to the United States Senate in 1789 and served until 1796. (U.S. Senate 2020)

[76] James Ross, a lawyer, was a Pennsylvania native and a delegate to the state constitutional conventions in 1789 and 1790. Elected as a pro-administration (later Federalist) to the United States Senate in 1794 to fill the vacancy caused by the senate declaring the election of Albert Gallatin void. He was reelected and remained until 1803, serving as President pro tempore during the Fifth Congress. (U.S. Senate 2020)

As the letters are closed on great hurry, see that there are no inaccuracies. If Mr. Skipwith is confirmed, pray send Prevost off immediately. I repeat again that I put this business entirely under y'r care. You will readily conclude, if the report is entirely without foundation & which I most earnestly hope it is, that it will be best to suppress the whole.

To Edmund Randolph, Paris, December 18, 1794

Dear Sir,—Within a few days past English papers have been received here stating that Mr. Jay had points in controversy between that country and the United States: in some of those papers it is stated that Canada is to be ceded with the ports, that privileges are to be given in the West Indies and other stipulations which imply an alliance offensive & defensive as likewise a commercial treaty.[77] As this government has always felt uneasiness upon the subject of his mission, and which was greatly mitigated but not entirely done away by the solemn declarations I had made upon the authority of my instructions, that he had no power other than to demand the surrender of the ports & compensation for injuries, this recent intelligence has excited a kind of horror in the minds of those acquainted with it. And as it will probably get into the papers I fear the same sensation will be universal for a while. As it is that this accommodating disposition in the Cabinet of St. James, if it really exists, is owing to the successes of the French arms, the good under-standing between the United States and this Republick, and the decisive temper of our government as shewn in the movements and letters of Wayne, and which were previously published in the opposition papers here, it might perhaps be expected from a just and generous people that we would pursue the adjustment of our controversy with that country in concert with this: in any event that we would not bind up ourselves in relation to the present war, in any manner to prevent us from fulfilling existing stipulations if called on to execute them, or rendering other service to our ally which a recollection of past and recent good offices might incline us to render. But to take advan-tage of the success of the French arms, of the good understanding subsisting between this. Republick and our own, and which was created by the dismis-sion of a minister odious to all France, and the frank declarations which I made in obedience to my instructions in the presence of the Convention and in the view of Europe, of our attachment to their welfare and solicitude for their success, to part the two countries and draw us into the bosom of our

---

[77] This is the enclosure referred to in the James Madison letter of December 18, 1794.

mortal foe, would be an act of perfidy the example of which was perhaps never seen before.[78]

As yet I have not been spoken to upon this subject by the Committee nor do I expect to be, for reserve is the peculiar characteristic of that department, and from which it never deviates except in cases when the person in whose favor the deviation is, possesses their entire confidence. Notwithstanding the harmony of opinion which prevailed among all their parties here, in respect to my political principles and attachment to their nation for services in our revolution, yet this impenetrable cloak was for some time after my arrival, assumed even towards myself. It was laid aside by degrees only and upon their own experience of the verity of these reports: for so common are the cases of political depravity in the Courts of the European world, that they act as if nothing else were to be found any where. If then this report should be entirely discredited, or if it should be credited, I think I shall not be spoken to. In the former instance they will not offend me, by letting it be seen that they had even noticed it. And in the latter as they will be mortified for having given me a rank in their estimation more elevated than that of other political agents whom they class generally or in the mass as rascals, and will consider themselves as duped they will endeavour to hide it from me. So that in either case 'tis probable I shall not be spoken to on the subject. If credited it will be seen only by their relapse into the former state of reserve and which the first interview will decide.

On my part I entirely disbelieve it. I can readily conceive that the British administration under the pressure of the French Arms, and the decisive tone of our government will yield the ports and pay us for our losses, or rather it would be the endeavour of that administration to make us pay for it if possible by betraying us into some stipulation which would weaken our connection with France and stain our national character, for they know too well the temper of the publick mind to think it possible to connect us with them. And I can also readily conceive that our agent there would be well disposed to harmonize with that administration in an effort to weaken that connection, and that in the pursuit of this object he would not be over nice or scrupulous as to the means. But I rest with unshaken confidence in the integrity of the President and in the veracity of the instructions given me to

---

[78] Rumors circulating about the treaty, mostly from the British press, put Monroe in a difficult position. The French government felt an "uneasiness" concerning Jay's mission, which Monroe tried to alleviate by consistently repeating Randolph's assurance that Jay only possessed restricted powers to treat with the British. This new treaty, which rumors indicated might even include "an alliance offensive and defensive," elicited a "kind of horror" from the French. As a result, Monroe agreed to let the French view the treaty as soon as he received it from Jay. (Poston 105, 2012)

declare that he had no such power. When I con template the fixed and steady character of the President, cautious in his measures, but immoveable after he has adopted them, jealous of his honor & regardful of his fame, the precious acquirement of great services and of a long and venerable life, I cannot hesitate for a moment in pronouncing that in placing me here he meant what he said, and that I should be the organ of an honest and not a double and perfidious policy. Upon this point I am perfectly at ease. The only point therefore upon which I feel any concern, is the apprehension of the dish which may be prepared for the palate of those who have particular interests with us & which 'tis possible may be contrived with great art by Messrs. Pitt & Jay, the latter of whom would be useful in giving information how such interests might be acted on so as to make it irresistible. And what increases this apprehension is the report that several of the stipulations are provisional, to be executed hereafter whereby the hostage remains in the hands of Great Britain, it being only a project (and of course no violation of instructions in form tho' absolutely so in fact) to be offered for the approbation of the President and the Senate. By this he would keep his ground in England, harmonize with the administration, and aid it in the means of attacking the integrity of our Councils. Upon this point I have my fears for I knew him play the same game upon the subject of the Mississippi. I instructed to enter into no stipulation which did not open that river and fix the boundaries according to our treaty with Great Britain. He should therefore not have heard a proposition on that subject: on the contrary he absolutely entered into a stipulation which shut the river up, or according to his own language forbore the use of it and left the boundaries to be settled by Commissaries to be appointed by both countries, as I understand is the case with some of the litigated points in the present case. The analogy in the project reported to be now de pending with that I have here recited (and which I have often wished the President would peruse from beginning to the end) together with my own perfect knowledge of the principles and crooked policy of the man disguised under the appearance of great sanctity and decorum, induce me to pay more attention to those papers than I otherwise should do.[79]

---

[79] While numerous reports speculated on the various aspects of the negotiations, from a long-range perspective the treaty would arguably be a success, but in the short term it presented serious problems. To his credit, Jay secured the definite withdrawal of British troops from their fortifications in the territories ceded to the United States in the Treaty of Peace and arranged for the arbitration of certain rather vaguely defined boundaries in those territories. He also arranged for the arbitration of American claims against the British for their past illegal maritime seizures, and he opened the British East Indies and, to a limited extent, the British West Indies to American shipping. But, on the downside, and against Southern interest, he failed to obtain compensation for the manumitted slaves and agreed to the arbitration of American debts to British creditors before joint commissioners in London. Moreover, in abandonment of the Madison–Jefferson policy

If any thing of this kind should have taken place I know the dilemma into which you will be all thrown. The western ports are offered you, compensation for losses; free trade to the Islands under the protection of the all powerful British flag; Canada is or will be given up, whereby the fisheries become more accessible; Engl will no longer support Spain in favor of the Mississippi &c. This will be resounded in the public papers and the impudence of the British faction become intolerable. But will it not be perceived that whatever is offered cannot be deemed the amicable concession of England but is already prosperous fortunes of your ally, & the decisive of your own councils? Will you take therefore in breach of plighted faith, and expense of our national character, and of an amicable concession of England what may be obtained without loss, and is in truth due to the merits of our ally? I will candidly own that I do not think it in the power of Messrs. Pitt and Jay to succeed in any project they can contrive where by to weaken our connection with France & put us again under the influence of England, for such would be the case provided that connection was weakened.[80]

I have written you freely upon this subject as well to state the report and explain the light in which such an adjustment would be received here, as to put you on your guard in relation to transactions in England, a country which will never smile upon but to deceive you. Tis impossible to be closely connected with both these countries if no other considerations prevented from the animosity, and frequent wars that will take place between them, and which must terminate from the superior strength of this in the ruin at least to a certain degree of the other: unless indeed we should now abandon our ally to prop the declining fortunes of hers and our adversary. I write to you in confidence that you will make no improper use of this & that from the necessity of retaining a copy you will excuse its being dressed in the character of a friend.

With great respect and esteem, I am dear Sir very sincerely yours,
Jas Monroe.

---

of retaliatory discrimination, and against the interest of the American shipping industry and of France, he conceded that, contrary to an existing act of Congress, British goods need no longer pay an additional 10 percent tax when carried in British ships, and he agreed that British trade be placed on a most-favored-nation basis. Worse, from both the American shippers' and the French points of view, he abandoned the principles to which the United States had previously committed itself in treaties: that neutrals were entitled to trade freely with belligerents in noncontraband goods and that the list of contraband must be narrowly confined to war-making items. Instead, Jay agreed to the inclusion of timber and other raw materials for shipbuilding as contraband, and to the right of the British to deflect American vessels from blockaded enemy ports and remove enemy property from the vessels. Finally, the treaty omitted any reference to the impressment of American seamen. Viewed as a whole, the treaty so offended Virginia interest that its publication caused a partisan Republican uproar. (Lynch 1999, 140-141)

[80] Monroe's candor is clearly on display, as he suggests that the entire matter is nothing less than a connivance between British Prime Minister William Pitt and John Jay.

To the Committee of Public Safety, Paris, December 27, 1794

I was favoured this morning by yours of yesterday, intimating that the report of a treaty, said to have been concluded by Mr. Jay, envoy of the United States of America to England, with that nation, derogatory to the treaties of alliance between those States and this Republic, had given you some disquietude and requesting information from me upon that point.[81] I obey the invitation with pleasure because I well know that a candid policy is that alone which becomes Republics, and because it is likewise most correspondent with the wishes of the American government and my own feelings. Having already communicated to you the limited object of Mr. Jays mission, it only remains for me to inform you what I know of the result. All that I know upon this subject is comprized in a letter received yesterday from Mr. Jay of November 25th., in which he says that he had fulfilled the principal object of his mission, by concluding a treaty, signed on the 19th. of the same month, which contains a declaration. "That it should not be construed, nor operate, contrary to our existing treaties, and that, therefore, our engagements with other nations were not affected by it." He adds that as the treaty is not yet ratified, it would be improper to publish it. I am altogether ignorant of the particular stipulations of the treaty, but I beg leave to assure you that as soon as I shall be informed thereof, I will communicate the same to you.

I take it, however, for granted, that the report is without foundation; for I cannot believe that an American minister would ever forget the connections between the United States and France, which every day's experience demonstrates to be the interest of both Republics still further to cement.

Jas Monroe.

---

[81] As indicated, it should be noted that Monroe did not initiate this correspondence; rather it is a response to the Committee's December 27th missive to him that states, "We are informed, Citizen, that there was lately concluded at London a treaty of alliance and commerce between the British government and Citizen Jay, envoy extraordinary of the United States. A vague report spreads itself, that in this treaty the citizen Jay has forgotten those things which our treaties with the American people and the sacrifices which the French people made to render them free, gave us a right to expect on the part of a minister of a nation which we have so many motives to consider as friendly. It is important that we know positively in what light we are to hold this affair. There ought not to subsist between two free people the dissimulation which belongs to courts, and it gives us pleasure to declare that we consider you as much opposed personally to that kind of policy as we ourselves. We invite you then to communicate to us as soon as possible the treaty whereof there is question. It is the only means whereby you enable the French nation justly to appreciate those reports, so injurious to the American government, and to which that treaty gave birth." (Tracy 1915, 30)

1795

To the President [George Washington], Paris, January 3, 1795

Dear Sir,—Your favor of the 5 of June did not reach me till a few days past or it sho'd have been sooner answered.[82] I am happy now to answer it because I am able to give you details of the lady in question which will be very agreeable to you. I had advanced her near 2000 dol'rs when I was advised here by Jacob Van Staphorst that you had plac'd in the hands of his brother for Madame La Fayette the sum of two thousand, three hundred & ten guilders & which had never been rec'd. At this time she was soliciting permission to leave France with a view of visiting & partaking with her husband the fortune to which he was exposed. I had given her a certificate that her husband had lands in America & that the Congress had appropriated to his use upwards of 20,000 dol'rs, the am't w'h was due for his services in our revolution, & upon which basis her application was founded & granted. I made known to her the fund you had appropriated for her use & which she readily & with pleasure accepted, & which served to defray the expense of her journey. She pursued her route by Dunkirk & Hamburg to which places I gave & procured letters of recommendation, & at the former of which she

---

[82] Monroe did not initiate this correspondence, either. This is a response to Washington's letter of June 5, 1795, that stated, "The regular and detailed accounts, which you receive from the department of state, of occurrences as they arise with us, leave nothing to be added. As a private concern I shall take the liberty of troubling you with the enclosed, requesting that it may be presented or forwarded, as the case may be, to Madame de Lafayette. The papers are under a flying seal, that, seeing the scope and design of them, you may (if the money therein mentioned should not have reached her hands, of which I have received no information,) be enabled to assist her in obtaining it; the favor of doing which I beg you to render us both. My best respects are presented to Mrs. Monroe. With esteem and regard, I am, dear Sir, &c." (Sparks 1858, 29)

---

was rec'd in the house & entertained by our consul Mr. Coffyn. I assured her when she left France there was no service within my power to render her & her husband & family that I would not with pleasure render them. To count upon my utmost efforts & command them in their favor. That it was your wish & the wish of America that I should do so. To consult her husband as to the mode & measure & apprize me of his opinions thereon. She departed grateful to you & our country & since which I have not heard from her. She had thoughts of visiting in person the Emperor & endeavoring to obtain the release of her husband; but whether she did or not I cannot tell. It was reported sometime since he was released & afterwards that she was admitted with her family into the same state of confinement with him; the latter of which I believe to be true. Before she left this I became responsible in her favor for 9000[83] upon a month 's notice (in specie) the object of w'h was to free a considerable estate from some encumbrance & which was effected upon my surety, as yet I have not been called on to pay it. As soon, therefore, as I rec'd the draft on Holland for six thousand dol'rs in her behalf, I wrote her by two different routes to assure her that I had funds for her & her husband's support & upon which she might for the present draw to the am't of £250. ster'g, & afterwards as occasion might require & to which I have rec'd no ans'r.

What may be the ultimate disposition of France towards Mr. Lafayette it is impossible now to say. His integrity so far as I can find remains unimpeached, & when that is the case the errors of the head are pardoned as the passions subside. It is more than probable I may be able to serve him with those by whom he is confined, & that I may do this without injury to the U. States here; acting with candor and vowing the motive, since it is impossible that motive can be otherwise than approved, especially if the step be taken when their aff'rs are in great prosperity. For this, however, I shall be happy to have y'r approbation, since if I do any thing with the Emperor it must be done in y'r name, if not explicitly yet in a manner to make known to him the interest you take in the welfare of Mr. Lafayette. Young Lafayette is I presume now under y'r auspices.

Within a few days past a truce or armistice was concluded between Pichegru & Jourdan on the one side & Clairfayt & Wurmser on the other as it is said for three months: this was of course subject to approbation or rejection of the gov't on each side. I hear that it was rejected on the side of France, orders being sent by the Directoire to pursue the war without cessation. Both armies are in the neighborhood of Mayence where the country is almost

[83] Madame de Lafayette, with her two daughters, joined her husband in the prison of Olmutz in October, 1795. (Cooper, 1825, 321)

entirely devastated. In Italy the Austrians are completely routed & their whole army nearly demolished. 'Tis said that 8000 prisoners are brought to one of the French villages.[84] Mrs. Monroe desires her best respects to be presented to yourself & Mrs. Washington, who we hope enjoy good health. If there is any thing in which I can be serviceable to you here, any article of curiosity or taste you wish to possess & which can be procured, I beg of you to make it known to me that I may procure it for you.

With great & sincere respect and esteem I am, Dear Sir, your most ob't & very humble servant, Jas Monroe.

P. S. There are many articles of tapestry the most beautiful that can be conceived, & w'h are intended for the walls of rooms, for chair bottoms &c, some of which perhaps wo'd be acceptible to the Com'rs of the federal town, & which if permitted by you or them I wo'd immediately procure & forward.

To the Secretary of State [Edmund Randolph], Paris, January 13, 1795

Sir,—I have the pleasure to inform you that upon the report of the united committees of Public Safety, Legislation, Commerce and Finances, a decree has passed the Convention since my last, whereby it is resolved to carry into strict execution the treaty of amity and commerce between the United States and this Republic. I beg leave to congratulate you upon this event, and particularly the unanimity with which it passed the Convention, since it demonstrates the good disposition of that body and of the nation generally towards us. I was always satisfied, as hereto fore intimated, that if I could have brought the subject in the first instance, before the Convention, I should have succeeded immediately in the object in view: But as the Committee was the department organized for such business this was impossible, without commencing a species of warfare upon it, and which was equally improper, as it might tend to increase their own dissentions. Happily by pursuing the object patiently with the Committee, removing doubts, and obviating objections, aided by occasional changes of the members, this has not only been avoided, but I have the additional pleasure to assure you, that it was finally accomplished, without the least difficulty and without exciting the animosity of any one.

After my late communications to the Committee of Public Safety, in which were exposed freely the object of Mr. Jay's mission to England, and

---

[84] This is a reference to the November 1795 engagement at Loano where the French army of Italy led by Barthélemy Schérer defeated the combined Austrian and Sardinian forces under Olivier, Count of Wallis. Shortly thereafter, Schérer's campaign was brought to a standstill by bad weather and lack of supplies. (Markkam 1954, 15)

the real situation of the United States with Britain and Spain, I had reason to believe, that all apprehension on those parts was done away and that the utmost cordiality had now likewise taken place in that body towards us. I considered the report above recited, and upon which the decree was founded, as the unequivocal proof of that change of sentiment, and flattered myself that in every respect we had now the best prospect of the most perfect and permanent harmony between the two Republics. I am very sorry, however, to add, that latterly this prospect has been somewhat clouded by accounts from England, that Mr. Jay had not only adjusted the points in controversy, but concluded a treaty of commerce with that government: Some of those accounts state that he had also concluded a treaty of alliance, offensive and defensive. As I knew the baneful effects which these reports would produce, I deemed it my duty by repeating what I had said before of his powers, to use my utmost endeavours, informally to discredit them. This, however, did not arrest the progress of the report, nor remove the disquietude it has created: For I was finally applied to directly by the Committee in a letter which stated what had been heard, and requested information of what I knew in regard to it.[85]

As I had just before received one from Mr. Jay, announcing that he had concluded a treaty, and which contained a declaration that our previous treaties should not be affected by it, I thought fit to make this letter the basis of my reply.[86] And as it is necessary that you should be apprized of whatever

---

[85] From the Committee of Public Safety to Monroe: "December 27, 1794. We are informed, Citizen, that there was lately concluded at London, a treaty of alliance and commerce between the British Government and Citizen Jay, envoy extraordinary of the United States. A vague report spreads itself abroad, that, in this treaty, the Citizen Jay has forgotten those things which our treaties with the American people, and the sacrifices which the French people made to render them free, gave us a right to expect on the part of a minister of a nation, which we have so many motives to consider as friendly. It is important that we know positively in what light we are to hold this affair. There ought not to subsist between two free people, the dissimulation which belongs to Courts; and it gives us pleasure to declare that we consider you as much opposed personally to that kind of policy, as we are ourselves. We invite you then to communicate to us as soon as possible the treaty whereof there is question. It is the only means whereby you can enable the French Nation justly to appreciate those reports so injurious to the American government and to which that treaty gave birth." (Hamilton 1899, 169)

[86] Jay's November 24, 1794, letter to Monroe: "Sir, It gives me pleasure to inform you that a treaty between the United States and His Britannic Majesty was signed on the 19th., instant. This circumstance ought not to give any uneasiness to the Convention The treaty expressly declares that nothing contained in it shall be construed to operate contrary to existing treaties between the United States and other powers. I flatter myself that the United States, as well as all their ministers will, upon every occasion, manifest the most scrupulous regard to good faith; and that those nations who wish us well, will be pleased with our preserving peace and a good understanding with others." On November 25th, Jay again addressed Monroe: "By a letter written and sent a few days ago, I had the pleasure of informing you that on the 19th., instant, the principal business of my mission was

has passed here on this subject, I now transmit to you copies of these several papers and which comprize a full statement thereof, up to the present time. I cannot admit for a moment that Mr. Jay has exceeded his powers, or that any thing has been done which will give just cause of complaint to this Republic. I lament, however, that he has not thought himself at liberty to give me correct information on that subject; for until it is known that their interest has not been wounded, the report will certainly keep alive suspicion, and which always weakens the bonds of friendship. I trust therefore you will deem it expedient to advise me on this head, as soon as possible.

I apprized you, in my two last letters, of an informal communication between the diplomatic members of the Committee and myself, upon an interrogatory of theirs, whether it would be possible for France to obtain aid from, or within, the United States, for the purchase of supplies; and of my effort upon that occasion to interest this Government in support of our claims with Britain and Spain; and to which I was stimulated by intelligence that Mr. Jay's mission had failed; and that we were on the point of war, or actually engaged in it, with Britain; as likewise by the knowledge that Spain was covertly seeking a separate peace. I was satisfied that if France would embark in our cause, in the present state of things, and which I found her well disposed to do, and without the prospect of much aid in return, that the object in each instance would be secure. I therefore thought it eligible in that state of things, and with that view, to leave the door open for a communication on the subject with you. But as soon as I understood that Mr. Jay had adjusted the points in controversy with that nation, the object on my part was at an end. I was aware that if the adjustment was approved, we could render no such service: Indeed I doubted whether in peace the government possessed the power to render it. I called, therefore, immediately upon those members with whom the previous communication had been and suggested the same to them. They had anticipated the idea, and were prepared to answer it by a peremptory assurance, that it was not their wish to create embarrassment in this or any other respect: On the contrary, that regard should be shown in all cases to our actual situation; and with respect to the point in question, that the minister about to depart, should be instructed not even to mention it if you forbade it. So that this business stands upon a

---

concluded by a treaty signed on that day. It contains a declaration, that it shall not be construed, nor operate contrary to our existing treaties; as therefore our engagements with other nations remain unaffected by it, there is reason to hope, that our preserving peace and a good understanding with this country, will not give uneasiness to any other. As the treaty is not ratified, it would be improper to publish it. It appears to me to be upon the whole, fair, and as equal as could be expected. In some respects, both nations will probably be pleased, and in others displeased." (Hamilton 1899, 170)

footing, as indeed it always did, whereby under a particular state of things, some benefit may be derived from it, and no detriment under any.

The operations of this government continue to progress in the same course they have done for some time past. During the time of Robespierre, a period of the administration which is emphatically called the reign of terror, much havoc was made not only in the rights of humanity, but great confusion was likewise introduced, in other respects, in the affairs of the government. It has been the systematic effort of the administration to repair this waste, and heal the bleeding wounds of the country, and, in this, great progress has been made. By the same report which proposed the execution of the violated articles of the treaty of amity and commerce with the United States, it was likewise proposed to open wide the door of commerce to every citizen (excluding them from navigation only) and which was adopted: So that, at present, any person bringing productions into the ports of this Republic, may sell them to whom he pleases, and generally with astonishing profit. The Agents of the Republic stand upon the ground of other persons: They are preferred only by out-bidding them. In my judgment no region of the world presents such an opening to the enterprize of our countrymen as this does. The restraints upon their own navigation, operate in the degree as a bounty to ours; and the government and citizens of France seem equally pleased to see ours preferred to that of any other nation. The restraints, likewise, which are imposed in other countries, on account of the war, upon a commerce with the French citizens, produce, in other respects, the same effect. It is the interest of the latter to employ our countrymen in ordinary mercantile transactions, and especially with foreign nations; whereby they get into their hands a great proportion of the whole trade of the Republic. The profits which those on this theatre have already made, and continue to make, surpass what you have any idea of. I sincerely wish that this was more generally known, that more might be induced to embark in it, not only for the purpose of diffusing more generally the immediate emoluments, but for the more important one of gaining an interest in the commerce of this Republic, which may be of lasting advantage to the United States. Before the Revolution, the English possessed this advantage, as they did in most other countries: But now that interest is annihilated; and if the Americans step in, aided as they will be by the preference of the government and people in their favour, they may occupy the ground, and retain it forever afterwards. Permit me to add that nothing will more essentially forward this object, than an extensive and numerous appointment of Consuls. In every port an agent should be placed: and I should suppose the object of sufficient importance to induce our countrymen to accept of these offices. If a prudent and creditable person, the appointment attaches to it confidence, and gives him the command of Capital. I am satisfied that any young man of good character, having the appointment in any of the ports, might immediately connect himself advantageously with the first house there, and gradually command elsewhere what capital he pleased. I have examined into this subject and have thought proper to give you the result of my researches into it.

Nor has this wise and humane system been limited to this object alone. It has already been extended to many branches of national policy and promises to embrace the whole. A decree was not long since passed by which the seventy-one members, formerly of the Brissotine or Girondin party, and who had been confined on that account, were all at liberty, and called into the Convention. And a few days afterwards our countryman, Mr. Paine, was likewise restored to his seat in that body, with marks of the most respectful attention. These events have given satisfaction to the community at large. A decree also, which had excluded the nobles and foreigners (the Americans excepted) from Paris, and the seaports, has likewise been repealed. This latter act, though comparatively of apparent little importance, has notwithstanding produced an excellent effect: For as it breathes a spirit of humanity and on that account captivates all, so it has contributed, by passing in review many members of the ancient order of nobility (and who have not forgotten, and never will forget, old habits) to present before the public, and much to the credit of the Revolution, the strong and interesting contrast between the manly character of the French nation at the present day, and the miserable effeminacy, foppery and decrepitude of former times.

A decree has likewise passed, by which a general amnesty has been proclaimed in the Vendu; and a report has been since received from the deputies who were sent to carry it into effect, that all those to whom it was announced, had lain down their arms, and arranged themselves under the banner of the Republic; and that they were likewise satisfied it would terminate the war; a war heretofore, beyond example, bloody and destructive, and whose origin, support and means of continuance, appear even yet to be but little understood. Freed from this embarrassment, the Republic will acquire new vigor in all its enterprises; it will certainly have under its command, for other purposes, a considerable force which was hereto fore employed there.

But in retracing the ground, to repair in detail the injuries which the reign of terror had inflicted, it was impossible to behold the havoc it had made, with out feeling some indignation for the authors of so great and complicated misery. This propensity, however, and which was equally incited by the obligations of justice and humanity, was strongly opposed from the period of

Robespierre's death to the present time, by a sentiment of extensive impression, that it were better to prevent the further effusion of blood, and to cover with a veil the atrocities which had passed, so far as they could be covered, than to punish those of greatest enormity. For some time this sentiment prevailed, and though often irritated and disturbed by the remaining leaders of the opposite party, who courted danger and provoked their own fate, yet it appeared probable it would finally preponderate and confirm the administration within that limit. The trial, however, of the Nantois, a long train of respectable citizens at Nantes, who were arrested under the administration of Carrier, in his mission there, and brought lately before the tribunal of Paris, opened the scene again, and revived the sensation of horror, which had before in some measure subsided.[87] Such enormities were disclosed in the course of this trial, that it was impossible otherwise to appease the public mind than by submitting Carrier, and his accomplices to the tribunal in their turn. Condemnation was the sure consequence of his trial; and it was expected, so clear was the case against him, that all those formerly of that party, would now separate from and yield him to his fate. From such a line of conduct some merit might have been arrogated, and the public censure thrown in a great measure on him alone; by whose punishment too the public resentment might possibly have been satisfied. But Billaud de Varennes, Collot-d'Herbois, and even Barrère, a man heretofore noted for skillful movements obviously and from the beginning, made Carrier's cause their own; not only by supporting him in the Convention, as far as it was possible, but by exciting the Jacobins to take part in his favour; thereby attaching themselves to the declining fortunes of that Club, and likewise making some unseasonable motions which bore on their face the complexion of that party. The separation required at best a dexterous management; but by these means they presented themselves out as an object, invited the public attention, and, in the degree, the public resentment. Whether they will finally escape is now doubtful. Lecontre, who has shewn himself sufficiently prone, upon a former occasion to commence the attack, took advantage of one of these moments of indiscretion to renew it, and with better effect. This motion was sent to the

---

[87] Forty-two per cent of the death sentences during the entire Terror were passed in the various special courts established in the Loire Inférieure, Nantes's department. This accounted for 3,548 capital sentences. Moreover, the citizens of Nantes, repeatedly threatened by insurgents who reputedly gave no quarter, raised little objection to such methods, or to the hundreds of shootings of armed rebels that Carrier also authorized. (Doyle 1990, 257) Hamilton notes that it is impossible to image the difficulty Monroe must have felt when (as America's representative) he was obliged to cultivate France's friendship and to "conciliate her Councils in their every sensitive whim and disposition" without taking offense when faced with the "cruelties and the horrors of the French Revolutionists," especially when it was to France's murdered king that American gratitude was due. (Hamilton 1899, 175)

Committee of Twenty-One, heretofore organized to report, whether there was just ground of accusation, and there it now is.

Another signal victory was obtained over the Spaniards since my last, and in which the two commanding generals, with many men, were slain, and nine thousand taken prisoners. And in the north, since the ice, nearer approaches are made to Holland, which will most probably soon be taken. Within a few days past deputies arrived from the Stadtholderian party, to negociate a separate peace: But at the same time others came from the patriotic party to oppose it, and who pressed the Committee to order forward the troops immediately, to assail and enter Amsterdam; and to which effect orders were accordingly issued. I am satisfied that peace will not be granted to the Netherlands, although a revolution should take place there, on any other condition than that of their uniting in the war against England.[88] It is conceived that a peace to that power, on other terms, would be more favourable to England than its continuance in the war; for thereby the British troops might be withdrawn, and great advantage gained in other respects from its neutrality. This it is thought is the object of England in assenting to their peace; but in rejecting the offer, France opens a trait in her views that will add much to the weight of the ministerial argument for a continuation of the war. No argument is so strong as that of necessity, and if France will not make peace it will be impossible for England to do it. In my judgment it is the determination of this Republic to pursue the war, until the maritime strength of England is broken; and when the actual state of things is regarded, with that of the comparative population, force and enterprize of the two nations, I do not see how it can be prevented. A single victory at sea accomplishes the object, and the rapidity with which ships were built, and fleets equipped here is inconceivable. Within few weeks past, the Brest fleet has been out twice (indeed it is now out) consisting of thirty-six ships of the line, fifteen frigates, fourteen sloops of war and cutters, giving the defiance to its antagonist, which continues close locked to the land. More latterly, however, some indications were seen on that coast of a disposition to take the sea, and hazard the fate of the Island on a battle, so that it is probable something decisive may take place soon.

---

[88] In 1795, the Dutch Republic was literally trampled by the French troops. On every level, from village administrations to the Estates General, revolutionaries seized power. Stadtholder William V fled to England. In the Netherlands the revolutionaries established a new constitution, and thus the Batavian Republic was born. Politically, the situation remained troubled, chiefly because of the strong opposition between the Federalists, who wanted to preserve the Estates General as it had been under the former republic, and the Unitarianists, who aspired to a unified state modeled after the French example. The Batavian Republic lasted until 1806, when the Netherlands became a kingdom under Louis Bonaparte, brother of Napoleon I. (Dekker 2003, 130)

With respect to the other powers nothing definitive has yet been done in regard to peace. It is certain that several wish it, and particularly Spain and Prussia; but yet some difficulties have occurred in regulating the commencement and manner of the negotiation. England opposes it, because she knows she will not be included; and they on that account wish it to be private, merely to avoid the imputations that would arise if it were known; and this cannot well be accommodated under the present organization of the French Government. It is said that a Minister from Prussia is at Basle, in Switzerland, with power to treat; and that they all have agents there for the same purpose is likewise probable.

I will endeavour, if possible, to forward by this opportunity a report rendered me by Mr. Skipwith, upon the subject of American claims. Be assured that every possible attention has been, and shall be paid to this subject. With great respect and esteem, I have the honor to be, dear Sir, your very humble servant, Jas Monroe.

P. S. I had omitted to mention the official communication by the Committee of Public Safety, of the decree of the Convention for carrying into effect the treaty of amity and commerce between the United States and France: The polite terms, however, in which it is expressed merit attention.

To John Jay, Paris, January 17, 1795

Sir,—Early in December last, English papers were received here, containing such accounts of adjustment with the British administration, as excited much uneasiness in the councils of this government, and I had it in contemplation to dispatch a confidential person to you, for such information of what had been done, as would enable me to remove it. At that moment, however, I was favoured with yours of the 25th., November, intimating, that the contents of the treaty could not be made known until it was ratified; but that it contained nothing derogatory to our existing treaties with other powers. Thus advised I thought it improper to make the application; because I concluded the arrangement was mutual and not to be departed from. I proceeded, therefore, to make the best use in my power of the information already given.

Today, however, I was favoured with yours of the 28th of the same month,[89] by which I find you consider yourself at liberty to communicate to

---

[89] The letter, dated London, November 28, 1794, stated: "Sir: Within this week past I have written to you two letters to inform you that on the 19th, instant a treaty between the United States and his Britannic Majesty was signed. The design of this letter is chiefly to introduce to you Mr. [Samuel] Pleasants of Philadelphia, whose connections there are respectable, I have not the pleasure of being personally acquainted with this gentleman, but as a fellow citizen I wish to do him friendly offices; and I am persuaded that a similar

me the contents of the treaty, and as it is of great importance to our affairs here, to remove all doubt upon this point, I have thought it proper to resume my original plan of sending a person to you for the necessary information, and have in consequence dispatched the bearer, Mr. John Purviance for that purpose.[90] I have been the more induced to this from the further consideration that in case I should be favoured with the communication promised in cypher, it would be impossible for me to comprehend it, as Mr. Morris took it with him. Mr. Purviance is from Maryland, a gentleman of integrity and merit, and to whom you may commit whatever you may think proper to confide with perfect safety. It is necessary, however, to observe, that as nothing will satisfy this government but a copy of the instrument itself, and which, as our ally, it thinks it self entitled to so it will be useless for me to make to it any new communication short of that. I mention this that you may know precisely the state of my engagements here, and how I deem it my duty to act under them in relation to this object.[91] I beg leave to refer you to Mr. Purviance for whatever other information you may wish on this subject, or the affairs more generally of this Republic.

I have the honor to be with great respect your most obedient servant, Jas Monroe.

To the Committee of Public Safety, Paris, January 25, 1795

Citizens,—I have thought proper to present to your view, in the enclosed paper, the situation of the United States in relation to the situation of the river Mississippi, and respecting which a negotiation is now depending with

---

disposition on your part will insure to him such a degree of attention as circumstances may render proper. As Mr. Pinckney has a cypher with our other ministers in Europe, either he or I will shortly use it in communicating to you the principal heads of the Treaty confidentially. You need not hesitate in the mean time to say explicitly that it contains nothing repugnant to our engagements with any other nation. With the best wishes for your health and prosperity I have the honor to be, Sir, your most obt and hble servant. John Jay" (Hamilton 1899, 180)

[90] John Henry Purviance was secretary and interpreter to Monroe in Paris, 1794–1796, and secretary of the American legation in London, 1804–1810. (Purviance 2020)

[91] Although Monroe asked Jay for a copy of the treaty. He, perhaps foolishly, told the pro-British Jay that "nothing will satisfy this government but a copy of the instrument itself." Jay refused. Though he originally promised to send Monroe a copy, Jay now elected not to do so, as he did not believe it proper to send an un-ratified treaty to a foreign government, however friendly. Arguably, Jay was in the right in terms of diplomatic protocol. A foreign nation had no right to inspect a proposed treaty between two other powers. Accordingly, to permit France to do so would make the United States appear supplicant to their interests. Diplomatic protocol did not overly concern Monroe, who continued to believe that a closer alliance with France could only enhance American prestige. (Poston 2012, 105)

the Court of Spain.[92] This paper opens fully this interesting subject in its relation to both Republics, and which it is proper you should be correctly informed of, at the present time. France can only assist in opening the river, by inviting the American Minister, Mr. Short, to act in concert with her when she shall conclude her treaty with that power, and which by her permission, I can easily accomplish; or by comprising it in her own treaty. I have no power to treat upon this subject otherwise than by bringing it thus before you for the purpose of ascertaining what your disposition is upon it; and which with any comments you may be pleased to make, I shall be happy immediately to communicate to the American government.

Jas Monroe.

Notes Respecting the River Mississippi
Communicated to the Committee of Public Safety
Paris, January 25, 1795

The river Mississippi extends from about the forty-eighth degree of north latitude to the twenty-ninth, where it empties into the Gulph of Mexico, running nearly a north and south course and through a tract of the most fertile country in the world.

It bounds the United States to the west, from latitude thirty-one, to its source; an extent, pursuing the course of the river, of about two thousand miles.

Many rivers empty into it from the west, of which the Missouri is the most important. This latter has never been traced to its source; although voyagers have passed up it above one thousand five hundred miles: It is however believed that it penetrates further into the bosom of the continent than the Mississippi itself.

The whole of that portion of the United States lying westward of the Alleghany Mountains, and which comprizes about one half the territory within the said States depends upon this river for the export of its productions to foreign markets. It comprehends a portion of the territory of several of the existing States: Perhaps one third of Pennsylvania, Virginia, North Carolina, and Georgia; the whole of Kentucky and an immense tract of vacant

[92] President Washington nominated Thomas Pinckney of South Carolina, then United States minister in London, to be envoy extraordinary in Madrid. The designation authorized Pinckney to pursue a treaty to address the navigation of the Mississippi and all other matters in dispute between the United States and Spain. His commission was dated November 24, 1794, interestingly, the same day John Jay in London wrote to Monroe in Paris that a treaty between the United States and His Britannic Majesty had just been signed. (Rives 1898, 73)

territory, lying between the Ohio and the Mississippi, and which has already been laid out into five separate States, and which are to be ad mitted into the Union with the same rights as the old States, when they shall respectively attain a certain number of inhabitants. Of these it is proposed to settle one only at a time, and of which the first has already been commenced.

When we examine the extent of this territory; its fertility, superior to that of the old States; the felicity of its climate, lying all within the temperate zone; the kind and quality of its productions, such as hemp, flour, corn, in short everything necessary in human life, protected in its infant settlements by the government of the United States, and admitted as soon as it shall attain a certain degree of maturity to equal membership with them, we are compelled to appreciate it more highly than any other vacant tract known upon the globe.

Its settlement is of importance to all those European countries whose inhabitants are engaged in manufactures; because it will furnish in abundance rude materials for every species of manufacture: To those which have occasion at times for the supply of provisions; because it will furnish an exhaustless source of every species of provision; but it is of peculiar importance to those which have islands in the West Indies; because it lies in the neighbourhood of those islands, the mouth of the Mississippi being nearly in the same latitude; and will furnish everything in demand there, such as lumber, provisions, &c.

But the commerce of this country when settled, will depend upon the navigation of the Mississippi, and of course the settlement itself will depend upon the same cause. This was secured by a treaty of peace between the United States and Great Britain in 1783, but has hitherto been prevented by Spain from motives equally unjust and illiberal. A negotiation the object of which, on our part, is to open it, is and has been depending with that power since that time.

At the time our peace was made with England, the importance of this country was little known in her councils: It is said that her negociators did not even know on which side of the lakes, and of course within whose jurisdiction, the forts, which have since been the subject of contention, lay. But its importance was soon afterwards understood, and from which time it is certain that Britain has regarded it with particular attention, in hopes either of gaining it to herself, or otherwise making it subservient to her schemes of policy. With this view she refused to surrender the posts, excited the Indians to make war on our frontiers, encouraged Spain to refuse our right to the navigation of the Mississippi, and did us other injuries of the same kind.

It is certain that the western people will sooner or later open this river, either by negotiation or by force, and more than probable that England, retaining as she still does her resentment against the old states for their independence and against France for the aid given in that war, will watch the uneasiness of the western people, on account of the obstruction of the navigation of the river, and improve it into an opportunity of separating the new from the old States, and connecting them with her interest in Canada, by undertaking to open the Mississippi to both countries. And with that view it is said that she has long had agents there to treat upon this subject; and that nothing has prevented her success, but the attachment the people have to their brethren in the old States; their repugnance to become the sport of foreign politics, and which would follow their separation; and the particular enmity they bear to that power. Next to Conquest Separation would be the most advantageous arrangement for Britain; for in consequence, and especially if opened under her auspices, she would become the ally of the western States and play them off against the eastern; whereby their importance and weight in the scale of nations would be diminished, if not destroyed. Many believe, and with this view, that she was at the bottom of the late insurrection on the frontier and which grew out of the discontents proceeding from the occlusion of the river.

But the same motive which inclines England to promote the separation of the new from the old States should dispose France to prevent it. As they now stand, the whole are the allies and the friends of France, and whilst they remain united they will continue so: By the separation, therefore, Britain might gain but France could not.

It is then the interest of France to keep the whole of this territory under the same government: But this cannot be done unless the intrigues of England be defeated, and the Mississippi be opened under the patronage of the United States. It is therefore the interest of France to yield her aid to her ally, to open this river, and which at the present crisis would most probably produce a decisive effect. Nor would her retribution be limited to those considerations only, which have been already mentioned. Experience has shewn that those alliances are not only the most beneficial but likewise most durable, which are founded equally in the affection and the interests of the parties, and by this act of friendship France would establish a claim to the gratitude of the American people; which by pervading every quarter would reach the heart of every citizen. It would be known to the present race and remembered by posterity, that by the aid of France, the old States were enabled to gain their independence, and that like wise by her aid the new States commenced their settlement, grew up to the enjoyment of their rights, and attained their maturity. In the present state of the war with Spain, it is presumed, that France may obtain what is here proposed; and indeed, infinitely more, either in the Islands or even in South America, and without the least difficulty. Her system is a system of freedom to the world, as well in respect to the rights of nations as of men: It is therefore hoped she will avail herself of the present opportunity, not only to verify that fact; but to manifest at the same time the pleasure with which she embraces every opportunity that occurs to promote the interest of her ally.[93]

To the Secretary of State [Edmund Randolph], Paris, February 1, 1795

Sir,—I was lately informed by Mr. Jay that it was his intention to communicate to me the contents of his treaty with the British administration, and as I knew the good effect which correct information upon that point would produce upon our affairs here (admitting it to be as heretofore represented) I thought it my duty to endeavour to avail myself of it as soon as possible. But as the communication promised was to be in cypher, and Mr. Morris had taken his copy with him, I knew that I should not be able to comprehend it in case it was received. I therefore deemed the acquisition of it an object of sufficient importance to authorise the expense of an especial dispatch to London to obtain it, and have, in consequence, committed that trust to Mr. Purviance of Baltimore, who left this immediately after the receipt of Mr. Jays letter and who was likewise instructed to bring me a copy of Mr. Pinckney's cypher for future use. By his return I hope to be able to remove all uneasiness upon that head and in which I am the more confident from a knowledge that the government here is well disposed to view it with the utmost liberality.

I was also lately informed by a letter from Mr. Fenwick that he understood that Mr. Muscoe Livingston[94] who had lately arrived from Lisbon that Colonel Humphreys had sailed thence for Algiers upon the business, as was presumed, intrusted to him with that Regency; and that prior to

[93] Monroe received the following acknowledgment from the Committee of Public Safety: "We acknowledge by the solicitude which you show in the negotiations of this affair, that nothing which can tend to confirm the bond of friendship and harmony between the two first republics in the world, is strange or indifferent to you. We thank you for the ideas you have communicated to us: We will examine them profoundly, and we will communicate to you with out delay our observations upon your note. But we appreciate beforehand the motives of this loyal communication. (Hamilton 1899, 186)
[94] Muscoe Livingston, a native Virginian, was a ship captain based in London who frequented the various European mercantile cities. In 1768 he referred to himself "Master of the Baltic Merchant." (Tyler 1905, 263)

his departure he had committed to him a message for me, to be communicated in person. Mr. Fenwick adds that Mr. Livingston was taken sick and in consequence deprived of his senses just as he was about to set out from Bordeaux for Paris; whereby he was not only rendered unable to proceed on his journey, but even to communicate to him the purport of his message to me. Thus I am left in perfect ignorance equally of Colonel Humphrey's wishes, the time of his departure and plan of operation. I intimated to you before that although I had written to Colonel Humphreys for information upon that point and with the view of forwarding his wishes to the utmost of my power; yet I am fearful in consideration of those embarrassments which were inseparable from the war, it would be difficult to con cert any plan of harmonious operation which should commence and proceed from such distant points whereby the aid of this Republic could be yielded us in that negotiation. Under present circumstances therefore you will readily perceive that it has become altogether impossible.

The French troops have at length entered Amsterdam whereby the whole of the province of Holland was brought immediately under the power of this Republic, as, indeed the whole of the seven United Provinces most probably soon will be. This was announced a few days past to the Convention by a letter from the deputies in that quarter; two of whom, it is said, are on their way to render an account in detail of this very important acquisition. It is reported that Breda and Bergen-op-Zoom have surrendered: Indeed the general idea is that no further opposition will be made there to the French arms, and of course that this Republic will become possessed of the fleet and immense stores of every kind.[95] The Prince of Orange, with his family, accompanied by several members of the States General, had made their escape; but by what route and whether for London or Berlin is unknown.[96]

After the entry of the French into Amsterdam was certain and in consequence the entire conquest of the Seven Provinces more than probable an effort was made by the States General to yield the same thing upon terms for the purpose of putting the Republic in possession of the country by treaty instead of conquest; and with this view an agent who arrived here about a

---

[95] A week earlier, French troops had entered Amsterdam, while the Dutch fleet in Ijsselmeer was captured by France. By the end of January, France effectively occupied Holland. (Crook 2002, 223)

[96] In reality, the French invasion of 1795 was almost like a carnival, being "happily conducted," as one British observer noted, the towns bedecked with tricolour flags and revolutionary posters as well as the black cockades of the Patriots. There was remarkably little violence against the persons or property of fleeing Orangist dignitaries such as William V, Prince of Orange, who exiled with his family in London. (Israel 1995, 1120)

fortnight before that event was dispatched, and who offered, as I am well assured to surrender all the important fortifications of the country and to provide at their own expense and for the residue of the war quarters and provisions for such force as should be deemed adequate to hold them. To yield immediately twenty-five sail of the line, and likewise to pay at stated times convenient for both parties the sum of three hundred millions of florins. But it was known by the Committee that without an accident as much might be gained and perhaps more by conquest: That the latter mode which knew of no condition, freed them from fetters, and of course from the possibility of any future breach of treaty and of violated faith. The agent however, who was an ancient minister of that government here, was suffered to remain and treated with respect, whilst orders were issued to the troops to advance, and which were obeyed.

There arrived at the same time a deputation from the patriots who associating with Mr. Van Staphorst, and one or two others of those who were banished from their country in 1787, endeavoured to counteract the movements of the agent from the States General and to attract to the patriotic body the attention of the Convention. Before the entrance into Amsterdam they wished admittance to the bar, as well for that purpose, as to sound the disposition of the Convention in regard to the future state of Holland. But in that stage it was evaded, perhaps from policy; perhaps from the real impropriety of expressing any opinion upon that point in the then state of affairs, or perhaps indeed from the impossibility of forming one. But, since that event, they were admitted, and with an address founded on it, though in other respects adapted as was before intended. The answer of the President was respectful, but cautious; for whilst it breathed a spirit of patriotism, and of particular regard for the ancient virtues of the Belgic Confederacy, and of course, left them no cause of complaint, it carefully avoided all compromitment of the government itself.

What will be the future fate of those provinces is altogether uncertain, and must be in a great measure dependent on events. At present I am satisfied there is no settled plan on that head, nor indeed, is it possible there should be, within so short a space of time. Many members and among them some of distinguished weight in the Convention seemed disposed to extend the future boundary of the Republic to the Rhine; and, of course, to comprehend within its limits all that part of those provinces lying on this side of that river. This idea was lately avowed by Boissy d'Anglas,[97] a member of the

---

[97] François Antoine Boissy d'Anglas had put forth the idea that executive power ought to have been equal (in power and dignity) to the legislative power and argued that no

Committee of Public Safety in a speech delivered apparently by authority of that body, and for the purpose equally, of sounding the Convention upon the conditions of peace, to ascertain what terms they would approve of; as to announce in that informal, and of course not obligatory, manner, to the parties concerned, the ultimata upon which they might expect it. In this he proposes that the Republic shall be hereafter bounded only; "by the ocean, the mountains and the great rivers." Be this, however, as it may, I think it certain unless the fortunes of war should inspire other councils, that the whole of these provinces will be retained in the hands of this Republic until its termination, and be made, in the progress, as instrumental to that event, in its favour, as circumstances will admit of.

But even in case they be not dismembered, a revolution in their government seems to be unavoidable. Their strong posts, their harbours, perhaps their fleet, will be under the control of France, and, of course, their councils likewise will be so. Ancient forms may for a while remain, but it is not possible, under circumstances of this kind, that they should be more than forms. Half the political regulations of the country, perhaps the whole, will proceed from the representatives of this Republic with the army: Nor will any of its inhabitants, other than those of decided patriotism, be employed by them in any office of trust or profit. Thus the weight and authority of the government will be gradually transferred to the popular scale. The people at large will soon take the admonition, and from that moment the ancient fabric, which was before tottering, will be levelled to the ground. The ordinary allurements of freedom are sufficiently great to the mass of mankind to require no additional recommendation in its favour, and the hand of power must be strong where it is not pursued with effect; but in the present instance, the additional inducement will be great; for as it is well known, that this Republic can repose no confidence in the existing government, and especially in the house of Orange, and which might not be the case, and most probably would not, with that which would succeed a revolution; so it must be equally obvious that its continuance will furnish a strong argument here for the dismemberment. This consideration, therefore, will add a new stimulus to all those who incline rather to preserve the independence of their country, than become reduced into a few departments of France.

Before this great achievement, and which resembles more an exploit of the ancient Roman empire, than those of modern princes, there was a collection of diplomatic characters, formal and informal, from several of the powers

genuine balance of the two could exist as long as the government remained weak and lacked the necessary authority required to properly discharge its role. (Craiutu 2012, 138)

at war, and others friendly to some of them, at Basle in Switzerland, and who expected to be met there by some agent or agents from this Republic, to commence negotiations for peace. But as soon as they heard of this event, that prospect vanished, and it is said that some of them have retired home, and others arrived here to confer more directly with the government itself. Count Carletti,[98] from Florence, and Baron Stahl[99] from Sweden, men, said to be friendly to the French revolution, are those only who are known, and the latter is supposed rather to expect, than to have brought his credentials with him.

I herewith transmit to you some communications received from Mr. Skipwith, and which will shew the state of the Bordeaux and St. Domingo claims, and I beg of you to be assured of the unremitted attention which I shall continue to pay to these concerns, and indeed to every other in which my countrymen are interested.

With great respect and esteem, I have the honor to be your most obt. and very humble servant, Jas Monroe.

5th February, P. S. Since the above was written, some details have been received of the success of the French in the United Netherlands, and by which it appears that every thing which was predicted in that respect has been verified. Williamstadt, Breda, Gorcum, Bergen-op-Zoom, and the fleet, the held by ice in the Texel, are all taken. I enclose, however, the papers containing those accounts.

To the Secretary of State [Edmund Randolph], Paris, February 12, 1795

Sir,—I was honored with yours of the 2nd. December, three days since, and by which I find that my third letter only had then reached you, although the two preceding, with duplicates, were forwarded according to

---

[98] François Xavier Carletti had been appointed by the Grand Duke of Tuscany to be his envoy at Paris. He was not well received and was described by one member of the Directorate as nothing "but a courtier, the ambassador of a petty Italian State." The Directorate soon ordered the dismissal of the ambassador Carletti "whose political conceit had made him forget what was due to the Government of the Republic." (Duruy 1895, 19)

[99] Baron de Stael Holstein, chamberlain to the queen of Sweden, had resided in Paris for some years, first as counsellor to the Swedish embassy and afterwards as ambassador. He frequented the society of the French liberals, was a friend of the former French finance minister Jacques Necker and enjoyed the reputation of being an amiable and honorable man. (Lardner 1839, 305)

their respective dates, and by opportunities which promised security and dispatch.[100,101]

---

[100] Randolph's letter clearly reflected the Administration's disappointment with Monroe's sentiments, as well as offering considerable insight into the real desires of the secretary. "With the frankness of friendship," wrote Randolph, "I must discharge the obligation of my office, by communicating to you the opinions which we entertain here concerning the speech which you made on your introduction into the National Convention. When you left us, we all supposed, that your reception, as the minister of the United States, would take place in the private chamber of some Committee. Your letter of credence contained the degree of profession which the government was desirous of making; and though the language of it would not have been cooled, even if its subsequent publicity had been foreseen; still it was natural to expect that the remarks with which you might accompany its delivery would be merely oral and therefore not exposed to the rancorous criticism of nations at war with France. It seems that upon your arrival the downfall of Robespierre, and the suspension of the usual routine of business, combined perhaps with an anxiety to demonstrate an affection for the United States, had shut up for a time the diplomatic cabinet, and rendered the hall of the national convention the theatre of diplomatic civilities. We should have supposed that an introduction there would have brought to mind these ideas. The United States are neutral: the allied powers jealous: with England we are now in treaty: By England we have been impeached for breaches of faith in favor of France: Our citizens are notoriously Gallican in their hearts: It will be wise to hazard as little as possible on the score of good humour: And therefore, in the disclosure of my feelings something is due to the possibility of fostering new suspicions. Under the influence of these sentiments we should have hoped that your address to the national Convention would have been so framed as to leave heart-burnings nowhere. If private affection and opinions had been the only points to be consulted, it would have been immaterial where or how they were delivered. But the range of a public minister's mind will go to all the relations of our country with the whole world. We do not perceive that your instructions have imposed upon you the extreme glow of some parts of your address; and my letter in behalf of the House of Representatives which has been considered by some gentlemen as too strong, was not to be viewed in any other light than as executing the task assigned by that body. After these remarks which are never to be interpreted into any dereliction of the French cause I must observe to you that they are made principally to recommend caution; lest we should be obliged at some time or other, to explain away or disavow an excess of fervor, so as to reduce it down to the cool system of neutrality. You have it still in charge to cultivate the French Republic with zeal but without any unnecessary eclat; besides the dictates of sincerity do not demand that we should render notorious all our feelings in favor of that nation." In future correspondence Randolph took a more conciliatory tone and Monroe believed that he would never have written so severely if all the dispatches had reached him in due order. (Hamilton 1899, 193)

[101] Monroe responded to Randolph's criticism by explaining exactly why he took such drastic action. He reminded the secretary of state of the strained state of relations between France and the United States upon his arrival; the treaty of 1778 had been violated, American commerce harassed, and the previous Minister removed. Monroe described to Randolph how "connections between the two countries hung, as it were, by a thread." All in all, it appeared to Monroe that without drastic action the relationship between the two republics might deteriorate completely. Therefore, he thought his duty was to act in such a way that assured the French public and the members of the National Convention that the United States supported their Revolution. Furthermore, Monroe argued, the scheme had worked. With the French people and the National Convention on his side, the Committee of Public Safety had relented. Monroe informed Randolph that his actions had also gained massive concessions from the French, including their agreement to discontinue the seizure of American ships. (Poston 2016, 293)

I read, with equal surprize and concern, the strictures you deemed it necessary to make upon some particulars of my conduct here; because I think it did not merit them, and trust upon a further view of all circumstances, you will entertain the same opinion. Of these, by this time, you will possess a general view: A more particular detail, however, I think proper now to communicate.

It is objected that I addressed the Convention with a glow of sentiment not warranted by my instructions. Secondly; that I made public what was intended and policy dictated, should be kept private. And thirdly, that I compromitted the government, by saying, that it was willing to tolerate injuries, which it was not disposed to tolerate; whereby an important interest to our country was slighted or given up.

Whether my address contains a single sentiment or expression different from what my instructions and the declarations of the legislative branches contain, is to be determined by comparing the one with the other. I had them before me at the time and drew it by them; of course I thought it did not, and I now think so. The force, however of this objection is, I presume, comprized in the second; for if the communication had been in private and not in public, the objection most probably would not have been made. Upon this point, therefore, a more thorough explanation is necessary, and for this purpose a full view of the circumstances and motives which influenced my conduct equally so.

Upon my arrival here, I found our affairs, as it was known they were before I sailed, in the worst possible situation. The treaty between the two Republics was violated: Our commerce was harrassed in every quarter, and in every article, even that of tobacco not excepted. Our seamen taken on board our vessels were often abused, generally imprisoned and treated in other respects like the subjects of the powers at war with them. Our former minister was not only without the confidence of the government, but an object of particular jealousy and distrust: In addition to which it was suspected, that we were about to abandon them for a connection with England, and for which purpose principally, it was believed that Mr. Jay had been sent there. The popular prepossession too in our favor had abated, and was in some measure at a stand; for the officers of the fleets from America had brought unfavourable accounts of our disposition towards them. Thus the connection between the two countries hung, as it were, upon a thread; and I am convinced, that if some person possessing their confidence had not been sent, it would have been broken.

My first reception was marked with circumstances which fully demonstrated these facts, and shewed how critical the ground was on which we stood; for it is unquestionably true, that notwithstanding my political principles were subscribed to, the Committee, or the governing party in it, were disposed to delay my reception, throw me entirely out of view, and destroy altogether the effect of my mission. It was said that as my principles were with them, I ought on that account to be the more dreaded; for if they confided in me, I should only lull them asleep as to their true interest, in regard to the movements on foot; and under this impression I was viewed with a jealous eye, and kept at the most awful distance. This deportment towards me was so observable, that it attracted the attention of the representatives of the other powers here, and was most probably communicated elsewhere.

Into what consequences this policy, which was hostile to us, might lead, I could not readily perceive; but I was alarmed on that head; for I well knew that an avowed enmity by this government, against our executive administration, and in which shape it threatened to break out, pursued with passion as I had reason to apprehend it would be, would not only injure our national character, but likewise disturb our internal tranquility, and perhaps involve us in war. The interval between such a step and the existing state of things was small, and in the tide of their fortunes which were prosperous, I was fearful it would be taken. Thus circumstanced what course did policy dictate that I should pursue? Did it become me to look on as a tranquil spectator of machinations that portended so much mischief to my country; or was it more wise, more consistent with the obligations of the trust I had accepted to make a decisive effort to defeat them? And, in adopting the latter counsel, in what line should that effort be directed, or by what means enabled to succeed? The doors of the Committee, as already mentioned, were closed against me: And had it been otherwise, knowing as I did the disposition of that body towards us, would it have been prudent to have deposited those documents under its care, since they furnished the only means by which I could counteract its views? Or was it to be presumed, that the declarations of friendship which they contained, would produce in the councils of that body any change of sentiment, advised as it had been, and armed as it was, with a series of contrary evidence, and in which it would place a greater confidence? I can assure you and with great sincerity, that after taking in my mind, so far as I was able, and with perfect calmness (for the imputations against me were not of a nature to inspire zeal) that range of our affairs in their general relation to those of other powers, and in which you deem my conduct defective, that the measure I adopted appeared to me not only the most eligible one; but that in the then juncture of affairs, I thought it my indispensable duty to adopt it. Nor was I disappointed in any of the consequences upon which I had calculated; for by this public demonstration of our regard for this nation and its revolution (though indeed the word was not used) the people at large were settled on the right side. The abettors of a contrary doctrine were in a great measure confounded; and as soon as the impression upon the public mind had time to react back upon the public councils, aided by the little incidents I caught at to inspire confidence, together with a change of the members of the Committee, was the object, even in that body, though slowly, yet finally, completely accomplished.

But you intimate that I ought to have shunned this publicity, from the fear it might injure our depending negotiations with Britain and Spain. Had I seen cause to apprehend that consequence, I should certainly have been more averse to the measure: But there was none; on the contrary that it would produce the opposite effect, was in my opinion certain. In demonstrating this, permit me to develope, according to my idea of it, the object of Mr. Jay's mission, and the contingencies upon which his success depended. This will shew the relation which mine had to his, and more satisfactorily than I can otherwise do, the motives in that respect of my conduct.

I understood that the sole object of Mr. Jay's mission was to demand the surrender of the posts, and compensation for injuries, and was persuaded that his success would depend upon two primary considerations; the success of the French arms and the continuance of a most perfect good understanding between the two Republics. If we were disappointed in either of these events, I concluded that his mission would fail; for we knew that a long and able negotiation for the first object had already proved abortive, and we saw that in the preceding year, when Toulon, was taken and fortune seemed to frown upon the arms of this Republic, that an order was issued for those spoliations of which we so justly complain. We likewise saw afterwards when the spirit of this nation was roused and victory attended its efforts, that that order was rescinded and some respect was shewn to the United States. Thus it appeared that our fortune, at least so far as depended upon Britain, and of course the success of Mr. Jay's mission, depended upon that of France.

But the success of France could not redound to our advantage, and especially in the negotiation with Britain, without a good understanding and concert with the French government: For without that, we could neither count upon success in negotiation, nor in case it failed, upon the fortunate issue of arms, if war should be appealed to. By negotiation we could not hope with Success otherwise than from the apprehension in the British cabinet, than if we were not accommodated, we would join in the war against them. We could not accept it at the price of an equivalent, and thus pay again for what was already our due: Nor could we expect it from the affection, the justice or the liberality of that court; for we well knew that if it had possessed those virtues, we should have had no cause of complaint. But we could not join in the war, nor even avail ourselves of that argument in nego-tiation, without a con cert with France; for without such concert, we might commence at the moment she was about to conclude; whereby we should be left alone to contend with that power; who would probably be supported by Spain. If then our good understanding with France was broken, or the necessary concert between us incomplete, Britain would only have to amuse us 'till the crisis had passed, and then defy us.

If this doctrine is true, and it is admitted, that the success of Mr. Jay's mission depended upon a good understanding with the French Republic, it follows, that the more cordial it was, and the more generally known, the happier the effect would be; and of course, that by exhibiting this public proof of it, instead of retarding, I forwarded essentially the object of that negotiation: And such, indeed, was my idea at the time; for I knew that the movement would be so understood on the other side of the channel; and in consequence, believed it would produce a good effect, and in which I was the more confirmed by the information of several of my countrymen, who were in England when the embargo was imposed, and who assured me that if it had been continued, Mr. Jay's success would have been immediate.

That the English administration would complain of this movement, and of me, was what I expected; but I knew that I was sent here not to subserve the views of that administration, and trusted that whilst I rested on my instructions, and performed my duty with integrity, although my judgment might occasionally err, as those of most men sometimes do, that no conces-sion would be made to my discredit, in favour of that administration: On the contrary, that I should be firmly supported against its attacks by those who sent me here. I trust that this has been the case in the present instance, and upon which point I am more anxious, upon public than upon private considerations; because I well know, that if any such concession has been made, it was immediately communicated by its instruments here, and for the purpose of weakening the confidence of this government in our own; a prac-tice systematically pursued heretofore, and with the hope of separating, or at least of preventing any kind of concert between the two countries.

Had the fortunes of France been unprosperous upon my arrival, the motive for greater caution would have been stronger. But the case was in every respect otherwise. Her fortunes were at the height of prosperity, and those of her enemies decisively on the decline. It was obvious that nothing was wanting to preserve tranquillity at home, and to ensure success in our foreign negotiations, but the good wishes and the good offices of this Republic towards us. By the measure therefore, I thought that every thing was to be gained and nothing to be lost.

Upon the third point little need be said. I have some time since transmitted to you a decree which carried the treaty into effect, and yielded the point in question. Satisfied I am, too, it was greatly forwarded if not absolutely obtained, by the manner in which it was urged: For a generous policy is better calculated to produce to good effect here, than a strict one: And other than in that light my declaration can not be considered. Surely I did not concede the point, nor intimate an indifference upon it: On the contrary, I laboured, with the greatest force of which I was capable to demonstrate the interest we had in it as well as themselves: Nor did I condescend in that or any other transaction. In general I know I am more apt to err on the other side; and I am persuaded, that in the present instance you will find, upon a reperusal of the paper in question, that although it contains expressions of friendship, it certainly betrays none of condescendsion.

I have thus answered the objections contained in your strictures upon my conduct, by stating the circumstances under which I acted, with my motives of action; and I presume satisfied you that I did not merit them. But I cannot dismiss the subject without observing; that, when I review the scenes through which I have passed, recollect the difficulties I had to encounter, the source from whence they proceeded, and my efforts to inspire confidence here in our administration, and without which nothing could be done, and much mischief was to be apprehended, I cannot but feel mortified to find that, for this very service, I am censured by that administration.

You have already seen by the course of my correspondence, that however difficult it was to succeed, yet at certain times, we were completely possessed of the confidence of this government; and that, at those times, I had the good fortune to accomplish some objects of importance to us. But it is likewise my duty to inform you, that I was at the same time enabled to penetrate more accurately into what would most probably be its policy towards us, in case we continued to possess that confidence unimpaired: And I now declare that I am of opinion, if we stood firmly upon that ground there is no service within the power of this Republic to render, that it would not render us, and upon the slightest intimation. In the interval between the period of those communications which were made by me to the committee, explanatory of our situation with Britain Spain, &c., and the arrival of the intelligence of Mr. Jay's treaty, the indications of this disposition were extremely strong: for at that time I had reason to believe, that it contemplated to take under its care, and to provide for our protection against Algiers; for the expulsion of the British from the western posts and the establishment of our right with Spain to the free navigation of the Mississippi, to be executed in the mode we should prefer, and upon terms perfectly easy to us; terms, in short which sought only the aid of our credit to obtain a loan from our own Banks for an inconsiderable sum, to be laid out in the purchase of provisions, within our own country, and to be reimbursed, if possible by themselves. But by that intelligence, this disposition was checked, but not changed; for it is with the course of opinions as with that of bodies, and which are not easily to be forced in an opposite direction, after they have decisively taken a particular one. I mention this for your information, not indeed in relation to the past, but the future measures of the Executive; for I am still inclined to believe that if the arrangement with England, or the negotiation with Spain should fail, it is possible, provided a suitable attempt be made here before a peace is closed with those powers respectively, to accomplish the whole through the means of this government, and upon terms which would perhaps require on our part no offensive movement, or other act which would rightfully subject us to the imputation of a breach of neutrality. Well satisfied I am that the full weight of its fortunes might be thrown with decision into our scale and in a manner that would enable us to turn those fortunes to the best account in negotiation.

I am happy to inform you that Mrs. Lafayette was lately set at liberty; and although I could not make a formal application in her favour, yet it was done in accommodation with that which was informally made. She attended immediately at my house, to declare the obligations she owed to our country, and of which she manifested the highest sensibility. Unfortunately she is, and has been for some time past, destitute of resource, and in consequence required aid not only for present support, but to discharge the debts that were already due, and for which she applied to me and was accordingly furnished with a sum in assignats equivalent to about one thousand dollars in specie. I made this advance upon the principle it was my duty to make it, as the representative of the United States, and in the expectation, that the like sum which should be paid to my order by our Bankers in Amsterdam, would be taken from the fund appropriated to the use of her husband by the Congress in the course of the last year. Is this approved, and may I upon that fund make future advances adequate to her support, and for which the interest will perhaps suffice?[102]

---

[102] This was approved. Six thousand dollars were taken from Lafayette's fund, then in the hands of Thomas Pinckney, and sent to Monroe for the use of Madame de Lafayette. (Hamilton 1899, 205)

A treaty of peace or rather of Amity with Tuscany with the progress of a revolution in Holland, and which has been more rapid than I expected it would be, are the only events worthy notice, that have taken place since my last, and for more particular details respecting which I beg leave to refer you to Mr. Adet, to whose care the present is committed.

With great respect and esteem, I have the honor to be, dear Sir, Your, most observant, Jas Monroe.

P. S. I herewith enclose you a report from Mr. Skipwith upon some cases, that were noticed in your last despatch; as likewise upon some others upon which application will most probably be made to you, and whereby you will be enabled to give satisfactory information to the parties concerned.[103]

To the Committee of Public Safety, Paris, February 17, 1795

Citizens,— I accept with great pleasure the opportunity offered, of writing to the American minister at Madrid, and with equal pleasure transmit the letters enclosed me in your last to his care; never doubting that whatever comes from you to me will equally promote the interest of both republics.[104]

Jas Monroe.

To James Madison, Paris, February 18, 1795

Dear Sir,—I was yesterday favored with yours of the 4th of Dec'r the only one yet rec'd. I had perfectly anticipated the secret causes & motives of the

---

[103] To be sure, Randolph's letter had stung deeply. And, astonished, infuriated, and confused, Monroe had reread his original instructions, then reread Randolph's letter of reprimand before sending this bitterly worded missive in justification of his actions, pointing out that his address had not contained a single word or phrase that differed from his instructions. And writing this lengthy exculpatory letter seems, at least to some degree, to assuage his initial anger, for Monroe ends his letter with a triumphant flourish: "I am happy to inform you that Mrs. Lafayette was lately set at liberty..."(Unger 2011, 119)

[104] The Committee's request to Monroe: "Citizen Minister, the Citizen Bourgoin, formerly minister of France at Madrid, informs us that he has asked of you to transmit into Spain, under your cover, two letters which he wishes to send there upon his own affairs. He also informs us that you are willing to render him this service, provided it is desired by the Committee of Public Safety. We have in consequence examined the letters in question and are satisfied that they contain nothing contrary to the interest either of the French or American people. It therefore appears to us that you may without difficulty transmit under your cover these letters of the citizen Burgoin, and which we now send you. We undertake to forward them to the frontiers with your dispatches by the first courier extraordinary which we shall expedite to the army of the Western Pyrenees." For the Committee, the request was signed by Cambacérès (Duke de Parme), Merlin (of Thionville) and Pelet (of Lozère). In connection with this letter to him, Monroe notes that it was the commencement of the negotiations for peace between France and Spain (Hamilton 1899, 205; Aulard 1910, 208, 215).

western business[105] and was extremely happy to find that the patriotism of the people in every quarter, left to its own voluntary impulse and without any information that was calculated to stimulate it, was sufficient to triumph over the schemes of wicked and designing men. I have been always convinced that this was a resource to be counted on with certainty upon any emergency, & that the more frequent these were, the sooner wo'd the possibility of success in such schemes be destroyed, & our gov't assume a secure and solid form. I likewise perfectly comprehended the motive and tendency of the discussion upon the subject of the societies but was persuaded that the conduct of the societies themselves upon that occasion, together with the knowledge diffused every where of the principle upon which they were formed, would give that business likewise a happy termination.[106] This was the case in one house and will I doubt not likewise be so in the publick mind if the discussion sho'd be provoked. The fact is, such societies cannot exist in an enlightened country, unless there is some cause for them their continuance depends upon that cause, for whenever you test them by the exigence and it is found inadequate they will fall: and if there is one an attack upon them will encrease it, for they are not even to be put down by law. I was fearful the conduct of the Jacobin society here would injure the cause of republicanism every where by discrediting popular complaints and inclining men on the side of government however great its oppressions might be. But that society was different from those that ever existed before; it was in fact the government of France, and the principal means of retarding the revolution itself; by it all those atrocities which now stain & always will stain certain stages of the revolution were committed, and it had obviously become the last pivot upon which the hopes of the coalesced powers depended. This society was therefore the greatest enemy of the revolution, and so clear was this that all France called for its overthrow by some act of violence. It is easy for designing men

---

[105] "Western business" was a reference to the Whiskey Rebellion in western Pennsylvania. While initially it was the immediate reaction to Treasury Secretary Hamilton's persuading Congress in 1791 to enact a federal excise tax on distilled spirits, the focus changed. Soon thereafter, resistance to tax collectors and violence against complying distillers mounted in several states, but especially in western Pennsylvania, culminating in 1794 with President Washington's leading an army of 13,000 across the mountains to quell unrest. (Formisano 2008, 47)

[106] Although Federalists hailed the armed response as a triumph of a strong central government acting against anarchist elements intent on undermining its authority, Jefferson viewed the federal government's response as an overreaction to a minor uprising. And, along with Monroe and Madison, believed that Hamilton, Washington's treasury secretary, used the rebellion to advance his own partisan political agenda, casting the Federalist Party as the party of law and order and the Republican Party as the party of rebellion and lawlessness. As Jefferson later (May 1785) summed up the affair, "An insurrection was announced and proclaimed and armed against, but could never be found." (Wood 2009, 138)

to turn the vices of one society, somewhat similar in its origin, and which became such only in the course of events by degenerating and losing sight of the object which gave birth to them, ag'nst all others, altho' the parallel may go no further than that stage in which they all had merit. As the conduct of the Jacobin society made such an impression upon Aff'rs here it became my duty to notice it in my official despatches: I accordingly did so by giving an historic view of its origin, progress, & decline, truly & of course under the above impression, & which I think will be found marked upon the statement to an observant reader: for in one stage viz. from the deposition of the king I say that the danger was from confusion alone, since the old government was overset & the new one intirely in the hands & exerted virtuously for the sole benefit of the people, and it is intimated in the close that however enormous the vices may be, provided treasonable practices be not discovered, that its over throw must be left to publick opinion only. It became my duty to notice this subject & I think I have done it with propriety, however examine it & write me what you think of it.[107]

I rec'd some days past a letter from Mr. Randolph containing a severe criticism upon my address to the convention & the publication of the papers committed to my care, and which justified that address & makes its defense ag'nst the attacks of that party with you. I was hurt at the criticism & equally surprised, for I did not expect it would be avowed that it was wished I sho'd make a secret use of them, giving them weight by any opinion which might be entertained of my own political principles, or in other words that I would become the instrument of that party here, thereby putting in its hands my own reputation to be impeached hereafter in the course of events. They were deceived if they supposed I was such a person. On the contrary I was happy in the opportunity furnish'd not only on acc't of the good effects I knew it would produce in other respects, but likewise as it furnished me with one of presenting to the eyes of the world the covenant which subsisted between them and me: by the publication they are bound

---

[107] This is a reference to Randolph's 1794 defense of Washington's conduct during the Whiskey Rebellion in some essays written under the pseudonym of "Germanicus." The thirteen essays also attacked the democratic societies, explaining that Washington had meant to condemn as illegitimate and dangerous the societies generally, along with any other self-constituted group that would undertake to "condemn" laws or otherwise to stir up Washington had refrained from proposing legislation to outlaw the societies not because this could not be done, moreover, but only because it was better to reserve that measure for the last exigency. And although the government thus reserved the right to resort to prosecution to eliminate the societies if necessary, Washington in effect kept the prospect of prosecution in his back pocket even as he relied on more informal measures, Randolph put the best face on the matter by asserting that it was "an epoch in the annals of liberty that opinion can vanquish a public mischief, without the assistance of legal penalties." (Chesney 2004, 1570-1571)

to the French nation & to me to observe a particular line of conduct. If they deviate from it, they are censurable and the judicious part of our countrymen as well as posterity will reward them accordingly. The fact is I would not upon my own authority make those declarations of their sentiments, & therefore I was glad to embrace the opportunity to let them speak for themselves. I felt some concern for Mr. Randolph because I feared it would expose him to some attacks, but I concluded he would despise them for in truth I do not apply to him the above comments. I have answered those criticisms with suitable respect but as becomes a free and independent citizen whose pride is to do his duty but who will not yield where he is undeservedly attacked. I have reviewed the state of things upon my arrival & showed the necessity of some bold measure to retrieve it. What I have stated in my reply is true, I have many documents to prove it in each particular. 'Tis possible this business may end here, for I have since rec'd a letter in answer to my 2 first, which were not then rec'd by Mr. Randolph, in a different style; and to which latter I shall likewise write a suitable answer: but it is also possible it may not. I have therefore tho't proper to transmit to you a copy of it, that you may perfectly comprehend the state of this business with the ground upon which I rest. Perhaps it may be proper for you to show it in confidence to others but this is entirely submitted to you. I wish it seen by Mr. Jefferson & Mr. Jones[108]

The state of parties in America is as well known by the Committee of publick safety & other leading members as it is there. It was mentioned by some person to Merlin de Douai that Hamilton & Knox were going out of office & he instantly replied he would have it inserted in the Bulletin & communicated to the Departments, as an event auspicious to France as well as America. This, however was prevented, because the comm had been rec'd by one person only.

Fortunately the successes of this republick have been great even beyond the expectation of every one. The entire conquest of the 7 U. provinces closed in the midst of winter for a few months the last campaign: indeed so great has the success been that they have scarcely an enemy before them and I believe they may march whither they please in the course of the next. Their conduct in Holland too in other respects has done as much service to

---

[108] In his letter to Monroe, Madison had written, "The account of your arrival and reception had some time ago found its way to us thro' the English Gazettes. The language of your address to the Convention was certainly very grating to the ears of many here; and would no doubt have employed the tongues and the pens too of some of them, if external as well as internal circumstances had not checked them; but more particularly the appearance about the same time of the President's letter and those of the Secretary of State. Malicious criticisms if now made at all are confined to the little circles which relish that kind of food." (Hamilton 1899, 210)

the cause of liberty almost as their arms, a revolution which was immediately commenc'd has made a rapid progress there & will no doubt be soon
completed. I think if our sage negotiator in London had waited a little longer
till the victories of France were more complete (& it was certain they would
be so) he might have gained terms satisfactory to all his countrymen: but
perhaps being a conciliating negotiator, he could not take advantage of that
argument, perhaps he wished for the honor of Engl'd to deprive the republican party in America of the opportunity of saying his success was owing in
any degree to that cause.

I think upon the whole y'r prospects independent of foreign causes are
much better than heretofore: the elections have been favorable: but with the
aid of foreigners, they are infinitely so. We are well; our child is at school in
a French family & already speaks the language tolerably well. Joe is also at
school & rather in a line of improvement. I have little leisure & of course
am but little improved in the language. We desire to be affec'y remembered
to y'r lady whose esteem we shall certainly cultivate by all the means in our
powers. If a loan is obtained can it be laid out to advantage? Inform on this
head. Remember me to Mr. Beckley, to Tazewell, Mason & all my friends &
believe me sincerely y'rs, Jas Monroe.

P. S. Pinckney is ab't sitting out for Sp'n; suppose the peace with France
is made before his arrival, what success will he have?

To the Secretary of State [Edmund Randolph], Paris, Febru-
ary 18, 1795

Sir,—I have just been honored with your favor of the 5th. of December,[109]
and am much gratified by its contents. The preceding one of the 2nd. had
given me great uneasiness but this has removed it. I sincerely wish my two
first letters had reached you in the order they were written, as they would

---

[109] "Philadelphia, December 5th. 1794. Sir, Since my letter of the 30th. ultimo, which will
be conveyed by the same vessel with this, I have had the honor of receiving your very
interesting letters of August 15th and 25th. They are the more acceptable, as affording an
earnest of your attention to the kind of intelligence which is to us very important. We
are fully sensible of the importance of the friendship of the French Republic. Cultivate
it with zeal, proportioned to the value we set upon it. Remember to remove every suspicion of our preferring a connection with Great Britain or in any manner weakening our
old attachment to France. The caution suggested in my letter of the 30th, ultimo arises
solely from an honorable wish to sustain our character of neutrality, in a style which may
be a pattern for the morality of nations. The Republic, while they approve of the purity
of your conduct, cannot but be persuaded of the purity of our affection. The President
approves your conduct as to the national house, offered for your residence. Your interpretation of the Constitution is correct. But you are charged to make known his sense of this
evidence of respect. The affair of the Consul is noticed in my letter of the 30th, ultimo. I
am & c. Edm. Randolph, Secretary of State." (Hamilton 1899, 212)

have prevented yours of the 2nd. of December by preventing the impression which gave birth to it[110]

Be assured, I shall continue to forward by all the means in my power, the objects of my mission, and I am persuaded with the success which might be expected from those efforts, addressed to the Councils of a nation well disposed favourably to receive them. The object of this is to acknowledge the receipt of your last letter, and in the expectation that it will ac company, under the care of Mr. Adet, my last dispatch which was in answer to the preceding one.

With great respect and esteem, I have the honor to be your most ob' and very humble servant, Jas Monroe.

To the Committee of Public Safety, Paris, February 19, 1795

Citizens,—It is with infinite pleasure I communicate to you the grateful impression which the kind and fraternal reception given me upon my arrival here by the National Convention, as the representative of your ally and sister republick, the United States of America, has made upon our Government and my compatriots in general. You, citizens of France, who have proved to the world by a series of the most illustrious exploits how highly you estimate the blessings of liberty, can well conceive with what a degree of sensibility the account of this reception was welcomed by a free government & by a free people. I hasten in obedience to my instructions to make this communication, and which I do with the greater pleasure, because it furnishes me with an additional opportunity of declaring to you, the affectionate interest which the United States take in whatever concerns the liberty prosperity & happiness of the French Republic.[111]

---

[110] Clearly, Monroe was troubled by the earlier admonishment from Randolph. But it should be noted that Monroe's initial public speech was not the only instance in which he displayed diplomatic inexperience. In his September 3, 1794, letter to the Committee of Public Safety [the first discussions regarding French restrictions on America's trade], he bizarrely remarked that if France indeed benefited from preying on American commerce, the American government and its citizenry would understand and endure the consequences "not only...with patience but with pleasure." But now, in this letter, he responds to a new letter from Randolph, in his last weeks as secretary of state, who wrote privately to mollify Monroe. Indeed, what Randolph said could not have been more dissimilar to the earlier correspondence. Randolph stressed the "importance of the friendship of the French republic" and urged Monroe to "Cultivate it with zeal." Randolph went on to say that he did not prefer "a connection with Great Britain" and objected to any steps that would weaken "our old attachment to France." Unseasoned and alone, Monroe may have now thought that he had a friend in Randolph, someone with whom he could be quite candid. (Ferling 2018)

[111] Unsigned.

To James Madison, Paris, February 25, 1795

Dear Sir:—Being under the necessity of explaining the motives of my conduct upon my arrival, to the Executive, & in consequence of presenting a statem't of the circumstances under which I acted, I have thought I could not better convey my ideas to you on that head than by enclosing a copy of the paper. This will of course be kept from Mr. R. because of his official station & all others from whom it ought to be kept. I have sent a copy under the care of the minister, Mr. Adet,[112] who was to depart some days since; but as he did not & probably will not in some days, I have deemed it expedient to send a duplicate to the executive & likewise to yourself by Bordeaux to be forwarded by some American vessel. Three days after the letter above referred to was written, a second was likewise, & in a different tone. But being on the Executive Journal, my vindication ought to be there too. It is proper to observe that my first & second letters were intermediately rec'd by Mr. Randolph.

The revolution in Holland progresses with great rapidity & will most probably comprise the 7 provinces under a single gov't founded of course on the sovereignty of the people. Here greater tranquillity continues to reign; indeed it has never been other wise since my arrival than during the same space I presume it was in Phila. Bread is scarce in some quarters but the people are beyond example patient under it. I do not think a real distress is to be apprehended, but if such were to happen, I am convinc'd the yeomanry wo'd emulate by their fortitude, the bravery of their compatriots in the army.

Nothing is done yet with Prussia; the death of Gottz[113] in Switzerland interrupted a negotiation which was depending; 'tis reported that France demanded of that power the abandonment of Poland, & for which she proposed to give Hanover.

With Sp'n a negotiation is said to be depending. I am persuaded if Jay's treaty is rejected provided it contains any thing improper that we can not only get a decision of this Gov't to suppo't our claims there but with Sp'n. 'Tis possible this latter point may be aided from this quarter independent of

---

[112] Pierre Auguste Adet was French minister to the U.S., 1795–97, but his background was in the sciences. Adet was like many of the French philosophers whom Thomas Jefferson befriended in Paris. (Hayes 2008, 420)

[113] The King of Prussia desired the recognition that would be associated with becoming the pacificator of the other states of Europe that had been engaged in the war caused by the French revolution. Although moderated to some degree by his chagrin at the failure of his military escapades on the Rhine and the Vistula, he commissioned the Count Bernard Wilhelm von der Goltz [who died during the discussions] to travel to Basel to apprise the French plenipotentiary of the king's desire and to negotiate what eventually became the 1795 Peace of Basel. (Lucchesini 1821, 21)

the contents of that project, provided they are not very exception able, but the thing wo'd be certain in the opposite view of the case.

I trust he has gain'd all that we claimed, for that nothing could be refused in the present state of things, or indeed when the treaty was formed, must be certain, provided he did not convince the adm'n, that as he had adopted the conciliatory plan he would in no possible event change it.

We had some idea of procuring a loan in Holland to a moderate am't to be vested in land. Is this still y'r wish? I am persuaded it may be done; inform me, therefore, whether it is desirable, to what am't, and whether it would suit you to draw for it on such persons as I sho'd designate? What I intimated some time since is not meant to be derogated from here: for I can by loans, answer y'r drafts upon three months' sight for one, two & even three thousand pounds sterlg payable in Hamburg or Holld. I have rec'd but one letter from you to the present time, I wish the paper enclosed to be shown Mr. [Joseph] Jones & Mr. Jefferson; we are happy to hear you have added a particular associate to the circle of our friends & to whom you will make our best respects[114]

Sincerely I am y'r friend & servant, Jas Monroe.

Colo. Orr promised to procure my patent for a tract of land on Rock Castle, Kentucky of Capt'n Fowler for me. Will you be so kind as remind him of this & endeavor to get it to be deposited with Mr. Jones, or sent here, as I mean to sell it after I shall have quitted this station, the latter is preferred.

I have written by Adet to Burr, Langdon, Brown & some others.

The liberation of our country from the counsels of H. & K. had like to have been announc'd in the Bulletin. Be assured characters are well understood here.

To the Secretary of State [Edmund Randolph], Paris, March 6, 1795

Sir,—I avail myself of the opportunity by Mr. Adet, who leaves this to succeed Mr. Fauchet, of transmitting herewith some communications which have lately passed between the Committee of Public Safety and myself, upon the subject of our interfering claims with Spain; and which will serve not only still further to illustrate my former dispatches upon that point, but likewise to shew the precise ground upon which it now rests. I had thoughts of declining any further effort upon that head, until I was enabled to lay before the Committee the project of Mr. Jay's treaty with the English government,

---

[114] This was a reference to James Madison's marriage to Dolley Payne Todd on September 15, 1794. (Brant 1978, 278)

and which was and still is daily expected by the return of Mr. Purviance; but from this I was swerved by a report then current that the outlines of a treaty were nearly adjusted between the Representatives of this Republic with the Army, and some agent of Spain on the frontier; from the fear that the peace would be closed with that power before our differences were compromised. Thus circumstanced I deemed it my duty, in conformity with my instructions (and the more especially as they had no right to make any inference with respect to that project other than I had stated) to bring the subject more fully before them than I had before done. Among the papers enclosed, and which comprise the whole of what passed between us upon this subject, you will observe a note of Merlin de Douai,[115] and which though given by a single member, and in reply to an informal application, yet as it marks a remaining solicitude upon the transaction to which it refers, I have thought it equally my duty to transmit for your information.

No peace is yet made with Spain, nor indeed with any other power, Tuscany excepted, and which was before communicated: But it is still probable that one will be made with that power and likewise with Prussia It is, however, well known that England is against it, and that she exerts all the address which ingenuity, prompted by interest, can suggest to prevent it; and it is possible that those arguments which are used by the Minister in the House of Commons, to forward the preparations for war, may have weight in the cabinets of other powers, and incline them to protract any definitive arrangement with this Republic, until just before the commencement of the campaign, in the hope of profiting in the interim by such events as the chapter of accidents may throw in their way. But I cannot think, if the tranquillity which now reigns here, should remain undisturbed and the incidents of the interval, in other respects prove favour able to the revolution, that either of them, and especially Spain, will hazard the probable evils of another campaign, for any benefit she can possibly expect from it. In truth the objects of the war, so far as they were ever understood, are now entirely changed: If a dismemberment of the Republic was among them, that must of course be considered as abandoned. Or if the restoration of the ancient monarchy

---

[115] From Merlin de Douai, Representative of the People, to Citizen Skipwith, Consul of the United States of America, Paris, 3rd. Ventose, 3rd year of the Republic (February 22, 1795). "I have received, Citizen, the observations you have addressed to me, upon the navigation of the Mississippi. The ideas which they present are not new to me, nor the Committee of Public Safety; and I have reason to think they will be taken into profound consideration, in suitable time and place. I ought not to dissemble, that this may depend much upon the conduct which the American government will observe in regard to the treaty, which its minister Jay, has concluded with England. You know in effect, that there ought to be a reciprocity of services and of obligations between nations, as between individuals. I speak however, here as an individual." (Hamilton 1899, 218)

was the sole one, the hope of accomplishing it by arms must now likewise be considered as gone. Nations acting entirely on the defensive never dream of conquests. The only remaining source from whence the coalesced powers can derive the least hope of success, is founded in the possibility of some internal commotion being excited by the scarcity of provision; the derangement of their finances, or the divisions of their councils: Calamities it is true or either of them singly, provided it attained to a certain height which it is admitted would be sufficient to destroy any government. But whether France is threatened with real danger from this source, in either of those views, is the problem to be solved. Upon the two first points I do not pretend at present to be able to decide with certainty: Indeed the best informed can only conjecture. Bread I know is scarce in some parts; and it is possible much distress may be experienced in those quarters if foreign supplies are not obtained, and in great amount.[116] But these are expected from the North and from America. 'Tis probable too that this scarcity has been increased by the speculation of individuals, and in which case it will diminish as the exigency presses.[117]

Nor am I skilled in their financial policy. When I arrived the assignats were depreciated in comparison with specie, as three to one, and now they have declined to about five and a half for one. The amount in circulation, and the sums occasionally emitted, are wonderfully great, and the depreciation must follow as a thing of course. What measures will be taken with the paper is yet doubtful. Formerly it had depreciated in equal or greater degree, and then it was elevated to par, by striking out of circulation all the bills of a certain description; securing the payment of the liquidated amount by the mortgage of the National property, aided by the maximum law which regulated the price of every thing. Whether some measures of the like kind will be again adopted or whether any attempt will be made to appreciate the paper, is equally uncertain. Many consider the appreciation as an evil to be avoided, preferring a gradual decline till it shall finally expire, and adopting then a scale suited progressively to private contracts, and redeeming the whole at the rate it passed in the last stage of circulation. I think it probable this latter policy will finally prevail, as it is advocated with ability and

---

[116] For example, the 1794 Tallien report to the Convention noted that that the inhabitants of Bordeaux received a daily ration of a half-pound of poor quality bread over an eight-month period, in some cases eating bread made from dog grass. (Brace 1946, 665)

[117] Poor harvests in France from 1793 to 1795 opened French markets to American grain and flour. In June 1795, a cargo of flour sold in Bordeaux at $23 per barrel. One month later flour prices in Paris had risen to $40 per barrel and to $35 at most of the seaports. The French market was never as lucrative after 1795 because of declining relations between France and the United States and political changes taking place in Europe. (Hunter 2005, 517)

zeal by some who were tutored in our own school. The subject is, however, still under discussion and nothing absolutely decided on it. If this latter plan should be preferred, although no step be taken to appreciate the paper, or even prevent its decline, a considerable time will probably elapse before the final suspension; and after this the Republic will stand nearly upon the same ground on which it commenced. Its debt will be but small, and it will possess besides the ordinary resource of taxation, &c., national domains to an immense amount; equal by estimation to at least two hundred millions sterling, in specie; supported in its credit by Holland (from whence too other aids are to be expected) and by the reputation of its arms. I will, however, take a more accurate survey of this subject, and give you the results as soon as possible.

And upon the subject of those dangers which are presumed to menace the safety of this Republic from the division of its councils, I have but little to add at present to the details already furnished. The papers, herewith forwarded, contain the report of the Commission of Twenty-one, upon the denunciation of Barrère etc., and which finds cause of accusation. As soon as the report is printed the denounced will be heard before the Convention, who will decide, by what is called the appel nominal, for their acquittal or trial; and in the latter case they will, in a convenient time, be sent to the Revolutionary Tribunal, and in my opinion finally to the guillotine, unless they should previously abscond, as one of them (Vadier)[118] has already done, and which it is wished, even by those most active in the prosecution, they all may do. This particular incident will not be new to you, and in other respects the councils of the country bear the same aspect they have done from the time of my arrival.

In contemplating the possible effects of this prosecution, on what may be called a division of the public councils, the friends of the Revolution have cause to regret that since a decision upon the conduct of these members was to be taken, it was not sooner taken. If it had followed immediately after the execution of Robespierre, it would have occasioned less noise, and borne less the aspect of party collision. Its protraction too has exposed the government to dangers which would not otherwise have existed. For by the delay the two-fold crisis of the trial, and of famine, or rather the scarcity of provisions, will take place precisely at the same moment, than which there certainly could not be a coincidence of events more favourable to the views of the coalesced powers, or unfavourable to those of the Republic. But you have already seen by the course of this transaction, that although the preponder-

[118] Marc Guillaume Alexis Vadier was a member of the Committee of General Security who escaped the guillotine and eventually died in exile in Brussels. (Doyle 1989, 273)

ating party has denounced and may finally execute these members, it has, not withstanding acted rather upon the defensive than otherwise. Had the prosecution been undertaken with that degree of zeal and vigour, of which so decided a majority is always capable, they must long since have been carried to the scaffold. On this side then, there was obviously no plan; nor indeed is it probable there was any on the other: For I am convinced that the real object of at least four out of five, on both sides, has been to complete the revolution. The coincidence, therefore, must be deemed one of those unlucky, but fortuitous arrangements, forced by the course of events, not to be controuled, and under which the friends of republican government must con sole themselves with the reflection, that although in a possible view, it may prove injurious to their cause, yet if it glides smoothly by, it will produce a correspondent benefit, by demonstrating to the world, how deeply rooted the principles of the revolution are in the hearts of the people.

But does no danger threaten the Republic from this source? In my opinion (I speak of the present moment more particularly) none: For, from all those circumstances which have passed under my view since my arrival, I am satisfied that whilst the majority of the Convention is on the side of the revolution it will be supported by the people, and I am even persuaded that even if the majority was against it, although, in consequence, it would be able to occasion great confusion, and do in other respects much injury; yet it would not be able to restore the ancient monarchy. In advancing this position I reason not only from recent incidents, but from past events; and by which I see that the great mass of the French nation through all the vicissitudes of the war, and succession of parties, was always on the side of the revolution; supporting the Convention with an undeviating perseverance; not because it possessed their unbounded confidence, but because they believed it to be true to the main object, and was, of course, the only solid rock upon which they could rest with safety. A variety of circumstances, marked in strong characters and by great events in the course of the revolution (heretofore communicated and which on that account I forbear to repeat) tend to demonstrate the truth of this position. Nor have the citizens of this Republic merited, in other respects, the reputation for turbulence and licentiousness, often ascribed to them in foreign countries: For it is unquestionably true, that the great atrocities which have stained the different stages of the Revolution, and particularly the massacres of the 2nd. and 3rd September 1792, and the invasion of the Convention on the 31st May, 1793, which terminated in the arrestation and destruction of the Girondine party, did not proceed from a licentious commotion of the people.[119] On the contrary, it is believed that many of the immediate agents in the first were not inhabitants of Paris; but brought from a considerable distance, Marseilles, and some even from Italy, put in motion by some secret cause not yet fully understood. It is also affirmed that the great mass of the people of Paris were ignorant of what was perpetrating at the time of the transaction, and that those who knew of it were struck with the same horror that we were when we heard of it on the other side of the Atlantic. And the movement of the 31st of May, when they were embodied and arranged against the Convention, was a movement on their part in obedience to the law and for which they were regularly summoned and commanded by the ordinary officers. 'Tis said that the great mass knew nothing of the object for which they convened, or the purpose to which they were to be made instrumental: That the secret was deposited with a few only in the Convention; such as Robespierre, Danton, &c., who governed the operation, and the Mayor of the city; the General and some principal officers of the guards, and who marshaled the citizens out as upon an ordinary parade. The party in the house which controuled the movement knew how to turn it to good account. The Mayor, (a partizan of Robespierre, Danton, &c.,) had a few days before presented a petition demanding the arrestation of the twenty-two members, and it was now urged in the house by Couthon, a leading member of the same party, that the present discontents, and which he said occasioned the movement in question, and threatened the annihilation of the Convention, could not be satisfied unless those obnoxious members were arrested. And as the Girondine party did not control the movement, or know any thing about it, otherwise than as appearances announced, and which were tremendous, for Henriot was then also at the head of the guards, the declarations of the other party were believed

---

[119] Monroe did not believe that Frenchmen deserved the reputation for turbulence, lawlessness, licentiousness, which their actions during the past few years had won for them in foreign countries. "For it is unquestionably true," he writes, "that the great atrocities which have stained the different stages of the Revolution, and particularly the massacres of the 2d and 3d September, 1792, and the invasion of the Convention on the 31st May, 1793, which terminated in the arrestation and destruction of the Girondine party, did not proceed from a licentious commotion of the people. On the contrary, it is believed that many of the immediate agents in the first were not inhabitants of Paris but brought from a considerable distance and some even from Italy, put in motion by some secret cause not yet fully understood. It is also affirmed that the great mass of the people of Paris were ignorant of what was perpetrating at the time of the transaction, and that those who knew of it were struck with the same horror that we were when we heard of it on the other side of the Atlantic." Monroe then explains the 31st of May as a simple piece of finesse on the part of Danton, Robespierre and others, who used a popular movement that was perfectly legitimate for purposes quite other than those the people had in mind. The element of popular turbulence and ferocity disappears largely in the explanation. (Hazen 1897, 129)

to be true, and the members in consequence arrested. Thus by mere finesse, and under a dexterous management, the Girondine party was completely over whelmed, and the mountain party as completely established on its ruins, and by means of the people; who being exhibitted in dumb show by the latter were the object of terror, and the cause of the overthrow of the former, notwithstanding it was, at the time, the preponderating party in the Convention, and equally so in the public estimation.

These latter details may perhaps appear inapplicable to the subject: But as I consider them of some importance, as well to enable you to judge of the future fortune of the Revolution, as of those dangers which are supposed by many, more immediately to threaten the welfare of the Republic, I have thought proper to communicate them to you. The success of the Revolution depends of course upon the people: Whatever, therefore, unfolds the character and dis position of the people and especially in relation to that object, must be useful.

I was advised by your favor of the 2nd. December that Mr. J. Pitcairn of New York[120] was appointed Consul for this city, and upon which appointment some considerations have occurred which I have thought it my duty to suggest. Permit me to ask: Is he an American citizen, and if so, whether by birth or naturalization; and, in the latter case, whether he became such since the Revolution? If of the last description his arrival will subject me to great embarrassment, and for reasons given in my fourth letter of October 18th. last; and to which, with those from the Commissary of Foreign Affairs to me, transmitted at the same time, I beg leave to refer you. I candidly think, if his situation is known, being a person deemed by the English law a subject of that crown, he will not be recognized, or if recognized, not without great reluctance. Shall I announce him then, withholding a communication of the fact, admitting it to be a fact? In case I do, and it is afterwards discovered, what will be the impression of this government towards myself, and especially after what has passed between us on the same subject; finding that I had placed, without their knowledge, in office, and immediately in the presence of the public councils, a person of a description against which they had particularly objected? And that it will be discovered, and immediately, is most certain; for there are already letters for him here from England, and these will most probably be multiplied tenfold after his arrival: Besides, the character &c. of every foreign agent, and of every grade, being an object of systematic political enquiry, is always well known. In other views this

---

[120] Joseph Pitcairn, an American citizen from New York, was a seasoned diplomat. Prior to his nomination for the Paris posting, he had served as vice consul in Hamburg from 1790 to 1793. (Smith 1987)

subject merits attention: admitting the acquiescence of this government in his favor, it is to be observed that a great proportion of the business of our countryman here is transacted with the government: The adjustment frequently requires my official support: If he does not possess the confidence of the government, he will not only be unable to render that service to our countrymen which might otherwise be expected from one in his station; but as he will be brought officially into frequent and familiar communication with me, it will follow that precisely that portion of distrust to which he is subject will attach itself to meme and produce a correspondent effect, to a certain degree, upon every subject depending here in which we are interested. I know well that if my fourth letter had been received, I should not have been placed in this dilemma: But how to act in case he arrives I do not know. I console myself under the hope he will not arrive; but by delaying his departure until that letter was received, put it in your power to reconsider the appointment.

With great respect and esteem I have the honor to be, Sir, Your very humble and most obedient servant, Jas Monroe.

P. S. March 9. Since writing the above, I have been explicitly assured by Mr. Pelet, a member of the diplomatic section of the Committee of Public Safety; that in confidence Mr. Jay's treaty contained nothing which would give uneasiness here, they had expressly instructed their agent, now negociating with Spain, to use his utmost efforts to secure for us the points in controversy between the United States and that power. In consequence I thought proper to send in a short, supplemental note, explanatory of the several objects of that controversy, and which I likewise enclose with the report of Mr. Mountflorence[121] by whom it was delivered.[122] What the success

---

[121] James Cole Mountflorence had been sent to Paris in 1792 as a commercial and land agent for William Blount, governor of the territory that would soon become Tennessee. The proposal Mountflorence presented to the French government came at an opportune time. Already embroiled in war against Austria and Prussia in the fall of 1792, France faced a possible conflict with Spain as well. Mountflorence's letter to the French foreign minister called for French intrigue in Spanish Louisiana and a new treaty with the United States. Within a fortnight, French leaders decided to send Genêt on a strikingly similar mission. The resemblance and timing of this decision suggest that Mountflorence's proposal had an influence on French politics. (Campbell 2008, 780)

[122] The Mountflorence correspondence: "Sir, I delivered your note to Mr. Pelet at the diplomatic room of the Committee. After he had perused it, I told him that I had it in my charge from you to explain to him the nature of our demand on Spain, in case at a future period that overture should be made by that power, the French government should find it convenient to accommodate us. I then represented to him that the free navigation of the Mississippi being no anchorage in that river, and that the Spaniards holding both sides of it by the possession of West Florida as high up as the most northern extremity of

of their endeavours in our behalf may be is uncertain; but we cannot expect the conclusion of their own treaty will be long delayed on that account.

I had forgotten to notify you officially of the present I had made to the Convention of our flag. It was done in consequence of the order of that body for its suspension in its hall, and an intimation from the President himself, that they had none, and were ignorant of the model. I herewith send you a copy of my note accompanying it.

To the Secretary of State [Edmund Randolph], Paris, March 17, 1795

Sir,—I have just received a letter from Mr. Jay of the 5th of February, in answer to mine of the 17th January preceding, and by which he declines to communicate to me the purport of his treaty with the English government; although he had previously promised it. Ashe has explicitly declared himself to this effect, I consider the business of course closed between him and me; nor should I make a further comment upon it, were I not otherwise impelled by the style of his reply; which is obviously addressed more for your consideration than mine. To you therefore my comments upon that reply shall also be submitted.[123]

Mr. Jay says: That he has no right to communicate the treaty since it belongs exclusively to the Governments which form them, and by which I understand that the Minister has no discretion on the subject, being bound to communicate with his Government only. If this proposition is true and which (especially if no latitude is given him by his instructions) I am willing to admit, it follows that as the injunction of secresy applies to the whole instrument, it must of course to every part. It were absurd to say that in the gross or as an entire thing it must be kept secret, but yet in the detail it may be divulged. How then does his conduct correspond with his own doctrine;

---

the 31st degree of N. Latitude, we would have no place for storing our goods or to refit our vessels, and even no means of coming up the river from its entrance with our ships. He seemed to be perfectly well acquainted with the situation of the river, and to be sensible of the necessity of our having the freedom of New Orleans. I explained to him the limits we claimed by the Treaty with England of 1783, and the ridiculous pretensions of Spain respecting her territorial rights. He asked me the present situation of our Government's negotiation with Spain, and whether that last power had given us reason to expect a favorable issue. I answered him that I was perfectly ignorant of what had been done. He concluded by desiring me to assure you that should a negotiation take place with Spain, France would not forget the interest of America and would render her every good office in her power." (Hamilton 1899, 228)

[123] In this letter, Monroe categorically puts forth, at considerable length, his vexation with Jay's refusal to share copies of the treaty.

---

having in his three several letters communicated a particular article, and promised in the second the whole.

But he likewise says that the communication was intended to be confidential, or in other words to be kept secret; for such is the ordinary import of the word. But will his letters bear that construction? Does it appear as if the communication was intended merely to gratify on my part private curiosity; or for the benevolent purpose only of announcing to me an event favorable to our country? On the contrary, does it not appear from each of his letters that he had anticipated the disquietude of this government upon the subject of his treaty and wished to remove it; and that the communication promised was intended for me in a public capacity, and to be used for public purposes? In short had I been in a private station, is it probable he would have written or communicated any thing to me on the subject? In no view, however, could I consider the communication promised, though termed a confidential one, as imposing on me any other restraint than that of caution; whilst it exonerated him, and made me responsible for the blame of a disclosure, in case it was made, and produced any inconvenience.

As I really believed at the time I wrote to Mr. Jay, that he intended to make to me the communication in question, and likewise concluded from his own assurances, as well as from other circumstances, that the treaty comprized in it nothing that could give just cause of complaint here, I thought I could not better forward his own views, or the interest of our country (especially as Mr. Morris had taken his copy of the Cypher with him) than by sending a confidential person for it. You will, therefore, judge of my surprize when instead of the communication expected, I received his letter of the 5th of February, containing an absolute refusal to make it.

But in reviewing now his several letters, it is difficult to ascertain what he intended to do, or what his real object was in writing them. For he says in these that he was not at liberty to disclose the purport of his treaty, and yet promises it: That he will give me the contents or principal heads, to enable me to satisfy this government; but yet will give them only in confidence, and of course under an injunction that will put it out of my power to give the satisfaction in tended: And, finally when the application is made, upon the basis of his own letters for the information in question and for the purpose contemplated, as appears by the three letters then written, he not only refuses to comply with what he had promised, but criminates this government for entertaining any uneasiness or making any enquiry on the subject.

When one party offers a thing upon the principle the other has a right to it, as was the case in the present instance, the justice of the demand on the part of the latter is of course admitted. There may indeed be some merit in offering it before the demand is made; but to make the offer and then recede from it subjects the party thus acting to an additional proportional reproach. Had Mr. Jay, however, chosen to place himself in this dilemma, from me he would have heard nothing more on the subject. I should have lamented, it is true, as I now do, that I was not possessed of information that might be useful to our affairs here; but there the business would have ended, for both his promise and my application were, and still are unknown to this government. But to recede in the manner he has done, putting his refusal upon the ground of national dignity, &c., is neither consistent with candour nor the true state of things.

Had Mr. Jay confided to me the information in question and in due time, and which, it is obvious, he thought himself in duty bound to do, I should then have become responsible for a proper use of it: And, I am satisfied, admitting it to be as by him represented, good use might have been made of it: For I should not only have been enabled thereby to quiet their fears, and whose legitimacy he acknowledges by his efforts to remove them; and silence a thousand unfavourable insinuations whispered about by the enemies of both countries; but by making a merit of the frankness of the communication have con ciliated rather than weakened, the friendly disposition of this government towards us. I am likewise persuaded that if I had been authorized to declare generally from my own knowledge (being the minister on the ground and responsible for the truth of the declaration) that the treaty did not interfere with our engagements with this republic, but that being a mere project, subject to rejection &c., it ought not to be published; it would have been satisfactory. And had the communication been sent to me even in this last stage, such would have been my conduct, and most probably such the effect: In any event had I gone further against his request, upon me and not upon him, would the responsibility have rested. But this was not Mr. Jay's object: On the contrary, it is obvious, that he wished me to compromit my character, and through me, that of the United States with this nation upon the contents of his treaty, without letting me see it; or placing in this government or myself the least confidence in regard to it; and which I would not do, nor, in my opinion, ought not to have done.

Whether this government acted with propriety in asking for information upon the point in question, is a subject with which I have nothing to do. I am responsible only for the answer given and which you have. My application to Mr. Jay was certainly not founded upon theirs to me; for I had contemplated it before theirs was received. I had then gained such an insight into their councils, as to satisfy me, that all our great national objects, so far as they were connected with this country were more easily to be se cured by a frank and liberal deportment, than a cool and reserved one: That if we wished to preserve our neutrality with strict integrity, and avail ourselves at the same time of the fortunes of this country, without the least hazard on our part, in the negotiation with Spain as likewise in that with England (in case Mr. Jay's treaty was rejected) that this was the way to do it. In short that if it was necessary to gain the approbation of this Government to any thing in that treaty, which it would otherwise disapprove, that this was the way to do it. Nor can I see any condesension in such a line of conduct; On the contrary, between nations allied as we are, and especially, when past and recent circumstances are considered, I deem it the most magnanimous as well as the soundest policy. Mr. Jay, however, is now of a different opinion and for the future I shall not disturb him in the enjoyment of it.

The Vendee war is considered as completed.[124] Charette,[125] the commanding general, has surrendered with all the forces immediately under his command; and like wise undertaken to quell a small remaining body of about one thousand which yet holds out. 'Tis said the liberty of religion granted by a late decree terminated this war. A short time, however, will now disclose whether this compromise, or the general favourable aspect of the present moment, is real or delusive; since, if there is a force in the nation opposed to the revolution of sufficient strength to make head against it, and which I do not think there is, I doubt not it will soon shew itself.

You intimated to me in your last that Mr. Pinckney was commissioned as Envoy Extraordinary for Spain, upon the subject of the Mississippi; and you have seen by my last, how far I had succeeded in calling the attention of this government to that object. It is probable Mr. Pinckney will pass through France, and of course by Paris, on his mission. In case he does I will most certainly open to him everything that has taken place here on that subject, and endeavour, according to the plan he shall prescribe to render him in every respect all the services in my power. I have already intimated to Mr. Short, by a confidential messenger from Lisbon, the good understanding which subsists between this government and our own upon that point; so that there is in every view the most favour able prospect of a successful

---

[124] The counter-revolution of the Vendee was significant in and of itself. It was the first, and probably the most potent, concentration of provincial opposition to the Revolution. With as many as 100,000 rebels under arms in the section of western France south of the Loire, the revolt threatened the work of the new regime, hindered the prosecution of the external war, provided the occasion for enactment of some of the terrible legal instruments of the Terror, and continued to distract the central government from other tasks. (Tilley 1963, 31)

[125] François de Charette, a French Royalist, was one of the leaders of the revolt in the Vendee against the revolutionary regime. Sentenced to death by a republican court, he was publicly executed by firing squad. (Burton 2001, 180).

termination of this interesting business, the completion of which will reflect so much honour upon the administration by which it is accomplished.

With great respect and esteem I have the honor to be, Sir, your very humble and ob serv, Jas Monroe.

To John Quincy Adams, Paris, April 2, 1795

Dear Sir,—I have been honored with your two favors of the 12 & 23 ulto.[126] and should have answered the first sooner had I known the post was established between this and Amsterdam, or had I not been disappointed by the Dutch Commissaires who promised soon after its receipt to make known to me the period when their next courier should be dispatched. For the future however these difficulties will not intervene.127

The situation of Holland being exclusively neither an independent or conquered country, and subject in the interim in certain respects to the controul of two authorities, is a novel one in the political system; nor is it easy to decide by any circumstances known to me how soon it will be changed. As it is reasonable however to presume that the spirit of harmony which you intimate now subsists will continue to prevail reciprocally, it is, likewise so to conclude that the final adjustment will be formed upon principles equally sat is factory to both parties.

It was to be expected that whilst those provinces remained in their present situation, your duties would partake of the quality of the government and be as complicated as it might be.

In removing the embarrassment to which our Commission was subjected, it became indispensably necessary that application should be made to the competent authority, and to which your powers were certainly competent, whether French or Dutch; for unless that government was totally & permanently absorbed in this, it followed that you were the party thro' all the intermediate modifications, to whom it belonged to take cognizance of the affairs, and redress the grievances, if any there be, of our countrymen there. It gives me pleasure to hear that you have experienced no difficulty upon this head, because thereby the interest of the United States will be greatly promoted: I take it for granted you will experience the like facility in future, but if the contrary should be the case and any arrangement on the part of this government here appears to you necessary, to facilitate your operations & you will

---

[126] Adams had written concerning the friendly disposition of the Dutch government towards the United States and on its maritime power which was not sufficient, he thought, for the protection of the North Sea. (Hamilton 1899, 236)

[127] At this point, Adams was serving as Minister Resident for the Netherlands, a post he held from November 6, 1794, to June 20, 1797. (Office of the Historian 2020)

be pleased to communicate the same to me & point out the line in which I may be serviceable, be assured that I shall be happy to cooperate with you in obtaining it.

The trial of Barrere, Collot D'Herbois & B. Varennes ended yesterday by a decree of banishment.[128] A party from the suburbs of the city, calling itself the same which caused the revolution of the 31. of May attended in the morning & entered the convention en masse with a view probably of making a like revolution on the 1st of April. But the convention was firm. The alarm was sounded thro' the city & the citizens in general commanded by Pichegrue attended by the Deputies, [Paul] Barras & Merlin Thionville, immediately arranged themselves in order & repaired to its Hall in defense of the national representation.[129] By surrounding the palace, inhibiting the admission of others and cutting off the retreat of those within, thereby shewing that punishment was certain, in case they should proceed to extremities, the commotion was terminated without the effusion of blood. Several (8) of the mountain party were arrested after the hall was cleared, upon evidence furnished in the course of the day of being accomplices in the plot. Everything is now tranquil, and so far as it is possible to estimate the consequences of an event so recent, by the attending circumstances, it must be deemed favor able to the revolution.

With great respect & esteem I am Dear Sir y most ob & very humble servant, Jas Monroe.

I beg of you, to command me in all cases wherein I can be serviceable.

To the Secretary of State [Edmund Randolph], Paris, April 14, 1795

Sir,—I was lately favoured with a letter from Mr. Jay, of the 19th of February; by which I was informed that the bearer, Colonel Trumbull,[130] who had copied and knew the contents of his treaty with the English government,

---

[128] French Guiana had already been adopted as a site of banishment for those considered counter-revolutionaries during the 1790s, most notably Jacques Nicolas Billaud Varenne, who was exiled in 1795 along with Jean-Marie Collot d'Herbois and Bertrand Barère de Vieuzac. Billaud-Varenne refused to return to France and died in Haiti in 1818. (Forsdick 2008, 240)

[129] Increasingly hungry and desperate, Parisians blamed the Convention for their misery. On April 1, 1795 (12 Germinal, Year III), thousands of demonstrators, shouting "Bread and the Constitution of 1793!" invaded the Convention and held the deputies captive. General Jean Charles Pichegru [who defeated the Prussians at Landau in the Palatinate] was present in Paris when the crisis broke and was given command of the troops that crushed the uprising. Paul Barras and Antoine Christophe Merlin were both senior leaders of the Convention. (Connelly and Hembre 1993, 101, 121, 130)

[130] Colonel John Trumbull, of Connecticut, accompanied Jay to England and served as Jay's secretary when he negotiated the treaty. (Moore 1918, 311)

---

was instructed to communicate the same to me, because I was an American Minister, and in which character it might be useful to me; but that I must receive it in strict confidence, and under an injunction to impart it to no other person what ever. As I had explicitly stated to Mr. Jay, in my letter by Mr. Purviance, the only terms upon which I could receive the communication; and which I had done, as well for the purpose of covering my engagement with the committee, formed after the receipt of his first letter, and when I expected no further information from him on the subject, as of preventing the transmission of it, in case it contained the slightest circumstance which might be objection able here. I could not otherwise than be surprized by the contents of this letter. To withhold the communication at the moment when it was presumable the report of the contents of that treaty would excite a ferment here, and offer it, after the expiration of some months, and when it was expected from America, and upon terms upon which I had assured him I could not receive it, (to say nothing of the impossibility of comprehending how it could be useful to me, if it was to be kept a profound secret,) was unexpected: It was the more so, since it was obvious, that whilst the condition insisted on precluded the possibility of enabling me to promote thereby the public interest, it would unavoidably tend, in some respects, to subject me to additional embarrassment in my situation here.

I was likewise soon apprized, that Colonel Trumbull did not consider himself at liberty to make the communication in question, unless I asked for it; and by which it was understood, that I bound myself to accept it on the terms proposed, adding thereby to the injunctions of Mr. Jay, the additional obligation of private stipulation. The dilemma, therefore, with which I was threatened, was of a peculiar kind: For if I accepted and withheld the communication from the committee, I should violate my engagement with that body; and if I gave it, I subjected myself not only to the probable imputation of indiscretion, but likewise certainly to that of breach of promise. The line of propriety, however, appeared to me to be a plain one. I was bound to use such information as Mr. Jay might think fit to give me in the best manner possible, according to my discretion, to promote the public interest: But I was not bound to use any artifice in obtaining that information, or to violate any engagement by the use of it. My duty to the public did not require this of me, and I had no other object to answer. As soon, therefore, as I had made a decision on the subject, I apprized Colonel Trumbull, that I could not receive the communication proposed, upon the terms on which it was offered.

But the mission of this gentleman here, though according to my information of him, a worthy and a prudent man, produced an effect of a more serious kind. I was soon advised by a person friendly to the United States, and heretofore friendly and useful to me; that his arrival had excited uneasiness in the public councils, and would probably eventually injure my standing with the government, especially if I should be able to give the committee, in consequence, no account of the contents of that treaty: For it would hardly be credited after this, considering the relation between Mr. Jay and myself, that I knew nothing of those contents. Upon what other motive, it would be asked, could the secretary of Mr. Jay come here; since the pretence of private business in Germany, which lay in another direction, would be deemed a fallacious one? He added that the wisest precautions were necessary on my part, to guard me against any unjust imputation; since through that the interests of my country might at the present crisis be essentially wounded. As I had anticipated in some measure the effect, I was mortified but not surprized by the intimation. It became me, however, to profit by it, and as well from the delicate regard which was due to my private as my public char-acter, to place the integrity of my own conduct upon ground which could not be questioned. There appeared to me to be but one mode by which this could be done, and which was by making known to the committee what had passed between Mr. Jay and myself; to state the terms upon which he had offered the communication, and my refusal to accept it on those terms; with my reason for such refusal. This you will readily conceive was a painful task: But as I had no other alternative left, but that of exposing myself to the suspi-cion of having known from the beginning the purport of Mr. Jay's treaty, and uniting with him in withholding it from them, whilst I was using all the means in my power to impress them with a contrary belief, I was forced to undertake it. In consequence I waited on the diplomatic section of the committee, and made the representation as above, repeating Mr. Jay's motive for withholding the communication, as urged by himself: "That it belonged to the sovereign power alone to make it, &c." It was replied that it could not otherwise than excite uneasiness in the councils of this government, when it was observed that in the height of their war with the coalesced powers, and with England in particular, America had stept forward and made a treaty with that power, the contents of which were so carefully and strictly with-held from this government: For if the treaty was not injurious to France, why was it with held from her? Was it prudent for one ally to act in such manner in regard to another, and especially under the present circumstances, and at the present time, as to excite suspicions of the kind in question? I assured them generally, as I had done before, that I was satisfied the treaty contained in it nothing which could give them uneasiness; but if it did, and especially if it weakened our connection with France, it would certainly be disapproved in America. They thanked me for the communication; assured me they wished me to put myself in no dilemma which would be embarrassing, and thus the conference ended.

A few days after this, I was favoured with a letter from Mr. Hitchborn,[131] an American gentleman of character here (from Massachusetts) of which I enclose you a copy,[132] stating the contents or outlines of the treaty in question; as communicated to him by Colonel Trumbull, and with a view that he might communicate the same to me, for the information of this government. I was surprized at the incident; because I could not suppose that Colonel Trumbull would take this step, or any other, without the instructions of Mr. Jay, and it seemed to me extraordinary, that Mr. Jay should give such an instruction, or mark to him such a line of conduct. I was not surprized that Colonel Trumbull should confide the purport of the treaty to Mr. Hitchborn, for he merited the confidence; but I was surprized that Mr. Jay should write me it was to be communicated to me only as a public minister, &c., to be imparted to no one else, and that Colonel Trumbull, however deeply impressed he might be after his arrival here with the propriety of removing the doubts of this government upon that point, should consider himself at liberty to communicate the same to a third person, to be communicated to me, under no injunction whatever. I was, however, possessed of the paper in question; and it was my duty to turn it to the best account for the public interest, that circumstances would now admit of. It was, it is true, the most informal of all informal communications, and one of course upon which no official measure could be taken; yet the character of the parties entitled it to attention. Upon mature reflection therefore, and the more especially as I did not wish to meet the committee again on that point, until I heard from you,

---

[131] Benjamin Hitchborn graduated from Harvard College and became an eminent lawyer, Massachusetts state senator, and an associate of Paul Revere particularly with respect to civic activities. (Fischer 1994, 229)

[132] From Mr. Benjamin Hitchborn, to the Minister Plenipotentiary of the United States of America. Paris, March, 31st, 1795. "Sir, In some free conversation with Colonel Trumbull, on the subject of the late treaty between Great Britain and America, I could not avoid expressing the uneasiness I felt at the disagreeable effects, which had already shewn themselves, and the still more serious consequences which might result from that negotiation. And I must confess, I experienced a very agreeable surprize, when he assured me upon his honor, that the treaty had for its object, merely the adjustment of some matters in dispute between the two nations, that it secured to the Americans some rights in commerce which might have been doubtful by the laws of nations, and by which their intercourse with this country would be facilitated during the war, that it provided a compensation with those of either nation who had been injured, and finally settled all controversy respecting the boundary line and the western posts. He further declared that the treaty did not contain any separate or reciprocal guarrantee, of any rights, privileges or territory, or an engagement on either part to afford aid or supplies of any kind to the other, under any circumstances whatever. The treaty, he says, simply declares, that the parties shall remain at peace, and points out the mode, in which the matters of controversy between them shall be finally settled. If this information can be of any service to you in your public capacity, you may make use of it in any manner you may think fit. I presume the authenticity of its contents will not be called in question." (Hamilton 1899, 243)

---

lest I should be questioned why this new mode of diplomatic proceeding was adopted, I thought it best to send the paper in by my secretary, Mr. Gauvain[133] (a young gentleman who has acted with me, since the provisional nomination of Mr. Skipwith to the consulate) instructing him to assure the members, on my part, that they might confide in the credibility of the parties. The paper was presented to Merlin de Douay, with the comments suggested; and since which I have neither heard from the committee, Colonel Trumbull, nor Mr. Jay on the subject.

I intimated to you in my last, that I was persuaded if there was a force here able and willing to make head against the revolution, it would soon shew itself; but that I was of opinion none such existed. This presage has been since verified by a great and interesting example. The storm which I thought I then saw gathering, after rising to its height and expending its force, has past, and without doing any mischief. On the contrary, I am inclined to believe, from present appearances, it will be productive of good.

It was natural to expect, that the trial of Barrere, Collot d'Herbois, and Billaud de Varennes; three men, who were in the early stages, the associates, and in the latter, in some degree, the rivals of Robespierre's power, and who were, after his fall, unquestionably at the head of the mountain party, would excite some ferment. It was equally so, to presume, that if that party was not so completely crushed, as to preclude all hope of success, it would in some stage of the proceeding, make an extraordinary effort to save them. The epoch of this trial was, therefore, deemed by all an important one to France; and its several stages were marked by circumstances, which were calculated rather to encrease, than diminish, the general solicitude.

Under the banner of this party, and apparently in favour of the acquittal of these members, the discontented of every description were seen rallying; forming in the whole an extraordinary assemblage; being gathered from the various, and heretofore opposite, classes of society, but united now for the common purpose of disturbing the public tranquillity. The prisons, which were filled in the time of Robespierre, and opened under the more humane administration of the present day, had discharged upon the city an immense crowd of the ancient aristocracy, and who soon gave proof, that the severe discipline they had undergone had not eradicated the propensities that were acquired under the reign of the ancient court. As the present administration had rescued them from the guillotine, and to which they were otherwise inevitably doomed, it was at least entitled to their gratitude. This slight

---

[133] Michel Ange Gauvain served as a secretary to Monroe in Paris in 1795. He was in the United States by 1802, when Monroe introduced him in a letter to James Madison as "amiable, well informed, perfectly upright, and attached to our country." (Hamilton 1900, 347)

tribute, however, was not paid for that important service. On the contrary, these were among the most active in fomenting the present discontents. Another group, not less numerous, or turbulent; composed of the refuse of the lately disfranchised, or rather routed, Jacobins and their adherents were seen marshalled by its side, and acting in harmony with it. These two classes of people, and who were heretofore at endless war with each other, now combined, formed a force of some strength, and excited in the minds of many well disposed persons, serious apprehensions for the public safety.

The increasing scarcity of bread, and which menaced an unavoid-able diminution of the ordinary allowance, contributed much to increase the apprehension of danger. A deficiency in this article in Paris, under the ancient government, generally excited a tumult. It was, therefore, a primary object in every reign, and with every administration, to guard against such deficiency, as the greatest of public calamities. Abundant stores were, in consequence, always provided, when it was possible to provide them; and let the scarcity or price be what it might, in other quarters, the ordinary allowance, and nearly at the ordinary price, was distributed, as in times of greatest plenty, among the inhabitants of this city. Such, likewise, had been the practice since the change of government; so that a state of affairs which announced the approach of a deficiency, announced likewise that of a crisis extremely important in the history of the revolution. The most firm knew it was an experiment yet to be made; and from which, whilst they counted upon no possible benefit, they had many reasons to apprehend some real inconvenience.

It was foreseen, that if any movement was set on foot, the deficiency of bread, if that was the fact, would be made the pretext; and as the complaint, being addressed to the wants of all, would excite a general sympathy, it was feared that such deficiency would tend much to encrease the strength of the insurgent party. In every view, therefore, the crisis which approached was an interesting one: It was, however, at hand, and no other alternative remained, for those whose duty it was to sustain it, than that of yielding under, or meeting it with firmness, and passing through it as well as possible.[134]

As soon as it was known that a diminution of the ordinary allowance was unavoidable, it was resolved to make it known likewise to the people, that they might not be taken by surprise; and for this purpose Boisy d'Anglas,[135]

[134] The consequences of the new government policies were proving to be disastrous for the common people of Paris. Complaints and murmurs were becoming continually heard. The long delays in obtaining rationed bread, the shortage of flour, the high prices in markets and squares of bread, firewood, wine, coal, vegetables and potatoes, the prices of which were increasing daily, significantly added to the civilian unrest. (Rudé 1954, 261)

[135] Count François Boissy d'Anglas was an influential member of the Committee of Public Safety and bore direct responsibility for the provisioning of Paris. As such, he was an

of the section of subsistence committee of public safety, appeared at the tribune some days before it took effect. His discourse, was short, but explicit, began by exposing the enormities and vicious arrangements of the committees; whereby, he said, France had already been visited with many calamities, and was threatened with others; and concluded by observing that even famine was likewise one proceeding: that source; which neither the wisdom nor the industry of the present councils had been able altogether to avert: That he was happy, however, to assure convention, that as the most prudent measures long since taken to correct the abuses of that administration, the distress of Paris would be for a short term only. The communication was received by Barrere, Billaud de Varennes, &c. and by the members of the mountain party in general, with a smile of approbation. It was obvious they considered Boisy, as a welcome messenger, announcing to them joyful tidings. A few days afterwards, the deficiency so much dreaded took place, and, at the same time, the intrigues of the discontented began more fully to unfold themselves.

The movement was commenced by about four hundred citizens, from a section heretofore noted for its turbulence; and who, appearing without the hall, demanded admission to the bar of the convention. A deputation from the party, consisting of twenty members, was admitted, and who addressed that body in a style unusual; complaining of the want of bread, and declaring also, that they were upon the point of regretting the sacrifices they had made to the revolution. The answer of the President (Thibaudau)[136] was firm and decisive. To that part of the address which complained of the scarcity of bread, he replied, by stating the measures of the government to remedy it: And to that which exposed the temper of the party in regard to the revolution, he answered explicitly, that he knew the disaffected were at work to excite trouble, but that their efforts would be fruitless; for, enlightened by experience, and strong in the power of the whole nation, the convention would be able to controul their movements; and in closing, he addressed himself more particularly to the memorialists, saying, that the efforts of the people to recover their liberty would not be lost, whilst good citizens seconded the labours of their representatives; that despair belonged only to slaves; freemen never regretted the sacrifices they had made in such a cause. The answer, which was received with general applause, checked for awhile the turbulent spirit of the disaffected.

active participant in the quest for a political settlement which would stabilize the Revolution and end popular upheaval. (McPhee 2002, 160)
[136] Antoine Claire Thibaudeau was elected to the National Convention in 1792. A member of the Committee of Public Safety, he served as secretary and then president of the Convention for a short period. He voted for the death of the king without appeal and without reprieve. (Frey 2004, 135)

But this party had too much at stake, and its measures were probably too far advanced, to be abandoned in this stage. About a week after this, and which was on the 1st of April (12 Germinal) a more numerous body, consisting principally of workmen from the Faubourg of St. Antoine, presented itself likewise before the hall, demanding admission to the bar of the convention, and upon some pretext, and in violation of the usual forms, immediately forced its way into the hall of that assembly. The crowd increased, so that in the course of a few hours, there were in the hall, perhaps, three or four thousand; and in the vacant external space around it, as many more. The proceedings of the convention were suspended: The President, however, and the members kept their seats, declaring, that as their sitting was violated, they would do no business: Indeed it was now impossible to do any had they been so disposed; for the general and tumultuous cries that were raised by the invaders "for bread" for "liberty to the patriots," meaning some of the accomplices of Robespierre, could alone be heard. They continued thus in the hall about four hours, from two to six in the evening, offering in the interim no violence to any of the members; but behaving, in other respects, with the utmost possible indecorum. When they first entered, some circumstances were seen which caused a suspicion, that a good understanding subsisted between the leaders of the mob and some members of the mountain party: And it was likewise observed, that their final retreat was made upon a suggestion from that quarter; for as soon as an admonition to that effect was given from that quarter it was obeyed. Many believed it was intended to lay violent hands upon all the leading members of the preponderating party, and either murder them in their places, or send them to prison, to be murdered afterwards, under the form of a trial; as was the case in the time of Robespierre; whereby the preponderating scale would be shifted to the other side, and the reign of terror revived again for awhile. Be the plan, however, what it might, it was soon frustrated; for, as the movement was that of a mob against the civil authority, its operations were irregular and disorderly: It had no chief to lead it on to acts of violence: The time was therefore, whiled away in senseless uproar, till at length the putative authors of the movement were as uneasy about the issue, and as anxious to get rid of it, as those at whom it was supposed to be pointed. In the interim too, the means that were adopted without, tended not only to secure the general tranquillity of the city; but most probably to influence in a great measure the proceedings within. By order of the committees the tocsin was sounded, and the citizens in every section called to arms; so that the appeal was fairly made to the people of Paris, whether they would support the Republic, or rally under the standard of those who were for a change. Nor was the question long undecided; for as soon as the government acted in its various functions it was obeyed: The lapse of a few hours gave it the preponderance, and the lapse of a few more, not only freed the hall of the convention from the invasion with which it had been seized, but dispersed the crowd from its vicinity.

At six in the evening the convention resumed its deliberations; beginning by declaring its sitting permanent, and progressing by a review of the move-ments of the day, which were well understood and freely discussed. By this time too, it was fortified by accounts from every quarter, that the sense of the city was decisively pronounced in its favor, and against the rioters, and that the inhabitants of those sections, whence the disorder proceeded, were returning to their duty. The sitting continued until six in the morning; in the course whereof a decree of banishment was passed against the accused members, and of arrestation against eight or nine of the mountain party; which latter list was afterwards increased to about eighteen; and both of which decrees have since been carried into effect, by sending the former to the Isle of Oleron, and the latter to the castle of Ham in the department of Somme; and thus ended the commotion which was so long gathering and which menaced at one time, not to arrest the progress of the revolution (at least such was my opinion) but to occasion much trouble and stain its page with new atrocities.

In the course of this day, the services of General Pichegru, who happened to be in Paris, and was appointed commandant of the national guard, were of great importance to his country. His activity was great, for he was always on horse, and passing from one quarter of the city to another; and his arrange-ments in disposing of the cannon and military force were wise: His name too was of great utility, for it tended equally to elevate the hopes of the friends, and depress those of the enemies of the public tranquillity. I do not think if he had been absent, the event would have been different; but I am satisfied, that his presence contributed much to hasten the restoration of order, and to preserve it afterwards.

By this event, which is called the complement of the 9th of Thermidor, and which forms the catastrophe of the mountain party, tranquillity appears to be established, not only in this city, but throughout the Republic in general. The scarcity of bread, it is true, still continues, but yet, no murmuring has been since heard on that subject. The moderate party, and which, in prin-ciple, I deem the same with that which was overwhelmed on the 31st of May, will therefore commence its career under auspices extremely favourable to its own reputation, and to the liberty and prosperity of France. The fate of its late antagonist, if there was no other motive, and which was precipitated by the general wish of France, and of all other nations, not in league against the French Republic, must furnish a solemn and lasting admonition to shun its example. The opposite principles too, upon which it is founded, being the avowed patron of humanity, justice and law, and equally at variance with the opposite extremes of aristocracy and anarchy, whose partizans were lately combined in an effort to crush it, promises to secure in its measures some stability in the observance of those just and honourable principles which it professes.

For some time past, the views of this party have been directed towards the establishment of the constitution, and some motions to that effect are now depending before select committees appointed to prepare the several organic laws necessary to introduce it. An opinion is likewise entertained by many, that the constitution in question is very defective, and ought to be amended before it is put in force. A discourse to this effect was lately delivered by Pelet, a respectable and well informed member, and the same sentiment was then avowed by others. But whether an attempt of this kind, should it be formally made, will succeed or whether the general solicitude to put the constitution in force, however defective it may be in the hope of amending it afterwards, will prevail, is yet uncertain.

Since the fortunate issue of the late commotion, a treaty of peace was concluded with Prussia, at Basle, in Switzerland, of which I enclose you a copy. The import of the fourth and fifth articles, give cause to suspect, that some stipulations exist which have not been communicated, and it is believed by many, that it is agreed between the parties, that France shall retain the Prussian territory on the left of the Rhine, in lieu whereof, she is to take and cede Hanover. Should this be the case, it is probable, if the war continues another campaign, that Prussia will be seen arranged as a party in it on the side of France. The latter considers the old connection with Austria as broken, and wishes to supply it by one with Prussia; and provided satis-factory arrangements are or shall be hereafter formed for that purpose, will become interested in raising the latter power at the expence of the former, as well as that of England. The negotiation with Spain is also said to be far advanced, and will most probably soon be closed. 'Tis likewise reported, that a person, or more than one from England is now in Paris, upon the pretext of treating for an exchange of prisoners, but in truth, for the more substantial one of treating, or at least of sounding the disposition of this government for peace. Upon this point, however, I hope to be able to give you in the course of a few days more correct information than I now can.

I have the honor to be, Sir, with great respect and esteem your very humble serv, Jas Monroe.

To the Secretary of State [Edmund Randolph], Paris, May 17, 1795

Sir,—I was yesterday honoured with yours of the 8th of March, the only one received since that of the 5th of December, and was at the same moment favored with the company of Mr. Pitcairn, who having just arrived, had called to present his commission of vice-consul for this city, to be recognized as such.

I informed you in my letter of the 6th of March, and for reasons that were in part before explained, that the arrival of this gentleman would subject me to an unpleasant dilemma, for if it was known that he was a British subject, although he had likewise become an American citizen, I doubted much whether he would be received: That in strict propriety I ought to communicate the fact if it was so, for after what had passed between us, upon a subject analogous to this, if I announced him with-holding the fact, and it was discovered afterwards, I should expose myself to the imputation of the want of candour, and that in any event, if he were established, however correctly I might personally act, the circumstance of his being a British subject, would not only lessen his weight and to the prejudice of our commercial affairs here, but to a certain degree, and from causes that are obvious, lessen mine likewise, the ill effects of which might be felt, and especially at the present moment upon concerns of more general importance. By his arrival, therefore, this embarrassment was realized: The commission of the President is the law to me, and upon every principle it is disagreeable to suspend its force; but yet the nature of the trust reposed in a public minister, seems to imply in him a discretionary power, to controul according to his judgment, incidents of this kind, wherever it appears that thereby he may promote the public interest, and which becomes of course the stronger, when necessary to prevent the public detriment. Upon mature consideration, therefore, I thought it best to withhold the official communication of his appointment from the government, until I should hear from you in reply to that letter; and the more especially, as it might now be expected in the course of a few weeks. In consequence, I communicated this decision to Mr. Pitcairn, with the motives upon which it was founded, and was pleased to observe, that he appeared to be perfectly satisfied with the propriety of it.

I observe by this letter, that the treaty concluded by Mr. Jay with Great Britain, did not arrive before the 5th of March, and in consequence would not be submitted to the Senate before the 8th of June, and in the interim would be kept secret. I regret equally this delay and secrecy; the delay because if it is not approved, it may become more difficult in the probable course of events on this side the Atlantic, to obtain a remodification of it: and the secrecy because the jealousy which was at first imbibed by this government of its contents will of course remain for the same space of time, and which cannot otherwise than be somewhat hurtful in the interim of our affairs depending here. Having too explained the object of that mission, whilst its issue was uncertain, they think it strange that the result should be now withheld. Upon this point, however, I have nothing new to add. I have already communicated to you whatever I had to communicate upon it, and waiting the issue, I shall continue by my assurances to endeavour to inspire this government with a confidence, either that the treaty in question contains in it nothing improper, or that it will not be ratified in case it does.

Your last letter gave me the first intelligence upon which I could rely, that Colonel Humphreys was in America. He will of course return fully possessed of your views with respect to the piratical powers on the African coast. I assure you long since that it would be easy to obtain from this government its aid upon that point, and it is certain that its aid with each, and especially Algiers, with which regency this republic is in the strictest amity, would be of great effect. Those powers hear that France is at war with Austria, Spain, England, Portugal, &c. and defeats them all, and in consequence conclude that she is more powerful than all united, and respect her accordingly. I have frequently been told in private conversation by the members of the committee, that they were ready to render us all the service in their power in that respect, and I should long since have requested the government to make our peace there in pursuit of the plan commenced by Mr. Morris, had I not been instructed that the business was in the hands of Colonel Humphreys, and feared by such interference I should embarrass the views and measures of our own government. I shall be ready however, to act in whatever line you may think proper to direct, and shall endeavour, and without any particular compromitment on our part, to keep the committee in the same state of preparation.

In general our commercial affairs progress as well, all things considered as could be expected. Transactions of old standing, I have not lately formally pressed, because I know that the government is embarrassed at present on the score of finance, and because I think it would be better to wait the issue of the business depending with you in June next. Mr. Skipwith, however, does everything in his power to forward those objects, and perhaps with as much effect, as would be possible under any pressure that could now be made. But in the direct or current commerce, our countrymen enjoy all the privileges that the government can give them; and although delays are sometimes experienced, and especially in the payment of contracts, that were formed in America, yet the transactions are generally closed in a manner satisfactory to the parties. The profits which some of them have made, and continue to make, according to report, are great, beyond example. In truth our countrymen are generally planting themselves in commercial houses throughout the Republic, and engaging in the commerce of France to an extent which, whilst it promises to be profitable to themselves, will likewise be of great and permanent utility to both nations: for by means thereof not only personal acquaintance and connections are formed by the citizens of each with those of the other respectively, but their common wants and common capacities will be better understood.

The claim of 15,000 dollars I mentioned long since would be admitted without a word, and that it ought to be so understood at the treasury.[137] I omitted it in my more early applications to this government, because I wished to progress with the greater objects first, and more latterly, for the reasons above suggested. I conferred, however, on the subject with Mr. Adet, and presume he will allow it as a thing of course; but if he does not, upon notification thereof to the committee, and which I will immediately make when so advised by you, he will certainly be instructed to do it.

Since my last, Paris, and the Republic in general, have enjoyed a state of perfect tranquillity. Every little disturbance which ensued for a time the movement of the 2d April (12th Germinal) and there was one or two of the smaller kind which did ensue, subsided almost of itself, and in each instance without force, and of course without bloodshed. Thus the authority of the convention prevails, although it is supported by the common sense, and the common interest of the citizens of Paris only; a thing heretofore deemed impracticable under similar embarrassments. Certain it is, that if the government had been in the hands of a king, or any other description of persons than that of the people themselves, we should have seen in the course of a few weeks past, a succession of many revolutions of the ministerial kind, and which perhaps would have dethroned eventually any king that ever reigned here. The distress of the people on account of the scarcity of bread, since that time, has been like that of a besieged town. They have been constantly upon allowance, and which was latterly reduced to two ounces and sometimes less per day. My family which consists of 14 persons is allowed two pounds of bread per day. I mention this that you may have a just idea of the distress of others, and particularly the poor; for at a great expence (nearly 40 dollars specie per barrel) I am supplied. The accounts which we have of the distress

---

[137] As mentioned in Randolph's initial June 10, 1794, instructions to Monroe, the U.S. Congress had passed an act in February 1794 providing $15,000 for the relief of refugees from Santo Domingo who were seeking asylum in the United States during the Haitian Revolution. The funds were to be charged against the American debt to France. (Dusenbury 2014, 30-50)

---

of the aged, the infirm, and even of children are most afflicting; yet calmness and serenity are seen everywhere; complaints diminish, and that ferocity which was observable on the 12th of Germinal, on the part of those who forcibly entered the convention, and which was excited by the animosity of contending parties, and most probably encreased by foreign influence, has entirely disappeared. In this moment they all look to America for bread, and most fervently do I join them in prayer, that our countrymen may speedily bring it to them. If they can make out for six weeks they are safe; for by that time the rye will ripen, and from present prospects they may be in a better situation in the interim than they now are, and most probably not in a worse.

In the line of negotiation, nothing has been concluded since the treaty with Prussia, and which was ratified by both parties soon after it was signed. Sir F. Eden[138] came to Rochefort, from whence he notified his arrival to the committee and requested permission to come to Paris. They had him conducted to Dieppe, where he was kept under guard until the arrival of an agent from the committee, who was instructed to receive and report his propositions to that body, provided they embraced any other object than an exchange of prisoners; but in case they did not, to request his departure in twenty-four hours. The agent attended, asked his business, and was answered, he came to treat for an exchange of prisoners. Have you no other power? Let us settle this point first; we shall be together, and may afterwards talk on what we please. But have you no other power? Your answer to this question may settle this and every other point in a word: If you have I will receive what you will be pleased to communicate; if you have not, our business is at an end. Mr. Eden replied, he had none; and thus they parted, the agent for Paris, and Mr. Eden for London, the latter being apprized what the wish of the committee was in that respect.

The negotiation with Spain is still at a stand. The Spanish court is strongly inclined to connect itself with this Republic; but in so doing it foresees the necessity of an accommodation with us in respect to the boundaries and the Missisippi; and against which it thinks itself secure by adhering to England, who it is believed gives assurances to that effect. Of the views of England, however, Spain is and always was jealous, so that it is not improbable an accommodation will soon take place. 'Tis said that the king of Spain makes a provision for the children of the late king, the object of his care: That he wishes to have them delivered up to him, with the view of giving them an establishment in property somewhere in his kingdom, and to the

---

[138] Sir Frederick Morton Eden, the eldest son of Sir Robert Eden, governor of Maryland. His mother was Caroline Calvert, sister and co-heiress of the last Lord Baltimore. (Hamilton 1899, 41)

boy the title of Duke, and that this point in some form or other will probably be agreed.

'Tis said that a treaty is lately concluded with the commissioners from Holland, by which the independence of that country is acknowledged, and an alliance offensive and defensive formed, upon terms which promise to be satisfactory to the parties. I will enclose a sketch of these which has been published.[139]

General Pichegru has crossed the Rhine and with a considerable force; but probably at present for the purpose only of quartering his army in the enemies' country. He is now in the neighbourhood of Mayence, which is still besieged. The campaign, however, cannot be considered as fairly opened: Perhaps it is not definitely settled, against whom in the Empire, the forces of the Republic will be directed; for the door which was opened to receive propositions from the Princes of the Germanic body, through the king of Prussia, was not an idle provision. Advantage, I am told, has already been taken of it, and that it will most probably prove the means, and to the credit and interest of the king of Prussia, of promoting in the Empire the views of France.

At sea, in the excursions which were made in the course of the winter, by tempest great loss was sustained, and considering that the war will hereafter be directed principally against England, less attention was for sometime paid to the navy than ought to have been expected. At present, however, the attention of the executive branch seems to be turned more to that object than heretofore; so that 'tis probable the waste of the winter will soon be repaired.

The assignats continue to depreciate, and the frequent discussions which take place upon the various propositions made to raise their credit, always produce the opposite effect of depressing them. Many, however, think the depreciation a blessing to the country, and that their total fall would be among the happiest of political events; especially if they can be kept up through the summer. At present their depreciation is by the standard of gold, or foreign exchange, as fourteen to one.

---

[139] This was the Treaty of the Hague signed on May 16. By design the French, considering that they were in military occupation, interfered relatively little in internal Dutch affairs. The French aim was still to use Holland in the war against Great Britain. This aim did not constitute forcible interference, since many Dutch were in favor of it. Nevertheless, when the terms of the treaty between the French and Batavian republics became known, many in the Netherlands were disappointed. The Batavian Republic was required not only to declare war on England but to maintain a French occupying army at Dutch expense, to accept French paper money, to cede Flushing and the mouth of the Scheldt, and to pay an indemnity of 100,000,000 florins. This was severe treatment for an alleged ally, but not severe enough to alienate Dutch revolutionaries from France since they saw no alternative except capitulation to England and the House of Orange. (Palmer 1954, 23)

The mass of wealth in national domains, is affirmed by those who ought to know, more than double what I supposed; being, after restoring the property of those who were illegally condemned, according to a late decree, about four hundred millions sterling. A deputation was lately sent to Holland, of Sieyes and Reubell, to press for money, and 'tis expected they will succeed, at least in such degree as to answer present exigencies.

I am happy to hear that the President approves my conduct in the instance mentioned,[140] and I beg you to assure him that for the future I shall continue to be neither less attentive nor assiduous in the discharge of the duties of the trust reposed in me, to all its objects, that I have heretofore been.

With great respect and esteem I have the honor to be, Sir, Your most obedient servant, Jas Monroe.

P.S. Since writing the above, I was informed personally by one of the agents who attended Mr. Eden at Dieppe (for there were two) that he (Mr. Eden) had power to treat on other subjects than that of an exchange of prisoners, and that he not only communicated this, but likewise his propositions, and which were sent to the committee and peremptorily rejected. That the treatment given Mr. Eden, was polite and respectful, and with which he appeared to be perfectly satisfied. What the propositions were I know not; but that they contemplated peace cannot be doubted.

To William Short, Paris, May 30, 1795

Sir,—I was favoured, about ten days past, with yours of the 4th instant, and should have answered it immediately, had I not previously done so by anticipation, in some measure, in one of the same date through the armies, or had I not waited for the arrival of Mr. Pinckney, who was then on his way from Dunkirk for this place.[141] By him this will be forwarded; indeed, by him alone would I hazard what I deem it necessary to communicate to you. Previously therefore, permit me to assure you, that this government will admit of no intermediate or third parties in its negotiations, but will only treat with its enemies themselves, or directly. The only power whose good offices they

---

[140] I have the pleasure to inform you, wrote Randolph, that the President much approves your attention to our commerce; and the merchants who are immediately interested, and to whom I have communicated your measures, think them judicious. (Hamilton 1899, 264)

[141] On December 19, 1792, Short had left for Madrid, having been appointed Commissioner Plenipotentiary, in conjunction with William Carmichael, to treat with Spain concerning Florida and the Mississippi boundaries, the navigation of the Mississippi River, commercial privileges, and other open questions. He arrived in Madrid about the February 1, 1793. After Carmichael's untimely death from illness, Short's negotiation for a treaty with Spain dragged for so long that the American Government became impatient with him and sent Thomas Pinckney, the American Minister in London, as Envoy Extraordinary to conclude the treaty. Pinckney reached Madrid about July 1, 1795, and with Short's assistance, succeeded in completing the treaty. Immediately after the signing of the treaty on October 27th, 1795, both Pinckney and Short left Madrid. (Short 1920, 311)

ever thought of accepting was the United States; but the negotiation of Mr. Jay with England has, by its manner, and particularly by withholding with such care the result, inspired such distrust in our friendship for them, that they are disposed not even to accept of ours. This is a fact of importance, which I did not chuse to hazard through the route of the armies; since if it was known to the Spanish government it might lessen our weight in our negotiation with that court; for I always knew that an opinion of a good understanding between us and this government would greatly forward our own depending negotiations elsewhere. You must therefore (or rather Mr. P.) must press the object of your negotiation to a close as soon as possible, counting with certainty, that although, in general, we stand well here, yet we are to have no agency in the affairs of France, and of course are to derive, from that consideration, no aid to the advancement of our own.

It is proper to inform you, that just before the report of Mr. Jay's treaty reached us, this government, whose attachment to us was daily increasing, had it in contemplation to extend, by all the means in its power, its fortunes to us, in our depending negotiations elsewhere; and that even since that report, upon the presumption everything is right, they have instructed (as I am told) their minister, negociating with Spain, to secure in their treaty the points insisted on by us.

This instruction was given just before the report of Mr. Pinckney's appointment was known, and I am inclined to think, that although it was not in Mr. Pinckney's power (not being able to explain Mr. Jay's treaty to them without which it would have been indelicate) to ask their aid, that the instructions still continue in force. In any event Spain will have all possible proof, and from this government itself, that they wish us well, and rejoice in our prosperity, and therefore, although they keep their own affairs to themselves, yet the Spanish Court will find, that a good understanding with France is not to be expected or preserved without a good understanding with us.

I have heard that Mr. Jay has stipulated something in his treaty respecting the Mississippi; whereby upon the ridiculous pretence of a guarantee to us, an extension of territory is substantially given to Britain, and she in consequence admitted to the Mississippi. The fact of a guarantee by Britain to us must excite the indignation of Spain towards her, though ready to yield the point to us: But the extension of her territory so as to comprehend the source of that river, and thereby entitle her to its navigation, will produce a more serious and alarming effect. I think it will tend greatly to separate Spain from England, and to force the former into a more intimate connection with France and the United States; the first step towards which, is an accommodation to their present demands.

Another circumstance which will facilitate this object is, that England, through Sir F. Eden,[142] has absolutely and very lately attempted, upon the pretext of an exchange of prisoners, to open a negotiation for peace with this Republic. I suspect Spain knows nothing of this, but I am assured, by authority in which I confide that it is the truth. He was received at Dieppe, and detained whilst his terms were sent to the committee, and an answer received peremptorily rejecting them. If true, I presume the fact will be made known to Spain; so that the latter power ought to reject all delicacy towards the former in its transactions with it.

I have one other observation to make, which shews the necessity of dispatch, if possible, in our negotiation with Spain. Suppose her peace made with this Republic; she is of course, relieved from the pressure which disposes her to accommodate us. Shall we not afterwards stand of course nearly upon the same ground that we stood in that negotiation, from the epoch of the one which was conducted by Mr. Jay with Mr. Gardoqui, which had well nigh ended (though managed by the former with great skill, and according to the rules of ancient diplomacy) in the occlusion of the river and dismemberment of the continent; which negotiation has certainly deluded the Spanish government, from that time to the present day, into an opinion, that half America wish it shut: At least to me (who was in the Congress during the pendency of that negotiation, and who have since seen your correspondence) such appeared to be the case.

The above are hints upon the real state of things here, upon which Mr. Pinckney and yourself will take your measures. If I could satisfy this government that Mr. Jay 's treaty contained nothing with which they have a right to complain, every thing would be easy here; we might forward the views of the two countries in which we reside, which in respect to this, I ardently wish to forward, making previously those of our own secure. But can any motive of interest, on the part of France, induce her to accept such offers from us, until she shall receive such satisfaction? Where the interest of our country can be advanced, or there is a possibility it may, I am willing to attempt any thing in concert with you, and shall, therefore, be always happy to hear from you in these respects.

I enclose you a letter from a friend of yours in this country, being assured it contains nothing of a treasonable nature: No intelligence of the march of armies or preparations against Spain, which it is the interest of this government to keep secret.

---

[142] Sir Frederick Morton Eden adamantly believed that British naval supremacy was central to England's security and prosperity and any compromise to those rights was courting disaster. He saw British rule of the seas as a conqueror's right. (Bickham 2012, 54)

To James Madison, Paris, June 13, 1795

Dear Sir,—I was sometime since fav'd with yours of the 11 of March being the second since I left America. You were I presume soon after the date of that in possession of several from me, of two more especially which opened fully the state of things here under the impression of Mr. Jay's treaty, and which state has not been essentially varied since: for as all communication upon the subject of that treaty has to this moment been withheld from me, it was impossible I sho'd alter the impression that was at first made by the reports concerning it. In the interim, therefore, the opinion of this govern- ment is suspended in regard to us. The chagrin, however, w'h applied in the first instance to the author of the treaty only, upon acc't of the distrust which was shown of this government in withholding its contents even from me, has by the continuation of the system, been extended in a great measure to the Executive itself. It is considered here even by the rep's of the neutral powers as making a particular harmony with Engld and w'h ought to ex cite uneasi- ness. You will, therefore, readily conceive how well disposed the minds of all are to criticise upon that transaction whenever it transpires: and you will likewise be enabled to form a just estimate of the pain & distress of my situ- ation here, & which promises to be increased in case that transaction is not approved.

As soon as the treaty was signed in Engl'd Mr. Jay wrote me it was signed observing that it contained an article which stipulated our other engage- ments sho'd not be affected by it: and sometime after this, he wrote me that he intended to communicate to me in confidence the principal heads of the treaty for my use as a publick minister. Upon this, as I found we were losing ground in consequence of that event, I sent to him for it, stating my promise to the gov't to shew to it whatever he sent me: hoping that in case it cont'd any thing improper he wo'd not send it. Upon this application he was greatly wounded upon the score of national dignity &c, said we were an independent, people &ca and sent nothing, but wo'd write to the Execu- tive & take its orders, it being obvious that before he could receive which, he wo'd embark for America, as it really happened. After this again he sent Colo. Trumbull here (the Colo. having in truth, some private business also in Germany) to offer a verbal communication of the contents of the treaty upon condition I wo'd not disclose it. As I had promised to communicate what I sho'd receive upon the subject & when I sho'd receive it, and which promise was made after my first letter from Mr. Jay & which stated that he co'd not communicate it, and of course in the expectation that I sho'd hear nothing on the subject till I heard from America, it followed that I co'd not accept it upon the terms offered by Colo. Trumbull. His mission here, however, excited the displeasure of this government & encreased my embarrassment, for it was suspected that he came upon some business of the English administration (as was published in the Engl'h papers) and was calculated to create a belief that thro' him I was possess'd, if I had not been before, of the contents of Mr. Jay's treaty: so that I was plac'd in a dilemma of not only not being able to remove the doubts of the gov't as to the contents of this treaty, but likewise of defending my own character from the suspicion of having been acquainted with the negotiation from the beginning & of being of course in great political harmony with Mr. Jay. As I had always fortified myself ag'nst this very unjust suspicion by frank communications, so I deemed it equally necessary in this instance, & in consequence exposed to the Committee the proposition of Mr. Jay thro' Mr. Trumbull & my refusal to accept it.[143] By this line of conduct together with the concur rent report of all Frenchmen who now are or have been in America, I believe I am free in the estimation of the gov't from unjust suspicions: and I likewise believe I shall be free from them let the issue in America (now depending) be what it may. Whether I shall have any weight, in case the thing is approv'd & is improper, upon the sentiment & measures of the gov't here is doubtful.

I find by Mr. Randolph's letter that mine of the 18th of Dec'r has reached him. I hope you rem'd in Phil'a till the 8th of this month & were possess'd of the other letter alluded to above explaining more fully the impression of this gov't towards us, for certainly your counsel in that interesting business wo'd be of great use to our country, and especially as you would be confided in by many from the Easterward. I will possess you by some safe hand of the correspondence with & respecting Mr. Jay. I will now send you a letter from Mr. Short showing that if we stood well here we have every thing under our control with respect to Sp'n as we certainly had with respect to Engl'd had it not been thrown away as I fear it has been. This letter is an important document and oversets all the reasoning of those who are opposed to the necessity of harmony here to give effect to our negotiations elsewhere.[144]

---

[143] Monroe had detailed his presentation before the Committee of Public Safety in his April 14, 1795, correspondence with Randolph.

[144] Don Manuel Godoy, Duke de la Alcudia and First Secretary of State of Spain, was not quite satisfied with Spain's political situation, especially when Prussia made peace with France in the spring of 1795. He therefore made advances to William Short [now the sole chargé d'affaires of the United States at Madrid] with a view to getting the American minister at Paris, Monroe, to assist Spain in their efforts to treat directly with the French government. It was Godoy's "real and sincere wish," according to Short's May 4th, 1795, letter, to conclude immediately a treaty with France; but he desired to conduct the negotiation in such a manner "that there should be no suspicion of it on the part of England, or the least possible ground of suspicion, until the conclusion and ratification of the treaty." If the French government preferred to send a confidential agent to Madrid, Godoy suggested that the agent should pass as an American. At the same time, he gave

The movements of the 12 of Germinal & 1st of Prairial have terminated favorably to the objects of the Revolution by strengthening the hands of Gov't & promising some change in the constitution of 1793, upon our principle, a division of the legislature into two branches, &c. which it is expected will be reported by the Committee of 11 who now have that subject under consideration.[145]

I beg of you in particular to show my communications always to Mr. Jefferson, who I suspect declines intentionally a correspondence from a desire to enjoy free from interruption the comforts of private life; and likewise to Mr. Jones & with respect to others I leave you to act as you please. We are well & desire to be affec'y remembered to Mrs. M. y'r father & his family.

The derangm't of Holland by the conquest puts it out of Von Staphorst's power to advance me money tho' I am convinc'd a loan may be obtained to purchase land if any bargain offers & of w'h you will advise me.[146]

Sincerely I am y'r friend & servant, Jas Monroe.

A treaty with Holland is made whereby those states are independent, paying 100,000,000 of florins for the expenses of the same &ca.

To the Secretary of State [Edmund Randolph], Paris, June 14, 1795

Sir,—It seemed probable, after the movement of the 12th Germinal (2nd of April) and which terminated in the banishment or rather deportation (for the hand of government was never withdrawn from them) of Barrere, Billaud de Varennes and Collot d'Herbois, and the arrestation of several of the leading members in the mountain party, that the convention would be left at liberty to pursue for the future the great object of the revolution, and without further molestation; and the calm which ensued, for a considerable time, that movement, although the scarcity of bread continued, gave

Short "the fullest assurances" that all the matters in controversy should be "settled to the satisfaction of the United States." (Rives 1898, 73-74)

[145] The French Constitution of 1795 was more conservative than the abortive democratic Constitution of 1793 and established a liberal republic with a franchise based on the payment of taxes, similar to that of the Constitution of 1791; a bicameral legislature to slow down the legislative process; and a five-man Directory. The central government retained great power, including emergency powers to curb freedom of the press and freedom of association. (Campbell 2020)

[146] At the time, Nicholas van Staphorst was a principal of the Holland Land Company which pursued land speculation efforts in the United States. Organized by six Dutch bankers who purchased over five million acres of land principally in New York and Pennsylvania, they eventually resold the properties in small parcels directly to settlers at a profit. (Barrow 1985, 248)

strength to this presumption.[147] But a late event has shewn that the victory which was gained upon that occasion by the convention, over the enemies of the present system, was not so decisive as there was reason to presume it would be; for within a few days after my last, which was of the 17th of May, another attempt was made upon that body, and which menaced for a while at least, in respect to the personal safety of the members, the most alarming consequences. I am happy, however, to be able now to assure you that this has likewise failed, and without producing, according to present prospects, and in regard to the main course of the revolution, any material effect.

The circumstances which characterize this latter movement were in general the same with those of that which preceded it; except that it was attended with greater violence and its views were more completely unfolded. On the 20th of May, a party from the Faubourgs of St. Antoine and St. Marceau, armed, and consisting of several thousands, approached the convention early in the morning, having previously circulated a paper that their object was a redress of grievances; of which the scarcity of bread was the principal, and which could only be accomplished by the establishment of the constitution of 1793, and the recall of Barrere and his colleagues; or, in other words, the revival of the reign of terror. As these measures could not be carried into immediate effect, without the overthrow of the preponderating party, so the movement appeared to be directed unequivocally to that object. The centinels of the convention were forced upon the first approach, and in an instant the party, preceded by a legion of women, entered and spread itself throughout the hall of that assembly. The sitting was broken and everything in the utmost confusion. In a contest which took place between Ferraud,

---

[147] This letter seeks to detail the events surrounding 1 Prairial Year III and the most recent popular uprising. Acutely aware of the danger of a renewed insurrection, the convention's military committee had summoned troops to Paris. As in July 1789, however, the soldiers showed an alarming tendency to sympathize with the people. Members of one unit swore that "they were not going to kill people half-dead from hunger." On 30 Floreal Year III (May 19, 1795), a printed pamphlet titled "Insurrection of the people, to obtain bread and reconquer its rights" circulated in the streets. It urged the citizens to march on the Convention. The germinal uprising had been a demonstration; but the effort that took place a few days later, on 1 Prairial Year III (May 20, 1795), was a genuine attempt to replace the government. The anonymous authors of the "Insurrection of the people" summoned the men and women of Paris to act on behalf of the entire nation. Justifying their revolt on the grounds that the Convention was "making the people die inhumanely from hunger," they demanded the immediate arrest of all the members of the Convention's governing committees, implementation of the Constitution of 1793, immediate national elections, and a new assembly. In the meantime, Paris would be put under a state of emergency: the city's barriers were to be closed except for those bringing in provisions and all public officials suspended from office. "The people will not stand down until it has ensured the subsistence, the happiness, the tranquility and the freedom of all the French," the document promised. Although defeated, this was the last popular revolt of the French Revolution. (Popkin 2020, 443)

one of the deputies, (a gallant and estimable young man) and some of the party, for the protection of the chair and person of the President, which were threatened with violation, the former was slain, and soon afterward his head, severed from his body, was borne on a pike by the perpetrators of this atrocious crime, in triumph, into the bosom of the convention itself.[148] It really seemed for sometime, as if that body, or at least the leading members in the preponderating party, were doomed to destruction, or safety to be secured only by disguise and fight. During this conflict, however, the whole assembly behaved with the utmost magnanimity: No symptoms of fear were betrayed: No disposition to yield or otherwise dishonor the great theatre on which they stood; and Boissy d'Anglas, who happened to preside, not only kept his seat, but observed in his deportment a calm ness and composure which became the dignified and important station which he filled. This state of con fusion lasted until about twelve at night; when it was terminated by the decisive effort of a body gathered from the neighbouring sections, planned by the united committees of public safety, sureté generale and militaire, and led on by several deputies, among whom were most distinguished, Kervelegan, Anguis, Mathieu, Delmas, Freron and Legendre. They entered precipitately the hall, attacked the intruders, sabre and bayonet in hand; nor did they cease the charge until they had rescued it from the profanation. A little after twelve the convention was re-established, and proceeded, as upon the former occasion, to a review of what had passed, in the course of the day.

Whilst the insurgents were in possession of the reins of government, and after Boissy d'Anglas had retired, they placed the President Vernier, in the chair by force,[149] and began an organization upon the principles that were first avowed. They repealed in a mass all the laws that were passed since the 9th Thermidor; recalled Barrere, Billaud de Varennes and Collot d'Herbois; took possession of the tocsin and the telegraph; ordered the barriers of the city to be closed, and were upon the point of arresting all the members of the comunittee of the executive branch, having appointed a commission of four deputies, to take their places and with full power to act in their stead; so that in truth the reign of terror was nearly revived, and with accumulated force.

[148] Jean Bertrand Féraud, a Jacobin, had been close to Robespierre. A deputy of the Convention, on May 20, 1795, angry crowds broke into the Tuileries Palace, demanding among other things that an emergency food committee be formed and that Jacobin leaders be released from prison. When attendants tried to drive them out with whips, someone shot and killed Féraud. The people put his head on a pike and waved it in the face of the president of the Convention. Intimidated, the deputies passed laws to meet the crowd's demands. (Connelly and Fred Hembree 1993, 121)

[149] Hamilton suggests that this is a mistake. That if Vernier relieved Boissy d'Anglas upon his own pressing solicitation, it might then appear that Boissy d'Anglas was exhausted. (Hamilton 1899, 275)

At this moment, however, the plan of the committees, who had continued their sitting, was ripe for execution and fortunately the stroke was given before the system was completed.

But the commotion was not ended by the expulsion of the insurgents from the hall of the Convention itself. They retreated back to the faubourgs to which they belonged, and where, for a while, they opposed its authority. In the course, however, of the succeeding day, a considerable force was collected, under the authority of the Convention, from those sections who voluntarily offered their service, amounting, perhaps, to 20 thousand; and which being marched against them in different directions, surrounding, in a great measure, both faubourgs, reduced them immediately to order, and without the effusion of blood.

On the same day an insurrection took place at Toulon of the same kind, and with the same objects in view, and which for several days wrested that port and its dependencies, the fleet excepted, from the authority of the government. Upon that theatre too, some outrages were committed, and fatal consequences in other respects were apprehended. But this was like wise lately suppressed by the efforts of good citizens, drawn by the representatives in mission there, from Marseilles and the neighbouring country; a report to that effect being yesterday presented to the convention by the committee of public safety: So that order may be considered as completely established, the authority of the convention being triumphant everywhere.

As soon as the Convention resumed its deliberations, the punishment of those who had offended in the course of the commotion was the first object which engaged its attention. Whilst the insurgents were in possession of the hall, and enacting their short but comprehensive code of legislation, several members of the mountain party not only retained their seats, but joined in the work. Four were appointed to the commission, which was designed to supercede the executive administration, and who accepted the trust. These circumstances, with many others which occurred, created a belief that the movement was in harmony with that party. It was therefore concluded, that more decisive measures ought to be taken with those members, and with the party generally, than had been heretofore adopted; and in consequence, about 30 of them were arrested on that and the succeeding days, within the course of a week, and who are to be tried according to a late decree, in common with others charged with offences, said to be committed in the course of the commotion, by a military commission appointed at the time, and invested with full power for that purpose.

It is to be observed, that the character of this movement was decisively anti-monarchical. Its success, if it had succeeded, would have revived the reign of terror, and most probably carried all the aristocrats, with the leading members of the preponderating party, to the scaffold. Bread and the Constitution of 1793, were written upon the hats of many of the insurgents;[150] and whilst the hall and its vicinity resounded in favor of the patriots, meaning Barrere, &c. the feeble voice of one solitary aristocrat only was heard in favor of the constitution of 1789. Indeed the aristocrats, who had before the 12th Germinal contributed much to foment the discontents which broke out on that day, in the hope that if a commotion took place and the Convention was overthrown, the standard of Royalty would be erected, and the monarchy re-established, and who were in the interval, from the dubious character of that movement, which was crushed before it had fully unfolded itself, of neither side, for, nor against the Convention, were observed in the commencement of this, to remain in the same state of inactivity, greatly agitated, but taking no part. As soon, however, as the object of this latter movement was understood, and it became obvious, that in case it succeeded, terrorism, and not royalty, would be re-established, the disposition of this party towards the Convention changed. It no longer shewed an in difference to its welfare; on the contrary, it became active in its support. But in truth, the force of this party in this City, and especially upon the late emergencies, did not appear to be great. The most gallant of its members are either upon the frontiers, at war against the republic, or have fallen already in the cause of royalty. These, too, consist of those who were of sufficient age to take their part in the commencement; for the young men of Paris, who are descended from it, or from others of the more wealthy inhabitants of the city, and who have attained their maturity during the revolution, or are now growing up, have imbibed the spirit which it was natural to expect such splendid examples of patriotism would create upon young and generous minds, and are in general on the side of the revolution.

That there should be a party of any force within the republic, or rather of sufficient force to disturb the government in the manner we have seen, disposed to subvert the present system, and establish that of terror, must excite your surprise. You will naturally be inclined to ask of what character of citizens is it composed; what their numbers and ultimate views; since it is to be presumed that a system of terror, as a permanent system of government, cannot be wished by any one? You have seen that the movements in

---

[150] What seems insightful in Monroe's account is the abundant evidence of the connections these insurrectionary forces were making between subsistence issues and political and constitutional matters: Bread and the Constitution of 1793. Indeed, clear evidence that rights to subsistence and welfare were guaranteed [at least from a public perspective] by the Declaration of the Rights of Man and Citizen of 1793. (Levy 2000, 807)

question proceeded principally from the two faubourgs of St. Antoine and St. Marceau; the enquiry, therefore, will be satisfied by exposing the character of those two sections. In general, I am told, they are artisans, and among the most industrious in Paris. Many of them are said to be foreigners, Germans, and which explains the motive of their partiality for the constitution of 1793, which naturalizes them. That they are opposed to monarchy is certain, for such has been their character from the epoch of the destruction of the Bastille, in which they had a principal hand, to the present time. Indeed, upon this point, the late movements speak with peculiar force; for if those movements were spontaneous, and commenced by the people themselves, it follows, as they cannot be suspected of any deep political finesse, and of aiming at royalty through the medium of terrorism, that the latter, and not the former, was the object. And if they were set on by foreign influence, as is believed by many, the conclusion must be the same; for as royalty is unquestionably the object of those persons who are suspected of such interference, it is to be presumed, that, if practicable, they would have taken a more direct course to promote it, by an immediate declaration in its favour, since thereby they would rally under its standard all those who were the friends of that system. Whereas, by declaring in favour of terrorism, the opposite effect was produced; for the royalists themselves were thereby driven into the expedient of using their utmost endeavours to save the Convention, as the only means whereby they could save themselves. In every view, therefore, they must be deemed enemies to royalty, and as such it is natural to expect they will feel a great sensibility upon all those questions, which, in their judgment, have a tendency to promote it Whether any such have been agitated or contemplated is, perhaps, doubtful: I have thought otherwise, and still think so. But that many circumstances have presented themselves, in the course of the collision of parties, that were sufficient to create a suspicion with persons of that portion of discernment, which laborious artizans usually possess, that the leading members of the preponderating party were prepared to abandon the republican scale, and incline towards monarchy, is certain. The inhabitants of these faubourgs having sided always with the mountain party, have of course, brought upon themselves the particular enmity of the royalists. They have, therefore, or rather their leaders have been, in their turn, persecuted by the royalists. But they have likewise thought themselves persecuted by the present preponderating party, with whom they were engaged in uninterrupted warfare, before and since the time of Robespierre. In this respect, therefore, they saw the present preponderating party and the royalists acting apparently in harmony together, and concluded that the former were likewise royalists. They have likewise seen, under the administration of this party, the royalists enlarged from prison, and other measures of that kind adopted, which have probably fortified them in this belief. A report, too, which has been circulated through the city, that under the name of organic laws, it is contemplated by the committee of eleven, to introduce some important changes in the constitution of 1793, has, no doubt, tended in a great measure to increase their disquietude. In an attempt to explain the cause of these movements, the above circumstances have appeared to me to merit attention, and, with that view, I have presented them.

But that there was no real harmony of political views between the present preponderating party and the royalists, even with respect to the terrorists, is a fact of which I have no doubt. The reign of terror continued until it could last no longer: It was necessary to suppress it, and it was suppressed. That the royalists wished this event, and gave it all the aid they could, is certain; but that their efforts were of any service in that respect is doubtful: Indeed, I was persuaded that for some time they produced the opposite effect, and for reasons that are obvious: For as the preponderating party sought the estab-lishment of the Republic, and knew that the mountain party had the same object in view, it was reasonable to expect, that after the former had gained the ascendency it would be disposed to exercise towards the latter some degree of moderation and humanity; and equally so to presume, that the same spirit of magnanimity which inculcated this disposition towards its antagonist, chiefly from a respect for its political principles, would dispose it to reject with disdain the aid of the royalists who were enemies to both. This sentiment I think is to be traced through all the measures of the convention, from the 9th of Thermidor to the 1st of Prairial; for we behold, through that interval, the preponderating party rescuing from the guillotine and prison, the royalists, whilst they reprobated their principles, and terminating in other respects the reign of terror; whilst they avoided, as far as was possible, the punishment of those who had been the principal authors and agents under that reign. Indeed this party has appeared to me to be, and so I have often represented it to you, as equally the enemy of the opposite extremes of royalty and anarchy; as resting upon the interest and the wishes of the great mass of the French people, and who I have concluded, and from those data the revolution itself has furnished, as well as from my own observations since my arrival (the latter of which, it is true, has been confined to a small circle) are desirous of a free republican government; one which should be so organized as to guard them against the pernicious consequences that always attend a degeneracy into either of these extremes.

You will likewise ask; what effect have these movements had upon the public mind, in regard to the present system? Is it not probable they have already wearied the people out, and in consequence inclined them to royalty merely from a desire of repose? That they are all wearied is most certain, and what may be the course of events, in the progress of time, I do not pretend to determine: These lie beyond my reach, and indeed beyond the reach of all men. I only undertake to deduce immediate consequences from the facts which I witness; and when I see that these movements have produced upon the royalists themselves the opposite effect, and forced them, at least for the present, to renounce their creed and cling to the convention for their safety, I cannot presume that the moderatists, who are republicans, will quit the safe ground on which they rest, their own ground too, and become royalists. Royalty, therefore, I consider at present as altogether out of the question. But that these convulsive shocks, and which proceed from the opposite extreme, may produce some effect, is probable. In my opinion they will produce a good one; for I am persuaded they will occasion, and upon the report of the committee of eleven, some very important changes in the constitution of 1793; such as a division of the legislature into two branches, with an organization of the executive and judiciary upon more independent principles than that constitution admits of: Upon those principles indeed which exist in the American constitutions, and are well understood there. Should this be the case, the republican system will have a fair experiment here; and that it may be the case, must be the wish of all those who are the friends of humanity every where.

On the day that this late commotion commenced, Mr. Pinckney arrived here on his way to Madrid, and was a spectator of the great scene it exhibited to the close: A few days after which he pursued his route, by the way of Bourdeaux, where before this he is probably arrived. Whilst here, I presented to his view what had passed between this government and myself, upon the subject of his mission, assuring him from what I had heard and seen, that I was of opinion, that in case he would explain himself to the committee upon that subject, and express a wish they would give what aid they conveniently could, in support of his negotiation; satisfying them, at the same time, that they were not injured by Mr. Jay's treaty, they would do it. I likewise shewed him a letter I had just received from Mr. Short, written at the instance of the Duke de la Alcudia; to request that I would promote, by certain communications to this government, a negotiation between Spain and this Republic; he having previously and positively assured Mr. Short, that our demands should be yielded and adjusted at the same time. Mr. Pinckney was sensible of the benefit which the aid of this Republic could yield in his negotiation, and wished it; but, upon mature consideration, was of opinion he could not request such aid without having previously exposed to its view Mr. Jay's treaty, and which he did not chuse to do, for considerations delicacy forbade me to enquire into. It was, however, equally his and my wish, that his journey through the country should be marked with all those circumstances of recip-rocal civility between the government and himself, which are always due, and generally paid, when the minister of a friendly power passes through the territory of another; and in consequence I announced his arrival to the committee,[151] and obtained for him an amicable interview with the members of its diplomatic section, and by whom he was received with the most perfect attention.

You have already seen that England and Spain are each, and without the knowledge of the other, seeking a separate peace with this republic. What the motive for such secrecy on the part of the former is remains to be here-after unfolded: But what it is on the part of the latter is easily understood; for, as she apprehends, in case a peace is made with France, a declaration of war from England, and, of course, in case the attempt to obtain a peace is known, some new pressure from that power ; it follows, that she must wish the arrangement to be complete, to guard her against the ill consequences which might otherwise attend such an event, before any thing upon that head transpires. As soon, however, as it is known to Spain, that England seeks a separate peace, her jealousy of the views of England will be increased; as, likewise, will be the motive for an immediate accommodation with this Republic. The period, therefore, when a good understanding, embracing, perhaps, the ancient connection between the two nations, will be revived cannot be considered as remote. Whether our claims upon Spain will be attended to, under existing circumstances, in that adjustment, is a point upon which it is impossible for me to determine: for, as I was not possessed of Mr. Jay's treaty, and could give no other information on that head, than I had before given, I have latterly forborne all further communication with the committee upon that subject. Mr. Pinckney will be able, soon after his arrival at Madrid, to ascertain the temper of the Spanish court in regard to our demands, and the means by which his negotiation may be forwarded; and, as he likewise knows the state of things here, he will be able also to

---

[151] Monroe's announcement: To the Committee of Public Safety. "Paris, May 22nd, 1795.—I have to notify the committee of public safety, that Mr. Pinckney, minister plenipoten-tiary of the United States at London, and envoy extraordinary to the court of Spain, is now in Paris, on his way to Madrid, upon a particular mission from the United States to that court. He intends to pursue his journey by land, and wishes the passport of the committee, to secure him that safety and protection which is due to the minister of their ally, whilst within the jurisdiction of the French Republic. Mr. Pinckney will be happy to bear any commands which the committee may have for the quarter to which he is going." Pinckney's passport was certified and delivered by the Committee of Public Safety on May 31. (Hamilton 1899, 284)

---

point out the line in which, if in any, I may be serviceable; and, in the interim, I shall not only be prepared to co-operate with him in what ever movement he may suggest; but to obey, with promptitude, any instructions you may be pleased to give me in this, or any other, respect.

Since my last, the treaty with the United Provinces [of the Netherlands] has been concluded and ratified, of which I send you a copy, and the garrison of Luxembourg, consisting of 12,000 men, with an immense amount in military stores, cannon, &c. has surrendered. The achievement of this post, one of the strongest in Europe, has opened the campaign on the part of France with great brilliancy: As it was taken, too, after a long siege, and when all possible efforts to raise it had proved abortive, it not only demonstrates the superiority of the French arms in the present stage of the war, but furnishes satisfactory ground whereon to calculate, according to the ordinary course of events, its ultimate issue.

You will, perhaps, have heard before this, that the British have recommenced the seizure of our vessels laden with provisions, destined for the ports of this republic.[152] An American, just from Hamburg, charged with other articles, informed me the other day, that he was boarded on his way by two frigates, whose officers informed him, they were ordered to take in all vessels thus laden.

Within a few days past, the son of the late king departed this life.[153] A minute report will be published by the government of his decline, having

---

[152] While the Jay treaty was concluded in November 1794, its ratifications were not exchanged until October the following year, and meantime the British orders (in council) directing seizure of American vessels and provisions bound to France were being so well enforced that Secretary of State Randolph was compelled to issue a July 1795 warning that the Jay treaty had not yet been ratified by the President; "the late British order in council for seizing provisions is a weighty obstacle to ratification. I do not suppose that such an attempt to starve France will be countenanced." Every endeavor was made by the United States to secure a repeal of the admiralty order, but without success, and finally John Quincy Adams, then resident American minister at The Hague, was sent to London with instructions that if, after every prudent effort, he found it could not be removed, its continuance was not to be an obstacle to the exchange of ratifications. The order was not removed or modified; and indeed ratifications of the treaty were exchanged. (United States Court of Claims 1886, 11)

[153] Louis Charles, Louis XVII, Duke of Normandy, was the younger son of King Louis XVI and Marie Antoinette. Upon the death of his older brother, he became the new Dauphin, heir apparent to the French throne. After the execution of his parents, he was held in Le Temple, a converted 13th century fortress that functioned as the royal prison of Paris. A mere child but the legitimate king of France, his presence on the throne would reconcile the nation to its government and in his name, under a revived Constitution of 1791, the new rulers of France could exercise power without fear of a counter-revolution and therefore without terror. Boissy d'Anglas, whose role during the days of prairial had marked him out as the key man of the new order, was cautiously preparing the way for a return to constitutional monarchy, when, on June 8, 1795, the child on whose life so many hopes for France rested, died of tuberculosis, exacerbated or caused by his ill-usage

lingered for some time past, and of the care that was taken to preserve him. They are aware of the criticisms to which this event may expose them, and suffer, on that account, an additional mortification. His concession to Spain, as was contemplated, made his life, with the government, an object of interest; since it would have forwarded, in some respects, its views in the depending negotiation.

I have just been honored with yours of April 7th, and shall pay due attention to its contents.[154]

I have the honor to be, Sir, with great respect and esteem your very humble serv, Jas Monroe.

P. S. I am sorry to inform you of the death of Mr. Coffyn, consul for the port of Dunkirk. His loss is to be regretted, as he was able, diligent and faithful in the discharge of the duties of his office. His son is very desirous of succeeding him, and certainly if any one, not an American, is appointed, it will be impossible to find for it a more suitable person.[155] In my opinion, however, Americans only should be appointed. In any event, I think the merits of the father, who was distinguished for his services and attachment to our country, entitle his memory to some attention, and doubt not your letter of acknowledgment, addressed to his son on that head, through me, will be gratefully received.

To Thomas Jefferson, Paris, June 23, 1795

Dear Sir,—Your first enquiry will be, upon what basis does the revolution rest? Has it yet weathered the storms that have beaten against it, and taking all circumstances into view that merit consideration, is there ground for a well founded hope that it will terminate happily for France & of course for mankind? I will give you concisely the actual state of things, by comparing

---

in prison. Numerous conspiracy theories surrounded the death of Louis XVII. (Cobban 1961, 241-242)

[154] In the letter Randolph had stated, "the invariable policy of the President is to be as independent as possible, of every nation upon earth; and this policy is not assumed now for the first time...but it is wise at all times, and if steadily pursued, will protect our country from the effects of commotion in Europe.... [W]ithout a steady adherence to principles no Government can defend itself against the animadversions of the world, nor procure a permanent benefit to its own citizens." (Clifford 1972, 303)

[155] At the beginning of the American Revolution, Francis Coffyn was appointed by the American commissioners at Paris to be their agent at Dunkirk. In 1777, he assisted with the transshipment of two cargoes of gunpowder to Philadelphia—which arrived when the Continental army had barely three rounds left. He also helped in the shipment of numerous brass field cannons, all of which were safely received at various American ports. He was appointed American Consul at Dunkirk, December 10, 1794, but died shortly thereafter. He was succeeded, however, by his son, of the same name, who held the office for many years. (Ingram 1929, 4)

which with those great events which have preceeded and are known every-where, you will be enabled to form as correct a judgment upon that point as can now be formed upon it.156

To say that the Convention maintains its authority over the whole inte-rior of the republick, notwithstanding its late difficulties, would give you but a superficial view of the subject, without developing in some degree the nature and probable consequences of those difficulties. Internal convulsions where they happen try the strength of parties, and demonstrate what their real object is, as well as that of the society in general, in regard to the points in controversy. Fortunately such have happened here, and of a character to furnish respectable data whereon to calculate not only the strength of parties, but likewise the probable issue of the revolution itself. Fortunately, permit me to say, for as political truths depend upon experiment, so we have reason to rejoice in those experiments which prove what it is the wish and the interest of mankind to see proven.

Within less than two months past I have seen the Convention twice assailed by a considerable force and which was in the latter instance armed, & upon both those occasions, have seen that force foiled, in the first without the effusion of blood, and in the second by the death of one man (Ferrand, a deputy) only. Many circumstances too were combined to make those move-ments formidable and to create a belief that they would shake the revolution; if there existed in the society a force able and willing to shake it: for the first took place at the moment when the city was agitated by a twofold crisis of famine, & the trial of Billaud de Varennes, Collot d'Herbois & Barrere, leading members of the mountain party: and the second, when the famine was at the height and the distress of the people beyond what was ever seen on our side of the Atlantic. For several hours on both days, the proceedings of the Convention were interrupted, & on the last the rioters were in abso-lute possession of the hall and in a great measure of the government itself:

---

156 Monroe was eager to allay concerns in America that the French Revolution might have strayed too far from the American path and descended into chaos. He minimized the impact of two consecutive uprisings and, with significant candor, forwarded Jefferson this optimistic "Sketch of the State of Affairs in France." Here, Monroe once again predicted the revolution's fast approaching "happy close. under a government founded upon principles which when completed and resting firm, must cause a similar revolution everywhere." Later, Monroe would also send copies of this letter to Aaron Burr, George Logan, Robert R. Livingston, and John Beckley, and asked them to have it published anonymously in the *Aurora*, in order that the community at large might be more correctly informed of the progress of the revolution than they would be from reading British publi-cations. However, Monroe's letter to Logan fell into the hands of the new secretary of state, Timothy Pickering, who would forward it to President Washington as "proofs of sinister designs," along with the cabinet's recommendation for Monroe's recall. (Ziesche 2010, 104)

so that in truth the superiority of active force was on their side, and danger only on the side of the members and the friends of the government. At such a moment as this, when the functions of the government were suspended, or exercised by the insurgents only, there was surely a fair opportunity for those who were in favor of a change, to pronounce themselves on that side: and the presumption is reasonable that all those who were in favor of it, or at least who were willing to hazard anything in support of it, did pronounce themselves on that side. It was the epoch upon which foreign powers and the royalists had fixed their attention & upon which it was understood they would unite their efforts to bring about a counter-revolution nor was there any army at hand or other force to oppose the enterprise than the citizens of Paris itself. Upon a fair appeal, therefore, to the interest and the wishes of the in habitants of this city, the issue was put, and the experiment in both cases and particularly the last proved that the strength of those who were for a counter revolution was, comparatively with that of those against it, like that of an infant against Hercules. Upon the first occasion the commotion was crushed, before the movers in it got the ascendancy, but upon the second it was otherwise, so that their force was fairly ascertained & shewn to be nothing.

Nor was the issue more unfavorable to royalty, if we may judge from what appeared, than the success of the party would have been if it had succeeded: for the principle upon which the movement was undertaken by the great mass of those who acted in it, was not to favor royalty but to oppose it, being impressed with an opinion that the prevailing party were disposed to re-establish that species of government, and against which they declared themselves affirming that their object was, liberty to the patriots (the members of the mountain party who were under prosecution) & the establishment of the constitution of 1793 & which certainly has in it none of the attributes of royalty.

In the course of these commotions the royalists did not display them-selves to advantage: they shewed neither enterprise nor decision. In the commencement they were active by intrigue only, fomenting, by all the means in their power, the discontents of the laborious poor, and which proceeded from the famine which oppressed them, contrasting their present distress with the abundant ease of former times &c. &c., but when the moment of danger arrived, they took no part so as to make themselves responsible in case the effort failed. And upon the latter occasion, when the party got possession of the convention and began for a while to rule, & were about to re-establish terrorism and not royalty, the royalists shifted their ground in a moment and became very vociferous against popular commotions, &

equally pathetic in support of the Convention & of the law, which a few hours before they disdained and endeavoured to subvert. In truth they saw that their own safety was involved in that of the Convention, and in consequence became interested in the welfare of that body from the strongest of all possible motives, a regard for themselves.

Upon the whole, therefore, I am of opinion that these movements have tended rather to strengthen than to weaken the foundation of the revolution, for they have shewn that the mountain party which so long governed France, altho' it has latterly lost its influence, has not abandoned its principles, and that if it had recovered its authority, it would not have introduced royalty but on the contrary a greater degree of rigor against the royalists than humanity al lows, or the present preponderating party is disposed to exercise. Of this truth even the avowed royalists are already admonished; is it not, therefore, reason able to conclude that those who were before wavering what part to take will for the future, cease to hesitate.

But you will ask is there not a party in the Convention itself favorable to monarchy, are not some of the leading members in the preponderating party inclined to that system of government? If the fact were so, these late movements would have a tendency to check that bias: but I have no reason to think that the fact is so, with many I am personally acquainted, and from what I have seen of their conduct, for some time past, in publick and in private life, I can assure you that whilst I have nothing to say against any of these members, I consider many of them as among the most enthusiastic admirers and advocates of the pub lick liberty that I have ever known. I have seen them too in situations where it was impossible to dissemble. Time &circumstances, it is true, may produce changes, & against which I do not pretend to reason: I only argue from data within my view, & deduce those consequences from them which according to the ordinary course of events are probable. So much then upon the state of parties and their respective views, & by which it appears that the publick liberty will not be endangered under the auspices of either.

In other respects the prospect has become more favorable to a happy termination of the revolution than was heretofore promised. The people of France may conquer their liberties & merit to be free, but without a good government it will be impossible to preserve them. This truth has latterly been more deeply impressed upon the Convention than it formerly was, and in consequence the attention of that body seems now to be principally turned to that object, a committee consisting of 11 members having been appointed for more than six weeks past, to report what changes it will be necessary in their judgment to make in the existing one of 1793 & whose report is daily expected. It is believed that this committee will propose some important changes in that constitution and that the Convention will adopt them, such as a division of the legislature into two branches &c. after the model of the American constitutions. I have heard many deputies confer on this subject & who were unanimous in favor of this change, & which is certainly of greater importance to the preservation of their liberty than any other that has been spoken of. As soon as this report is presented, I will transmit it to you.

The external view is still more favorable. The achievements of the last campaign surpassed every thing that the modern world has witnessed: in every quarter their arms were triumphant, but where the greatest danger pressed there the grandeur of their exploits was most conspicuous. Spain and Holland bear testimony in favor of this assertion, for the close of the campaign left the republick in possession of extensive territories belonging to the former & of the whole of the latter. The armies of the Emperor, too, were often beaten & finally forced to abandon the field. Those of Prussia experienced upon several occasions the like fate; & as for the British, they retreated till they came back upon sea, where hurrying on board the ships that were prepared to receive them, they took their flight upon the element upon which alone they could hope for safety. From these successes you have already seen that France has gained the most solid and durable advantages. From an enemy Holland has become a friend and ally. In that country the government only was conquered & by whose conquest the people became free: for upon the ruins of the miserable oligarchal tyranny which reigned there, we find a sister republick reared, marshalled by the side of France, & preparing to fight with her for the common liberty of the two people. Prussia has withdrawn from the war and is now in the closest amity with France. Spain is negotiating & will probably soon have peace. Austria is known to wish it, & England has absolutely made overtures secretly thro' the medium of Sr. Fk. Eden, whilst the ostensible object of his mission was an exchange of prisoners only. Exploits like these become a free people, nor are any but a free people able to perform them.

Such was the actual state of things when the campaign was lately opened on the part of France by the achievement of Luxembourg one of the best fortified and strongest posts in the world. The siege was closely continued for more than six months, and finally succeeded after the provision was exhausted & it was seen that the coalised powers could not raise it. At this post 12,000 men were taken with great amount in cannon & other warlike stores. Upon Mayence the whole pressure now is, nor is it probable that that garrison will long be able to sustain itself. Upon Spain also some recent advantage has been gained: indeed it is well known that the troops of this republick can make what impression they please in that quarter.

Under these circumstances it is not probable that the war will be long continued upon the continent. The coalised powers have latterly placed their only hope, in the possibility of a counter-revolution here, upon account of the dissentions in the publick councils, & the scarcity of bread: but the late events & which I have already communicated, will shew how unproductive a resource the former has been and promises to be; and the revolution of a few weeks only, within which space the harvest will ripen, will I think likewise demonstrate that the latter was not less so. The war then will soon be narrowed to a contest between this republick and England, I mean such is the present prospect, & this will of course be a maritime one only, unless the former succeeds & in which case, the government of England will be conquered as that of Holland was. Among the maritime powers there is not one (unless Russia forms an exception & which is not absolutely certain) which does not wish to see the naval force of England broken or at least greatly diminished: whereas on the side of France there is Holland already embarked and Den mark & Sweden are unquestionably in the same interest; nor is it improbable that past and present injuries may force them to declare in support of it, for latterly the orders of the 6th. of Novr. have been revived by the Ct. of St. James, for seizing all neutral vessels laden with provision for France & under which many have been seized of theirs as well as ours. It is likewise probable that Spain will eventually be on the same side, for as she wishes not only to get rid of the war, but to revive with France her ancient connection, and which contains on the part of France a guarantee of the Spanish possessions in So. America, and which it will otherwise be difficult to accomplish, I cannot well perceive how Spain will be able to avoid declaring herself on the side of France. Such is the external & internal state of things, & upon which you will be able to form your own conjectures of the probable issue.

But you demand what ground does America occupy upon this great and interesting scene of affairs? How does she stand in the estimation of her generous & victorious ally? As we were never called on to bear a part in the controversy upon the issue of which ours as well as her liberty was dependant, but were left to enjoy in peace the abundant fruits of our industry, whilst she defied the storm alone, I am not surprised that you should feel solicitous upon this point. A few lines will give the sketch you wish. Preceding unfavorable impressions, and which were known to exist, were erased by the declarations of the present minister when he was introduced into the Convention, supported by the documents which he presented, and upon which basis the ancient and close amity which had formerly subsisted was rapidly reviving and growing up. Some changes of importance were accomplished in our commercial affairs with this republick, and in particular the treaty of amity &commerce, which in pursuit of the policy of England had been violated, was put in activity, & whereby our trade is not only free in every article (strict contraband excepted) & to every country even to England herself, altho' it furnished her with the most productive means for the support of the war, but likewise the trade of England is protected under our flag, & whilst it yields no protection to that of France. Such was the actual state of things when the report of Mr. Jay's treaty with the English government transpired, and by which it was circulated that a new connection was formed between the United States & that power, beneficial to the latter & probably hurtful to France. This report operated like a stroke of thunder & produced upon all France amazement. What the treaty really is, is not yet known, but most certainly the bias in our favor has been greatly diminished, nor is it possible that the cordiality should be great under such circumstances. If the treaty is rejected, or contains in it nothing strictly objection able, in either case we shall stand well here: but if it is adopted and does contain any thing which a just criticism can censure, be assured we shall hear from this government in terms of reproach. By this time you know what the treaty is, and therefore know according to its fate in what light we shall be considered here. If the treaty is not precisely what we wished it to be, most certainly the most favorable opportunity that was ever offered to make a good one, has been thrown away: for as France was successful, & a good understanding subsisted between us and France, it was really in our power to dictate what terms we pleased, provided we could make the English government believe that in any event we would take part against it. Accomplishing that point, everything would have been accomplished; for of all possible calamities with which they are threatened, a war with us is that which they most dread: not so much indeed from the fear of our maritime force, as the effect it would produce upon their commerce by which alone they are enabled to support a war. Such was the actual state of things at the time this treaty was formed, but a new scene has since been opened and which will shew how little confidence we ought to place in treaties with that power. For latterly and as I presume in violation of that treaty the same system of depredation & of plunder has been recommenced.

By the above hasty but true picture of affairs here you will perceive that this republick is rapidly rising or rather has already obtained a decided preponderance not only in the scale of Europe but indeed in that of human affairs. Having combatted alone and with success all the great powers of

Europe, the superiority of her strength over theirs, at least whilst that of the latter is weilded by the heavy and expensive governments which exist there, is well established. Nor is it probable that this superiority will be soon diminished especially when it is considered that the revolution of the one is approaching fast to a happy close, under a government founded upon principles which when completed and resting firm, must cause a similar revolution every where. To stand well with this republick is therefore now the interest of all nations, nor indeed do any of them seem at the present moment to entertain a contrary opinion: for they have all made approaches and shewn their solicitude for peace, notwithstanding they know the danger that will probably overwhelm them in that event and especially if France gets a good government, since they deem that danger more remote and less terrible than the one which immediately threatens under the pressure of the French armies. Upon every principle, therefore, it were greatly to be regretted if America should lose in any degree the ground upon which she hath heretofore stood in the estimation of her ally.

To the Secretary of State [Edmund Randolph], Paris, June 26, 1795

Sir,—Since my last, it is reduced to a certainty, that the British government has revived its order of the 6th of November, 1793, and commenced, on this side of the Atlantic, the same system of warfare and pillage upon our commerce, that was practised on it by that government, at that very calamitous area. Between 30 and 40 sail destined for the ports of this Republic, charged with provisions, have been already taken from their destination, and carried into those of that Island: and: as the period has arrived, when the invitation which the distresses of this country gave to our merchants here and at home, to embark their fortunes in this supply, is likely to produce its effect, it is more than probable that other vessels, and to a great amount, will share the like fate. Among those of our merchants who are here, this measure has created a kind of panic; for they think they see in its consequences little less than the ruin of their trade; and under which impression many are about to abandon it for the present, and send their vessels home in ballast.[157]

---

[157] Monroe's seems to be referring to a naval engagement that occurred just three days before, on June 23, when Lord Bridport, commander of the British Channel Fleet with 14 ships of the line, sighted a French squadron of nine ships of the line under Admiral Villaret Joyeuse, which immediately retreated towards Lorient. A general engagement began when the British overtook the French near Île de Groix off the Breton coast. The French failed to maintain a cohesive formation and three of their ships surrendered. Bridport, content merely to claim these prizes, broke off action, enabling Villaret Joyeuse to reach Lorient with his remaining force. (Fremont-Barnes 2007, 79)

What effect this measure will produce upon this government, under existing circumstances, I cannot pretend to determine. Formerly it adopted the same measure, for the purpose of counteracting its enemy; but the impolicy of that procedure was afterwards discussed and demonstrated, and the measure itself, in consequence, abandoned. At present, the distress of the country is great, and the government will, no doubt, be mortified to find, that, whilst our flag gives no protection to its goods, nor even to our goods, destined for the ports of this Republic, the whole of which become the spoil of its enemy; that it does protect not only our goods destined for the English ports, but likewise British goods destined equally for those, and the ports of other countries. The measure has obviously excited a kind of ferment in their councils; but which, I presume, will be directed against their enemies only. Be assured I shall do every thing in my power to give it that direction, and to enforce those arguments which were used upon the former occasion: But, should they fail in producing the de sired effect, and a less amicable policy be adopted, which, however, I think will not be the case, I shall deem it my duty immediately to advise you of it, by a vessel (in case none other offers) to be despatched for the purpose.

It will obviously attract your attention, that this measure was so timed by the British cabinet, that it might have no influence in the decision of the senate upon the treaty of Mr. Jay; nor can the motive for such an accommodation be less doubtful; for in case it be rejected, they will deem the stroke a lucky one; since thereby, they will say, they had fortunately gained so much time; and if it be adopted, they will probably presume, that so much time will be consumed in convening the Congress, should that measure be deemed expedient, that the course of events here may render it impossible for our efforts to produce a favorable effect; and which consideration, they will likewise infer, will be an argument against convening the Congress.[158]

---

[158] Upon receipt of the document, President Washington had called a special session of Congress that the Senate might consider the treaty. From June 8 until June 24, 1795, the Senate debated Jay's handiwork. But the public knew nothing of the terms of the treaty as both its provisions and the Senate debates were secret. For the most part, the friends of the treaty dominated affairs in the Senate. Yet on the morning of June 24, Senator Henry Tazewell of Virginia introduced a series of resolutions urging the rejection of the treaty. It ought to be defeated, argued Tazewell, because it "hath not secured that satisfaction from the British Government for the removal of negroes, in violation of the treaty of 1783"; because "the rights of the individual States, are by the 9th article of the treaty [which assured the restoration of confis-cated loyalist property], unconstitutionally invaded"; because "the Treaty asserts a Power in the President and Senate, to controul & even annihilate the constitutional right of the Congress of the United States over their commercial intercourse with foreign nations"; because the treaty was likely to damage Franco–American rela-tions; and because it destroyed American independence from Great Britain. Herein were the basic arguments which the treaty's opponents were to refer to again and

This kind of policy, however, shews not only the profligacy, but the desperation of that government, and will probably precipitate the crisis, which, notwithstanding all its follies and enormities, might yet have been postponed for some time to come. I think the measure will give new vigor to the French councils, and will probably bring immediately upon its authors, Denmark and Sweden: Upon this latter point, however, I am authorized to say nothing; for, as I was not instructed to confer with the representatives of those powers here, I have carefully avoided several conferences, that were sought of me by Baron Stahl from Sweden, soon after his arrival; because I knew nothing could result from them, and was fearful, as I presumed the result would be known to the committee, it might produce an ill effect there.

Your measures will, no doubt, be greatly influenced by the probability of the early termination or continuance of the war with this Republic, and upon which some information will of course be expected from me. You will, however, perceive the disadvantage under which I must give any opinion upon that point, and estimate it accordingly; for as I am authorized to say nothing to this government of what we will probably do, in case the war continues (for the revival of the order of the 6th November could not be foreseen) you will of course conclude it is impossible for me to sound it upon that topic. Indeed I was fearful that, by my former communications upon a similar occasion, slight and informal as they were, I might embarrass you, and was therefore extremely uneasy on that account, after I heard of Mr. Jay's treaty, and until I had obtained a conference with the committee on the subject. My judgment must, therefore, be formed upon general and external circumstances, and by which I perceive no prospect of an early accommodation of the war between France and England. On the contrary, the preparations on both sides seem to go on with all possible activity, for its continuance. The fleet of England is said to be raised to a height beyond what it ever attained before, and efforts are still making to keep it there, if not to increase it: And France is exerting her utmost endeavours to increase hers, and which are the more necessary, in con sequence of the improvident excursions of the last winter, by which it was greatly injured in the Atlantic, as well as the Mediterranean sea. 'Tis expected, that by a continuance of those endeavours, the Brest fleet will be ready to take the sea by the fall: The Mediterranean is said now to be at sea, and in good order. 'Tis likewise expected that the

---

again: its failure to obtain compensation for stolen slaves, its revival of loyalist property claims, its infringement upon congressional control of foreign trade, its potentially damaging effects upon the friendship of France and the United States, and especially its realignment of the United States within the British sphere. Federalist forces easily defeated the Tazewell resolutions, and that afternoon the Senate consented to the treaty with England. (Farnham 1967, 76)

Dutch fleet, at least to the amount stipulated, will be in readiness in time to co-operate with that from Brest; for great efforts were latterly made, and are still making, by that government, to equip it. Add to these the fact (and I am assured by unquestionable authority that it is one) that the overtures made by Sir F[rederick Morton] Eden were repulsed, and in a manner which immediately closed, under the powers possessed by the parties respectively, all further conference on the subject. From consideration, therefore, of these circumstances, I am led to conclude that the war between these powers will be continued for some time to come, and most probably till some change, by battle or otherwise, is wrought in the fortunes of one or both, so as to dispose them for peace.

If Denmark and Sweden, and especially if they are joined by Spain, unite with France and Holland, they will probably have the preponderance and must bear hard upon England. In any event, the enormous expence to which she is unprofitably exposed, if continued for any time, must not only exhaust her resources, but excite great discontents among the people. They have been allayed latterly, by the assurances of the minister, that the people of France would be starved, and that the government must in consequence accommodate, and which were countenanced by the movements which took place here sometime after those assurances were given. But when it is seen that the crisis has passed, and that the people after bearing unexampled distress, and upon the whole with unexampled patience, are quiet and in the possession of the fruits of a plentiful harvest, as promises soon to be the case, it is doubtful whether a change will not soon take place in the temper of those on the other side of the channel.

What part it becomes our country to take at this crisis belongs not to me to say. Peace is a blessing which ought not to be wantonly thrown away. But whether sufficient sacrifices have not been already made to preserve it, and the time arrived, when the duty we owe to ourselves, and the respect which is due to the opinion of the world, admonish us that the insults and injuries of Britain are to be no longer borne, and that we ought to seek redress by again appealing to arms, and putting the issue of our cause upon the event of war, is a point which will no doubt be wisely decided by those who have a right to decide it. Permit me, however, to express a wish, that in case any active measure is taken, or likely to be taken, in consequence of these aggressions, that you will immediately apprise me of it; that I may, without delay, begin to make a correspondent impression upon the councils of this government.

I omitted in my last to transmit to you a copy of the letter from Mr. Short, which I mentioned was shewn to Mr. Pinckney; and which, as it demonstrates how completely we may command success in our demands upon Spain, provided France aids us in that respect, ought not to be withheld, and especially in the present state of affairs. I make to you the communication with greater pleasure; because at the same time that it furnishes a document of importance for you to possess, it will reflect honor on Mr. Short, upon account of the able and comprehensive view he has taken of the subject.

I have the pleasure to inform you, that the committee of 11. have at length reported a plan of Government, of which I herewith enclose you a copy. The discussion upon the merits will commence in a few days, and as soon as the question is finally decided I will transmit to you the result.

With great respect and esteem I have the honour to be, Sir, your very h and ob serv, Jas Monroe.

To Thomas Jefferson, Paris, June 27, 1795

Dear Sir,—Of the above hasty view I have sent a copy to one or two other friends. Since it was written the Committee of 11 have reported a plan of govt. as suggested of 2 branches, the one to be called a council of 500, consisting of so many members, the other of 250, called the council of ancients.[159] The age of the 1st to be 30 & of the 2d 40. They are to be chosen each for 2 years but to be supplied annually by halves. The Executive to be composed of 5 members to be elected for 5 years, but so arranged that only one withdraws annually. Each member is to have a salary of abt. £5000 sterg. pr. ann. the object whereof to receive & entertain foreign ministers &c. The council of ancients cannot originate a bill. If possible I will procure & send you a copy of the plan.

The British have recommenc'd the seizure of our vessels as formerly under the order of the 6th of Novr. 1793, near 40 being carried in by our last & which were the first accts. This has produced an extreme ferment here, & it will be difficult under the irritation existing in consequence of Jay's treaty, to prevent a revival of the same practice on the part of France.[160] And if we do nothing when it is known in America, but abuse the English and drink toasts to the success of the French revolution, I do not know what

---

[159] The "plan of government" was included in the new constitution of the first French Republic that was drawn up by the National Convention during the last year of its session and after it had passed under bourgeois influence. This constitution went into effect in 1795 and is known, therefore, as the Constitution of the Year III (of the Republic). In it, the bourgeois distrust of the lower classes showed itself again by restricting the electorate only to taxpayers who had lived in one place for at least a year. (Hayes 1916, 512)

[160] A secret order-in-council was issued to British naval officers on April 25, 1795, instructing them to seize all provision ships which they may have reason to believe were bound for France. (Rice 1937, 474-475)

step they will take in regard to us. My situation since the report of Mr. Jay's treaty has been painful beyond any thing ever experienc'd before, and for reasons you can readily conceive, I have, however, done everything in my power to keep things where they shod. be, but how long this will be practicable under existing circumstances I know not. Denmark & Sweden will I think be active.

I have just received a letter from Mr. Derieux[161] with one for his aunt; if possible I will now answer it; but in case I cannot, I beg you to tell him that I waited on her last fall with Mrs. Monroe, having previously written her repeatedly in his behalf, & after a long and earnest solicitation in his favor & returned without obtaining any thing for him. She had promised something before I went, & the dinner she gave us, was to pave the way for retracting & which she did. The old lady has about her (as I suspect) some persons who are poor, & who prefer their own welfare to his. By the law of France the property cannot be devised from her relations, but 'tis possible these people will help to consume the annual profits; which latter, however, she says in consequence of the depreciation are nothing.

We wish most sincerely to get back & shall certainly do it, as soon as a decent respect for appearances will permit, especially if the present system of policy continues. I wish much to hear from you having written you several times but recd. not a line since my appointment here. Is there any thing in this quarter you wish to command of books or any other article; or can I serve you in any respect whatever? You will of course command me if I can be serviceable.

I have requested Mr. Madison to shew you some letters of mine to him. I wish to know much in what state my farms are. We are well: our child speaks French well & she & Mrs. M. desire to be affectionately remembered to yourself & daughters, to whom as well as to Mr. R. & Mr. C. as likewise to my brother & neighbours be so kind as remember me.

With great respect & esteem I am, Dear Sir, yr. affectionate friend, Jas Monroe.

---

[161] J Justin Pierre Derieux was the son-in-law of Philip Mazzei, an Italian historian who was also a close friend and neighbor of Jefferson. After serving in the bodyguard of Louis XVI, Derieux emigrated to America in 1784, settling on an estate near Monticello. He seems to have been pursued by misfortune, such as real estate disputes and exploitation by unscrupulous entrepreneurs, but Mazzei does not appear to have acted with justice towards him. Jefferson, Madison, and Monroe were equally interested in his welfare and made many appeals in his behalf. (Hamilton 1899, 341; Jefferson 1908, 20)

To James Madison, Paris, June 30, 1795

Dear Sir,—I send herewith a copy of the constitution reported by the committee of 11 & which will be discussed in the course of a few days. A doubt arises with many upon the propriety of the Executive organiz'n, & some wish and with a view of strengthening it that the number be reduc'd to 3; but this wo'd certainly produce the opposite effect, for the annual rotation by the withdrawal of one & the speedy shift of all, w'h wo'd follow the change, wo'd in a great measure prevent the existence of an esprit de corps & that system of Executive operation, w'h the plan in the draft admits of: for with only three the preponderance of the legislature wo'd be complete, especially when it is considered that they are to be elected by the legislature. For my own part, however, I do not think either plan really dangerous; but I wo'd prefer having 6 members, changing 2 annually, the presiding members losing the right of voting. This wo'd be safer upon every principle. But I have no time to criticize.

You will be surprised to hear that the only Americans whom I found here were a set of New England men connected with Britain and who, upon British capital, were trading to this country: that they are hostile to the French revolution is what you well know: but that they sho'd be thriving upon the credit which the efforts of others in other quarters gain the American name here you could not expect: that as such they should be in possession of the little confidence we had and give a tone to characters on our side of the Atlantic was still less to be expected. But such was the fact. With a few exceptions the other merchants are new made citizens from Scotland. Swan who is a corrupt unprincipled rascal had by virtue of being the Agent of France and as we had no minister & he being (tho' of the latter description) the only or most creditable resident American here, had a monopoly of the trade of both countries. Indeed it is believed that he was connected with the agents on one side and the Minister on the other. I mention this as a trait worth your attention. You will confide the view to Mr. Jefferson only. But good may come from it, and especially if the allurement here will draw them off from the other side of the channel.

I candidly think if we bear this aggression from Engl'd without an immediate decl'n, at least by the seizure of all her property, ships, certificates &ca., that our reputation is gone beyond recovery, most certainly it will be difficult & the work of time to recover it. We shall certainly lose our estimation here. If we were to take the measure suggested, of seizing British property, prohibiting the importation of her goods & which I wish was perpetual, laying hold of the ports, fitting out privateers &c we sho'd indemnify ourselves & incur but a trilling expense: for Brit'n wo'd not land a single soldier on our coast &

wo' d be driven to extremities. But if we are amused, we are deceived & will be despis'd. I am told that the most humiliating explanation & apology was made to Bernstorff[162] for the measure at the moment the order was issued. But it is thought he will show more decision & respect for the character of his country than to be the dupe of such finesse. Probably the same thing is done with us, but surely we are not sunk so far as to bear it.

With great esteem & respect I am y'r friend & servant, Jas Monroe.

To the Committee of Public Safety, Paris, July 5, 1795

Citizens,—The injuries which the piratical powers on the African coast have rendered and continued to render to our commerce, are known to this Republic; because it takes an interest in our welfare, and because those injuries cannot otherwise than be eventually hurtful to the commerce of France likewise.[163,164]

It was foreseen, at the moment when we became an independent nation, that we should be exposed to the piracies of those powers; and the spirit of amity which disposed the then councils of France, in obedience to the wishes of the people, to aid us in that struggle, disposed them likewise to assure us of their support in our negotiations with each respectively. But unfortunately no treaty has yet been formed with any of those powers (Morocco excepted) and in consequence our commerce has been interrupted by their cruizers and especially those of Algiers; whereby many of our citizens were also taken, and who are now detained in slavery.

It is the wish of the United States to make an effort, at this present moment, to conclude a peace with those several powers, and to pursue that object in harmony with this Republic, that its aid may be extended to them in their negotiations with each; and for which purpose I have now the pleasure to in. form you, that Mr. Humphreys, minister of the United States at Lisbon, has just arrived here with full power to commence and conclude such treaties. It may be necessary further to premise, that suitable provision

[162] Count Andreas Peter von Bernstorff, Danish Minister for Foreign Affairs and President of the German Chancery. (Hamilton 1974, 111)

[163] For months, Monroe had sought French assistance in negotiations with the Barbary States over their ceaseless preying on American shipping. He stressed that French intercession was good not only for American interests, but that "some other powers" [any Frenchman could guess who they were] "would not be pleased to see us at peace with these regencies." (McGrath 2020, 149)

[164] On July 4, 1795, the day before this missive, Monroe had sought to win the hearts, souls, and stomachs of French government officials with the first celebration of American Independence Day ever held at an American embassy. He invited members of the Convention, the government, the diplomatic corps, and prominent Americans in Paris to the sumptuous affair. (Unger 2011, 120)

has been made for those treaties, according to our idea of what would be suitable, and so far as we were able to make it; and of course, that the only aid which we wish from this Republic is that of its good offices and influence in the councils of those powers.

If the committee is disposed to render us this aid, our future measures will be in concert with the committee; because it best knows how it may be most efficaciously rendered, and with least inconvenience to itself. In that view we will be happy to open to the committee our funds, &c. that by knowing completely our real situation, the concert and harmony may be perfectly complete; and in consequence the best arrangements taken, that circumstances will admit of, to ensure success in the negotiations contemplated.

As we have reason to apprehend the interference of some other powers, who would not be pleased to see us at peace with those regencies, permit me to suggest the propriety of great secrecy in respect to the present, and such future, communications as may take place between us, upon this interesting subject.

Jas Monroe.

To the Secretary of State [Edmund Randolph], Paris, July 6, 1795

Sir,—About three or four weeks past, one of our vessels[165] which touched at Havre from England, was taken in charge by the government, and the captain and passengers confined, upon a suspicion they had brought false assignats[166] with them, with a view of circulating them through the country, and thereby subserving the views of its enemies. Complete search was made upon the vessel, but no assignats were found. As I knew that the suspicion which was entertained, ought not to be extended to three young men who were passengers, I immediately applied to the commissary of foreign relations for their dis charge, and obtained an order for it, though fortunately, they were released by the municipality at Havre before it reached them.[167] But as I was not acquainted with the character of the captain, or any others belonging to the vessel, and was aware of the right the government had to protect itself

---

[165] Seized on May 27, 1795, the vessel was the sailing brig *Jane*. The owner and master was Richard Cowell. (Williams 2009, 197)

[166] Assignats were a monetary instrument issued during the time of the French Revolution. The notes were secured by a pledge of productive real estate and bore interest to the holder at three per cent. (White 1933, 7)

[167] The three individuals were William Bache (Benjamin Franklin 's grandson), William Boys and Adam Leyberts, who were travelling to France for the purpose of pursuing their medical studies. (Hamilton 1899, 318)

from injuries of every kind, and from every quarter, and of course to search the vessel, and as I also hoped in case the suspicion proved to be groundless, it would prevent the like in future, and especially upon frivolous sugges-tions, I did not chuse, in that stage, to apply likewise in their behalf. After the search was made, and the government satisfied it had suspected without cause, the Captain was put at liberty, and the vessel offered back to him. But, being mortified in having been suspected, and as his vessel and cargo were somewhat injured by the search and neglect which ensued his arrestation, he seemed disposed rather to throw the whole upon the government, and demand an indemnity for it, and with which view he lately came here to confer with me. I advised him to gather up what he could of his own prop-erty, and pursue his voyage according to the original destination, limiting his claim merely to the damage sustained, and leaving that to be pursued by the consul here under my direction. As yet he waits his pro test and other docu-ments from Havre, reserving to himself the liberty of acting after their receipt as he pleases, and according as the light of preceding examples of the like kind, and whose details he will in the interim acquire, may admonish him will be most for his interest. I shall endeavour to obtain justice for him upon sound principles, and have only mentioned the case, that you may know such a one has happened, and what the circumstances of it are.

The jealousy which is entertained by this government, of the commerce carried on by our countrymen between the ports of this republic and those of England has latterly shewn itself in a more unpleasant form than heretofore, and I am fearful will yet produce some more disagreeable effect. A Mr. Eldred was lately apprehended at Marseilles, and sent here under guard, upon a charge of having given intelligence to the British of some movement in the French fleet. Upon enquiry I found he had my passport, granted too, upon the most substantial documents, proving him to be an American citizen: But I like wise found that, in truth, he was not an American citizen; for, although born in America, yet he was not there in the course of our revolution, but in England; nor had he been there since. From what I hear of him, he is not a person of mischievous disposition, nor one who would be apt to commit the offence charged upon him, but yet I do not see how I can officially interfere in his behalf; for when once a principle is departed from it ceases to be a principle.

More latterly I was requested by the commissary of foreign affairs, to prohibit our consuls from granting passports, and which was immediately done. I was afterwards requested by him, to furnish a list of the Americans actually in Paris, and to render a like list every decade of those who should in the interim arrive, and which was promised, and will be punctually executed. I herewith send you a copy of my instructions to the consuls, and correspondence with the commissary on this subject.[168]

---

[168] *The Commissary of Foreign Relations to Monroe:* [undated] The commission have had repeated opportunities of being convinced, that American consuls in France, and even sometimes their agents, grant passports or certificates, giving the qualification of citizen of the United States to the bearers of them, and by means of which these travel through France, and even go out into foreign countries.

I cannot help observing to you, that, according to our laws and the laws of nations, foreign ministers having alone the right to grant such passports, and to attest the political existence of the individuals born in their respective countries, those given by the consuls or their agents are totally useless; since, to travel in the interior of the Republic, the passport of the municipality of the place of landing is sufficient, and that to leave the territory, the only admissible passport is that given by the minister of their nation.

I must add, that if the individual who wishes to leave the territory of the Republic has come in consequence of ordinary commercial transactions, he does not need a passport for that purpose; if, on the contrary, he has been brought in by the ships of the Republic, having been found in an enemy's vessel, in that case, his position, which is almost always dubious, deserves attention, and ought to be submitted to the examination and determination of the minister alone.

Persuaded, Sir, that you will find these observations just, and that you will please to communicate them to the consuls of your nation, recommending it to them to conform to them, it is with the fullest confidence that I submit them to you.

Monroe to the Commissary of Foreign Relations: Paris, June 19th, 1795. Your letter of the 22d Prairial communicates to me your observations relative to the passports and certificates granted by different consuls of the United States, and their agents in the ports of the Republic; and agreeable to your desire, I have informed them thereof in my circular letter of the 18th instant, of which I enclose you a copy. I beg you to be persuaded, citizen, of my sincere desire to adopt all such measures as may be deemed necessary to the welfare of this Republic; confident that in so doing, I shall always have the approbation of the government of the United States.

***

Circular to the Consuls of the United States in France: Paris June 18th, 1795. Complaint has been made to me by the commissary of foreign relations, that our consuls, and in some cases their agents, have granted passports and certificates, under the authority of which, the bearers are permitted to travel through the interior of France, and likewise into foreign countries. He observes, that by the law of France, and of nations, no person, other than the minister of a foreign power, has a right to grant such passports; and that it is likewise unnecessary, since, for the interior passage, the passport of the municipality of the port where such persons land is sufficient, and for the exterior, or to go without the Republic, that of the minister alone ought to be granted: For, if the party desirous of withdrawing enters the ports of the Republic in the ordinary course of trade, none is necessary to enable him to withdraw from it; and if he was brought in by the ships of the Republic, taken on board those of its enemies, then his case, which is always doubtful, merits attention, and should be examined, and determined upon the evidence furnished by the minister alone, who is more immediately responsible to the government in that respect. These observations appear to me to be just, and according to the law of nations: I have therefore thought it my duty to make known to you the desire of this government upon that subject, and to request your punctual observance of it.

In those cases where our fellow citizens are permitted to depart from the Republic, by existing decrees, in the ordinary course of trade as above mentioned, but are improperly impeded by some circumstance or other, you will of course observe, by application to the municipality, or other suitable authority, that the benefit of those decrees be extended to them; and in all those cases where my passports are necessary, and the parties are not able to attend here in person, you will be pleased to represent to me their pretensions, provided you think them well founded, with the evidence to support those of each applicant. In such cases it will not be necessary to transmit copies of each certificate or other document laid before you: It will be sufficient that you state in a certificate, under the seal of the consulate, the purport of each item of testimony; by whom furnished, and whether by Americans or foreigners: The former of which are always to be preferred; because, as the citizens of the United States have an interest in the character of their country, so it is to be presumed they will always be on their guard not to injure that character, by imposing on its representative here.

In describing the pretensions of those who ask for passports, you will be pleased to state how they came into the Republic, and what their occupation is: You will likewise observe that as there are two descriptions of persons whose claims are deemed inadmissible by the government here, so it will in general be unnecessary to bring them forward. The first of these consists of those, who having become citizens of some state since our revolution, have left us, and now reside in the country from whence they emigrated; for such persons, being likewise subjects of the power where they were born, ought to be deemed here citizens of that country only, to which they have given the preference by residence. The second consists of those who were refugees in the course of our revolution, and who having never returned, or acquired the right of citizenship since, cannot be deemed citizens, whether born in America or elsewhere. In all doubtful cases, however, you will be pleased to submit the pretensions of the parties to me, that, regarding principles, I may pay all possible attention to them, that circumstances will admit of.

Your ordinary commercial concerns, in which my support may be deemed necessary, I will thank you to communicate with me as heretofore, through Mr. Skipwith the consul in this city: For as he is charged with those concerns, and obtains redress if possible, without my intervention, he is thereby enabled officially to report to me correctly those cases in which he cannot succeed, and of course, in which my interference may be useful; which report forms generally the basis of my application.

***

The Commission of Foreign Affairs to Monroe: June 21st, 1795. The commission has received with your letter of the 1st of this month, the copy of the circular you have been pleased to address to the consuls of the United States in the ports of the Republic. I must beg you to accept my thanks for the attention you have paid to the observations which I thought it my duty to present to you. The manner in which you develop in that circular the principles concerning the preservation of good order, are a new security of your care to maintain it. I could only have wished, that in establishing, as you do, that persons arrived in the ports of the Republic in the common course of commercial transactions, and who wish to leave it, need no passport for that purpose, you had added this restriction, if they are not at a distance from the ports where they landed.

The Commission of Foreign Affairs to Monroe: June 24th, 1795. The commission knowing your readiness to concur in whatever tends to preserve good order, propose to you with confidence the measures which may contribute to that object. They beg you consequently, to be so good as to communicate to them, each decade, a certified list of your fellow citizens arrived in Paris. It is important to the government to know the foreigners who reside in this commune; and it must be advantageous to themselves, that their abode here be known.

Monroe to the Commissary of Foreign Relations: June 27th, 1795. Being extremely solicitous that the rights which my countrymen enjoy here should be strictly confined to themselves alone, I shall be happy at all times to adopt such measures as may be deemed necessary to make known to your government those who are my countrymen. With this view, therefore, I shall, with pleasure, cause to be furnished you every decade the list of those to whom passports or certificates are granted, according to your request. In guarding the welfare of the Republic, I pray you to propose to me always, with freedom, those measures in which my co-operation may be useful; since you may always calculate upon my concurrence, in forwarding an object, which it is upon all occasions my most earnest wish to forward.

The Commission of Foreign Relations to Monroe: July 1st, 1795. The commission has received your letter of the 6th instant; by which you inform them, that, adopting the measure they proposed to you by theirs of the 6th, you are willing to transmit to them each decade the list of your fellow citizens who may have obtained passports. They beg leave to observe to you, that by means of the certificate which they annex to the passports given by the foreign ministers, they have full knowledge of those delivered; but that the request they have made you has for object to know the Americans arrived at Paris, and who cannot but present themselves to you. They beg of you, therefore, to send them a list of these each decade.

The commission has communicated to the committee of public safety, the readiness which you have shewn in whatever tends to preserve good order. The committee fully convinced of your active attention in this respect, has not doubted but that you would favourably regard every means of concurring in it. They consequently direct the commission, to invite you to communicate to them a list of all your fellow citizens now in Paris. The government being thus made acquainted with the Americans that are within this commune, and with those who may arrive hereafter, will be better enabled to secure to them efficaciously the protection which the American government extends to them.

Monroe to the Commissary of Foreign Relations: July 3d, 1795. I have received yours of the 13th Messidor in answer to mine of the 27th of June, and to which I beg leave now to reply.

The note which I wrote to you ought to have comprized those to whom certificates are granted, as well as passports; for to many certificates are granted merely to authorize a residence in Paris, and its vicinity. This change will comprize all those of whose arrival I have, or can have, any knowledge.

It is true, that all the Americans who arrive in Paris ought to call immediately upon me and take the protection to which they are entitled from the minister of their country. But the fact is otherwise; for many never call until they are about to depart, some of whom have thus remained for five, six and eight months. In the interim they are protected by the passports they have from the municipalities in the sea ports, and other authorities which they find adequate: For if they were not adequate, they would of course apply to me, for the protection they otherwise did not enjoy. You will readily perceive that it is my business only to give protection to my countrymen entitled to it; beyond which my authority cannot extend: That it is the business of the government to see that those who are not possessed of that protection, shall not be deemed such, and of course be treated accordingly. I suggest this idea for your consideration, that weighing it you may shew what step I shall take to avoid the inconvenience complained of, if possible on my part; or propose to the committee such measure as will remedy it on theirs.

In case any new regulation is adopted, I beg of you to apprize me of it, that I may give the necessary notice thereof to my countrymen, that they may sustain no injury from a measure which is calculated to secure them the enjoyment of their just rights, by preventing others from imposing themselves upon this government as their compatriots, to the injury of France and the dishonor of America.

I will see that the list of those in Paris be made and furnished you as soon as possible. (Hamilton 1899, 320-324)

You will readily perceive, that this jealousy proceeds from the circum- stance; that many of those, who are actually engaged in this trade, are of that description of persons, who, having latterly become citizens of the United States, are likewise subjects of England; nor can you be surprised when that circumstance is considered, without any imputation on the character of the parties, that this jealousy should exist: They are English themselves, their connections are so, and in England their profits will probably ultimately settle. It is natural that a communication of this kind should draw after it suspicion, or rather it would be unnatural if it did not produce that effect. To the people of America this is an evil of serious import: For by it, it is obvious, that the confidence which is due to our national character is daily dimin- ished. Nor can the mortification which is incident to such a situation, be otherwise than heightened, when it is considered, that we are most a prey to this evil, at the moment when the government to which these persons belong insults our national dignity, and tramples on our rights. Be assured I shall do everything in my power to guard us against injuries of this kind, by excluding all who are not, and upon the principles agreed upon my first arrival here, strictly entitled to our protection; and by which line of con duct I hope I shall succeed, in a great measure if not altogether, in the accomplish- ment of an object so important to our welfare.

As connected with this subject, permit me to mention another, which I deem equally important, and more remediable. We have at Hamburg, as consul for the United States, a Mr. Parish[169] and who has held that office for some years past. This gentleman is an English subject, and was, as I am assured, never in America. All the Americans who have been at Hamburg and who come here unite in representing him to be (comparatively with England) as unfriendly to America; as absolutely unfriendly to France and the French revolution, and which traits are said to be often discernible in his public conduct. It is affirmed, that he is likewise an agent of England, and that, in particular, the Prussian subsidy passed through his hands. Upon these facts you may rely (and especially the latter, into which I have made more pointed enquiry) for they are agreed in by all the Americans, and, I am sure, have been stated to me by at least 50. Without observing how wide a door is here opened for England to benefit herself, and injure France through us, even whilst its use is confined to that range, which, without any impu- tation on the morality of this gentleman, national prejudice alone would allow, there are other considerations, which, at the present moment, make this appointment worthy your attention. Since the commencement of the

---

[169] John Parish, native of Great Britain, was confirmed by the Senate February 20, 1793. (Hamilton 1899, 325)

present war, a great proportion of the commerce of the north, and from every quarter of the world, has centered at Hamburg, and will probably continue to center there, till its close; from whence it issues again in different directions: France, Holland, England, &c, &c. That this commerce is capable of a serious impression by the public agents of different countries there, and especially by those of the neutral powers, whose connection is sought with great avidity by the subjects of the powers at war, cannot be questioned; nor can it be questioned, when it is considered who this gentleman is, that the impression which he makes upon it is a British and not an American one. In addition to which it may be observed, that as he resides in the dominions of an independent power, and where we have no Minister, it is in some measure his duty to grant passports to Americans travelling elsewhere. This circumstance, therefore, and especially at the present moment, increases the importance and delicacy of the trust. In justice, however, to this gentleman I must add, that I do not know any instance in which he has betrayed it in this respect, and that, in others, I only apply to him general principles, and bring to your view the complaints of our countrymen. Personally, I never saw or had any communication with him. There are at present at Hamburg several Americans worthy of this trust, among whom are Joel Barlow and William A. St. John, son of him who, by his writings, is well known; but, in truth, so profitable is the post, that there are but few American merchants in Europe who would not accept it. In general, permit me to suggest for your consideration; whenever a vacancy takes place, or whenever it becomes necessary to supercede an existing Consul, whether it would not be advisable to advertise the fact, that candidates might offer for the post; for sure I am, that it would rarely happen that suitable candidates, American citizens, did not offer. In Europe such may generally be found.[170]

Since my last, the French have sustained a loss at sea of three ships, which arose partly from accident not to be guarded against, and partly from misconduct. It occasioned the immediate dismission of Dalbarade,[171] minister of marine, who gave way to a successor believed to be better qualified for the post. The British have likewise landed on the French coast near Nantes, about 6,000 emigrants, and who being joined perhaps with some of their own troops, and since by some fanatic priests, are said to make up a force

---

[170] Monroe later received a June 13, 1796, letter from Secretary of State Timothy Pickering [who replaced Randolph] stating, "On full consideration of the case of the Consulate Hamburg the President has determined to make a change, as soon as a proper person can be found to supply the place of Mr. Parish; the substitute if possible to be an American citizen." (Hamilton 1899, 327)

[171] Jean Dalbarade was a brilliant privateer whom, shortly after his appointment as Minister of Marine, found himself simply overcome by the size of the task before him. (Fremont-Barnes 2006, 380)

of about 10,000 men. It is supposed the British government might hope, that by putting these people in the neighbourhood of the Chouans or Ven deans, they might, by encouraging a rebellion there, combine a force capable of making some impression: But a wish to rid themselves of these unfortu-nate men, whose support became daily more burdensome, is believed to be the more influential motive. All parties unite here in the sentiment that they are sacrificed, and consider the act of landing them, as an act of barbarity, excelled only by those which were formerly perpetrated in the same neigh-bourhood by the infatuated Carrier.

It is believed that a treaty has taken place between England and Russia, in which the former has stipulated not to take the side of Poland against the latter; in consideration whereof, Russia is to furnish England a certain number of ships during the residue of the war.[172] It is likewise believed, that England has announced to Spain, that in case the latter makes peace with France, she will commence immediate hostilities upon her. This may possibly keep Spain in a state of suspence some time longer. On the other hand it is obvious, that the connection between France and Holland, Denmark and Sweden becomes daily stronger; whilst Austria, paralized by the peace and movements of Prussia, which threaten an entire change in the Germanic system, and such an arrangement of its parts as will give an entire prepon-derance to Prussia, scarcely knows what part to take; whether to make peace or continue the war. It is the interest of Prussia that Austria should continue the war; for the pressure of France upon the Empire, which is the conse-quence of it, tends to favour the views of Prussia, by throwing the members of the Empire into her arms, with a view of securing their peace with France, through the intercession of Prussia.

In conversation a few days past with Baron Stahl, Ambassador from Sweden, he informed me of a communication formerly made by the court of Sweden to Mr. Pinckney at London, for our government, and upon which no answer was given, although it was much wished. I desired his communica-tion in writing, that I might forward it to you, and which was accordingly given, and is herewith transmitted. I have no doubt that whatever he says to me is known to the committee, as I was informed by some of its members in the beginning of the winter, and before the Baron arrived, that such an application had been made to us from that quarter. It belongs to me only to forward this paper, and which I do, not doubting that I shall be instructed, relative thereto, in the most suitable manner.[173]

---

[172] On February 18, 1795, at Saint Petersburg, England had entered into a defensive alliance with Russia. (Corbett 1818, 207)

[173] Randolph retired from the office of Secretary of State on August 19, 1795. Thomas Pickering (Secretary of War) served as interim Secretary of State from August 20, until

Colonel Humphreys has just arrived, and, upon due consideration, I presented last night a paper to the committee, opening, as far as was expedient, the object of his visit; and upon which subject generally I shall be more full in my next, when I hope to be possessed of an answer to it.

With great respect and esteem, I have the honor to be, Sir, your very humble servant, Jas Monroe.

To James Madison, Paris, July 26, 1795

Dear Sir,—I had begun a long letter to you in cypher, it appearing the British have commenc'd seizing my letters, but which not being complete I forward the enclosed[174] by the present private opportunity[175], & which being on the moment of departure prohibits more being added than that the com'n is intended as a friendly deposit in your hands & for the purpose of guarding my reputation from unjust attacks whether published or private, always observing that whatever you receive is to be shown, when opportunity offers, to Mr. Jefferson & Mr. Jones. We are well & desire to be affec'y remembered to Mrs. M. Jas Monroe.

---

formally commissioned on December 10. 1795. Pickering responded to Monroe's on October 9: "Sir, this serves merely to ac knowledge the receipt (on the 7th instant) of your letter of the 4th [6th] of July with its inclosures. The President is now at Mount Vernon. This forbids my saying any thing on the subject of Baron Stahl's application. Besides, I do not conceive that the Executive could even attempt to negotiate about it until Congress should provide the means of rendering an agreement efficient. The proposition with a copy of the Convention between Sweden and Denmark I find were transmitted from London by Mr. Pinckney in his letter of the 8th of last May: it does not appear when they were received at this office." Relative to joining the convention between Denmark and Sweden of March 27, 1794 "for the maintenance of the rights of neutral navigation," Washington submitted the question to his Cabinet in July, 1794. Randolph was in favor of it, Hamilton, Knox, and Bradford against it. "There may be a state of things" wrote Knox in his answer, "operating upon Denmark and Sweden, essentially different from that operating upon America. States as well as individuals often have secret motives for their conduct. I dread being linked in with the follies or vices of European powers. In my weak judgment, our bark is in a fair train of reaching her destined port, unless by some error of our own she should be thrown out of her course. The mass of the people of England are now our friends, and they will probably prevent their government from making war upon us. But let us combine with the European powers, the case will be different. National pride will be excited in England, to which Justice and even their own interests may be sacrificed." (Hamilton 1899, 329)

[174] This included Monroe's correspondence with John Jay concerning the treaty. (Hamilton 1899, 330)

[175] In a later [October 24, 1795] letter to Madison, Monroe reveals that the "private opportunity" with which he had previously sent copies of the Jay–Monroe correspondence was with a "Mr. Perkins of Boston." This was Thomas Handasyd Perkins, an influential Boston merchant who was exploring business opportunities with the revolutionary government in Paris. (Seaburg and Paterson, 1971, 109-110)

To the Secretary of State [Edmund Randolph], Paris, August 1, 1795

Sir,—I was sorry to find, some days after my last, that the disquietude which I intimated existed in the councils of this Republic, and to which the communication between its ports and England had given birth, assumed a form still more unpleasant, in regard to us, than I then apprehended it would do; for, whilst the subject was under discussion between the commissary and myself, and, as I thought, approaching towards a close, the committee interposed, and taking the business out of his hands, addressed me on the same subject, and to the same effect, laying, at the same time the draft of a decree before the Convention, the principal object of which was, to preclude all those, who were not born within the jurisdiction of the neutral powers, from the protection of the ministers of those powers here. The decree, you will observe, was made general, as was the letter which preceded it from the committee. I had, however, seen too much of the business, not to know, that in regard to others it was formal only, whilst it was, in reality, pointed against a particular description of our own citizens, and of Englishmen, who, by means of American passports obtained elsewhere, and, no doubt, by fraud, sometimes passed for such.

As I presumed it was not the intention of the Committee or Convention, that the decree should be construed and executed strictly, because I knew upon principle it could not be supported, and because I likewise knew, that many of those whom it would thereby comprehend, were resident, and valuable members of our community, and had been, and now were, by their commerce, useful to France, I demanded immediately an explanation from the committee[176] of the decree, and soon afterwards obtained an interview with that body; in which I was explicitly assured, that they did not mean to call in question any principle insisted on by us; that their only

---

[176] Monroe's demand: "To the Committee of Public Safety. Paris, July 14th, 1795. Citizens, I sent you yesterday a list of my compatriots in Paris, according to your request of the 20th instant (Messidor) and shall continue to furnish a like list every decade whilst you deem it necessary.

In rendering this list, it becomes necessary for my future conduct, that I should ask of the committee an explanation of a decree of the convention of the 23d instant (Messidor) upon this subject: For I observe by that decree, that such citizens as are born within the jurisdiction of the powers in alliance and friendship with the French Republic, and who are acknowledged by the representatives of such powers here, are designated as entitled to protection, and by which it may be inferred, that all those who are not born there, are to be excluded from such protection. Permit me to ask; whether such is the import of the decree? The following considerations incline me to believe that it is not.

1st. Because it denies the right of expatriation, admitted by this Republic, and which cannot be denied without supposing a man attached to the soil where he was born and incapable of changing his allegiance.

---

wish was to exclude Englishmen and such as by their residence ought to be deemed Englishmen:[177] and that, in regard to myself, they meant to impose on me no restraint, in granting passports, I had not already observed. Thus, this business has happily terminated precisely where it ought to do, without producing any real change here, or other effect any where, which can be hurtful to us.

I have the pleasure to inform you, that the full aid of this government will be given in support of our negotiation with Algiers, &c. Upon this you may, I think, count with certainty, as I have been assured of it by the committee, and am furnished with all the light which their past negotiations with that regency enable them to give us on the subject. Difficulties, however, of a new kind arise, and which may possibly create some serious embarrassments. The fund destined for this business is, I understand, in England, and the English intercourse law prohibits, as I hear, and under the penalty of death, the payment of drafts from this country, in favor of any person in France, or who has been in France since the commencement of the war between the two nations. Perhaps this law may not be deemed applicable to this case: Perhaps, if it does, the inconvenience may yet be remedied somehow or other, so as to prevent the failure of the treaty on that account. Colonel Humphreys is still here upon this business; and, as we devote our unremitted attention to it, you may be assured that no measure, necessary to its success, will be omitted, that we are capable of.[178]

Within a few days past, the emigrant army, which lately landed in the Bay of Quiberon, under the auspices of Great Britain, has been completely defeated, and its whole force, amounting to about 10, 000 men, either slain or taken prisoners; of which about 4,000 were slain. Many of those who

---

2d. Because it denies the right to all governments to confer the privilege of citizenship, and incorporate into its society any person who was born else where, and which is admitted and practised every where.

3d. Because, as the first member of the fourteenth article of that decree al lows even the subjects of the powers at war with the Republic, who came in before the 1st January 1792, to remain here, it would follow, if such were the construction, that many of the subjects of those powers would be put on a better footing than many of the citizens of those who are your friends and allies.

From these considerations I am inclined to think, that such is not the import of the decree, and that the term was intended to mean political as well as natural birth; but as it is capable of a different construction, I have thought it my duty to ask of you an explanation on that head: For, at the same time that it is my wish to extend protection to all those of my countrymen, who are deemed such by the laws of my country, it is likewise my wish to do it in such manner and upon such principles as will be satisfactory to the French Republic." (Hamilton 1899, 332)

[177] The material addition is omitted in the print as given in Monroe's *View* and in American State Papers.

[178] This paragraph, in the original, is in cipher. (Hamilton 1899, 333)

composed that army are said to have been raised by compulsion, from among the French prisoners, and who were of course set at liberty when taken. By the law, all the others are doomed to suffer capital punishment; but it is to be hoped, as many of them are weak and misguided men, its rigour will be moderated, at least in regard to them.

Within a few days past, also, a peace was concluded with Spain; whereby the whole of the Island of St. Domingo is ceded to France, the latter yielding her conquests made in this quarter since the war. That there are some secret articles is more than probable. I herewith send you a copy of the treaty,[179] as likewise of the details which attended the defeat and destruction of the emigrant army, according to the report thereof rendered by Tallien, who was in mission there.

You will perceive that our claims have not been provided for in this treaty with Spain: relative to which claims I have heard nothing, since mine to you of the 14th of June last. 'Tis possible I may soon hear something on that subject, either from this government or from Mr. Pinckney and in which case I will immediately advise you of it. 'Tis likewise possible, a war may soon take place, in consequence of that treaty, between England and Spain, and in which case it will, no doubt, be the wish of the former to involve us in it on her side: But this, I hope, will not take effect; because, under existing circumstances, it would not only produce many unhappy consequences; but because I am of opinion, if Mr. Pinckney finds difficulties, that the object may yet be attained, by the intercession of this government, as soon as I am enabled to shew, that Mr. Jay's treaty stipulates nothing injurious to this Republic. Doubtless France will now have great weight in the councils of Spain; and, most certainly, if we continue in friendship with France, and of which there can be no doubt, it will be possible to avail ourselves of it, in support of our claims there.[180, 181]

---

[179] The Peace of Basel was actually separate two peace treaties signed in Basel, Switzerland, between the French Republic and two of the participants in the first anti-French coalition, Prussia and Spain. On April 5, 1795, the treaty between France and Prussia was signed, according to which Prussia recognized French annexation of the left bank of the Rhine. Prussia recognized French control of the west bank of the Rhine, pending a cession by the Imperial Diet. France returned all of the lands east of the Rhine captured during the war. On July 22, a treaty between France and Spain was signed. By the terms of this accord France received the Spanish part of the island of Haiti. Further, those parts of Catalonia and Navarre and the Basque Provinces occupied by French troops were returned to Spain. The Basel treaties with Prussia and Spain, in effect, eliminated the alliance between the nascent French Republic's two main opponents. (Clercq, 1864, 233-235)

[180] This paragraph, in the original, is in cipher. (Hamilton 1899, 334)

[181] Monroe later provided considerable insight into his thought processes at the time: "Whilst Spain adhered to England, she rejected our pretensions to the Mississippi, & c. and listened to them only when she was about to secede from England, and connect

These two great events must certainly produce the most important consequences, as well in securing tranquillity at home, as in cutting off all remaining hope of success, on the part of the powers still at war with this Republic. Indeed, the probability is that peace will soon be made with the Italian powers, and even with Austria: But with England, so peculiar is the relation between the two countries, that it is impossible to say when peace will take place between them, or even to hazard any plausible conjecture upon that point. An adjustment, however, with all the other powers, may possibly induce an accommodation between these, sooner than present circumstances authorize the expectation of.

About the time of the debarkation of the emigrant army, some symptoms were seen here, which gave cause for suspicion, that there was a party in Paris, which felt at least in unison with that army. Lately, a song called the Reveil du Peuple, composed in reproach of the reign of terror, had become very fashionable among those who had suffered under that reign, and by some accidental circumstances was placed in a kind of rivalship or of rather opposition to the Marseillese Hymn. The young men of Paris, the relations of many of whom had suffered under the reign of terror, formed a party who were in general in favour of the Reveil du Peuple; often calling for it at the theatre in preference to the Marseillese Hymn, and which circumstance never failed to give uneasiness to many who were present.[182] Light as this circumstance was, yet it seemed, at one time, to menace some serious ill consequences: The presumption whereof was indeed so strong, that the enemies of the revolution, who were said to stimulate the young men on, seemed to count upon it

herself with France. As this latter policy gained strength in her councils, her disposition to accommodate us likewise increased, as appears by Mr. Short's letter, referred to in mine of the 26th of June, 1795, and many other circumstances; since at that period she solicited our aid to promote her peace with France, promising that our claims should be adjusted at the same time. Standing well then with France, it followed that our controversy with Spain was permanently at an end, and upon our own terms. Mr. Pinckney arrived at Madrid precisely at the moment when things were thus circumstanced, and commenced and closed his negotiation, whilst that state of things lasted; the Spanish government being impressed with a belief that we were not only well with France, but that France supported our claims against Spain: And to which accommodation it is probable her then separation from England, and the danger of a war with that power, likewise contributed. Had Mr. Pinckney arrived a few months later, after France had seen our treaty with England, and adopted her present policy in consequence of it, I think his mission would have failed." (Hamilton 1899, 336)

[182] Defenders of the Reveil du Peuple described it as the song that had confirmed the victory of 9 Thermidor and which "makes vile and infamous terrorists quake." Like the proponents of the Marseillaise hymn, they recognized that some negative associations attached to their song; in this case, because it had accompanied reactionary violence and assassinations in the south. But, like their opponents, they argued that this meant only that one should acknowledge both the positive and negative associations of the Reveil and end by performing both songs. (Mason 1996, 144)

as a source from whence something in their behalf might be expected. Occasionally some excesses were committed by the young men, and in which they thought they had a right to indulge, even in contempt of the authority of the Convention itself; upon which body they presumed they had some claim, for services rendered in the late commotions. It was, in truth, obvious that the range which they took at this time, when tested by the standard of strict propriety, or indeed of law, could not be justified. It might, on the contrary, have been called an insurrection, and a little rigor would have made it one. The Convention, however, acted more wisely, by considering it for a while as a frolic; and finally, by issuing a proclamation telling them calmly of the folly and impropriety of their conduct, since thereby they exposed to danger the revolution, and of course their own safety; neither of which could it be their interest or their intention to endanger. This mode of proceeding produced the happiest effect; for even before the reduction of the emigrant army and peace with Spain, tranquillity was in a great measure established; but since those events, it has been completely so.

The Convention is still employed upon the subject of the constitution, which will probably be gone through in the course of two weeks more. As soon as it is adopted, and of which there can be no doubt, and upon the principles generally proposed in the project reported by the commission, I will forward you a copy.

I have lately received a letter from a Mr. Cazeau, an unfortunate Canadian who attached himself to our cause when we invaded Canada, whose name you will find in the journals of the Congress of 1783 or '4, at Annapolis, and which letter I now transmit to you.[183] The journal of that day explains the nature of his demand touched on in this letter. As I was of the committee upon this memorial, I am well acquainted with the nature of his claim, and think, in the issue of the business, that justice was not rendered to him; as the order of Congress in his behalf was not executed. He is here, and I believe supported by the nation, in the expectation we will do something for him. The minister of this Republic with our government having been instructed to patronize his claim there. May I request your attention to it?

I likewise enclose you a letter from Mr. Leach,[184] with one from several respectable Americans here, recommending him for the consulate at

---

[183] Francois Cazeau, of Montreal, was a man of property and influence who had suffered financial and personal ruin as the result of his support for the American cause. He would eventually file a formal claim for indemnity and compensation for losses sustained, and services rendered to the United States. (Hamilton 1898, xxviii)

[184] John Leach, who enjoyed a reputation as an aggressive American privateer during the war, was a sea captain and merchant from Boston who was then residing in Paris. (Morris 2000, 615)

Dunkirk, and to which I likewise beg that attention to which you may deem it entitled. My acquaintance with him is of late only; but he appears to me to be an honest and deserving citizen.

I am, Sir, with sincere regard your very h & ob serv, Jas Monroe.

To the Secretary of State [Edmund Randolph], Paris, August 17, 1795

Sir,—I have not been honoured with any communication from you since that of the 2nd May last though, doubtless, others are on their way, and which I shall soon receive.

Within a few days past, Philadelphia papers were received as late as the 3d of July, containing Mr. Jay's treaty, together with such proceedings of the Senate upon it as were then published. As the gazettes are circulating everywhere, I conclude some of them are in possession of the committee of public safety, and that the details they contain will likewise soon find their way into the papers of this city: Indeed, it is said, they are already published at Havre. As yet I have heard nothing from the committee upon the subject of this treaty; nor do I expect to hear any thing from that body upon it, let the impression be what it may, otherwise than in reply to such communication as I shall make in regard to that transaction, and in respect to which it may be proper to add, that I shall take no step without your particular instruction: For as I presume that some ulterior plan is or will be adopted in regard to that treaty, and upon which, in its relation to this Republic, my con duct will be particularly marked out; so I deem it my indispensable duty to avoid in the interim, any, the slightest, compromitment either of you or myself upon that subject. I mention this that you may distinctly know how completely the final result of this business, so far as it depends on me, is, as indeed it ought to be, under your control.[185]

As I have had no communication with this government upon the subject of this treaty since its contents were known, it is of course impossible for me to say what the impression it has made is.[186] It is as easy for you, with the lights you have, to form a correct opinion upon that point in Philadel-

---

[185] Monroe later put forth additional insight: "At this time the treaty was not ratified by the President, nor was it known that it would be: And, if ratified, I expected to be able to state (if complained of by the committee) how long the commercial part would remain in force; whether we were willing to make a new treaty of commerce, and upon what principles, with France, with a view to conciliate; but no such instructions were given me. As to my calling the attention of the committee to it (now that they were possessed of it without my aid) without orders from the administration, it appeared to me to be an act of folly which nothing could justify." (Hamilton 1899, 340)

[186] On July 14, Randolph would write Monroe, "The Treaty is not yet ratified; nor will it be ratified I believe until it returns from England, if then.... The late British order for seizing

phia, as for me to do it here. One circumstance, however, I think proper to bring to your view: Soon after the British government had recommenced the seizure of our vessels, destined for the ports of France, it was notified to the committee by a secret agent of this government, who had just returned from England; that he had been advised there, through a channel to be relied on, that the English administration had said, they knew that measure would not be offensive to our government; or, in other words, that it was a case provided for between the two governments. I treated the communication with contempt, and was happy to hear that it was considered nearly in the same light by the committee itself.

But since the arrival of the treaty, I have under stood that, in connection with that report, the attention of many has been drawn with some degree of solicitude to the contents of the second paragraph of the 18th article,[187] and who say, that as that article leaves the law of nations unsettled, and provides payment for seizures in cases of contraband, and of course for those which are not contraband, whereby the com plaints of our citizens are prevented, and the British construction by implication countenanced, this Republic has a right to complain of it. I mention this objection to you, that you may be aware of it, in case it should ever be brought forward on this or your side of the water; and that it will be brought forward, I think probable, if those seizures are not noticed in some very pointed manner. 'Tis painful for me to give you a detail of this kind; but being an interesting fact, I do not see with what propriety it can be withheld.

It is said that the constitution will be complete in the course of a few days, and of which I will immediately afterwards forward you a copy. The discussion upon this very important subject has been conducted with great temper, and the harmony of opinion throughout greater than could have been expected. The report of Pichegru having crossed the Rhine, as heretofore intimated, was without foundation: The height of the water occasioned by continual rains has hitherto prevented it: 'Tis however said, that he has orders to cross it, and is now making the necessary movements for that

---

provisions is a weighty obstacle to a ratification. I do not suppose that such an attempt to starve France will be countenanced." (Rives 1858, 2343)

[187] The article: "And whereas the difficulty of agreeing on the precise cases in which alone provisions and other articles not generally contraband may be regarded as such, renders it expedient to provide against the inconveniences and misunderstandings which might thence arise: It is further agreed that whenever any such articles so becoming contraband, according to the existing laws of nations, shall for that reason be seized, the same shall not be confiscated but the owners thereof shall be speedily and completely indemnified; and the captors, or, in their default, the Government under whose authority they act, shall pay to the masters or owners of such vessels the full value of all such articles, with a reasonable mercantile profit thereon, together with the freight, and also the demurrage incident to such detention" (Fish 1873, 389)

---

purpose. The enemy are on the opposite side, watchful of his measures; but from his skill, the strength and enterprize of his army, success is counted on as certain.[188]

No indication presents itself of an approaching peace between England and France, or even of a negotiation for it. The only indication is to be found in an English ministerial paper, which speaks of the convention in very respectful terms, and of peace as a desirable object. ' Tis probable, however, when a negotiation commences, it will be short: For as I presume the over-ture will come from England; so it is equally presumable that none will be made ' till her administration is disposed to accede to the terms of France. These, I presume, are in some measure known to England, at least I expect so; a consideration which I particularly suggest at present, with a view of turning your attention to those symptoms which may be discoverable on the other side of the channel, as data by which you may estimate either remote or immediate approaches towards this import ant event.

I have the honour to be, with great respect and esteem, Sir, your very obedient and humble servant, Jas Monroe.

To the Commissary of the Marine, Paris, August 30, 1795

Citizen,—I observe by yours of the 7th Fructidor (24th August) that you complain of an intercourse which is said to be carried on by some Americans from the ports of this Republic, to those of England; whereby a correspon-dence by letters is kept up, money exported and English people carried out of the country: You likewise complain, that the captains of those vessels ask exhorbitant prices for the transportation or passage of French citizens from England here; whereby they subject themselves, in addition to the suspicion of intelligence with your enemies, to the charge likewise of extortion from the unfortunate; and in remedy of these evils you request of me, 1st. To instruct

---

[188]After the military successes of 1794, there were hopes that the year 1795 would see the French armies pressing into the valley of the Danube and bringing the Austrian monarchy to terms. But the campaign of 1795 went to pieces. The generals were perceived to be were nearly as venal as the politicians. For example, Jean Charles Pichegru, Commander-in-Chief, Army of the Rhine, failed to support Jean Baptiste Jourdan, who had recently completed the successful Siege of Luxembourg. As a result, the French armies at the close of the summer were no further than the Rhine. Preparations were made by the Directoire to retrieve this comparative failure; the campaign of 1796 was to see a strong offensive against the Austrians to the north and to the south of the Alps. Jourdan and Jean Victor Marie Moreau, the latter displacing Pichegru, were once more to attempt to penetrate towards Vienna by the valley of the Danube. At the same time, a smaller army was to invade Italy and, from the valley of the Po, perhaps lend a helping hand to the armies in Germany. With Moreau's endorsement, Napoleon Bonaparte was selected for this last command. (Johnston, 1909, 241-242)

the consuls to prohibit the captains of our vessels from landing either men or cargoes, until a return of both is given to the maritime agents of the ports where they touch; as likewise a declaration of the port from whence they came. 2d. That I will arrange it so, that every captain shall take from me or the consuls his register, or other adequate proof of his vessel being American; by virtue of which alone, she shall be deemed such, and he entitled to the privileges of an American citizen.[189]

Permit me to assure you, that whatever regulations this Republic finds it for its interest to adopt, and which allow to my countrymen the rights of nations and of treaties, in common with the citizens of other neutral powers, I shall not only be satisfied with; but endeavour, by just and suitable representations there of to produce a similar impression upon the American government; being persuaded, that as well in the character of nations as republics, it is the mutual interest of both to cultivate each the friendship of the other. With the same view and upon the same principle I shall be always happy to adopt, so far as depends on me, such regulations as may be calculated to promote that desirable end.

The several particulars of your complaints are comprised in that of the intercourse between the two countries; if this were done away the others would cease; no correspondence of the kind could afterwards be kept up; no money could be exported, or English subjects carried out of the country; nor could any extortion be practised upon the unfortunate French citizens, who

---

[189] The indifference with which the government in Washington treated Monroe's recommendations was felt especially in the consular situation. The appointment as consuls to France of persons unacceptable to the French government, without any previous consultation with Monroe, caused him much embarrassment. For example, he asked for the removal of Pitcairn, an English subject who had been appointed consul at Paris, alleging that he would not be received by the French government, and that such a condition of affairs would be most detrimental to American business interests. After Pitcairn's arrival, Monroe again complained of the appointment. He withheld the consul's credentials until he should receive further instructions from Washington. Contrary to French law, the consuls frequently gave passes to Englishmen who pretended to be Americans merely to obtain the privileges enjoyed by Americans in France. Upon the complaint of the French government, Monroe had issued a circular designed to stop this practice by requiring American consuls to take the utmost care in approving passports. All doubtful cases were to be submitted to Monroe's personal decision. Nevertheless, the trouble continued, however, until the Commission of Foreign Affairs asked for a list every ten days of the Americans in Paris. Monroe complied, but continued to be frustrated by the numerous Englishmen who had obtained American passports under false pretenses. France also began to complain that certain Americans actively pursued or continued their various relationships with England. Monroe was, therefore, asked to have the consuls give a register of each captain and to prevent any seamen from landing from any American ship until the list had been approved by the French government. This last request he was unwilling to grant unless such a regulation fell equally upon the vessels of all neutral nations. (Vincent 1907, 42-43)

were imprisoned there. Is it in my power to prevent this intercourse? If it is, and this government wishes it to be prevented, then I should think I merited censure if I did not. But you will admit, that this is a measure to which I am not competent, and that it belongs to the French government alone to do it, as to regulate in all other respects its commerce: Regulations of mine upon that point would be disregarded by our mariners, who would consider me as usurping a power I had no right to exercise; they might likewise be censured by this government whose interest it might be to encourage such trade.

If then I cannot prohibit this intercourse, it follows, that I can subject it to no restriction. The same power which has the right to prohibit, has likewise the power otherwise to regulate it; and this belongs of course to the French government, and to it alone. Nor have our consuls any such power; their duties are regulated by a convention between the two nations, and which excludes every authority of the kind: Indeed the exercise of such an authority by a consul of either nation, within the jurisdiction of the other, would be deemed a derogation from the sovereignty of such nation, and therefore could not be tolerated. Our consuls are placed here, as yours are placed in America, for the advantage of our citizens respectively; to see that they enjoy the benefit of treaties, and the rights of nations; not to impose on the citizens any new and oppressive regulations.

If it is the interest and wish of this Republic to prevent such intercourse, admitting that it does exist, but of which I know nothing otherwise than by your letter and the public gazettes, which latter speak equally of the vessels of other neutral powers, as of those of the United States, and it does prohibit it, provided the prohibition be general I shall never complain of it, however decisive the regulation, or severe the penalty for infracting it. Whatever laws this government makes upon that subject, it is the duty of my countrymen to obey, and if they violate them, they must submit to the punishment such violation merits.

With respect to the two regulations which you mention; permit me to observe, that I deem the first, proceeding from your government, by arreté of the committee or decree of the convention, to be published and sent to all the ports, as a very suitable one, whether the intercourse is prohibited or not. Such a one exists in all cases with us: No vessel can land its cargo in the United States, without rendering an account thereof to the authority of the port; nor ought it to be done here, either in the case of cargo or passengers. With respect to the second, I have to add; that by the laws of the United States, it is already the duty of every captain of a vessel, to have a register from the government of the United States or some consul, describing his vessel, her burden, etc., and of course the object, which is herein sought, is already provided for: For you are not bound to consider any vessel as American, unless she produces some such adequate proof that she is such. I have thus answered, Citizen, the particulars of your letter with the same freedom with which it was written, and beg, likewise, to assure you, that if any further explanations are deemed necessary, I shall be happy to give them.

Jas Monroe.

To James Madison, Paris, September 8, 1795

Dear Sir,—Yours of the 2d of May is the last with which I have been fav, tho' most probably this is owing to the seizure of our vessels by the British & the full use I hear they make of my correspondence.

Since my last to you Mr. Mason's copy of the treaty with such proceedings of the Senate upon it as were published up to the 3. of July have arrived here: and since which we have seen the discussions at Charles town, Boston & New York, & which comprize all that I have seen on it.

Comments upon this instrument from me will I know be useless to you; but as they can do no harm I will suggest those that have occurred, beginning with the 9th. article[190] & which not only relaxes or cheapens the character of citizenship among us & introduces a new &contradictory (at least with the existing law) principle in our law of descents, but tends in the degree to incorporate the two countries together & to the benefit of England only; for I presume we have little land there & shall have less daily, whereas by the stock jobbing measures of many individuals among us they have much with us. The 10th.[191] disarms us of a principal weapon of our defence & perhaps the best security we have in peace agnst the commission of those outrages heretofore practiced upon us: We have no fleet or other means of preventing the Bh. from robbing us at sea, than by retaliating upon land; but this deprives us of that resource In the principal there is no difference, indeed most people had rather be robbed on land than sea, the former being a civil operation carried on like any other civil process & the latter a hostile one. Besides when plundered at sea, the parties, privateers or others, as the treaty acknowledges & provides agnst, may become insolvent & which most prob-

---

[190] Article 9 of Jay's treaty confirmed the titles of "British Subjects who now hold Lands in the Territories of the United States, and American Citizens who now hold Lands in the Dominions of His Majesty," further stating that "neither they nor their Heirs or assigns shall, so far as may respect the said Lands, and the legal remedies incident thereto, be regarded as Aliens." (Fish 1873, 385-386)

[191] Article 10 prohibited the confiscation of assets belonging to subjects of Great Britain or citizens of the U.S. (Ibid, 386)

ably would not be the case with a State. The 12th.[192] was still more extry for by it we shod be associated with the coalesced powers in the plan of starving this nation & likewise give a deep stroke to our own navigation, for it is a fact that at the present moment we are the principal carriers of W. India produce not only for France but for Holland and all the countries depending upon Hamburg & which you know are of great extent: indeed if this article was in force not a ship of ours co: cross the ocean without submitting to a search from the Bh. cruisers. The 13th.[193] gives nothing we do not now enjoy, & which of course it is to be presumed their interest prompts them to grant. The 14. 15. & 16. fetter us without a motive.[194] The 17.[195] confirms by positive stipulation the old law of nations & is the more odious at present on acc of the opposite principles contained in our treaty with France & which is completely in force or rather activity. The 18.[196] enlarges I think in the 1st paragraph the scale of contraband & in the 2d by admitting the law of nations to be doubtful when provisions were so & providing for payment of such as are seized on that principle, and of course for such as are seized against that principle, for it was not intended to put the latter on a worse footing than the former, and provision being made in no case agnst seizure, it seems as if the point insisted on by England was fairly yielded, and that she was authorized to seize when she pleased, paying us "a reasonable mercantile profit with the freight &c". At least I think it would be difficult to resist the argument which this article furnishes her in favor of that right. It may be said, it is true, that this article authorizes seizure only according to "the existing law of nations"; but from a view of the whole, ought not this phrase to be considered as inserted rather as a palliative to silence complaints agnst. the true import of the stipulation & which it required little sagacity to foresee wo be raised in America & here, than as controuling or forming the import itself: for if it was not intended to give the complete controul of this business to the Bh. govt. with right to seize at pleasure & for the consideration stipulated wo'd it not have been more correct to have begun with a specification of those cases, in which provisions either were or were not contraband, providing for such payment in cases where they were & leaving

---

[192] Article 12, in part prohibited U.S. ships from carrying American or British West Indian molasses, sugar, coffee, cocoa, or cotton to countries other than the U.S. (Ibid.)
[193] Article 13 admitted U.S. ships to British East Indian ports. (Ibid, 387)
[194] Monroe notes that, in the future, these may well impact American interests to some unknown degree. Article 14 generally permitted trade between Great Britain and the U.S.; Article 15 prohibited discriminatory tariffs; and Article 16 provided for the appointment of consuls. (Ibid, 388-389)
[195] Article 17 recognized enemy property in neutral ships as lawful prize. (Ibid, 389)
[196] Article 18 defined contraband. (Ibid.)

out of the provision cases where they were not? The 19th.[197] is not worth mentioning either way. The 20th.[198] serves to introduce the 21.[199] which is another stroke at France & derogates from the rights of our citizens. The 22.[200] is like the 10th. as it gives Engl time after seizing all our vessels to with-draw her property from the U. S. while we are negotiating for reimburse-ment. It will not be easy to point out any benefit we are to get from the 23. 24. & 25. articles.[201] Whilst the two latter are certainly calculated to irritate if not to injure France. The privilege given British subjects to remain with us in case of war by the 26.[202] is calculated to keep alive in that State the British party, whose influence in peace was perhaps the principal cause of the war. The 27.[203] is not worth a remark & the 28.[204] merits one only on account of the limitation given by it to the 12. & which proves that the construction insisted on above of it, was properly conceived. You will observe that in the above comments I began with the 6th. article; but I will likewise add some-thing now on those which precede. The permission to hold the posts till June 1796[205] & as it was to be presumed till the pressure of the present war was over was a great attainment for Engld for it not only secured her from any trouble on our part & on that account during that time, but enabled her to refuse to surrender them afterwards upon the slightest pretext & especially if the experiment made by the other articles to weaken our connection with France shod. prove unsuccessful. The cession of the free use of our portages to the British of Canada &c. are sacrifices on our part without any consider-

[197] Article 19 provided for compensation for damages inflicted by ships of war or privateers. (Ibid, 390)

[198] Article 20 required that pirates be punished and excluded from British and American ports. (Ibid.)

[199] Article 21 made citizens of the U.S. and subjects of Great Britain who accepted military commissions or letters of marque from enemy countries punishable as pirates. (Ibid, 391)

[200] Article 22 prohibited Great Britain and the U.S. from authorizing acts of reprisal for damages until the injured party "shall first have presented to the other a Statement thereof, verified by competent proof and Evidence, and demanded Justice and Satisfaction, and the same shall either have been refused or unreasonably delayed." (ibid.)

[201] Article 23 provided that warships of Great Britain and the U.S. "shall at all times be hospitably received in the Ports of the other"; Article 24 prohibited the arming of enemy privateers and the sale of prizes captured from one of the signatory powers in the ports of the other; Article 25 admitted warships, privateers, and prizes of Great Britain and the U.S. to each other's ports and denied refuge to those of their enemies. (Ibid, 391-392)

[202] Article 26 allowed that, in case of any future war between Great Britain and the U.S., merchants of one country resident in the other could not be expelled for a year after the outbreak of hostilities. (Ibid, 392)

[203] Article 27 provided for extradition. (Ibid, 393)

[204] Article 28 declared that the first ten articles were permanent, article 12 would be in effect for two years after the conclusion of the present war, and the remaining articles would be in effect for twelve years after the Jay treaty's ratification. (Ibid.)

[205] These comments are drawn from Article 2, which provided for the British evacuation of posts in U.S. western territories. (Ibid, 380)

ation on theirs.[206] I was in Canada in 1784 & assured by the merchants of Montreal that if the treaty was executed & we were admitted to free use of the Lakes, they wod. abandon the former & move within our jurisdiction, for comparatively between a commerce thro' the Hudson & the S: Lawrence the difference was at least 25 per cent: & wh. they wod. not encounter. You will observe that this opinion was founded upon the idea each country was to enjoy exclusively the benefits of its own situation, & to turn them to the best account for its citizens alone: for at that time all intercourse between Canada & the States was prohibited & so it was expected it would remain afterwards, especially in the respect abovementioned. But by this stipulation that difficulty wo: be at an end. & enjoying all the advantages of our situation, the Bh. govt. wo easily be enabled to make up for the difference to their merchants by bounties &c. which the mere circumstance of residence in Canada might occasion. Indeed to the province of Canada 'tis difficult to estimate at present the extent of the benefit which would be hereby gained: it would however certainly be great. The extension of the line from the Lake of the Wood, so as to admit the Bh into the Mississippi is calculated to admit her into the carriage of the immense export from our western country by means whereof as by extending her settlements westward upon that line, she would encircle us almost completely & thus communicate in some degree to our western settlements the same influence which she now enjoys upon our eastern.[207] The concession in the 6th[208] that we had violated the treaty of peace & the assumption to pay for the injuries supposed to result therefrom by delay &c. to be assessed by Commissioners, whilst the violation on her part in detaining the posts & carrying off the negroes was unprovided for and unnoticed, was still more extraordinary. The only remaining trait to be noticed in this project is, that by omitting to adjust principles by w the courts of admiralty were to be gov; if indeed a submission to such courts was to be tolerated at all, all reparation for spoliations seems to be abandoned. Had Mr. Jay been promised that those C's should decide as he wished, yet accepting a treaty without such stipulation, gave it up, or provided in case the decision was otherwise

---

[206] This is a comment on Article 3, which allowed British subjects and American citizens free navigation of North American waters, while excluding American ships from the Hudson's Bay Company's territory and the majority of waters in other British territories. (Ibid.)

[207] Article IV of the Jay Treaty stipulated that if the frontier did not intersect the river, the two parties should settle by amicable negotiation the boundary question and all other points in conformity with the intent of the 1783 Treaty of Paris. In effect, the article provided for the adjustment of the boundary to provide access to the Mississippi River from British territory, a permission not contemplated in 1783. (Ibid, 382; Teclaf 1963, 703)

[208] Article 6 established a commission to examine compensation of British creditors for pre-Revolutionary debts owed by U.S. citizens. (Fish 1873, 382)

any complete and even if the decision should be according to his views yet the omission to stipulate it, sacrificed our honor to preserve that of Engl'. In examining therefore this project from the beginning to the end & impartially I do not find one single stipulation in our favor, or which certainly improves our condition from what it was before. Whilst on the other hand it most certainly contains a series of stipulations many of which are extremely unfavorable & disgraceful, & others at best indifferent. When therefore I consider the circumstances under which the negotiation commenced, sometime after the Battle of Fleurus when the preponderance of the French arms was established[209] & the troops of the coalesced powers flying in every quarter before those of the republick; when the dominion of the sea was contested by the French & after a severe contest in which proofs of prowess were given by the latter that struck terror into their enemies, tho' rather the superior in that contest & when every day to the moment of the close of this negotiation improved the fortunes of France, I must confess I think this treaty in which it terminated, one of the most extraordinary transactions of modern times. No body will I presume attempt to vindicate the head which dictated it: the heart however may be free from taint or that pollution which is too often found among political agents: of this however the people of America, who are a just & a benevolent people, ought to be satisfied; and I doubt not will be satisfied.

If this treaty had parted us from France the views of Engl wod. have been completely answered; and believe me there were moments when I had the most disquieting apprehensions upon that point, for the opinion of its contents, with a variety of other circumstances, which inspired here a belief we were about to abandon this republick for a connection with Engl excited at different times a degree of irritation or rather indignation in their councils of a very menacing aspect A single unfriendly act being committed by this gov towards us wo have led to others: this wo. have produced recrimination from our quarter & which might have ended in we know not what. Governments too in a course of revolution as they act much from the heart of those who fill them, are susceptible of more sensibility than in other times; this made the danger under existing circumstances the greater. Believe me that since the reports of that treaty transpired I have rested on a bed of thorns: I was often fearful the subject wo be taken up in the Convention, & thus

---

[209] The French war with the First Coalition of Austria, Prussia, England, Holland, Spain began to take a favorable turn with General Jean Baptiste Jourdan's victory at Fleurus in southern Belgium on June 26, 1794, followed by the capture of Brussels on July 10. This was the first of many dramatic interplays between the erratic course of external war and the vicissitudes of the political struggle in Paris. In this instance, military victory prepared the ground for the relaxation of the revolutionary regime. (Mayer 2000, 563)

progress from one thing to another. I am however happy to inform you that none of these evils have happened. On the contrary the storm appears to have passed, leaving us the prospect of a fair and durable calm. This republick has not only refrained from degenerating into the unfriendly policy formerly practiced agnst. us, but has in this interval done us some acts of service, one in particular is just on the point of being placed in a train hence & which if it succeeds will be sensibly felt by all our country men. As this has been discussed and arranged, Jay's nomination; the business of Algiers.[210] Since the intelligence above referred to from Philadelphia arrived, it furnishes cause to hope (that notwithstanding the extreme dislike they have of the Treaty) they will continue to observe the same friendly policy towards us, in the hope we will sooner or later return it.

I consider this treaty as forming an important epoch in the history of our country. It fully explains the views of its author and his political associates; views which were long known to many and charged upon him & them, but denied, & by one artifice or other discredited. But this is an act which speaks for itself, & fortunately it is one in which not he alone is compromitted. This however is not the only benefit resulting from it, for having the sanction of the Senate & being presented for ratification to the President, whilst by Mr. Mason it was submitted to the people at large, the opinion of the latter will be before him at the same time, whereby he will be enabled to act as the voice of his countrymen admonishes, assisted too in his reflections by the light they may throw on it. If he rejects it & which I conclude he will, the publick opinion will afterwards perhaps be pronounced with still greater decision on that side. This therefore will form a basis upon which our republican system &connection with France may not only rest with safety, but hereafter in the latter instance be greatly improved. This is a reflection which will naturally occur to you & wh. will doubtless be held in view in the measures of the ensuing session.

You will have seen by my past communications that the affair of the Mississippi was lost or rather taken from this government by the mission of Pinkney, that before he past here the French minister was instructed to secure

[210] When Monroe was appointed as minister to France, on June 6, 1794, before leaving, he wrote to Thomas Jefferson, his mentor, from Philadelphia and asked him to send their code for their correspondence: "I feel extremely anxious upon the subject of a cypher. Our former one is in a small writing desk at my house, can you get & send it after me in case I do not see you before I sail?" This was followed up with a June 17, 1794, letter from Baltimore: "The urgent pressure of the Executive for my immediate departure has deprived me of the pleasure of seeing you before I sailed. I sincerely regret this for many reasons but we cannot controul impossibilities. Will you forward me a cypher & letters for yr. friends remaining in Paris to the care of Mr. R [Edmund Randolph] as soon as possible." This code had also been shared with Madison by Jefferson. (Tomokiyo 2014)

it in the treaty with Spain & which has been since confirmed to me by the Minister himself. But as P. passed thro here without mentioning the subject and which he could not do without shewing the treaty above mentioned it was concluded their interference would be deemed impertinent & so givin up to his care. The friendship shewn in the other instance proves it would have been in this if asked. Indeed the manner in which this Algerine business is conducted is calculated to take the aid of France without giving her the credit of it; for altho' we pursue her plan in everything and our agent goes hence with her passport and under her patronage and I am authorised to declare and have declared in my communications that without her aid we have no prospect of success within our resources, yet our agent Mr Hichburn[211] takes his commission from our minister at Portugal (now here) and to whom at Portugal he will render an account of his mission if it succeeds to be ratified conditionally by that minister there subject to the approbation of the president and Senate. Thus it will appear as if the whole proceeded from him at Portugal and France will appear to have had as little to do with it, even by circumstances as if it had proceeded from the moon. This however is a piece with all our other European transactions: we strive to filch the aid of this government in all cases where we can without letting the world know it deceiving the latter by pompous missions which appear to rest on ourselves alone. The above fact however if it succeeds with respect to Algiers ought to be made known in America. You will agree with me that to ask a favour under existing circumstances and without being able to explain the contents of a certain treaty is not a very dignified system of policy.

What course will be taken with respect to *England* under existing circumstances it is difficult to forsee.[212] *I have long since made it known that in case the treaty* was *disapproved it* wod. *be easy to secure the aid of this government* in *support* of *our demands upon England.* Nay I am convinced that *if our deportment was* such *in regard to England* as to inspire *confidence in France* she wod. make *no peace which* did not *go hand in hand with a proved ground for our claims and injuries. The negotiation however should be* in the hands of *a person in whom this government can confide* and be conducted *where the French negotiation was conducted either here or at Basle.* Suitable measures too shod. be taken at home *by laying hold of their property vessels &c and by taking the posts if* not *invading Canada.* This wod. be acting *like a nation and we should then be respected* as such *here and in England.* Nor wod. such *a measure in my opinion lead* to *war. On the contrary I think*

[211] Colonel Benjamin Hichborn, a native of Massachusetts and Harvard Law School graduate, had taken a prominent role in revolutionary New England. He was then in Europe pursuing business opportunities. (Buel 2011, 167)
[212] Italicized text in this letter was originally in cipher. Decoded text provided by the National Archives. (Mason and Sisson 2020)

they would promote a general peace by forming a seasonable *diversion in favor of* and which cod. not be *resisted at present. If the president would adopt measures of this kind separating himself* completely from *the advocates of the treaty everything might yet be retrieved.*

The Constitution reported by the Committee of Eleven is finally adopted & on the principles of the report. It is now before the primary assemblies which were opened three days past & will be closed tomorrow. It will pass with almost an unanimous vote. The Convention in a decree subsequent to the constitution required that 2/3ds of the Convention should be reelected, a principle incorporated in the constitution for the future. Tis probable this injunction will be disregarded & that in consequence some difficulty & delay may take place before the Const is put in force: for if some adopt that plan and others do not it will take some time to arrange matters as to get these in the same line again & which I presume will be that which the majority approve. The deliberations in Paris are conducted with calmness & perfect good temper—and every circumstance that I have heard of promises the happiest result, tho the royalists have looked to this epoch as one from which they were to hope a revolution in their favour.

The negotiation with the empire is going on & which perhaps is the cause Pichegru does not cross the Rhine. A peace is made with the Prince of Hesse whereby his troops, 6000, in Enl pay are withdrawn from the army of the Emperor.[213]

Very sincerely I am dear Sir y friend & servant, Jas Monroe.

To the Secretary of State [Timothy Pickering, Acting] Paris, September 10, 1795

Sir,— A private letter of the 31st of May, is the last with which I have been honoured from you, and as more than three months have since elapsed, I am inclined to believe that some of your despatches are carried into England, and treated with the same violence that mine were by the admiralty at Halifax.[214,215] It was, doubtless, an object of importance with the British government to know what were the ulterior measures of the President in

---

[213] A reference to the Peace of Basel.

[214] This entire letter was originally in cipher. Decoded text provided by Hamilton. (Hamilton 1899, 359)

[215] Timothy Pickering was appointed by President George Washington as interim Secretary of State on August 20, 1795, and would be formally elevated to the position of Secretary of State on December 10, 1795. To Monroe's consternation, Pickering would follow a staunch pro-British agenda and did not share Presidents Washington's and Adams' qualms about political entanglements with warring European powers. This in addition to the fact that ratification of the Jay Treaty worsened U.S.-French relations due to its preferential treatment of Great Britain. (Office of the Historian 2020)

regard to England, after the decision of the Senate upon the treaty of Mr. Jay, and as I presume you wrote me fully upon that head, and immediately after the decision was taken, so I cannot otherwise account why your letters have not yet reached me.[216]

I sincerely wish to hear from you as soon as possible upon that subject; because if in the further pursuit of our claims upon England, it is wished to derive any aid from this Republic, either by harmonious co-operation or otherwise, it is obvious from a variety of considerations that the sooner an attempt is made to adjust the mode whereby such aid is to be rendered, the better the prospect of success will be.[217] You know that France viewed with anxiety the late negotiation with that power, and waited the result not without unpleasant apprehensions of the consequences: and you likewise know that the moment when that anxiety ceases, and especially if there is any thing mingled in the cause producing the change, which argues an attachment for France, is the moment to make a suitable impression on her councils. Oftentimes incidents of this kind in private life encrease the friendship and cement the union between the parties; and the principle is the same with nations as with individuals, where the government is in the hands of the people. But the moment must be seized, otherwise the prospect diminishes, and every day becomes more remote; for where a cool ness which has once taken place is suffered to remain for any time, after the cause which gave birth to it ceases, that circumstance becomes a new motive for chagrin, and which, especially if afterwards encreased by mutual slights, often ends in mutual enmity. In addition to which, it may be observed, that if such aid is wished from France, the state of the war is such as to require, on our part, dispatch; for it is always presumable, when its substantial objects are secured on the one side, and the hope of gain in a great measure abandoned on the other, as is actually now the case, that its close is not very distant.

I am still of opinion, that if a timely and suitable attempt be made to engage the aid of this government in support of our claims upon England, it may be accomplished, and upon fair and honourable terms. But under existing circumstances, peculiar and extraordinary care becomes necessary

---

[216] On September 12, 1795, Pickering wrote to inform Monroe that the office of Secretary of State was vacant. Monroe received this information December 6, 1795, so that until this latter date, he was not aware "officially" of Randolph's retirement. On September 6, 1795, Jefferson wrote Monroe, advising him of Randolph "retiring perhaps from the storm he saw gathering." (Hamilton 1899, 360)

[217] Here, Monroe again urges the necessity of knowing, as soon as possible, the fate of the treaty. It was an increasingly difficult situation. Although he depended upon the home government for instructions as to how he might meet the anticipated complaints of the French government against the Jay treaty, official communications steadily grew more infrequent. (Bond 1897, 54)

in the arrangement to be adopted; otherwise the attempt will fail. Our negotiation must be in harmony, and possess the confidence of this government, or it will not support it; for no government will support a negotiation it suspects will terminate in a treaty injurious to itself. For this purpose, then, the person to whom we commit the trust, should possess the confidence of this government, and, in my opinion, the negotiation should be carried on at the place where the French negotiation is carried on; either here or at Basle, at which latter place it is reported, Mr. Eden has lately presented himself, the same person who was not long since at as it was said.[218] On the contrary, suppose any person was sent directly to England on this business, what would be its effect here? It is admitted that such a person might be sent, as would create no alarm here, of injury to this Republic from the consequence of such negotiation; but the manner would be deemed inharmonious, and would, of course, be considered as declining all claim upon this government for its support. England would know this, and profit by it. Indeed, no co-operation, under such circumstances, could be pursued. What are the objections to such an arrangement? I can see none. If we were at war with England none would be urged by any one; for such was the case when we were at war with her. If, then, remaining at peace another country is willing to give us the fortune of its arms, in support of our claims against a common enemy, ought we to decline an arrangement which would be adopted in war, especially when it is considered, that peace is the lot we prefer, and that our success depends upon its success, unaided by any effort of our own? Would it excite disgust in England? On the contrary, it would command her respect. Without compulsion we know we shall not gain from her what we are entitled to; and if this compulsion is to be procured from France, will it not be more efficacious, when she sees that our harmony with France is complete, and beyond her reach to disturb it? But can we accomplish what we wish by the fortunes of France, by any kind of negotiation we can set on foot, without any effort of our own; and if any such effort is to be made, of what kind must it be? To this I can give no answer, other than by referring you to my former letters on that head; for latterly I have had no communi-

---

[218] International animosity had lessened little since May 1794, when the Convention ordered that no quarter should be given to the English, a decree which the army refused to execute. There were, however, recriminations respecting the treatment of prisoners which were, perhaps, exaggerated. While in France it was alleged that French prisoners were fed on dead cats and dogs, the British were subsequently informed that at Dunkirk the English captives had very few blankets, at Amiens none, and that at Brest sixty captains or passengers of merchant vessels were debarred exercise and in want of necessaries. Sir William Eden [afterwards Lord Auckland] went to Dieppe in May 1795 to propose an exchange of sailors, but the Convention would only agree to an exchange of naval officers. Eden returned to London empty handed. (Alger, 1889, 230)

cation with this government on it. If it can be done, the above is the way to do it; but to secure success, by our embarking this government with full zeal in our behalf, and striking terror into England, it will be necessary to lay hold of her property within the United States, take the posts, and even invade Canada. This would not only secure to us completely our claims upon Britain, and especially if we likewise cut up her trade by privateers; but by making a decisive and powerful diversion in favour of France, promote, and very essentially, a general peace.

The state of the war is the same as when I wrote you last. Pichegru is still on this side of the Rhine, and the pressure upon Italy is less forcible since, than it was before the peace with Spain; a circumstance which gives cause to suspect, that negotiations, promising a favourable issue, are depending with the powers in that quarter. A similar consideration may likewise impede the movements of Pichegru; for it is generally understood, that not only the Empire as a body, but several of its members separately, are negotiating for a peace with this Republic; of which latter fact we have lately seen an example in a treaty with the prince of Hesse Cassel; whereby six thousand of his troops in English pay, are withdrawn from the army of the emperor.

I lately sent you, by Bordeaux, a copy of the Constitution which was adopted by the convention, and which is at present before the primary assemblies for ratification, and I now send another copy of that act by Havre. The attempt which was hereby made, not simply to amend, but absolutely to set aside the former constitution, and introduce a new one in its stead, differing, too, from the former, in many of its great outlines, and especially in the character of its legislative and executive branches, under the circumstances which existed when it was commenced, being at the moment when the trial of Barrere and his associates was depending, and Paris afflicted by famine, was an enterprize, you will admit, of great moment. So far as it was a dangerous one, it proves that such danger was encountered, from motives equally benevolent and patriotic. And as the constitution which this attempt has produced, comparatively with the other, is infinitely preferable to it, and forms, of course, in case it be adopted, a new bulwark in favour of republican government, it is fair to conclude, that such, likewise, was the object of it.

The primary assemblies were convened to deliberate on it five days, and this is the fifth; and in those quarters from whence accounts are already received, it appears that it is adopted, in some cases unanimously, and in all by great majorities. It was like wise submitted to the armies, and by whom it is said to be adopted almost unanimously. In the prospect, therefore, in this respect, before this Republic, one circumstance only presents itself, which darkens, in any degree, the political horizon. In putting the new constitution in motion, the Convention wished to transfer from its own body two thirds of its members to the legislative branches of the new government, and for which a decree was passed. A motive for this was, the advantage the republic would gain from keeping in office many of those in whose hands de pending negotiations were, and who in other respects are acquainted with the actual state of things. There may be, and doubtless are, other motives for this measure, and which will readily occur to you. This arrangement is, however, disliked by many, and, particularly, by the inhabitants of this city, by whom it is generally rejected. The presumption is, that a great majority of France will approve the decree, and in which case Paris will yield; but, should the majority prove to be on the other side, the presumption is equally strong, that the convention will yield; so that, from this source I do not see cause to apprehend any serious evil. Many, however, are of a different opinion, and count upon the division which exists upon this point, as the commencement of a counter-revolution. It is well known that the royalists are active, and using their utmost efforts to improve it in their favor, and it is also believed, that England and some others of the coalesced powers view it with the same anxious and favorable expectation. But it is usual for the royalists and those powers to catch at every circumstance which turns up, whereon to rest a hope; in general, however, their calculations upon the fortune of the revolution, have not been verified by events, and I shall be deceived if this is not the case in the present instance. Indeed, a sound reason may be given why Paris differs in this respect from the majority of the other departments, and without impeaching her attachment to the republican government. All the great atrocities which have stained the different stages of the revolution, were perpetrated here. Under every convulsion and change some of her citizens have suffered; and, with the preponderating party in the Convention, she is not popular as a department; so that it is natural she should wish a complete change of the members who are to compose the new government. With great respect and esteem I have the honor to be Sir your most obedient and humble servant, Jas Monroe.[219]

---

[219] After finally seeing the treaty's full text in September 1795, Monroe, in a September 8 letter to James Madison, lamented, "I consider this treaty as forming an important epoch in the history of our country. It fully explains the views of its author [Jay] and his political associates." To Monroe the treaty laid bare the Federalists' true colors. He believed that Jay had sacrificed the interests of both the country and the republican cause in order to preserve a relationship with monarchical Great Britain. But even against this backdrop, Monroe did not doubt that he could preserve the alliance with France. Unfortunately, his Federalist rivals had already set in motion his recall from Paris, and arch-Federalist Timothy Pickering's appointment as secretary of state all but sealed Monroe's fate. Pickering, who had determined that keeping an ardent Francophile as minister to France threatened both national security and

P. S. Respecting Algiers I will write you in my next. Since writing the above, it is announced in the Convention that Jourdan, who commands the army of the "Sambre and the Meuse," has crossed the Rhine, at the head of about 50,000 men, and in the face of about 40,000, well posted, and strongly fortified on the opposite shore. It is also said, that he at tacked and took by storm, immediately afterwards, the city and castle of Dusseldorf. Much applause is bestowed on the general and his army for this bold exploit, and which is deemed, under the circumstances attending it, among the most brilliant of the war.

To David Humphreys, Paris, October 3, 1795.

Sir,—By the enclosed extracts, if what they state is correct, it seems as if Mr. Donaldson had acted from himself, and without the aid of the French consul. If this be the case, he will doubtless explain to you the cause.[220] The price is higher than I expected it would have been. I could not call on Jean de Bry;[221] but Mr. Purviance did, the day before yesterday, on this business in my name, and was informed, that he had heard nothing from Herculais[222] on the subject, and that the only instructions heretofore sent him (being, indeed, those only which they could send him) were, to use the influence of this Republic with the Dey, to obtain a suspension of hostilities, on his part, against the United States. However, this you will understand better when you arrive at Lisbon. I shall notify the event, or rather the report, to this government, that it may, at least for the present, take no further measure in it.

With great respect and esteem, Your obedient servant, Jas Monroe.

---

the Federalist Party, eventually prevailed upon President Washington to replace Monroe. (Poston 2016, 293-294)

[220] Colonel Humphreys to had written to Monroe on October 4, 1795, informing him that Algiers had agreed to a peace treaty with the United States. He also mentioned that he had suggested to Joel Barlow that he travel to Alicante with presents that might be distributed in Tripoli and Tunis. Humphreys concluded, "I am clearly of opinion we must have one consul or agent for each one of the Barbary States. There must be a sufficient number of persons employed to perform the public services. The speedy conclusion of the negotiations with Tunis and Tripoli is of great importance. Pray then let us not suffer the business to languish or to be procrastinated, for want of agents, means or expenses." (Preston 2001, 51; Hamilton 1899, 367)

[221] Jean Antoine Joseph de Bry was a former president of the National Convention, then serving on the committee of Public Safety. (Archontology 2020)

[222] Louis Alexandre d'Allois d'Herculais was the newly appointed French consul to Algiers. (Cantor 1963, 180)

To the Secretary of State [Timothy Pickering, Acting] Paris, October 4, 1795

Sir,—I herewith enclose you extracts from several letters from Mr. Cathalan, our consul at Marseilles, and by which it appears, that a treaty on behalf of the United States is made with Algiers.[223] I have likewise since conferred with Jean de Bry, of the committee of public safety, who is charged with the American affairs, and by whom I am informed, that like intelligence is received by the Committee from their consul at Algiers; so that the verity of this report cannot be doubted. By these extracts, as by the communications of the consuls to the committee, as I am advised, it is to be inferred, that the movements of Mr. Donaldson were unconnected with the French consul, and, of course, that the aid of this Republic was not extended to us in that negotiation. From what cause this proceeded, if such is the fact, I cannot at present divine; but presume it will be fully explained to you by colonel Humphreys from Lisbon; where he doubtless is before this, having left Paris on his return there about three weeks since. It is, however, necessary for me to state to you what took place here in that respect, in consequence of colonel Humphreys' arrival, prior to the receipt of the above intelligence; as likewise what has been since done in consequence of that intelligence.

I was informed by Colonel Humphreys upon his arrival, that you wished to obtain the aid of this government in support of our negotiations with the Barbary powers; for which purpose, indeed, he had come, and that you wished me to ask for it, in case I thought it attainable. From particular considerations, and which will occur to you, I felt some embarrassment in making an application for aid of any kind at the present juncture; but as I was persuaded you had weighed these, and deemed them no obstacle, and

---

[223] In this letter Monroe explains to Pickering that he was in the process of making arrangements for French assistance in the negotiation of the Algerian treaty when word arrived that the Dey has agreed to the American terms. He explains that Joel Barlow is moving forward with the treaty negotiations and recommends Barlow as U.S. consul to Algiers. Barlow accepted the commission and immediately began to buy gifts for the Dey of Algiers which, according to custom, were essential to friendly relations with all the Barbary rulers. However. complications soon developed. On October 14, Monroe learned that Donaldson had concluded a treaty of peace with Algiers. Weeks of uncertainty passed with the need for the mission in doubt. Barlow interviewed Thomas Pinckney, the new Envoy Extraordinary to Spain, and Jefferson's protégé William Shor, both of whom had just arrived in Paris, but neither of whom had any knowledge of a treaty. Monroe sent a messenger to Lisbon in order to ascertain Humphrey's views. The reply encouraged him, as it doubted the accuracy of his information. Monroe then decided that the mission should be undertaken as planned. Even if the report proved true, it would be a valuable experience. Should there be a treaty, Barlow might rectify any textual errors. On the other hand, should none exist, he might initiate talks in that direction. No matter what the situation, Barlow would gain an insight into the policy of the Tripolian, Tunisian and Algerian powers that could prove to be of great advantage to the United States. (Preston 2001, 51; Cantor 1963, 174)

knew that the object was equally pressed by interest and humanity, I immediately resolved to bring the subject before the government, and ask for such
aid; stating it was not the aid of funds that we wanted, but simply the aid of
the amicable mediation and interference of this government, and which was
promised by our treaty of alliance, but never performed. Colonel Humphreys
and myself were agreed, that as credit for the service was to be a principal
motive on the part of France for embarking in it, so it would be expedient on
our part to make our arrangements such, as to give full force to that motive;
since thereby she would engage in it with greater zeal, and, in consequence,
with proportionably greater effect. It readily occurred, that the more direct
our measures were from this quarter, and the more united and harmonious
our councils were in this respect, with those of this government, the greater
its confidence in us would be, and of course, the better our prospect of
success. Besides, to give full effect to the influence of France in the councils
of the Dey, and thereby obtain the peace at the cheapest rate, it appeared
advisable that our agent should be cloathed with a French passport, and
be if possible a French citizen, and even appear to be an agent of France,
exhibiting ultimately our power when necessary to conclude. By this mode
it would seem as if France interfered as our friend and chiefly from motives
of humanity in regard to our prisoners; whereby we should avoid inculcating
any idea of wealth on our part (for wealth and imbecility are with them
strong temptations for war) and which would be further supported by the
long imprisonment of our people. In presenting, therefore, the subject before
the government, I left the mode or manner of the negotiation open for subsequent and less formal discussion; seeking in that step a decision only upon
the first point of aid, and which I was explicitly promised by the committee
and the commissary. I soon found however, in touching on the other part, the
execution, that our anticipation was correct, and that it was expected our
agent would depart hence by the route of Marseilles; shunning the countries
with which this Republic was at war, and at which place the government
would have a vessel provided for him to proceed to Algiers. In furtherance
of the object, I was furnished by the commissary with a list of such presents
as would be suitable for Algiers, &c., a literal copy of what they had last
presented themselves, with a specification of what suited the Dey and his
ministers in particular, and which presents, as introductory, he advised us
to commit to the agent, to be presented in the commencement according
to the usage of the place, and as their consul should advise. But Colonel
Humphreys observed to me, that he had left Mr. Donaldson at Alicant, with
power to correspond with the French Consul at Algiers, and act in harmony
with him; being further authorized, in case he was invited over by the consul,

to proceed to Algiers and conclude a treaty with that power. Here then an embarrassment occurred; for it was to be feared, and for the reasons above stated, that a mission from that quarter, under the circumstances attending it, would be less likely to succeed, than if it proceeded directly hence; and, on the other hand, it was likewise to be feared, that if we adopted the latter plan and despatched a person hence, the two agents might interfere with, and embarrass, each other. Upon mature reflection, therefore, and especially as Colonel Humphreys had instructed Mr. Donaldson not to act otherwise than in strict harmony with the French consul; nor then without an assurance of success, since he, Colonel Humphreys was coming to Paris to secure the aid of this government, it seemed as if the two modes might be incorporated into one; or rather as if we might proceed with the business here, counting upon no interference from Mr. Donaldson; providing however, in the arrangements, in case he acted before Colonel Humphreys returned, and which we concluded he would not do in such manner as to admit his falling in, incidentally, and harmonizing with the other agent; and to admit likewise, let him act as he would, provided he harmonized with the French consul, such an explanation as would be satisfactory to this government. Upon this principle therefore, and with the approbation and concurrence of Colonel Humphreys, I notified to the commissary of foreign relations, that we had committed the trust to Joel Barlow, who was a citizen of both Republics, and requested the passport of the government in his behalf, and also in behalf of Mr. Donaldson, who was eventually to be consul at Tunis and Tripoli, and whom we should associate with Mr. Barlow, to guard against accidents in the negotiation with Algiers; requesting likewise, that the committee would, in the most suitable manner, yield all the support in its power in favour of this negotiation. I stated also, that Mr. Barlow was here and would proceed by the most direct route in the discharge of his. trust, with the presents we had bought, and were buying, according to the list furnished me, for the said treaty; and was promised, that what I had asked should be strictly complied with: And thus stood the business when the accounts above referred to were received, and which I have thought it my duty to communicate, that you may be accurately informed of what was done here in relation thereto.

Perhaps you will ask, why Mr. Barlow or some other agent did not depart hence sooner, after the plan of sending one was agreed on? The fact is, it was impossible; for, owing to the state of things here at the time, about three or four weeks elapsed, after I applied to the government for the aid, before I obtained an answer; and after which, when it appeared expedient to purchase introductory presents, and for which purpose money was necessary, a doubt arose, and for reasons heretofore explained, whether Colonel Humphreys' draft from France would be answered, and which it was thought advisable to remove in the first instance. This consumed about three weeks more, and since which, every possible attention has been made to provide the presents, and forward the business, that circumstances would admit of.

When the news above noticed arrived, Colonel Humphreys was at Havre, on his return to Lisbon; and the first point to be decided on, was whether Mr. Barlow 's offices should cease; and secondly, what should be done in that case, with the presents already purchased. We were both of opinion, and for many reasons, that it was advisable he should notwithstanding, proceed, and take the presents with him. If any errors had been committed at Algiers, and which it is possible to rectify, we knew he would be able to do it; and we were also persuaded, that in other respects, a trip to that coast, whereby he would be enabled to gain an insight into the policy of those powers, could not otherwise than be of great advantage to the United States. Upon this principle I have asked his permission to intimate to you his willingness to accept the office of consul for Algiers, to which he has consented; and which I now do in a confidence, that no person can be found willing to accept that trust, in whom it can be so happily vested; and in which opinion I doubt not Colonel Humphreys will readily unite. Mr. Barlow leaves this place upon the plan above stated, in the course of a few days, and with the presents in question; and for further particulars respecting this interesting concern, I beg to refer you to Colonel Humphreys, who will, doubtless, be more particular in his details.[224]

Since my last Pichegru has also crossed the Rhine, and taken Manheim, and in consequence whereof, the siege is more closely pressed on Mayence. Since my last too, the Belgic is united by a decree to this Re public; in addition to which the mission of Mr. Monneron to England, ostensibly for an exchange of prisoners, but perhaps for other objects, is the only circumstance which merits attention.

With great respect and esteem, I have the honour to be. Sir, your most obedient servant, Jas Monroe.

---

[224] For the September 1795 peace, the United States paid a heavy price, ransom money, presents, and large commissions. In addition, it promised to furnish an annual tribute in naval stores amounting to $21,600. In the following year, the United States paid for a treaty with Tripoli and in 1797 for a more expensive one with Tunis. Although neither treaty called for additional tribute, Americans paid it in one form or another. This was the Mediterranean policy of the Federalist government which gloried in the slogan "millions for defense but not one cent for tribute." Yet, the treaties with the Barbary states were, in fact, worthless. All the rulers, when the opportunity arose, were anxious to break them and to prey on American commerce. The first state to repudiate its treaty and to launch large scale hostilities against the United States was Tripoli. In May 1801, less than three weeks after Thomas Jefferson had taken office as president, its Pasha declared war. (DeConde 1963, 85)

To the Secretary of State [Timothy Pickering, Acting], Paris, October 20, 1795

Sir,—The breach which I lately intimated to you had taken place between several of the Sections of this city, and the Convention, respecting two decrees of the 5th and 13th Fructidor, and whose object was to transfer from the Convention so many of its members, as would constitute two thirds of the legislature of the new government, continued daily to widen afterwards till at length all hope of amicable compromise was gone.225 A final appeal, therefore, was made to arms; and which took place on the 5th instant (13th Vendemiaire) and in which the Convention prevailed. The details of this contest, though very interesting, are not lengthy. In the morning of the 5th, a force was marshalled out by the revolting sections upon their respective parades, in concert, and under officers already engaged, and who led it on by different avenues towards the national palace; so that by four in the evening the Convention was nearly in vested on every side. Within the garden of the Thuilleries and around the national palace were collected the troops destined for the defense of the Convention; and which were advantageously posted with cannon to guard the several avenues by which approaches might be made. The members remained within the hall, prepared to await the issue of the day. The disposition, therefore, was that of besiegers against besieged, and which grew out of the disparity of numbers on each side; for on that of the Convention, taking the whole together, there were not more than 6, 000; whilst on the side of the sections, there were in activity at least 10,000, and a still greater body in arms, which was supposed to be on the same side, or at least neutral. The countenance too of the parties bespoke a strong sympathy for their respective situations; that of those without exhibited an air of cheerfulness and alacrity, and which nothing but the confidence of success could inspire, whilst that of those within was dejected and melancholy. The action commenced a little after five in the evening by the advance of the troops of the sections and ended about ten by their retreat. Wherever they approached they were repulsed by heavy discharges of artillery and musketry, which ranged and cleared the streets of their columns, as soon as presented. For some time, towards the close, the contest was sustained on

---

225 As general background, on September 12, Pickering had written Monroe a sharp rebuke for the he views that he had expressed in regard to the Jay treaty as being quite foreign to those of the government of the United States. Still, with the exception of this censorious letter, as of this date, it is noted that, while chiding Monroe for his past conduct, Pickering gave no guide for the future. Still, Monroe continued his conscientious efforts to keep the home government informed of what transpired in France and, whatever should happen, he would do his best to influence French opinion and foster feelings of good will. (Vincent 1907, 54)

the part of the sections, from the windows of the neighbouring houses; and from whence, perhaps, more of the troops were slain than from any other quarter. The loss on either side is unknown, and perhaps will continue so, and the reports are so various and contradictory, that they furnish but little data whereon to found a conjecture. Judging, however, from what I saw of the disposition of the troops who were presented at the corner of streets, or when advancing by the head of the column only, and of the time and nature of the action, which was by intervals, I cannot think that more than 500 were killed and wounded on both sides; though some of the reports make it as many thousands. It was generally understood by the assailants, that little or no opposition would be made, and that two of the regular regiments, in particular, were on their side, and that they would so declare themselves when the crisis approached. But in this they were mistaken; for all those troops behaved with great bravery and intrepidity, acquitting themselves as they had done before on the Rhine; having been drawn from the army of the north. Indeed, the probability is, the report was only circulated to inspire the troops of the sections with confidence, and to produce a suitable impression on the citizens of Paris in general. Many circumstances occurred in the course of the commotion, to countenance this opinion, of which the strongest is that, although it lasted until about 10 at night, yet by the citizens generally it was abandoned or feebly supported after the first onset, and repulse which immediately followed; and after which it was sustained principally by those who were really and truly the parties to it; for as such the great bulk of those who were in the rank ought not to be considered. This opinion is likewise countenanced by a train of incidents which attended this movement, from 10 at night to its close, and which was about 12 the next day. The troops of the Convention kept their ground all night, being unwilling to press as far as they might have done, the advantage gained; since it appeared, that by such pressure they might slay more of their countrymen, but not gain a more complete victory. On the other hand, the troops of the sections filed off gradually in small parties, as the darkness of the night or other circumstances favoured; till finally none were left, except those who were not properly of that description. By the morn everything was tranquil, as if nothing had passed. At the entrance of every street you saw the pavement taken up, and waggons and other impediments obstructing the passage; but not a centinel was to be seen. The only armed force, remaining in opposition to the Convention, was of the section of Lepelletier, consisting of a few hundred only, and which had in part retired and was retiring to its commune as a place of retreat, rather than of defence. But now the scene began to change and exhibit to view precisely the reverse of what was seen the day before, the besieged becoming the besiegers; for by this time the troops of the Convention were advancing towards the commune of this section, under the command of Barras, who had commanded formerly on the great epoch of the 9th Thermidor, and of Berruyer, who made regular approaches and by different routes, till finally this corps was completely surrounded. A peremptory summons was then sent to it to surrender, and which was immediately obeyed, by laying down their arms and submitting to the will of the conquerors; and thus was this movement crushed; the authority of the Convention vindicated, and Paris restored to complete tranquility, and within less than 24 hours after the action commenced. [What Monroe is describing here is the "Rise of the Sections."]

Such was the order, and such the issue of this contest: A contest, in many respects, the most interesting and critical that I have yet witnessed, and which promised, had the assailants succeeded, not perhaps essentially to impede or vary the direct course of the revolution; but, most probably, to involve the nation in a civil war; open a new scene of carnage more frightful than any yet seen, and deluge the country by kindred arms with kindred blood. In this view the character and object of the movement, on the part of the insurgents, merit some attention.

An explanatory note

[What Monroe is describing here is the "Rise of the Sections" and their surrender to the Convention]

With respect to political sway [particularly as applied to Napoleon Bonaparte] it would arguably emerge as one of the more significant events of Monroe's tenue in Paris. The Convention had created a five-member commission under Paul Barras to prepare the defense of the Tuileries. It called up 5,000 regulars and raised some 500 volunteers. Barras, who had been a Terrorist representative at Toulon in 1793, picked General Napoleon Bonaparte to command the defense. He felt Bonaparte would make maximum use of the Convention's meager forces and would not shrink from using all his weapons against the people. He knew Napoleon was ambitious and ruthless. The right man for the job. When Bonaparte took command, late on October 4, 1795, attack was obviously imminent. His first thought was to insure artillery support for his infantry. From a crowd of officers in the Tuileries, he picked cavalry major Joachim Murat, a tall, powerful, arrogant Gascon, and ordered him to take a troop of horsemen and seize the guns of the National Guard at Sablons, in the suburbs. Murat took his men on a wild ride through Paris and led them into the artillery park at Sablons at a full gallop.

The guards had no time to react. Before dawn on October 5 Murat had delivered forty cannon to Bonaparte, who placed them to sweep the approaches to the Tuileries. The general ordered the gunners to load them with canister (cans of small steel pellets), nails, links of chain, and scrap metal. Crowds began to gather on the morning of October 5, 1795 (13 Vendémiaire, Year IV), the sixth anniversary to the day of the march of the women to Versailles. All day the crowds built up on the streets north of the Tuileries, and by late afternoon perhaps 50,000 people had congregated, including about 10,000 National Guards. The Guardsmen were lightly armed, and the people, except for a few men with pikes, had nothing more than sticks, stones, and kitchen knives. At about 4:30 the mob, their courage fortified by wine, beer, and gin supplied by their affluent leaders, surged south toward the Tuileries gardens along the rue de La Convention, a roaring sea of bobbing Liberty Caps and pikes. Napoleon's gunners waited, torches lit, as the attackers closed in. Finally, with the crowd almost upon them, the order to fore came, and cannon blasts laid open bloody lanes in the people's ranks. They ran, trampling those in the rear and leaving the flagstones littered with dead and wounded. A few cannon were used in the Place du Carrousel, on the other side of the palace, and a few more stopped an attack from the Left Bank, both minor actions. The infantry, meanwhile, drove stubborn snipers from the Church of Saint Roch and broke remaining resistance in the sections. Bonaparte's "whiff of grapeshot" (as historian Thomas Carlyle labelled it) saved the Convention and allowed the Directory to take power. The National Convention dissolved itself by October 26, 1795 and was replaced by the new councils of the Directory. Bonaparte had quieted Paris, where mobs had ruled the streets and intimidated assemblies since 1789. His ascent to ultimate power had begun and the sections of Paris would not rise again until the Revolution of 1830. (Connelly and Hembree 1993, 124-126)

You have already seen that the decrees above mentioned were the ostensible, if not the real, cause of this controversy, and these you have. But to enable you to form a just estimate of its merits in other respects, and thereby of the probable views of the insurgents, it will be necessary for me to state other facts, and which preceded the final appeal to arms. These decrees, as you likewise know, were submitted with the constitution to the people, and according to a report of the convention by them adopted. But the verity of this report, of which I herewith send you a copy, was denied by the sections. By the report, however, you will perceive that the names of the departments voting for and against the decrees, were published some time since, and to which it may be added, that no department or commune has since complained; that the statement given of its vote was untrue. Still a doubt arises upon it, admitting that a majority of those who voted, was in favour of the decrees, whether those who did vote for them constituted a majority of French citizens entitled to vote, and upon which I cannot yet positively decide. The sections affirm the contrary, and likewise contend, that all who did not vote ought to be counted against the decrees. It is probable that some of the communes, foreseeing a storm gathering from that source, did not choose to vote for or against them, and therefore evaded the question by design, and it is certain that in others, it was understood by the people, that the question was taken upon the constitution and the decrees together; for latterly this was notified to the convention by several who had voted for the decrees, and particularly Nantes, to prevent a misapprehension of what their real intention was. I send you, however, the several papers which illustrate this point, and by which you will be enabled to form as correct an opinion on it, as present lights will admit: Observing further, that the report made by the convention respecting the decrees, was made, as you will perceive, at the same time with that upon the constitution; and that another report, containing a complete detail of the proceedings of every commune, is making out for the satisfaction of the community at large, and which was commenced by order of the Convention, immediately after the first one was rendered. It is to be wished that this had been some time since published; but when it is recollected that the publication must contain the proceedings of up wards of 7000 primary assemblies, many of which are, perhaps, lengthy; impartial people will perceive, that it could not be soon done, especially when it is also recollected, that the whole of the interval since the order was given, has been a time of unusual fermentation and trouble.

Under these circumstances, the electoral assemblies were to meet, and the day of meeting was not distant. The decrees, and the evidence of their adoption were before France, and would, of course, be before these assemblies: Nor were the electors bound by any legal penalty to regard them, if they thought they were not adopted, or even disapproved them. The presumption, therefore, was (and especially if they discredited the report of the convention) that every assembly, whose constituents voted against the decrees, would disregard them; and, rejecting the two thirds of the present Convention, vote for whom they pleased; leaving it to those who were elected, by the several departments, to the legislature of the new government, whether they were entirely new men, or partly such, and partly of the Convention, according to the mode that each department might adopt, to settle the point among themselves, and with the Convention, who should constitute the legislature of that government; or whether the whole proceeding should be declared void, and a new election called for; and which, in that event, would most probably have been the case. But the party opposed to the Convention, preferred a different series of measures, whereby to forward its views; the details whereof, so far as I have any knowledge of them, I will now communicate.

The primary assemblies were by law, to meet on the 10th of Fructidor, and dissolve on the 15th. In general, however, those of Paris prolonged their sit ting beyond the term appointed; and many of them declared their sessions permanent, and exhibited, in other respects, a tone of defiance and great animosity towards the existing government. Finally, however, the primary assemblies were dissolved; and after which the sections of Paris, to whom the same spirit was now communicated, became the channel, or rather the instruments, of the same policy; many of whom likewise declared their sessions permanent, and assumed, in other respects a tone equally unfriendly and menacing towards the Convention. The section of Lepelletier in particular, which is in the centre of Paris, and which always was, and still is, the theatre of its greatest gaiety and dissipation, took the lead in these councils. At one time it presented an address to the Convention, copiously descanting upon the horrors of terrorism, demanding that those who were called terrorists, should not only be inhibited the right of voting, but forthwith punished; and that the troops in the neighborhood of Paris should be stationed further off, although there were then in the neighborhood not more than 3,000 foot, and 600 horse, and which were there for six months before. At another time it placed, by its own arrêté, under the safeguard of the primary assemblies, all those who had delivered their opinions in those assemblies, and invited the other sections of Paris to form a meeting of 48 commissioners, to declare to all France the sentiments of this commune upon the state of affairs in the present juncture. On the 10th of Vendémiaire, this section resolved that a meeting of the electoral corps should be held at the Theatre Français on the next day, and admonished the other sections to a like concurrence; as likewise to escort the electors to the place of rendezvous, and protect the assembly whilst sitting, with an armed force, if necessary. A partial meeting was in consequence held there, and which continued its sitting for some time after a proclamation was issued by the Convention, ordering the electors to disperse. Indeed it was not without great difficulty that this proclamation was read before the door of that assembly. An armed force was then ordered out under General Menou, the commandant of the guard, to support the proclamation; but they were gone before he arrived. On the 12th, this section issued other inflammatory arrêtés; and on the night of the 12th, another fruitless attempt was made by the government to surround the commune of this section, and secure its members; for which failure, General Menou, who withdrew the troops after he had surrounded it, was degraded, and the command transferred to Barras. On the 13th, the catastrophe took place and ended as I have already stated.

That the party in question meant to subvert the revolution, and restore the ancient monarchy, and that the destruction of the Convention was the first step in the train of those measures, which were deemed necessary to accomplish it, cannot be doubted. A slight attention only to the above facts sufficiently demonstrates the truth of the assertion in all its parts. Even in the primary assemblies, a ground was taken incompatible with the present system. Some free latitude, it is true, the people have a right to take in those assemblies, however limited or special the object may be, upon which they are convened to decide. But as soon as the sections took the same ground, acting in harmony with the electoral corps, in contempt of the law, and in defiance of the convention, the case was altered. From that moment rebellion was announced in form, and the sword of civil war was completely unsheathed; nor could it be restored whilst the convention survived, or without a counter revolution, otherwise than by reducing the revolted sections to order. Fortunately, the latter was the issue, and in consequence whereof everything has since progressed as the friends of the revolution have wished. The revolted sections were immediately afterwards disarmed, and without opposition, and the electoral corps is now legally convened (those of it who have not, in dread of punishment, made their escape) and with a disposition to be more observant of the decrees, and accommodating to the existing government.

But, if this party had succeeded in its attack upon the convention, what would have followed? Would it likewise have succeeded in the other object, to which this was only a step? A conjectural answer can only be given to a suppositious case. My opinion then is, that although the impression would have been a deep one, yet the ultimate issue would have been the same. It is said, and perhaps with truth, that in case the attack succeeded, it was intended the electoral corps should immediately assemble, and place itself, in some measure, at the head of France. The overthrow of the Convention would have left the nation without a government or head, to influence public measures; and in which case, this corps, being a legal one, and at the head of this great City, would have had stronger pretensions to the public attention, than any whatever. 'T is not, however, to be presumed, that it would have assumed the reins of government; but it would have doubtless undertaken to admonish, and the probability is, that in such a state of things, its admonition would have been regarded. With this view, it is believed that the crisis was brought on, at that precise point of time, before the meeting of the electoral assemblies, to admit, in the interval, the communication of the event in case it were perpetrated) to all France, without allowing to the people sufficient time to recover from the dismay and confusion into which they would be thereby thrown. In such a state of things this corps might have made a great impression upon the whole nation, supported as it would appear to be, by all Paris; and as it really would be, at least to that stage, by a considerable portion. At the head of this corps was already placed the old ci-devant Duke of Nivernois, a man not without some literary merit, and whose character had been so free from enormity, and his temper so dormant, that, although imprisoned, and in the list of those who are deemed, under what is called the reign of Robespierre, a fit subject for the guillotine, yet he survived that reign, and received his life as a boon from those who were now threatened with destruction. It was said he declined the presidency; but it is also believed, that his modest disqualification was more the effect of an accurate calculation of chances, in the great game they were playing, than of principle; and of course, that if the blow succeeded, he might be prevailed on to serve. A majority of the corps, many of whom were likewise ci-devant nobles, was believed to be of the same principles. The nation would therefore have beheld, on the one side, the Convention overthrown, perhaps massa-cred, and whose members were, in general, known to be attached to the revolution; and on the other, the electoral corps, with this person at its head, and which it would, of course, conclude was decidedly of opposite political principles; the latter advanced forward upon the ruin of the former, and in some sort possessed of the reins of government. Surely no opportunity more favourable to the views of the royalists could have been sought, than this would have presented. How they meant to improve it, had for tune placed them in that situation, is not known, nor is it probable it will be; for it is to be presumed, that whatever the plan was, admitting there was one already formed for such an event, it had been concerted by the leaders only, and was not to be unfolded, until after the sections were thus far plunged into the same atrocity with themselves. There were two ways by which this oppor-tunity might have been improved; the first, by an immediate declamation in favour of royalty; the second, by electing their own deputies, and inviting the other departments to do the same, for the purpose of putting the constitu-tion in motion. Had the first been adopted, the nation would have, doubt-less, have been greatly confounded, and in the moment of dismay, the royal-ists would, most probably, have come forward, and the patriots lain quiet. Soon, however, in Paris herself, symptoms of discontent would have been seen, and perhaps even in some of those sections which were foremost in the late revolt; many of whose citizens had joined the opposition from principle, in respect to the right of suffrage; some because they had been persecuted, or censured as terrorists, and only because they were patriots; and others because they doubted the political integrity of the present house, and wished it changed. All of these would have been struck with consternation, when they heard that a king was proclaimed, and would have looked back with horror at the scene through which they had passed.

By this time too, some one of the armies would have been seen advancing towards Paris, and which would most probably have had little to do: For I am persuaded, that as soon as the citizens recovered from the extravagance into which they had been betrayed, they would be among the first to fall upon their betrayers. Had the second been adopted, it is probable it would have secured the elections in favour of the royalists; the decrees would have been of course rejected; nor would any of the present members have been re-elected. Soon, however, this would have been seen by the people, and being seen, half the danger would have been provided against. In the memory of those who were friendly to the revolution, (and the catalogue of its friends must be a long one, counting those only whose fathers and sons were slaughtered in its defence on the frontiers,) the destruction of the Convention, under whose banners they had bled, would form a moral cause that would hang heavy on the shoulders of the subsequent administration. The manner of the suffrage, though in form free, would be deemed an usurpation, and the slightest deviation afterwards become a signal for revolt. If they used their power with violence, the same effect would be produced as if a king were immediately proclaimed, and if they used it with moderation they might perhaps prevent the calamity of another crisis; and whiling away in office the time allotted by the Constitution, be enabled in the interim, so far to efface the memory of what had passed, as to secure to themselves afterwards a retreat which would exempt them from punishment. But in neither case would they be able to restore the ancient monarchy. You will observe that my reasoning is founded upon a belief that the army is sound; that the great bulk of the citizens of Paris are so likewise; and that the farmers or cultivators in general, if not decidedly in favor of the revolution, though in my opinion they are, are at least, not against it; and which belief, though perhaps erroneous, is the result of an attentive observation to such facts and circumstances as have appeared to me to merit attention.

But you will ask, if Paris is on the side of the revolution, how happened that such a force was formed there against the Convention, whilst so small a one was marshalled on its side? Let us first establish facts and then reason from them. Paris consists of 48 sections; and of 8 only were actually in arms against the Convention, three for it, and the others neutral. Of those too, who were sent by the eight sections, it is presumable from the peremptory manner of their retreat, and the ease with which they were afterwards disarmed, as likewise by their uniform declarations, at the time and since, that the greater number did not expect to be led against the Convention, or if they did, that they went with reluctance; so that, the real force which marched out for the purpose of actual hostility was in my opinion, inconsiderable. And this too, it is said, was in part composed of adventurers from other quarters, and in some in stances even of foreigners. Still however, there was an actual revolt by those sections, and at best a neutrality on the part of the others; the three who declared themselves for the Convention excepted. How account for this? That the royalists had gained the preponderance in some few of the sections, and particularly that of Lepelletier, is certain. But that this was not the case with many is presumable. It is well known that the inhabitants of Paris in general, wished to get rid of their present deputies, and for reasons heretofore explained. The opposition to the decrees, therefore, may be thus accounted for; and with the greater propriety, because it is certain they were op posed and even by the royalists, upon republican principles; the unalienable right of suffrage, &c. and by which an impression was made in the primary assemblies upon the audience, and thence gradually extended throughout the city. In the primary assemblies too every person was allowed to speak; and it happened, that among the royalists there were some good speakers, and who by taking popular ground, engrossed for the time the public attention; by means whereof they were enabled to practise more extensively upon the credulity of the less enlightened of their countrymen, than they were aware of. It often happens when a collision takes place between friends, and even upon a trivial cause, that one act of irritation begets another, till finally the parties become irreconcilable. How much more easy was it then for artful men, at the present moment, to prevail over the ignorant, and seduce them into error; especially when it is known that the latter already wished a change; that they thought they had a right to make it, and of which right they could not be deprived without the sacrifice of their liberty, in whose cause they had already so long contended, and so greatly suffered.

How explain the extraordinary phenomenon, why the very sections, who on the 4th of Prairial were on opposite sides, should now shift their ground, so as that those who then supported the convention, should now be against it, and those who opposed should now be for it? Taking the convention as the standard, it remains only in any case to explain the motive of such party as wanders from it; for that circumstance alone creates doubt, and of course alone requires explanation. No one will ask why such a party supports the convention, because there can be no motive for such an enquiry. In some cases a party yielding such support may have less honourable motives for it than another party had. I think I have seen such myself: But in no case can the object be a counter-revolutionary one. To this enquiry, then, in this view, I have already given a satisfactory answer, at least so far as I am able to do it; for I have already explained what I deemed in general the cause of the aberration of the sections upon the present occasion, as I did upon the former one; that of the Faubourg St. Antoine and whose present conducts warrants the opinion then given upon that head.

But how happened it, that so many of the disaffected were chosen into the electoral corps, as to give the royalists a preponderance there? How could a people attached to the revolution commit the care of it to those who were its foes, especially to such as, by their station and character, were universally known to be such? This touches a subject extremely interesting; for it leads to facts over which a veil has yet been thrown, but to which history will doubtless do justice; and in which case it will present to view a scene of horror, in some respects, not perhaps less frightful than that which was exhibited under the reign of terror. Behind the curtain, as it were, for it has made but little noise in several of the departments, the terrible scourge of terror has shifted hands, and latterly been wielded by the royalists; who, beginning with the subaltern, and perhaps wicked agents of the former reign, had persecuted and murdered many of the soundest patriots, and best of men. To such a height has this evil risen, and so general was the imputation of terrorism, that in certain quarters the patriots in general were not only discouraged, but in a great measure depressed. It is affirmed to be a fact, by those who ought to know, and who merit belief, that in some of those quarters, and even where the preponderance in point of numbers was greatly in their favour, none attended the primary assemblies; and that in others a few only attended, and who took no part in the proceedings. This, therefore, will account why the royalists took the lead in those assemblies, and why so many of them were chosen into the electoral corps.

But by what strange vicissitude of affairs was this effect produced? How could it happen under an administration unfriendly to royalty? In truth, the explanation is distinctly marked by preceding events, and has been in part unfolded, in preceding communications. Terrorism, or what was then called so, the persecution of the royalists, had gone to such a length, that it became indispensably necessary to end it. To this object, therefore, the whole force of the government was directed, and with effect, for it was accomplished. But in striking at terrorism, perhaps by the unguarded manner of the blow, perhaps by those consequences which are inseparable from such vibrations, and which I deem the most likely, an elevation was given for a while to the opposite extreme. The terrorism of that day was the excess of the passion for liberty, but it was countenanced by those in office, as necessary in their judgment, to bring about the revolution; nor were its acts displayed in private assassination. On the contrary, they were sanctified by public judgments and public executions. The most culpable, therefore, were those who expiated for their crimes on the 9th Thermidor. But with others in general, and even where the excess was criminal, the intention was otherwise. At that point, therefore, which discriminated between the vicious extravagancies of the moment, and the spirit of patriotism itself, should the scale have been suspended. And there by the law it was suspended; for I do not recollect any act of the Convention which passed beyond it. Special outrages were, it is true, specially corrected; but even in these cases I do not know an instance where the correction was disproportioned to the offence. But so nice was the subject upon which they had to act, and so delicate is the nerve of human sensibility, that it was perhaps impossible for the government under existing circumstances, to moderate its rigour towards the royalists, without giving, to a certain degree, an encouragement to royalty. In this view, therefore, it is to be presumed the late event will produce a beneficial effect; for as the views of the royalists were completely unmasked, and defeated, and which were always denied to exist, until they were thus unmasked, it cannot otherwise than tend to open the eyes of the community in that respect, and in the degree to repress the arrogant spirit of royalty. To your judgment, however, these facts and observations, in respect to the late movement, are respectfully submitted.

I have lately been honoured with your several favours of May 29th, June the 1st and 7th, and of July the 2d, 8th, 14th, 21st, 29th and 30th; all of which came to hand almost at the same time, and generally by the route of England; and to which I will certainly pay the utmost attention. As, however, this letter has already gone to an unreasonable length, and especially as I wish you to be correctly informed of the character and fate of the movement in question, I think it best to despatch this immediately, reserving a more particular reply to those favours for a future communication. For the present, however, permit me to add, that as yet no complaint has been made to me against the treaty; nor have I heard any thing from the committee on the subject, since the application requesting information, in what light they were to view the reports respecting it; and which was made soon after the treaty was concluded. If anything is intended to be said, I think it will not be said until after the new government is organized; nor then, until after it is known that the treaty is ratified; and in which case I have reason to apprehend I shall hear from them on the subject. I trust, however, let the event in that respect, or the opinion which the Committee may entertain of that event, be what it may, I shall find that the same amicable and dispassionate councils still prevail towards us, that have been shewn for some time past. To inculcate which disposition, not only by the documents and lights derived from you, but by such others as my own imperfect experience, and often too wandering judgment, have supplied has been, and be assured will continue to be, equally the object of my most earnest wishes, and undeviating efforts.

With great respect and esteem I have the honour to be, Sir, your very obedient and humble servant, Jas Monroe.

P.S. October 25th. As the vessel by which this will be forwarded will not sail until a gentleman, who is now here, arrives at Havre, I have kept the letter with me for the purpose of adding to it what might immediately happen before his departure. On the day after tomorrow, the new government is to convene, and the prospect is now favourable that it will then convene, and precisely on the ground stated in the preceeding letter. Some symptoms were latterly seen which gave cause for apprehension, that the expiring moments of the convention would be moments of great agony and convulsion. Some denunciations and counter-denunciations were made, proceeding from causes connected with the late movement; but happily they are over, without producing any serious effect. A commission of 5 was appointed to make a supplemental report, respecting that movement, and it was expected by many it would end in a proposal to annul the proceedings of several of the departments, whose primary assemblies were said to be under constraint by the royalists, and probably also in the arrestation of several deputies; but that commission has freed every one from uneasiness on that account, by a report just made; and which pro poses only some new provisions for the trial of offenders in that movement, and others in several of the departments, who have committed atrocities of various kinds, under the pretext of punishing the terrorists. Every moment must be deemed critical, in the existing circumstances of this country; being at the eve of a great revolution, a transition from one government to another; and especially when it is known, that there is a party, not despicable in point of numbers, and less so in activity and talents, always ready to seize every incident that occurs to throw things into confusion; and which party is connected, not only with the emigrants abroad, but with the sur rounding powers, by whom the necessary means are furnished for the purpose. But yet it seems as if the Convention would retain its strength to the last moment of its existence and transmit its powers unimpaired to its successors. The decrees are said to be universally observed, and the leading members of both sides of the house are in general re-elected; these are to elect the others, so as to make up the two-thirds of the new government.

Lately Jourdan received a check on the other side of the Rhine, and which occasioned his falling back to the Rhine, upon which river both his and the army of Pichegru are posted. The cause of this is not distinctly known; but certain it is, that the deputy of the military section of the Committee of public safety has been since arrested, upon a suspicion of treachery; as are three others, upon a charge of treasonable correspondence with their enemies; but with what propriety I do not pretend to determine. 'T is worthy of remark, that it was known in England and in Basle before it happened, that there would be a movement here at the time it happened; at which time too, the count d 'Artois landed from England upon the Isle Dieu, near the French coast, opposite the Vendee, where he still is.

A report was yesterday made to the Convention, of an important advantage gained in a rencounter in the Mediterranean, in which the French took a ship of the line and damaged greatly two others; and likewise took 14 merchant ships richly laden and estimated at an enormous sum. Two other advantages in other quarters are spoken of, still more signal than this, but not by authority.

Moneron is returned,[226] but whether by order of the French government (as I suspect, and in consequence of the fortunate issue of the late movement) or the failure of his mission, be it what it might, is uncertain. Be assured if Mr. Jay's treaty is ratified, it will excite great discontent here. Of this, however, I shall be able to speak with more certainty, after the new government is organized.

To James Madison, Paris, October 24, 1795

Dear Sir,—I wrote you yesterday with a view of sending the letter by the same vessel which takes the articles we purchased for you; but as an excellent opportunity, that of Mr. Murray,[227] a very worthy young man, offers, I shall avail of it not only to send the letter of yesterday but to add something to it. Perhaps these articles may likewise be sent by the same opportunity, altho' the vessel sails for New York.

[226] Jean Louis Monneron was a wealthy merchant who made his fortune in the French colonies in America and India. He also sat in the National Assembly as deputy for the East Indies. With his brothers, he formed a merchant bank in 1791 located in Place du Carrousel where he began issuing copper tokens and medals of exchange, notably of superior quality to official French coinage. His "mission" appears to have been related to prisoner exchange talks with the British. (Fischer 2020)
[227] G. W. Murray was a New York merchant. (Hamilton 1899, 401)

I herewith enclose you the copy of a letter to Mr. R[andolph], in ans'r to one of his; as likewise of my correspondence with Mr. Jay relative to his treaty, with such comments as I deemed it necessary to make to Mr. R. on that gentl'n's conduct in relation to that transaction. I sent you some considerable time since by Mr. Perkins of Boston a similar communication, & hope it has reached you; or rather I sent by him what respects Mr. Jay, having previously sent a copy of the other paper. My object was and is to put in y'r possession facts which may be useful in a certain view of things, perhaps to the publick &certainly to myself. So far as it respects Mr. R. the object is at an end for 'tis said he is withdrawn, but if he were not I have no reason to expect an attack from that quarter as it respects the other, however it may yet be useful. In any event you will become acquainted with another instance of the duplicity & finesse of that man, and find, at least I think so, how desirous he was of embarking my reputation here in support of his, and with a view of sacrificing it, in case his merited to be sacrific'd, and of which I had little doubt even at that time. I endeavored to act for the best advantage of my country under the circumstances existing & without compromitting myself in behalf of what he had done or might do: and I now find the benefit of that policy both in respect to the state of things here & with you.

I most sincerely hope the President has not & will not ratify this treaty, for if he does, I greatly fear the consequences here. From what I can learn we shall be deemed rather than otherwise in the scale of the coalis'd powers, and under such an impression it will require moderation in any gov't to withhold its resentment. How cautious, therefore, sho'd the President be in hazarding a step of this kind at the present moment, when the slightest circumstance is sufficient to excite indignation, & even to part the two countries forever. If the treaty is ratified, y'r situation is a difficult one: but even in that case do you not think the seizure on the part of Engl'd of our vessels since, a sufficient ground to declare it broken & void? Perhaps a distinction maybe taken that it was ratified after the seizure began, & of course that such seizure ceased to be a cause. But this is not sound, for if the President has ratified, I presume his motive was the advice of the Senate & w'h was given before the seizure was known. To that act therefore sho'd his ratification be referred & with it be dated. So that the Congress will be at liberty to act upon the seizure as a subsequent thing. In short you have a thousand grounds upon w 'h you may get rid of this treaty, and I sho'd be satisfied with the slightest of these had I a vote to give in the case. But if the treaty is rejected, say its advocates, you have war, & to w'h I reply that if so our dilemma is an unhappy one in consequence of that treaty. To be plundered with impunity was a hard thing, but to bear this treaty also, altho' we universally deem it a calamity, merely because we fear Engl'd is still worse. Surely that nation will not insist on such terms. She has too much regard for us, for Messr's Jay, Hamilton & comp'y, if not for our country to push us to such an extremity, especially when she knows we are so averse to fighting. But I think the conclusion by no means a sound one; for I cannot think it possible, let her menaces be what they may, that in the present state of things Engl'd will make war on us. We see that she is greatly exhausted, and it is the universal report of Americans & others from Engl'd, that there is no calamity yet to befall her which she dreads more than a war with us. Satisfied have I always been that, by a decent but yet determined pressure, we might not only obtain what we wanted & were entitled to, but likewise do it without war; indeed I have tho't it the surest way to avoid war. Still I am of this opinion.

The French have obtained a naval victory or rather advantage in the Mediterranean, in which a ship of the line was taken, & two others greatly damaged indeed 't is said they are run on shore) with 17 vessels, merchantmen richly laden under their convoy.[228] Two other similar advantages yet more signal are spoken of, but not authenticated. The late commotion was a terrible one, but it ended on the next day when everything was perfectly quiet & in w'h state it has since remained: some denunciations have followed but they have vanished in smoke, as yet, two cases only excepted, you will be astonished to hear that all Paris is disarmed, and by ab't 5000 men, & you will of course conclude that the sense of its citizens are for the measure, or it co'd not be done. Indeed it was by a decree only, for under it they disarmed themselves. If they were not for it the situation of the republick wo'd be an unpleasant one, for otherwise the citizens wo'd be deemed ag'nst the revolution, & w'h is certainly (I speak of a great majority) not the case.[229]

I write now in the evening of the 24. On the 27 the new gov't assembles, & as every moment of the interval is of importance I take occasion to let you know that all is yet well & promises to be so. For a few days past there was a prospect of some terrible denunciation of Julien ag'nst Boissy D'Anglas & others upon a suspicion that the latter had fav'd the late commotion & today

---

[228] This appear to be a refence to an October 7, 1795, naval engagement during which a French squadron led by French Rear Admiral Joseph de Richery captured a large British convoy of thirty-one merchant vessels. The British convoy, escorted by three ships of line and several frigates under Commodore Thomas Taylor, sailed from Gibraltar and were intercepted by the French squadron. During the action the French ships captured a British 74-gun ship of line and all but one merchantmen. (Corvisier and Childs 1994, 173)

[229] After the violence of early October, and with the active support of the Committee, Napoleon sought to disarm the National Guard as he did not believe that its middle-class rank and file would be able to maintain order and suppress future riots. In its place, he created a Municipal Guard of Paris, a full-time gendarmerie which was strongly militarized. In effect Paris had been placed under the control of the man who was also the commander of the home army, Napoleon Bonaparte. (Mansel 2001, 4)

it was expected they wo'd be made in form as a committee was appointed to rep't supplementally respecting that commotion. The report was made by Julien & I attended & heard it but it contained nothing of the kind, indeed it was conciliatory, I know B. D'Anglas and think him true to the revolution, as I likewise think Julien, whom I also know. After this I am persuaded nothing will intervene, & that the new gov't will commence under favorable auspices.[230]

An American just from London tells me that Mr. Pitt was at Deal & along the Eng'h coast during the late troubles here, and just before the C't D 'Artois was landed in the Isle Dieu close by the French coast opposite the Vendee where he now is.[231]

Very sincerely I am y'r friend, Jas Monroe.

P. S. I think it probable an attempt may be made to vindicate Mr. Jay ag'nst the imputations raised ag'nst him for his misconduct in the negotiation with Gardoqui. If such attempt is made it will be made by a publication of his reports in the office of State which contain his justification: but the true view is in the secret journal of Congress & which ought like wise to be publish'd in case the others are. There is no objection to publishing the journal (or so much as respects this topic) w'h does not apply to the publication of the reports with equal force: and to publish the one and not the other will be a partizan manaeuvre not very honorable to those who do it. They were in the Senate (I mean the reports) when I left it, & Mr. K[232] wanted them published, but I wanted the others also, & this put a stop to the business. I beg of you to attend to this for me, & give suitable notice thereof to my friends in that body.

The present is indeed an awful moment here; the change of the gov't & the momentary suspension of aff'rs makes it greatly so, especially when it is known, as it is, that foreign powers are, if not at the bottom, yet deeply concerned in every mov'ment. Gardoqui when he returned to Spain settled a secret service account for six hundred thousand dollars laid out in America; and a short time after our peace a man (an ancient Tory)[233] but a friend of his,

---

[230] On October 22, 1795, a Montagnard faction in the Convention, including Tallien, unsuccessfully tried to prevent the election of Boissy d'Anglas, as well as selected other moderates (and certain suspected Royalists) to the new Directory (Lefebvre 1964, 204)

[231] Encouraged by optimistic testimony from royalists within France and émigrés outside, British faith in the fragility of the revolutionary regime, the British landed a disastrous counterrevolutionary French expedition to Quiberon in 1795. William Pitt the Younger was a prominent British Tory statesman. (Walt 1996, 124)

[232] Rufus King (Hamilton 1899, 406)

[233] The "ancient Tory" is most likely Dr. John Connolly, who held the patent to a large body of land in Kentucky that had been confiscated as the property of a Tory during the American Revolution. After the confiscation of the Kentucky lands he became British agent and continued to delve in various American land-related intrigues, particularly the

& who came from France for the purpose offer'd Mr. Hichburn five thousand pounds sterling from Lord D[orchester][234], not to influence his opinion but presuming it w'd be right as a proof of friendship and who likewise told him similar tokens were intended for others whom he named to him also afterwards. The first fact depends on the authority of Littlepage[235] who told it to J. Barlow some time since on his return from Spain whither he was sent by the King of Poland. Barlow adds that Littlepage appeared to know nothing of the negotiation which had been on foot in America. The other fact is from the person himself. The French have received a check upon the Rhine w'h has caused a retrograde manaeuvre to the Rhine. It appears that the neutrality of some of the Eup. powers with whom peace was made, was broken by the opposite party & by wh, a wing of the French army was turned & w'h occasioned this mov'ment.[236] 'Tis not deemed a serious thing; two deputies, however, one of whom was in the military sect'n of the Committee of P. S. & the other suspected likewise of unf'r practices with their enemy, are arrested, as likewise is General Miranda.[237]

To the Secretary of State [Timothy Pickering, Acting] Paris, November 5, 1795

Sir,—On the 27th ultimo, the convention ended its career, by declaring that its powers ceased; and immediately afterwards the installation of the new government began in the same hall, by a verification of the powers of its deputies, and their distribution into two branches, according to the mode prescribed in the Constitution; and which was completed on that and the succeeding day.238 It was found upon inspection, that the decrees here-

Spanish conspiracy of 1788 which created a diversion in favor of King George. (Green 1891, 299)

[234] British General Guy Carleton was Lord Dorchester. (Valentine 1962, 493)

[235] Lewis Littlepage was an American diplomat who served in the royal court of the last Polish King, Stanisław August Poniatowski. (Davis 1957, 255)

[236] A reference to the Battle of Hochst, wherein Austrian forces engaged, then compelled General Jean Baptiste Jourdan's French army to retreat behind the Rhine. (Smith 1998, 104)

[237] Francisco de Miranda was one of the first of the Latin American revolutionaries. Fleeing from his Venezuelan homeland in the 1780s, Miranda eventually arrived in London in 1790. William Pitt rejected his plan for revolutionizing South America, so Miranda went to France, where rebels found better favor. He became a general officer but fell from power with his friends, the Girondists, and was cast into prison. (Perkins 1955, 111)

[238] In this letter, Monroe conveys to Pickering his impressions on the October 26, 1795, National Convention's self-dissolution and the subsequent and transfer of its powers to the new regime, the Directory. The constitution of the new government provided for a two-house legislative body, the Council of Elders and the Council of Five Hundred. The members of the legislature were to be chosen indirectly by individuals who could meet certain property qualifications. Elections were to be

tofore noticed, were universally obeyed; and that of the two-thirds of its legislative branches, who were to be taken from among the members of the Convention, more than a majority were elected by the department; so that the duty imposed on those who were elected, of supplying the deficiency by their own suffrage, became proportionably more easy and less objection-able. This, therefore, was immediately executed by ballot; and after which the interior organization of each branch followed, and which took up a day or two only; then the members of the Directoire, or executive, were chosen, and which was done on the 31st ultimo, and whereby the new government was completely installed.

When I observe that the scene, which was exhibited upon this great occasion, resembled in many respects what we see daily acted on our side of the Atlantic, in our national and state assemblies, you will have a better idea of the tranquillity and serenity which reigned throughout, than I can otherwise describe. Nor shall I be accused of an unbecoming partiality, if I draw from the increasing similitude in theirs and our political institu-tions, the most favourable hopes of the future prosperity and welfare of this Republic. The adoption of a new constitution, founded upon the equality of human rights, with its legislative powers distributed into two branches, and other improvements in the executive and judiciary departments, though still perhaps imperfect, yet certainly far beyond what past experiments here gave reason to expect, is an event of great importance, not only to France, but perhaps to mankind in general. Its complete inauguration too assures us that its merits will be tried. Though, indeed, under the existing circumstances of a war with the neighbouring powers, who are interested in its overthrow; of a strong party within, incessantly labouring to promote the same object; together with the derangement of the finances and other embarrassments

held annually for one-third of the members of the councils, but the first election would not be held until 1797. The Legislative Body of 1795-1797 consisted of many members of the former National Convention since by a so called "two-thirds decree" about two-thirds of the members of the latter would serve in the Directorial legisla-ture. This decree was widely criticized and was partly responsible for the so-called Vendemiaire October 5 uprising in Paris which was crushed by General Bonaparte's "whiff of grapeshot." As a whole, the legislature from 1795 to 1797 consisted of moderate and experienced men. There were various deputies, however, who felt that the powers of the legislature were too limited. The Council of Five Hundred could discuss and introduce resolutions while the Council of Elders adopted or rejected them. It also controlled finances, but it had no prerogatives in the realm of foreign affairs. The system of local government, as created by the National Assembly, was retained with the exception of the district which was abolished. But the Executive was given the power to appoint commissioners who supervised local administra-tions and secured the execution of the law. In many ways these men were the fore-runners of the prefects and subprefects of the Consulate and the Empire. (Homan 1972, 99)

which were inseparable from the difficulties they had to encounter; the experiment ought not to be called a fair one. If, however, it does succeed, and the republican system is preserved here, notwithstanding the various and complicated difficulties which opposed its establishment, and still shake its foundation, it will certainly furnish a complete refutation of all those arguments, which have in all ages and nations been urged against the practicability of such a government, and especially in old countries.

Reveillere Lepeaux, Ruebell, Sieyes, Le Tourneur and Barras are elected into the Directoire; and who are all distinguished for their talents, and integrity, as likewise their devotion to the revolution; a circumstance which not only furnishes reasonable ground whereon to estimate the principles of those who chose them, but which likewise tends essentially to give stability to the revolution itself.

I write you at present only to communicate this important event, and will hereafter, as heretofore, keep you regularly apprized of what shall appear to me to merit communication.

I have the honour to be with great respect and esteem, Sir, your very obedient Serv, Jas Monroe.

P. S. Sieyes has declined accepting his seat in the Directoire, and Carnot is appointed in his stead. Mr. Fauchet has lately arrived, and as he appears to be extremely dissatisfied with Mr. Jay's treaty with G. Britain, and is apparently well received by his government, I doubt not his communications on that head will be attended to.

To Thomas Jefferson, Paris, November 18, 1795

Dear Sir,—Your favor of the 26 of May did not reach me until lately, owing as I presume to its having been committed to some private hand and by whom it was retained to be delivered personally until that prospect was abandoned. I was extremely gratified by it as it led me into a society which is very dear to me & often uppermost in my mind. I have, indeed, much to reproach myself for not having written you and others of our neighbours more frequently, but I have relied much on you not only to excuse me personally, but to make my excuse to others, by assuring them how little of my time remains from publick & other duties, for those with whom by the strong claims of friendship I have a right to take liberties. Before this, however, you have doubtless recd. mine of June last and wch. gave a short sketch of affrs. here, so that culpable as I am, still I am less so than I might have been.

I accept with great pleasure your proposal to forward my establishment on the tract adjoining you, in the expectation, however, that you will give yourself no further trouble in it than by employing for me a suitable under-taker who will receive from you the plan he is to execute, that you will draw on me for the money to pay him, & make my plantation one of the routes you take when you ride for exercise, at which time you may note how far the execution corresponds with the plan.[239] With this view I shall look out for a model to be forwarded you as soon as possible, subjecting it to yr. correc-tion, & give you full power to place my house orchards &c. where you please, and to draw on me by way of commencement for the sum of 1,000 dols. to be paid where you please 3 months after it is presented. If to be paid without this republick 't is probable the draft will be most easily disposed of in sterg. money. This sum is all I can answer in the course of the ensuing year calcu-lating always on the possible contingence of a recall & upon which I have always calculated from the moment of my introduction into the Convention, & still calculate depending on the course of events on yr. side of the Atlantic. With this sum a suitable number of hands may be hired & oxen bought to draw the stone, which with you I prefer, put the ground in order &c. &c. to be in readiness to proceed with greater activity the year following. These hands may plant the trees, enclose & sow the ground in grass which is laid off & destined for the buildings of which, however, you will best judge observing that Hogg be instructed to give occasional aids with the other hands when necessary. Believe me there is nothing about which I am more anxious than to hear that this plan is commenc'd and rapidly advancing, for be assured, admitting my own discretion is my only guide much time will not intervene before I am planted there myself. I have mentioned the proposal you are so kind as make me to Mr. Jones, but as 't is possible my letter may unfold that item in my private affrs. not to him, but to some of my good friends in a neighbouring country, as my official dis patches have those of a publick nature, I beg of you likewise to communicate it to him as of my wishes in that respect.

---

[239] As background to the property discussion, it should be noted that Monroe had for some time desired to acquire property near Jefferson's Monticello. Indeed, on February 15,1789, he expressed his solicitous regard for his political benefactor: "It has always been my wish to acquire property near Monticello," adding, he had at last acquired "tolerably good" land near Jefferson's, so that "it puts it within my reach to be contiguous to you when the fatigue of public life, shod dispose you for retirement." His only uncertainty was over whether to move immediately or to wait for Jefferson's resettlement there. Here, upon the news of the availability of addi-tional land, Monroe again suggests his fealty when he states, "...make my planta-tion one of the routs you take when you ride for exercise." Similar entreaties would continue through the next decade, until Monroe finally made his estate habitable in 1797. Arguably, the property transactions were Monroe's possibly subconscious means of increasing his importance to Jefferson. (Burstein 1998, 398-399)

I have written La Motte & directed him to draw on me for what you owe him & have his answer saying he has drawn, for 3 or 4.00 £ but yet his bill is not presented. I likewise think him an honest man and deserving more than a mere official attention. I found him on my arrival in arrestation not because he had committed any positive crime but because the whole commercial class had drawn upon it, & often not without cause, the suspicion of being unfriendly to the revolution, & which in his instance was increased by the circumstance of his having married an Engh. woman. He was, however, shortly afterwards set at liberty & since he has exercised his consular func-tions. I will also procure you the books & other articles mentioned but shall not forward them till the spring for the reason you mention. I will likewise seek out those of yr. friends who have survived the storm, remind them of yr. inquiry after their welfare & apprise you of the result. A terrible storm, indeed, it has been & great its havoc especially among those in a certain sphere of life, but still I doubt not I shall find many have survived it among yr. friends.

I rejoice to hear that Short is to be our neighbour. By his last letter I am to expect him here in a week or two & with Mr. Pinckney, the latter having as I presume adjusted the affr. of the miss: & the boundaries. I suspect the relict of Mr. Rochfct. forms the attraction. If the Carters will take me for their pay master for what lands they have for sale & fix a price which you approve I will most willingly purchase the whole. I have western lands in possession of Mr. Jones for a part of which only he has been offered £2000 Pennsa currency & which I shod. be happy to vest near me: an idea equally applicable to the case of Collé.

You have I presume seen the new constitution & will I doubt not concur with me that altho' defective when tested by those principles which the light of our hemisphere has furnished, yet it is infinitely superior to any thing ever seen before on this side of the Atlantic.[240] The division of the legislature into

[240] The powers of the executive were rather extensive; it could declare war and sign treaties, appoint ambassadors, and organize armies. It also appointed the ministers who were to head the different departments and supervised much of the state's bureaucracy. Unfortunately, the powers of the legislative and execu-tive branches were too rigidly divided and there was nothing in the constitution that provided for a solution of conflicts between the two. Still, Monroe consid-ered that, perhaps with time and patience, the constitution could be made reasonably successful, and France might emerge with her first stable republican regime, noting that this constitution was "far better than the first experiments." Moreover, he believed it to be a great event for France and mankind in general. But, Monroe realized, there was little alternative. Most people in France had little enthusiasm for the Republic which had brought economic chaos and war. The Directory failed to solve these problems, and, consequently, its position became more and more tenuous. Already the election of the remaining one-third to the Legislative Body in 1795 reflected a degree of hostility to the Republic since most

two branches, one to consist of 500 & the other of half that number, will secure always in both due attention to the interest of the mass of the people, with adequate wisdom in each for all the subjects that may occur. The mode of election, too, & the frequency of it in both branches seems to render it impossible that the Executive shod. ever gain such an influence in the legis-lature, as by combination, corruption, or otherwise, to introduce a system whereby to endanger the public liberty: whilst on the other hand the Execu-tive by its numbers & permanence, one of 5 yielding his place to a successor annually only, seems in regard to this theatre, where the danger is always great & suspicion, of course, always at the height, well calculated to unite energy & system in its measures with the publick confidence, at the same time that it furnishes within itself a substantial guarantee in favor of the publick liberty. The judiciary too is better organized than heretofore. About 10 days past, the constitution was completely installed in all its branches & since each has been in the exercise of its respective functions. The effect which the change has produc'd is great indeed. The council of ancients occu-pies the hall lately held by the Convention, & the contrast which a tran-quil body, in whose presence no person is allowed to wear his hat or speak loud, a body who have little to do, & who discuss that little with temper & manners, is so great when compared with the scene often exhibited by its predecessor, that the Spectators look on with amazement & pleasure. The other day a demand was made by the Directoire on the 500. for a sum of money & which was immediately granted & the bill in consequence sent to the 250, who upon examination discovered there was no appropriation of it & for that rejected the bill. The Directoire then accommodated its demand to the article in the constitution as did likewise the council of 500 & whereupon the other council passed the bill. I mention this circumstance to shew the change in legislative proceedings whereby calm deliberation has succeeded a system which was neither calm nor deliberative. Since the govt. was organized, not more than two or three laws have passed & those of no great importance and the people go to rest of a night in tranquility consoling themselves with the grateful reflection, that now a strong impediment is opposed to the rage for legislation. They rejoice to find that their legislators have sup plied the place of action by reflection. Under this govt. too the spirit of faction seems to be curbed. Formerly when a member of any note rose and denounced another, it put his life in hazard, let his merit or demerit be what it might. But latterly some denunciations were threaten'd in the 500, & to which the parties menac'd rose and demanded that their accusers shod, put

of the new deputies were moderate-conservative men. And it was against this backdrop that Monroe penned this letter to Jefferson. (Homan 1972, 100)

in writing the allegations & sign them that they might prepare for & appear in defence, but this silenc'd the others, & thus tranquility seems to be established &confidence daily increasing.

The paroxysm which preceded the final dissolution of the convention & particularly that of the attack upon it on the 13 of Vendn. or of Octr, you will have heard long before this reaches you. In a few words, however, I will give you a general idea of it. The change of the govt. or transmission of the powers of govt. from one system to the other was a great experiment in the present state of affairs & which could not be made without some danger to the revolution; but yet such was the general solicitude to get rid of the revolutionary system that a refusal to make the experiment wod. likewise be attended with danger. All France seemed to call out for a stable government & this call was finally answer'd by presenting before the nation the constitution in question. But experience had shewn that each succeeding assembly had persecuted the members of the preceding one: a constituent especially was an object not less attractive of the rage of Rob.spr. than a ci-devant Bishop or even a chouan[241]. And reasoning from experience it was to be feared, that the deputies of the late Convention would be exposed in like manner to the resentment of those who took their places, & this creates in them a desire to keep their places & which was attempted by two decrees whose object was to provide for the restriction of 2/3ds of the legislature of the new govt. from among the members of the Convention, according to a principle of the constitution wch. applies hereafter & requires an annual change of 1/39 only, and which decrees were sub mitted with the constn. for the sanction of the people. By some of the primary assemblies these decrees were adopted & by other rejected: the Convention, however, reported & in my opinion with truth that the majority was for them & of course that they were obligatory on the Electoral assemblies. This was denied by the opponents to the decrees by whom a systematic effort was made to defeat them, first by newspaper discussion, next by section: arrets which defied the authority of the Convention, & finally by assembling in arms in great force to attack that body and which done on the day above mentioned.

I candidly think that this attack upon the Convention, as it failed, was of great utility to the revolution. The system of terror was carried to such a height by Robespierre & his associates, that in the vibration back which

---

[241] The term "chouan" loosely referred to members of any of the bands of peasants, chiefly smugglers and dealers in contraband, who rose in revolt in the west of France in 1793 and joined the Vendean royalists. The Breton word chouan, meaning "screech owl," is supposed to have been applied originally as a nickname to the nom de guerre of the Frenchman Jean Cottereau, leader of the unsuccessful revolt, and afterward extended to his followers. (Campbell 2020)

ensued, some danger seemed to threaten, not the overthrow of the revolution, but to put it a greater distance than there was otherwise reason to hope its happy termination; for when this vibration had gained its utmost point, it so happened that the govt. was to be transferred into other hands. In this stage, too, the royalists who were formerly persecuted more than was upon any principle justifiable, & in whose favor & upon that acct. a general sympathy was excited, & which was of course due to humanity & had no connection with their political principles, had gained an attention which under other circumstances wod. not have been shewn them. The probability, therefore, is that if the election had come on unaided by that incident, more than a majority of that description of people wod. have been thrown into the legis-lature. But as the attack failed, it produc'd in a great measure the opposite effect, for in consequence the decrees were not only strictly executed, but the former censure agnst. the royalists whose views were now completely unmasked, proportionally revived; many of whom and among those some who were candidates for the legislature & with good prospects of success, took refuge in the neighbouring countries or the Vendee, according as circumstances favored their escape.

On the side of the Convention there were 3000 foot & 600 horse of Pichegru's army & abt. 1000 or 1200 the citizens of Paris (the latter of whom were honored by their opponents with the title of terrorists) and on the opposite side there were perhaps in activity twice that number, whilst the other citizens of Paris were neutral. The battle was short for as soon as the assailants saw that opposition was made, their numbers diminished &continued to diminish by battalions till finally none were left but those who were too marked in their characters to hope for concealment; and which latter partly surrendered in a body on the next day at noon to the number of abt. 500. In the contest 4 or 500 on both sides were killed and wounded. It was extremely complained of on the part of the assailants that the Convention accepted of the terrorists, that it suffered cannon to be used in its defense, since they, the assailants, had none or but few, & where-upon they urged that the fight was not a fair one. You will observe that all Paris was agnst. the decrees, 2 or 3 sections only excepted, & because as many of their own Deputies were hereto fore cut off, they wod. be forc'd to elect their members from among those of the Convention belong'd to other departments, & because they did not like to choose even those of them who remained. This being the temper of the city in the commencement the royal-ists took advantage of it first by opposing the decrees & which they did with great address, contending for the unalienable right of suffrage which they said was thereby infringed & demanding wherefore had the good citizens of

France fought & bled so freely, & otherwise suffered so much if they were now to be enslaved, a slavery too the more odious because it was imposed by those who had assumed the mask of patriotism? One step led on to another till finally recourse was had to arms.

Before this event I doubted whether foreign powers had much agency in the interior movements &conventions of this republick, but by it I was satis- fied they had, for it was known in Engld. Hamburg & Balse before it happened that there wod. be a movement here at the time it took place: at which time, too, the Ct. d ' Artois approached the court from Engld. & between whom and the authors of that movement in Paris & the Vendee there was obviously the utmost harmony of measures. Something of the kind is to be trac' d in several pending events but not so strongly marked, at least not to my knowl- edge as in the present case. Yet the ordeal thro' which France has passed and is passing in the establishment of a republican system is called an experi- ment of that system, whose convulsions are contrasted with the gloomy & sullen repose of the neighb'ring despotisms, by the enemies of republican govt. & to the disadvantage of this latter species of govt. so often does it happen by the decrees of a blind fatality, that the authors of crimes not only succeed in exculpating themselves from the reproach they justly merit, but even in fixing the imputation of guilt upon the innocent.

The French were lately checked on the other side of the Rhine & which caused their retreat to the Rhine: but yet they hold the two posts of Manheim & Dusseldorph on the other side. 'Tis thought some serious rencounters will take place there soon & wch. may produce a serious effect likewise upon the war with the Emperor and on the continent. The late organization of the Directoire by wch. men of real talents & integrity, & in the instances of Car not & Barras of great military talents, are plac'd in it, the former of whom planned the last campaign, & the latter commanded the National Gds. in the great epoch of the 9th of Therr. when the tyranny of Robespierre was broken, and on the last event of the 13th of Vendre. is well calculated to secure a wise arrangement on the part of France.

In negotiation nothing has been lately done. Many negotiations were depending; they were doubtless suspended to wait the issue of the late elections & the organizatn. which ensued, in the hope on the part of the coalised powers that something wod. turn up from the struggles that were then expected to favor their views. But now that that prospect seems to be over 't is probable they will be commenc'd & peace their early offspring. An event which will be greatly promoted if Pichegru succeeds agnst. the Austrians, and still more so if his majesty of Engld. is agn, intimidated by the unfriendly grunts of his discontented & afflicted subjects. Unhappy old man![242] His reign has indeed been a reign of mourning & of sorrow to the world: for we trace upon its several stages in America, the East & in Europe no other vestiges but those which are marked by the blood of the innocent, who were slaughtered in all those various climes of the world & without regard to age, sex or condition. And yet we are told by many that he is a mild, an amiable and a piteous man, and that the govt. in which he presides & by means whereof these atrocities were perpetrated, is that model of perfection of which, thro' all antiquity, Cicero & Tacitus had alone formed only a faint idea, but with which the world was never blessed before. But you know I must not speak irreverently of dignities & therefore I will add no more on this subject at least for the present.

I hear that the French have just gained a consider able advantage over the Austrians on this side of the Rhine near Manheim. The Austrians crossed the R. in its neighbourhood to make a diversion there, were met by a body of French, defeated & driven back. Other particulars we have not. Mrs. M. & our child join in affectionate wishes to yr. self & whole family & pray you also to make them to my brother Joseph & all our neighbours & that you will believe me most affectionately yours.

(unsigned)

To the Secretary of State [Timothy Pickering, Acting Secretary] Paris, December 6, 1795.

Sir,—I was lately honoured with originals and triplicates of your favours of the 12th and 14th of September last. The duplicates are yet to be received. By the first of these letters, I learn that the President has ratified the late treaty with England: And by the second, the measures taken to vindicate our territorial rights, that were violated by the captain of a British frigate, in an attempt to seize Mr. Fauchet, the French minister, within our jurisdiction, on his return home; and to which communications due regard shall be paid, as occasion requires.[243]

That the treaty was ratified, was a fact well established, before the receipt of your favour. It was, indeed, generally credited before the arrival of Mr. Fauchet; by whom it was confirmed, and afterwards doubted by none.

---

[242] A reference to England's King George III. (Hamilton 1899, 421)

[243] Monroe was referring specifically to escapades of Captain Rodham Home of the HMS *Africa* who had flagrantly violated U.S. neutrality in waters off Newport, Rhode Island, in an attempt to capture the departing French minister Joseph Fauchet, who had been recalled to France after the execution of Robespierre. The Washington administration could do little to protect Fauchet [his ship eventually slipped away under cover of fog and he escaped] but revoked the authority of the British vice consul in Newport who had cooperated with Home. (Harper 2004, 159)

As I had no reason to presume, from any communication from your depart-ment, that the contrary would be the case, so I had never calculated on the contrary; nor had I given this government any reason to calculate on the contrary; having left it to form its own judgment on that point, according to its own lights; so that, in this respect, I have nothing wherewith to reproach myself on the score of discretion.

The effect which this incident produced in the councils of this country, through its several stages, may be traced in my former communications; and to which I beg to refer you. To these I have, at present, nothing material new to add. Symptoms of discontent, it is true, are still seen; but whether they will assume an aspect more unpleasant, I know not: If they do, or any thing else occurs of sufficient importance to merit your attention, I will certainly apprize you of it, and without delay.

You likewise saw, by my former communications, that I understood and acted upon that part of my instructions, which explained the object of Mr. Jay' s mission to England, differently from what it appears, by your favour of the 12th of September, and by Mr. Randolph's of the 1st of June preceding, it was intended I should understand and act on it; and whereby I was placed, by the course of events, in a very delicate and embarrassing dilemma; from which, indeed, I am not perhaps yet fully extricated; though I hope and think I am. Upon this head, I have only now to observe, that as soon as I had reason to believe, that Mr. Jay's instructions embraced objects which I had before thought they did not, I profited of what I heard, and acted accordingly; keeping out of view, so far as depended on me, what had before passed between the government and myself upon that subject, and to which I with pleasure add, that I have never heard the least intimation on it since. In reviewing this particular trait in my conduct here, you will, I doubt not, do me the justice to observe, that when I made the suggestion alluded to, it was not rashly done, nor without sufficient motive; on the contrary, that (paying due regard to the actual state of our affairs at the time) I was called on to make it by considerations the most weighty, and which ought not to have been dispensed with; considerations, however, which I now forbear to repeat, having heretofore sufficiently unfolded them.

I have the pleasure to enclose you the report of Mr. Skipwith, upon the subject of the claims of many of our citizens who were heretofore injured by the occurrences of the war, and in consequence intitled to indemnities; and by which you will find that many of those claims are settled; and derive useful information in respect to others.[244]

---

[244] In November 1795, thieves had broken into Fulwar Skipwith's Paris office, stealing three silver ingots valued at over $4,000. They were part of a $120,000 loan repayment

I likewise send you a letter from Mr. Fenwick, explaining his conduct in regard to the charge exhibited against him in your department.[245] As Mr. Fenwick has always proved himself to be an useful, indeed a valuable, officer in the station he holds, and as the error imputed to him might be the effect of judgment only, and which I think it was, I have thought I could not better forward your views or the interest of my country, than by continuing him in the discharge of the duties of his office, till the President shall finally decide in his case. He will, doubtless, communicate with you on the subject; so that the interval will not be great before I have the decision in question, and which will, of course, be duly executed.

Two days since, count Carletti, minister from Tuscany, was, in consequence of some offence given by him to the government, ordered to depart from Paris in 48 hours, and the bounds of the Republic in eight days. 'T is said the offence consisted in a demand made to visit the daughter of the late king, of whom he spoke in terms of extreme commiseration; and which was thought to be, not only an interference in concerns exclusively their own, but to have thrown some reproach on the French government.[246] The count, I hear, departs to-night by the way of Marseilles.

Soon after the government was organized, the minister of foreign affairs announced a day on which the Directoire would receive the ministers of foreign powers; and who were requested to rendezvous for that purpose at his house, to proceed thence to that of the Directoire. We did so, and were presented, without regard to precedence, to that body, and whose President addressed the whole diplomatic corps in a short discourse; the principal object of which was, to assure it of the cordiality with which it was welcomed here by the representatives of the French people, and which it contrasted with the pomp and ceremony of the ancient court; which, he said,

---

to the United States. Skipwith, who was responsible for the shipment, immediately notified both the police and Monroe, who duly reported it to Philadelphia. Federalist papers accused both Skipwith and Monroe of faking the burglary to buy their homes in Paris and speculate with the remaining money. In the spring of 1798, the Federalists in Congress would announce an official investigation into the affair. (McGrath 2020, 182-183)

[245] Joseph Fenwick, the American consul at Bordeaux, was charged with having French property under an American name. The French thought it proper that he should cease from his consular functions until an enquiry could be made. Monroe initially believed that the matter was more of a personal nature but, upon reflection, as it concerned the conduct of a public officer, that opinion was changed and, although Monroe personally supported Fenwick, he was asked to step down from his post, Monroe concluding that his discharge would ensure greater diplomatic peace. (Hamilton 1899, 424)

[246] Carletti represented to the Duchess d 'Angoulême that he, of all the foreign diplomats in France, was the most favorable to the French, and had been sent to take the first steps towards a better understanding between France and Tuscany, thereby paving the way for a peace between Austria and France. (Hamilton 1899, 425)

was neither cordial nor fraternal. I mention this latter circumstance merely to contradict the account given of the address by the journalists, and who made a particular speech for the President to each minister.

Manheim has certainly fallen again into the hands of the Austrians, with the garrison; the amount of which is not known, but presumed to be several thousands. But in Italy the fortune of the war is on the side of France; for the same day which announced the surrender of Manheim, announced likewise a great and decisive victory over the Austrians, in the other quarter. The details of killed and wounded are also not yet accurately known; but it is understood that 4 or 5, 000 are taken prisoners, many slain, and the whole army put completely to rout.[247]

Since the organization of the new government, the character and deportment of all the departments are essentially improved. The legislative corps, in both its branches, exhibits, in the manner of discussion, a spectacle wonderfully impressive in its favour, when compared with what was daily seen in the late convention. And the executive departments begin to shew an energy which grows out of the nice partition of their duties, and the greater responsibility that belongs to each. In truth, the vibration from the system of terror had, by the force of moral causes, gone so far, and produced so deep an effect, as to have greatly relaxed the whole machine of government. It was certainly felt in the departments, in the public councils, in foreign negotiations, and in the armies. A short space of time, however, will now shew how far the change, which has taken place in the government, will furnish the means of an adequate remedy.

Mr. Pinckney has, I hear, closed his business in Spain to his satisfaction; and is now on his route back, intending to take Paris in his way.[248] I trust this report is, in every respect, well founded; of which, however, you will doubtless be correctly informed, before this reaches you.

With great respect and esteem I have the honour to be, Sir, your most obedient and very humble Serv, Jas Monroe.

P. S. Count Carletti has notified to the French government, that he cannot depart without the consent of his own.

---

[247] The Battle of Mannheim [October 18-November 22, 1795] began when 17,000 Habsburg Austrians defeated 12,000 Republican French soldiers led by Jean Charles Pichegru. In the engagement, the French were driven from their camp and forced to retreat into the city of Mannheim where they surrendered after a thirty-day siege. (Smith 1998, 104)

[248] Thomas Pickney, the American ambassador to Britain, had been sent to Spain to negotiate a treaty regarding boundaries and U.S. navigation on the Mississippi River. On October 27, 1795, his efforts resulted in the Treaty of San Lorenzo, wherein Spain agreed to allow Americans to export goods through the Mississippi River. (Southwick 1998, 18)

To the Secretary of State [Timothy Pickering] Paris, December 22, 1795

Sir,—Since my last, I was favoured with yours of the 9th of October, with a quadruplicate of that of the 12th of September; of which latter, the original and triplicate were before acknowledged.249

Since my last, too, I have received a note from the minister of foreign affairs, complaining of the conduct of Mr. Parish, our Consul at Hamburgh, in granting passports for France to British subjects, equipping the emigrants, and acting in all cases as the English agent; a copy of which note, and of my reply, are herewith forwarded you.[250] I hear, also, that his conduct was even more reprehensible than is stated by the minister; for that he not only equipped the emigrants, but did it in American bottoms, with a view of protecting them under our flag. In calling your attention to this subject, permit me to add, that two American citizens, Benjamin Jarvis and Thomas Randall, both of New York, the former a respectable merchant, as has been represented to me, and the latter known to the President as captain of artillery in the late war, and lately as Vice-Consul at Canton in China, have requested me to communicate to you their wish to obtain appointments in the consulate, in any of the respectable ports of France, or other European ports connected with the trade of France; and that I have reason to believe they would, either of them, be happy to accept the appointment in question. In case Mr. Parish is removed, permit me further to suggest the propriety of giving to his successor two commissions; one for Hamburgh, and the other for Altona, in the neighbourhood of Hamburgh, but under the jurisdiction of Denmark. Much business is done at Altona, on account of the greater freedom of its trade; for Hamburgh, though in some respects a free and independent city, yet in others it feels the influence of the Emperor; and is therefore a less eligible port for mercantile transactions, and especially those connected with France.[251]

I sent you with my last a report of Mr. Skipwith, upon the cases submitted to his care, for adjustment with this government; and shall continue to give

---

[249] Pickering had been formally commissioned Secretary of State on December 10, 1795. (Hamilton 1899, 427)

[250] In 1790, President Washington appointed John Parish, a naturalized Hamburg citizen of Scottish birth, to the position of "vice consul for the port of Hamburgh." The U.S. Consulate in Hamburg was opened on June 17, 1790, as the eleventh American Consulate worldwide. John Parish lost his position as consul in 1796 after financing and organizing British troop movements against revolutionary France, the first U.S. ally, during the War of the First Coalition. (Public Affairs 2019, 5)

[251] Benjamin Jarvis was subsequently appointed to Altona, while Thomas Randall was not selected. Randall died in 1797 after a long maritime, governmental and philanthropic career. (American Philhellenes 2020; Richards 2016)

him all the aid in my power in those cases which remain unsettled, and apprize you regularly of the progress. To that of Mr. Girard, due attention shall certainly be paid.[252]

At present no symptoms of an approaching peace are to be seen; unless, indeed, the most vigorous preparations for a continuance of war be deemed such; and which sometimes happens. The Directoire has called on the Legislature for a supply of 600 millions, in specie, and which was granted immediately by a law which proposes raising it in the form of a loan; of which I send you a copy. The greatest possible exertions are making by that body, and which seem to be supported by the legislature, in putting the armies, the fleets and the interior into the best possible order; and so far as I can judge from appearances, these exertions seem to produce the effects that are desired from them; for to those who are friendly to the revolution they give confidence; and from those who are not, they command respect. 'T is said that Pichegru and Jourdan have lately gained several important advantages over the Austrians, in actions which, though not general, were nearly so; and that, in the result, they have resumed their station before Mayence. The former part of this report, I believe, to be depended on; the latter wants confirmation. In Italy the troops of this Republic continue to reap new successes; in which quarter indeed, since the victory mentioned in my last, they have met with but little opposition.

Latterly the views of Prussia have become more doubtful than they were before. The conduct of Prince Hohenloe, who commanded the Prussian troops at Francfort, in the neighbourhood of the French and Austrian armies, during the retreat of the former, and who were stationed there to preserve the line of neutrality in favour of Prussia, 't is said, could scarcely be deemed neutral. For the civilities which were shewn by him to the Austrians upon that occasion, 't is also said, he has been rewarded since by some complimentary attention from the Emperor.[253] The Dutch appear apprehensive that the

---

[252] Stephen Girard 's claims under the several classes of "French Spoliation Claims " were numerous. Some were settled under the Convention of 1803 and the Treaty of 1831 with France; but some have descended to the present day, being among those presented by the City of Philadelphia to the United States Court of Claims under the Act of Congress approved January 20, 1885, and for which payment has been provided, among other French Spoliation Claims, in An Act of Congress approved March 3, 1899. (Hamilton 1899, 429)

[253] Throughout the summer of 1795, French troops, under Jourdan and Pichegru, lay along the Rhine, hindered in their plans by lack of supplies and by the dissensions at home which kept the government fighting for its very existence. With the fall of Luxembourg and the failure of the invasion in Bretagne, the forces of the Republic on the Rhine found themselves in a position to open the long-delayed campaign. Their first offensive movement, the crossing of the Rhine, led to a violation of the demarcation line established by the treaty of Basel. Eichelkamp, on the east bank of the Rhine and within the line, was seized, despite the protest of the Prussian

king of Prussia will seize a suitable opportunity, if any offers, to favour the restoration of the Stadtholder; and 't is possible the conduct of the Prince Hohenloe, above referred to, may have increased that suspicion, by giving at least an insight into what might be the views of the Prussian cabinet, in case the retreat had continued; or any great reverse of fortune should here after befall the French arms. It every one is certain, however, that moments of difficulty are always moments of great jealousy; and that sometimes, upon such occasions, suspicion is thrown upon those who do not deserve it.

The Count Carletti, late envoy, &c. from Tuscany, left Paris for home 4 or 5 days since. He had refused going 'till he had heard from the Grand Duke; and remained notwithstanding the reiterated orders of the Directoire. Finally, however, he was ordered to depart in 24 hours (this was not done before, as I stated in my last) with intimation that force would be used to compel him, in case he did not. He still held out, however, the flag of defiance. The 24 hours expired, at which moment a commissary, with a carriage &c. from the government, waited to receive his orders for departure; or in other words, to take the Count by force, and conduct him safe beyond the bounds of the Republic; and which was accordingly done. The diplomatic corps was summoned, by a member either averse to this peremptory mode of proceeding, or friendly to the count, to interfere with the Directoire in his behalf: But several members of that corps were of opinion, that although sometimes a demand is made on the government of a minister who gives offence, to recall him; yet there is no obligation on the government offended, by the law of nations, to take that course; but that it may take any other, and even upon slight occasions, to rid itself of him, more prompt and summary, if it thinks fit; and in consequence no step was taken by the diplomatic corps, upon the subject.

I enclose you also a note from the minister of foreign affairs, complaining of the seizure and condemnation of the Corvette Cassius; which, he says, is in violation of the treaties between the two Republics; and to which I replied,

---

officers that such action violated the neutrality of the venue. The French had reckoned well on the weakness of the Prussians and their unwise confidence in French protestations of loyalty to their obligations respecting the Demarcation Line. With Eichelkamp in their hands, they were able to threaten the Austrian communications and force the Imperial troops into a retreat. The Prussian troops had practically all been withdrawn from the frontier into Prussian territory on the lower Rhine. The exception was the Prussian force under Prince Hohenlohe, which had drawn a cordon around Frankfort. Here it was that the French and Austrians both violated the neutrality line, and Prince Hohenlohe, feeling himself too weak to resist, contented himself with dignified notes of protest until ordered by his government to withdraw into Franconia.(Ford 1903, 105)

that I would present the subject to your view; and doubted not I should be enabled to give a satisfactory answer thereon.[254]

With sentiments of respect and esteem, I have the honour to be, Sir, your very obedient servant, Jas Monroe.

---

[254] Samuel Davis was a commissioned officer in the French navy, even though he held U.S. citizenship. On August 4, 1795, the French corvette the *Cassius* entered the port of Philadelphia as a public ship of war under Captain Davis's command. The next day, Philadelphia merchant James Yard filed a "libel" to initiate a civil case in admiralty in the District Court of Pennsylvania seeking to attach the *Cassius* and arrest Captain Davis. Yard alleged that Davis, who "pretended an authority from the French republic," had captured the schooner the *William Linsday*, which Yard owned, and that Davis was responsible for the financial loss that resulted when the *William Lindsay* and its cargo were wrongfully detained at Port de Paix. The Cassius was duly attached, and Davis arrested. Davis asserted immunity from the district court's jurisdiction on the grounds that he had acted as an agent of France. This was a significant legal case at the time, as it illustrated the diplomatic dance occasioned by litigation involving a foreign sovereign's property or the conduct of its officials. Further, the Cassius affair confirmed the U.S. Executive's consistent disavowal of the power to stop private civil proceedings against a nondiplomatic official. But it also shows a step toward more direct involvement, in the suggestion that applicable law precluded a French public ship from being rendered liable to civil process in the courts of the United States. But this "suggestion" of immunity for the ship was not accompanied by a similar suggestion of immunity for its captain, despite France's request. So, as the *Cassius* literally rotted in port, prevailing understandings about foreign official immunity continued to crystallize: first, that U.S. courts could compel nondiplomatic officials to respond to civil suits even if they claimed that their actions had been authorized by a foreign government; and second, that the Executive lacked power to order the dismissal of a civil suit against a nondiplomatic official, even though the Executive would maintain an active interest in litigation that gave rise to diplomatic protests. (Keitner 2012, 739-737)

1796

To James Madison, Paris, January 12, 1796

Dear Sir,—Yours of the 6th of April is the last I have rec'd, tho' since that period I have written you eight or ten at least. The theatre too on which you are has been & probably will continue to be an interesting one, for it is presumable the same subject which creates such solicitude among the people at large will produce a like effect among their representatives.[255] Certain it is that the temper which was shown upon that subject by the people with you, has produced a happy effect here, & moderated greatly the resentment which began to display itself before their sentiments were known, for

---

[255] This appears to be a reference to the escalating Republican resistance to the Jay Treaty in America that began with a meeting held at Boston's Faneuil Hall on July 13, 1795. In succession came similar meetings at Philadelphia, New York, Richmond, Baltimore, Portsmouth, Trenton, Wilmington, Charleston, and other places. The Boston gathering resolved that the treaty was "highly injurious to the commercial interests of the United States, derogatory to their national Honor and Independence, and may be dangerous to the Peace and happiness of their Citizens." Although the meeting's resolutions attacked almost every provision in the treaty, much of the argument centered on trade, including the complaint that the treaty "prevents the United States from imposing any further restrictions on British trade alone" [discrimination] and "surrenders all or most of the benefits of a commercial nature, which we had a right to expect from our neutrality in the present war." In other words, by granting most-favored-nation status to Great Britain the treaty denied the possibility of using discrimination to open the British West Indies completely, ending any ho pe for a truly free trade outside the old mercantilist restrictions. Moreover, by accepting a limited definition of neutral rights, including a broad definition of war contraband, the Washington administration appeared to be turning its back on the ideals of the revolution and the concept of free trade and the rights of neutrals. (Gilje 2013, 54)

as soon as this government saw that the people were dissatisfied with the treaty, and that a strong motive for their dis satisfaction proceeded from the interest they took in the welfare of France, from that moment it was obvious its chagrin diminished & that in sympathy with us again, it gradually lost sight to a certain degree of its own concerns, so far as they were supposed to be affected by that treaty & became instead of a party in, a spectator of ours. This is the external view of the effect which Mr. Jay's treaty & its incidents produced upon the councils & people of France, & more than the external view I cannot give you, for I deemed it upon every principle most suitable for me to stand aloof upon that subject, never touching on it except when mentioned informally to me, & then confining myself strictly within the limits observed by the other party, giving such explanations only as were sought & inculcating always good temper and moderation on the part of this government towards us, as the surest means whereby to unite forever the two republics. Whether therefore the subject has been acted on by the Directoire, or will be, or what will be the result in case it is I cannot tell you.

The progress of this government is so far wise, steady and energetic. Its outset was distinguished by an effort to introduce into every department of the administration the most rigid economy & whereby many abuses were reformed & the publick expenditure greatly diminished. The finances were in the utmost confusion, the assignats having depreciated almost to that point beyond which they would not circulate, & there was no other resourse. The Directoire exposed freely this state of the nation, demanding funds to carry on the war & adding without which it could not be carried on, recommending too at the same time the project of a forced loan whereby about 25 millions sterling in specie could be raised, & which was adopted.[256] By this project the assignats were to be redeemed or taken in, in discharge of the loan at 100 for 1 & which would consume of it about 12 millions sterling rather less than one half. Specie & produce only are admitted for the residue. This loan however forms a fund upon which they will most probably, for a while & un till some more complete system is adopted, be circulated again. By this paper I am told a great portion of the antient debt is discharged, so

---

[256] The Constitution of 1795 established an executive Directory from which the period has taken its name. There were five directors, one of whom was to be replaced each year, in an obvious attempt to avoid dictatorship, either collective or individual. Directors were elected by, but distinct from, the two parliamentary bodies, a Council of Five Hundred and a Council of Elders, the latter containing 250 deputies all aged over 40. The single chamber legislature was thus abandoned, though the checks and balances introduced by the new system might frustrate rather than preserve its liberal objectives. The reforms mentioned by Monroe, while adopted on December 10, 1795, by the councils of the Ancients and the Five Hundred, proved to be unpopular and ultimately unsuccessful. (Crook 2002, 24)

that by it the war has not only been carried on to the present stage (deducting the amount of the national domains that are sold and paid for) for nothing, but the nation exonerated from a considerable portion of that debt which depressed it before the war. This loan is now collecting and without exciting any great murmur among those upon whom it falls. The forms of business too in both houses are correct and discreet according to our ideas on the subject, and their attention seems so far to have been bestowed on the most urgent topics & in general the result such as might have been wished. In short in every respect the character of the public councils has greatly altered for the better; the effect whereof is plainly to be discerned in the publick opinions as well as public measures: for you observe among all classes an increasing opinion of personal safety, at the same time that the government displays a degree of energy that was never surpassed before. The royalists begin to despair for they know that the hopes of royalty are gone as their hopes were founded in the continuance of anarchy and confusion, to promote which of course all their efforts were united. Intemperate zeal too is restrained, but the restraint is always easy, indeed it is a self one, or rather it does not exist, when the administration possesses the confidence of the people & wields the government according to their wishes. I give you the aspect up to the present time & to which I add with pleasure that the probability is it will continue.

You will doubtless hear before this reaches you that there is a truce between France & Austria & which was asked by the Austrian generals. When a truce is asked & granted it argues that neither party has essentially the advantage over the other, or it would neither be asked or granted, and such was I believe the fact in the present instance.[257] The proposition from Austria was for a truce for three months, but admitted by the Directoire for one only. What the motives of Austria are is unknown: That peace is among them, perhaps the principal one is presumable. By some it is suspected that the message of the English King to his Commons,[258] was the immediate stimulus, since as the same persons suspect, that measure was taken in haste,

---

[257] The French signed an armistice with Austria in December 1795. It was considered a welcome reprieve, as the war was yet another, seemingly endless strain on a government whose administrative, economic, and social reforms were continually hampered by the chronic domestic violence that prevailed in many parts of the country. (Hanson 2009, 136)

[258] On December 8, 1795, British Prime Minister William Pitt, had delivered a message to the House of Commons from the George III, declaring, "His Majesty, on this occasion, thinks proper to acquaint the House, that the crisis which was depending at the commencement of the present session, has led to such an order of things in France, as will induce His Majesty (conformably to the sentiments which he has already declared) to meet any disposition to negotiation on the part of the enemy, with an earnest desire to give it the fullest and speediest

in accommodation with existing circumstances on the spot & of course without the knowledge of Austria, whereby, and especially as the former objects of the war were abandoned a disposition for peace avowed the jealousy of that power was excited. Perhaps however, it may be a mere financing project on the part of Austria, in the hope that by appearing to seek peace a loan for the next campaign may be more easily obtained from England. But my opinion is there is a negotiation for peace depending & which may probably have that issue with Austria, if not with other powers & the Southern more especially. The moment Austria makes up her mind to yield the Belgic the war with her is over, & the ruin of her army in Italy with other events may have inclined her to that measure, whilst the light advantages she has gained on the Rhine may have suggested the idea that now is the time to treat with some apparent credit. But with England there will probably still be difficulties, for I think France will never hear a proposition from her upon the subject of peace, that is not preceeded by a declaration that she will restore everything taken since the commencement of the war from herself & Holland, & which it is possible her present superiority at sea may prevent: certainly it would prevent it, if the discontents of the people there & which daily increase, on account of the scarcity of bread & the dearness of it, which latter proceeds not more from that cause than the superabundant circulation of paper, which raises the price of everything, & threatens more fatally to impair the manufactures &commerce of that country than even long & destructive wars by all their other evils.

You will also have heard of the demand of Count Carletti minister &c from Tuscany to visit the unfortunate daughter of Louis XVI,[259] who was on her departure for Basel to be exchanged for Barononville[260], & several of the deputies who were surrendered to the Austrians by Dumourier & of the manner in which that interference was resented by the Directoire. Suspending all intercourse with him & ordering him forthwith without the bounds of the republic. The Count explained & expostulated but without effect. The Diplomatic Corps convened & by some of whom it was urged

effect, and to conclude a treaty for general peace, whenever it can be effected on just and suitable terms for himself and his allies." (Ashton 1885, 32)

[259] In 1795, the French government released from prison in Paris Marie Thérèse, the eldest child of Louis XVI and Marie Antoinette, and later the Duchess of Angouleme, in exchange for five French noblemen held by the Austrian government. The actual exchange of persons took place in Jean Luc Legrand's home in Basel, as "neutral ground." In 1798 Legrand would become the first president of the Swiss Helvetic Republic. (Kurtz 2018)

[260] Pierre Ruel de Beurnonville, an army general and minister of war, was seized and conveyed to the headquarters of the Prince of Coburg until exchanged. Afterwards he sided with Bonaparte and was appointed ambassador to Berlin. (Hamilton 1899, 437)

that the Count could not be suspended or ordered without the Republic by any but his own sovereigns except in case of conspiracy: that the order to that effect was of course a violation of the rights of nations, and by others it was urged that every Government had a right to rid itself of a minister who gave offense & by its own means: that to demand his recall was, upon trivial occasions the ordinary usage, but that it was not prescribed by the law of nations, but by that of civility & good manners only. Was this however a light occasion, a demand by the representative of a foreign power to visit the unfortunate & thereby stigmatizing the revolution & reproaching France for that effort which she deems a glorious one? If demands of this kind are allowed from the representatives of other powers what kind of demands will be inhibited? And if it is meant to check such, is it not best to do it upon some such occasions & in such manner as the present, whereby the sense of the French Government being decisively pronounced, will be well understood at home & abroad.

The meeting broke up without a decision; not withstanding which it was published in all the gazettes that the whole diplomatic Corps had united in a re monstrance to the Directoire against its procedure in this case & without effect. Upon which another meeting was called & held for the purpose of expressing to the government the reason which the members of that Corps felt of the injury which was done them by that misrepresentation, & to request of the minister of foreign affairs, since he knew that no such step was taken, that he would contradict the report. Upon this proposal too no decision was obtained. By it however the spirit of some of the members of that Corps was checked & the body itself perhaps forced from like attempts to involve it in the interior & revolutionary politics of France & against the spirit of the revolution for the future. But the Count replied to this Government that he would not withdraw till he had the order of his own, upon which it was notified to him if he did not commence his route within 24 hours he should be sent out by force & to which a like reply was given. The 24 hours expired, at which moment a commissary with a carriage attended to take his orders for Basle, & by means whereof he was conducted to Basle & with all convenient speed. The communication of this event & its incidents was made by the French Minister to the Grand Duke & by whom it was well received, for instead of taking it in high dudgeon as was expected by many, he despatched immediately & upon the first intimation of it a minister pleni-potentiary for the express purpose of disavowing the demand of Carletti & declaring his respect for the French government, & so rapid were the move-ments of this Envoy, that he is already on the ground & has already made his disavowal to the minister of foreign affairs. By this measure therefore the

French Government has lost nothing without &certainly within & especially by the manner in which it has terminated it will acquire great respect. *I
am inclined to believe that England does not mean to execute the treaty & intends to justify
her evasion by any obstacles the H. of R. may throw in its way. If then any thing is done it
is to be hoped the administration will immediately change to give an opportunity to try the
effect of other councils it is late to do it but I think not too late.*261

Unsigned

To James Madison, Paris, January 20, 1796

Dear Sir,—I think I mentioned to you sometime since that Mr. Paine
was with me. Upon my arrival I found him in Prison, & as soon as I saw
my application in his behalf would be attended to, I asked his release &
obtained it.262 But he was in extreme ill health, without resources, & (affairs
being unsettled) not without apprehensions of personal danger, & therefore
anxious to avail himself as much as possible of such protection as I could
give him. From motives that will readily occur to you I invited him to take
a room in my house, & which he accepted. It was his intention at that time,
sometime in Octr 94, to depart for America in the Spring, with which view in
Feb' following, I asked permission of the Com. of P. safety for him to depart,
charged with my despatches for the Department of State, a motive which
I presumed would authorize them to grant the permission asked: but was

---

261 Italicized text in this letter was originally in cipher. Decoded text provided by the
National Archives. (Mason and Sisson 2020)

262 In fact, much of Monroe's waking hours were spent dealing with the travails of his
fellow Americans in France. "I found many of my Countrymen here laboring under
embarrassments of a serious kind," he related to Randolph. Once his arrival was
announced, Monroe was beset by Americans at his doorstep. Those who could not come
to him covered his desk with letters. Many lacked passports and money; others were
speculators looking for Monroe to expedite the wheels of business, and thereby their
own fortunes. S still others were languishing in prison cells, some perilously close to
death, or a death sentence. "Eight months I have been imprisoned, and I know not for
what, except that the order says— that I am a Foreigner." So wrote Thomas Paine to
Monroe from Luxembourg Palace, a massive ornate structure converted to a prison by
Robespierre when victims filled cells of other penitentiaries quicker than the guillotine
could dispatch them. Paine was confined to an eight-by-ten-foot cell on the ground floor.
Rainwater seeped through the walls and floor. Gouverneur Morris was unwilling to
risk helping such an ardent anti-Federalist. "Paine is in prison," Morris chortled, "where
he amuses himself with publishing a pamphlet against Jesus Christ." Monroe thought
otherwise. To him, Paine was not only a patriot and gifted essayist but a brother-in-arms.
Still, Monroe waited before replying to Paine's letters. He had received no instructions
regarding Paine from Randolph, nor did Morris have a thing to add before his departure. The prisoner was both an American and French citizen: How much leeway did
Monroe have to free a fellow American who was also a citizen of France? He decided to
explain the dilemma to Paine while assuring him that "to the welfare of Thomas Paine the
Americans are not, nor can they be, indifferent." Patience, Monroe counseled. He would
find a way, and indeed, he did. (McGrath 2020, 134-135)

---

answer'd it could not be granted to a deputy; tho' indeed he cod. scarcely be considered as such, having been excluded the Convention as a foreigner, & liberated upon my application as an American citizen. His disease continued & of course he continued in my house, & will continue in it, till his death or departure for America, however remote either the one or the other event may be. I had occasion soon after Mr. Paine's enlargement to intimate to him a wish, that whilst in my house, he would write nothing for the publick, either of Europe or America, upon the subject of our affairs, which I found even before his enlargement he did not entertain a very favorable opinion of. I told him I did not rest my demand upon the merit or demerit of our conduct, of which the world had a right to form & would form its opinion, but upon the injury such essays would do me, let them be written by whom they might & whether I ever saw them or not, if they proceeded from my house. He denied the principle, intimating that no one would suppose his writings which were consistent, were influenced by any one: that he was accustomed to write upon publick subjects & upon those of America in particular, to which he now wished to turn his attention, being able to depart thither & reside there for the future. But as I insisted that I owed it to the delicacy of my publick & private character to guard myself even by erroneous inferences, against any improper imputation or compromittment whatever & especially as I did not wish any impression to be entertained of me which I did not create myself, being the arbiter of my own measures & the guardian of my own name, & which I knew wo be affected thro. that door if it were opened, with many if not generally & therefore entreated him to desist. He then accommodated, more however from an apparent spirit of accommodation, than of conviction that my demand was reasonable or my argument sound. Thus the matter ended and I flattered myself I shoud, for the future, enjoy the pleasure of extending to Mr. Paine, whilst he remained here, the rights of hospitality & without exposing myself to the inconvenience I so much dreaded and laboured to avert. Latterly however an incident has turned up which has again disquieted me on the same subject. He had com mitted to Mr. Pinckney when here the other day on his return from Spain a letter from his bookseller in London, upon the propriety of carrying & delivering which unsealed Mr. Pinckney asked my opinion. I frankly told him, in his place I would carry nothing I did not see & approve of & as he was of the same opinion he desired me to communicate it to Mr. Paine & which I did. Mr. Paine owned that his letter contained an extract of one he was writing or had written to Frederick Muhlenburg in Philadelphia[263] upon english & american affairs & which he

---

[263] Italicized text in this letter was originally in cipher. Decoded text provided by the National Archives. (Mason and Sisson 2020)

---

intended sho' be published with his name. Mr. Pinckney returned the letter, not chusing to be the bearer of it. Upon this occasion I revived with Mr. Paine the argument I had used before, expressing my extreme concern that he pursued a conduct which, under existing circumstances, gave me so much pain, & to which he made little other reply than to observe, he was surprised. I continued of the same opinion I formerly was upon this subject. Whether he will send the one or the other letter I know not. I shall certainly prevent it in both cases if in my power. That to Engl' is not sent as yet. 'Tis possible the one for America has gone or will be sent. Let me entreat you therefore to confer with the gentlm to whom it is addressed & request him in my behalf if he receives such an one, to suppress it. In any event I have thought it necessary to possess you with these facts that you may use them as occasion may require to guard me against unmerited slander.

Since my last which was of the instant nothing new has occurred. Murmurs are heard against the forced loan, but yet the collection progresses, so that there appears no reason to doubt its execution. The armies on both sides keep their respective positions near the Rhine; nor is it probable the truce will be renewed, tho' on this point nothing transpires. 'T is known that Engl' is willing to leave France in possession of the Belgic & give up everything taken from her, provided she is permitted to retain the Cape of Good Hope etc. I say it is known because I have it from a respectable person who has had opportunities of knowing the views of the Engl' govt. But I think France will reject this with disdain, tho' indeed Holland has little claim on her to continue the war on that account, having made no effort whatever in her own behalf. This latter country presents to view a curious & interesting spectacle at the present moment. Its conquest by France was at the moment when the public mind was vibrating here from what was called Terrorism to the opposite extreme, the effect of antecedent & well known causes. Under this impression the Deputies in mission with the Armies in Holland were appointed & as they likewise felt and obeyed the same impulse, dreading terrorism as the worst of political evils (altho' there was no analogy in the situation of the two countries nor likely to be), it was natural they sho turn their attention to it where they were, as one it was Is more especially their duty to avoid. Such too was their conduct by means where of the early & flattering prospects of a complete revolution were checked. More latterly the error of this policy has been seen thro' & will doubtless be remedied so far as it depends now on the councils of France.[264] Unless the govt is placed

---

[264] From the very outset, the French revolution was an almost continuous succession of conflicts during which the various factions not only called on armed support from the street, but also sought to obtain the allegiance, and later the control, of the soldiers. After 1792 successive French governments had assigned representatives or

completely in the hands of the people there will be in the publick councils neither energy nor integrity to the cause of the people.

Your China will go from hence in the course of a few days when I will send you an invoice of it. It is a plain neat service, sufficient in number & cheap. If you will permit me I will procure for you in the course of the present year furniture for a drawing room, consisting of the following articles. 1. Chairs, suppose 12 or 18. 2d two tables or three after the taste which we prefer. 3d a sofa, perhaps 2. These all of tapestry & to suit, if to be had, the curtains we sent you, either one or the other sett. 4th a clock to stand on the chimney piece, & which chimney piece I will send also, of marble, if you wish it. I wish you to send me a list of what other things you want & especially of books, & I will provide & send or bring them with me when I return home. I will procure everything as cheap as possible, & adjust the amount when I have occasion for it. Mr. Jefferson proposes to have a house built for me on my plantation near him & to which I have agreed under conditions that will make the burden as light as possible upon him. For this purpose I am about to send 2 plans to him submitting both to his judgment, & contemplate accepting the offer of a skillful mason here who wishes to emigrate & settle with us, to execute the work. I wish yourself & M. Jones to see the plans &council with Mr. Jefferson on the subject.

Sometime since Mr. Ketland from Phila came here with Mr. Yards recommendation & which disposed me to shew him & his family all the attention in my power.[265] Indeed the circumstance of his having married Mr. M's daughter [Elizabeth] who was with him was of itself a good recommendation. Mr. K. however brought with him his sister who was an Engl subject as likewise was one of his servants for whom also he asked my passport. I told him I co grant it only to American citizens. He then asked me to demand it of this govt. & to which I replied that if I demanded it, I must do it as a favor. To ask a favor of this govt at the present time was not agreeable to me: to ask it in behalf of Engl subjects, in whose favor we were already suspected to be sufficiently biased was impolitick & against my uniform conduct, & in the rejection of the solicitations of Mr. Pinckney & Mr. Jay in many instances,

civil commissioners to the armies of France to oversee their conduct. Thereafter, the army primarily fought to protect and then expand the revolution against foreign adversaries, the ebb and flow of war greatly affected the fortunes of parties and factions in France where troops were used against domestic opponents. The 'bayonets', as they were called, increasingly determined the outcome of the near chronic schemes, plots, coups and countercoups, and dominated the last convulsions of the dying revolution. (Rothenberg 1989, 981)

[265] James Yard, of Philadelphia, was associated with American shipping interests. Elizabeth Meade was the daughter of George Meade, one of the largest provision merchants during the American Revolutionary War. She married Thomas Ketland, a successful British firearms manufacturer. (Hamilton 1899, 445; Dallas 1888, 47)

one only excepted & that where the party had his wife & family in America: His father & mother were American citizens & himself about to remove there. I told him however I wod. take charge of the cases & obtain pass-ports if possible without compromitting myself, & in case this could not be done I wod. ask for them. I requested in consequence an American citizen to state the case & make the application in behalf of his sister & the servant, & which was done with effect. I mentioned when Mr. Ketland first called on me that we shod be happy to see his lady &c. when convenient &c. being disposed to shew her all the civilities in our power. But she never called & in consequence we never saw her. It is the rule of Paris, applicable in all cases, that when a stranger arrives male or female, he or she visit those whom they wish to visit. This rule applies with greater force to publick ministers & their families & is universal throughout Europe & I believe the world, espe-cially on the part of the people of the countries they represent & for the obvious reason that in so great a city those resident would never know who arrived, if not thus advised of it. With this rule Mrs. M. complied herself on her arrival & many American ladies who have since arrived have also complied with it & who wo have cause of offence if she changed it in favor of any other. I mention these things that you may apprize Mr. Yard of them, that in case misrepresentation is given he may be aware of it. I do not know it was the wish of his family to be acquainted with us, or that any offense is taken. I presume the contrary is the case as I think you & Mr. Yd will upon the above statmt but as I know that misrepresentation is sometimes made I have thought proper to give this statement. I shall write Mr. Yd & D: Stevens in a day or two to whom & their families present our best respects. Our best wishes for your own & Mrs M' s health.

Sincerely I am yr fnd.

unsigned

Of the first paragraph of this letter I will send a copy to Col: Burr to go agnst accidents.[266]

I am satisfied we shall never have our just weight upon the scale of nations, nor command the respect which is our due or enjoy the rights of neutrality without a small fleet. It is astonishing what weight a beginning in that line of the decent kind will have. Let our coasts be well fortified & such

---

[266] The copy to Aaron Burr had the following postscript, "To A. B. You cannot conceive our solicitude to hear what passes on your side of the Atlantic. By the publick papers, as late as the 10 of Novr, we find that Mr. Jay's treaty has given much dissatisfaction in many parts of the U. States, & we wish to know whether that sentiment has abated or still continues, & in the latter case what its object is. Assure yourself that the temper which was shewn upon that subject by our citizens at large has produced a happy effect here, & moderated &c." (Hamilton 1899, 447)

a force of the kind be raised as will protect us from small detachments (and they will never send others) and we take an imposing ground immediately. This is worthy your most serious consideration.

To the Secretary of State [Timothy Pickering], Paris, January 26, 1796

Some weeks past the property of William Vans, a citizen of the United States, was attached by Joseph Sands, another citizen of the said States, in a tribunal of France at Havre; where the cause was sustained, and judgment rendered in favour of the plaintiff.[267] From this judgment the defendant appealed to the Superior Tribunal of the department at Rouen, where I believe it is now depending. As soon as the suit commenced, Mr. Vans applied for my interference, claiming, by the 12th article of the consular convention between the two republics, an exemption, at the instance of a fellow citizen, from the tribunals of the country: the cognizance of such controversies being, as he supposed, thereby exclusively vested in the consuls of each nation, within the jurisdiction of the other. I examined attentively the convention, and was of opinion, that the construction insisted on by Mr. Vans was found; but yet as the subject was import ant in respect to the principle, and questionable in point of policy, I wished to decline any interference in it, until I had your instruction. He continued, however, to press me; urging that if such was the import of the article, it vested in him a right which I ought to secure him the enjoyment of; the deprivation of which too in the present instance would be his ruin; for that the execution of the judg-

---

[267] This is an example of how Monroe took measures for the protection of American citizens in France. In view of the trouble caused by Englishmen who had secured passports under the guise of Americans, the utmost care was necessary in this matter, and Monroe promised the Minister of Foreign Affairs to scrutinize all cases closely. In extending this protection Monroe insisted upon the right of American citizens to a trial by consul. In the case of William Vans, an American residing in Havre whose property had been seized by Joseph Sands, another American, he called the attention of the Directory to their right of trial by an American consul. This demand, it must be conceded, was scarcely consistent with Monroe's defense of American violations of this stipulatiom. Upon the passage of a decree that all strangers not specifically exempted should depart at least ten leagues from Paris, Monroe asked that the one hundred and fifty Americans residing in the French capital should be excepted. As these American citizens were for the most part engaged in business, he asserted that it was for the interest of France, as well as of the United States, to allow them to remain. To carry out the purpose of the French government, he proposed that all passports made out previously to the decree be recalled, and new ones issued. Monroe also sent a list of Americans in Paris for whom he could vouch, expressing at the same time his willingness to aid in detecting frauds. This proposal must have been satisfactory to the Directory, as there appears to have been no further correspondence on the subject. (Vincent 1907, 58)

ment by the sale of the merchandize attached at Havre, where there was then no demand for it, would not only subject him in that view to a severe loss; but that he was likewise sued for the same debt in America, and where judgment would likewise be probably rendered against him. Finally, therefore, I did apply in his behalf, by a letter to the minister of foreign affairs, of which I send you a copy;[268] explaining my idea of the import of the treaty in the case in question; and requesting that the executive (so far as depended on that branch, and provided it concurred with me in opinion) might cause the same to be executed; and to which I have yet received no answer, though I am assured verbally, that the Directoire concur with me in the construction; and that a correspondent intimation thereon will be given by the minister of justice, to the court where the suit now is; and with whom it will probably be decisive. I state this case that you may apprize me how it is the wish of the President I should act in cases of the future, and even in the present one, if not finally settled before I hear from you; and which may possibly happen. If it be wished that such controversies should be decided by the courts of the country, I doubt not such a construction and practice will be agreeable to this government; but if the contrary is preferred, you will, I presume, see the necessity of prescribing by the suitable authority, how the consular courts are to be held; how their process is to be executed, and appeals conducted.

---

[268] The enclosure: "Citizen Minister, I observe by record of the proceedings of the Tribunal of Commerce at Havre, of which I send you a copy, that a dispute is introduced and sustained there between Joseph Sands and William Vans, two American citizens; relative to a bill of exchange drawn from America, and which belongs exclusively to one of the parties. The property of Vans was arrested by Sands, and condemned by the court of Havre, in satisfaction of the claim above mentioned; and from which decision it was carried by appeal to the Superior Court at Rouen, where it now is. In this stage I have thought proper to call your attention to the subject, that in case the executive government of this Republic should deem it proper to interpose, it may be able to do it with effect. By the 12th article of the consular convention between France and the United States, it is stipulated, that all disputes which may happen between the citizens of either party, in the dominions of the other, shall be settled by their respective consuls, and by them only. The article specifies in its close, some particular parties whose disputes shall be thus adjusted: But yet the true construction appears to include within it all disputes which may take place between citizens of either party, within the jurisdiction of the other. If such then is the true construction of the article, and which I apprehend it is, it necessarily follows that the proceeding of this court is in contravention of that article, and in that view merits the attention of the executive government, whose opinion will doubtless be regarded by the court. That the article was dictated by policy, and formed for the mutual accommodation of both parties, cannot be doubted. A principal object of it probably was, to prevent suits in both countries, between the same parties, for the same debt, and at the same time; whereby an innocent party might be doubly harassed, and to the general detriment of commerce. In this light, however, I do not think it necessary to discuss the subject. I think it my duty only to bring it before you, upon the principles of the treaty, and to ask that interference of the government in this case, which it may deem suitable." (Hamilton 1899, 448)

As connected with this subject, permit me to call your attention to another, and upon which I likewise wish to be instructed. For the port of Havre there are at present two consuls, or rather a consul and a vice-consul; both of whom, Mr. Cutting and Mr. Lamotte, are recognized by this government. Was it intended the latter commission should supercede the former, and in that case should I take in the former? or is it intended that both should exist at the same time; the power of the vice-consul being dormant only when the consul is present? I wish to know in what light I am to consider these appointments, since thereby I shall know to whom I am to look for the performance of the consular duties of the port.[269]

A third one of the same kind occurs, and which I think proper to mention to you. Sometime since, Mr. Pitcairn was appointed vice-consul for Paris, and in respect to which appointment, I deemed it my duty to present before you several considerations, growing out of his character, as a British subject, and the actual state of things here; which made it inexpedient to demand his recognition of this government, until after they were weighed, and I in consequence further instructed on that head. These were stated in my letter of the 17th of May last, and to which, as yet, I have received no answer. As Mr. Pitcairn probably expects to hear from me on this topic, I shall thank you for information of what I in to say to him, and how I am to act in that respect.

The collection of the force loan continues, and will, I think, succeed. But what its product will be, is a point upon which there is a diversity of opinion. Some think it will fall short of the sum at which it was estimated, whilst others carry it much beyond that estimation. Certain, however, it is that by means thereof the embarrassments of the government will for the present be relieved, and time given for the maturity and adoption of a more complete system of finance; which subject is now under consideration of the council of five hundred.

About the twenty-fifth of December last a truce was asked by the Austrian generals Wurmser and Clairfayt, of Pichegru and Jourdan, for three months, and granted, subject to the will of the Directoire; by whom it is said it was allowed for one only; the report at first circulated, that it was wholly rejected, being without foundation. Whether it will be prolonged, admitting

---

[269] Here Monroe also seeks advice regarding his task of appointing the American consuls for France. On April 14, 1792, a law was enacted which aimed to carry into "full effect" the convention between the United States and France. The duties of American consuls, as specified by the act, were mainly concerned with the protection of the interests of citizens of the United States, especially seamen. The uncertainty seems to be drawn from the fact that the act recognized the system established by Washington suggested that consular appointments were made separate and distinct from diplomatic appointments. (Robertson 1916, 562)

the term as here stated to be correct, is unknown; as likewise is the motive of Austria in asking, or of France in granting, it. The presumption is, it was to try the experiment of negotiation in the interim; and such is the report: And it is likewise presumable, that such an experiment was made or is now making; but from what I can learn, there is little prospect of its producing a peace. It will be difficult to part Austria from England, whilst the latter supplies the former with money to carry on the war; and which she will probably continue to do whilst she carries it on herself.[270] The present prospect, therefore is, that Europe is destined to sustain the waste and havock of another campaign; for, superior as England is at sea, with the recent conquest of the Cape of Good Hope, it is not probable, if she escapes an internal convulsion, the symptoms of which have diminished of late, that she will restore every thing on her part and leave France in possession of the Belgic; and without which, I think France will not make peace. A doubt, indeed, has latterly been circulated, whether England will make any sacrifice in favor of the Emperor; whether, in short she would agree to restore the possessions taken by her from France and Holland, as a consideration for the restoration of the Belgic to the Emperor. It is even added, that intimations have been given by her, that if France will leave her in possession of her conquests from Holland, she will restore everything taken from France, and leave her in possession of St. Domingo and the Belgic. If this is true, and is credited by the Emperor, it will certainly tend to weaken and perhaps absolutely to dissolve the connection between England and Austria.

I communicated to you in two preceding letters, the application of Count Carletti, minister from Tuscany for permission to visit the "unfortunate young Princess, &c." and the displeasure which that demand gave to the Directoire, who suspended his powers immediately; ordered him to leave the Republic forthwith; and, finally, sent him by force beyond its limits. It was apprehended by many, that this peremptory mode of proceeding would give offence to the Grand Duke; the contrary however, was the case; for as soon as he heard of the transaction, he despatched another Envoy to the Directoire, to disavow the demand of Carletti, and declare his respect for the French government; and such was the solicitude for his hasty departure, that he actually departed without the ordinary credentials, bearing simply a letter

---

[270] Here, Monroe reports that England has continued to help finance Austria's war against France. This was possible because a key element in British success was its ability to mobilize the nation's industrial and financial resources and apply them to defeating France. Although the UK had a population of approximately 16 million against France's 30 million, the French numerical advantage was offset by British subsidies that paid for many of the Austrian and Russian soldiers, peaking at about 450,000 men in 1813. (Kennedy 1989, 128-129)

of introduction from the Grand Duke himself. Thus, therefore, this business has ended without producing any injury to the French Republic, whilst it is a proof of the energy of its councils and of its decision upon the delicate subject to which it refers.

On the 21st instant, being the anniversary of the execution of the late King, the members of the legislative corps of the Directoire, and all public officers, took a new and solemn oath to support the Constitution, or rather of hatred to royalty. The Directoire gave, on the same day, what is called a fete in the champ de Mars; where an amphitheatre was erected, and from whence the President, surrounded by the other members and all the ministers of the government, delivered an oration suited to the occasion, to a numerous audience. It seems to be the policy of the existing government to revive the zeal of the people in favor of the Republic and of the revolution; and measures of this kind are certainly well calculated to produce that effect.

With great respect and esteem, I am, Sir, y' very humble Servant, Jas Monroe.

P. S. Since writing the above, I have heard, through a channel that merits confidence, that the term of the truce is prolonged, and which strengthens what I intimated above, that a negotiation is depending with Austria. The recent departure too of one of the Dutch Ministers for Holland, after a conference with the Directoire, and which took place about the time the truce was probably prolonged, is a circumstance which I think proper to communicate; since it gives cause to suspect, if a negotiation is depending, it treats for a general and not a partial peace.

To the Secretary of State [Timothy Pickering], Paris, February 16, 1796

Sir,[271] —I think it my duty to state to you, and without delay, a communication made me yesterday by the minister of foreign affairs, of a very interesting nature. I called to represent to him, the distress of several of my countrymen, occasioned by the protest at Hamburgh of bills given them for supplies, rendered the government; and to request his aid with the Directoire to obtain them relief. This application was intended to harmonize with one, that was making informally by our Consul General with the Directoire, and which was arranged in a manner to present the demands of the claimants before that body, in a forcible manner; and at the same time without wounding its feelings. But before I entered on this subject, my attention was

---

[271] This letter was originally in cipher. Decoded text provided by Hamilton. (Hamilton 1899, 454)

called to another more important; and upon which he seemed pleased with the opportunity of addressing me. He observed, that the Directoire had at length made up its mind, how to act in regard to our treaty with England: That it considered the alliance between us, as ceasing to exist, from the moment the Treaty was ratified; and had or would appoint an Envoy Extraordinary, to attend and represent the same to our Government; that the person in view was known and esteemed in our country, and who would be specially commissioned on this business, and whose commission would expire with it: That Mr. Adet had asked and obtained his recall; but did not say whether any other minister would be appointed in his stead, for the present; though, as connected with Adet's resignation,[272] it is reported that Maret,[273] lately returned from captivity with the Austrians, is to succeed him. The minister added some general observations on the Treaty, tending to shew, that it was considered as throwing us into the scale of the coalesced powers; observing that he should hand me an official note on this subject, being ordered so to do by the Directoire. As no specific objection was stated, I could make no specific reply. I expressed to him, however, my astonishment and concern at the measure spoken of, and inculcated in the short time I remained with him (for he was upon the point of going out) the propriety of candour in the discussion of the Treaty, in its several parts, and the benefit of great moderation towards us in all cases, since we were certainly their best friends. To this he made no reply, and whereupon I left him. I have since heard nothing from him nor on the subject. I mean to see him however to day; and, in case he permits me to act on the communication, to demand an audience of the Directoire, to endeavour to divert it, if possible, from the measure contemplated; of which, and of the business generally, I will write you again in a day or two.

With great respect and esteem, I am, Sir, y' most ob' and humble serv, Jas Monroe.

---

[272] Pierre Auguste Adet was a diplomat and chemist who was sent by the French Republic to the United States in 1795 as minister plenipotentiary. As a revolutionary diplomat, Adet attempted to restore the Franco–American alliance with the help of American Republicans, by leaking the contents of the Jay Treaty, by recruiting foreign revolutionaries for the French army, and by intriguing in the presidential election of 1796. Adet's services terminated in December 1796. (Conlin 2000, 479)

[273] Hugues Bernard Maret, Duke of Bassano, was a French statesman, diplomat and journalist. (Stephens 1911, 103-104)

To the Secretary of State [Timothy Pickering], Paris, February 20, 1796

Sir,—Immediately after my last of the 16th February was concluded, I demanded and had a conference with the minister of foreign affairs, upon the communication given in that letter.

I represented to him, that the information he had given me, of the intention of the Directory to appoint an Envoy extraordinary, to repair to the United States, to declare to our Government the dissatisfaction of this, in respect to our treaty with Great Britain, and other acts which they deemed unfriendly to them, had penetrated me with the deepest concern; because I feared from a measure so marked, and conspicuous, the most serious ill-consequences, both to them and to us. I stated to him, that such a mission was calculated to make an impression in America, and through out the world; not only that they were deeply dissatisfied with us, but that even the issue of war and peace was suspended on the issue of the mission; that their and our enemies would rejoice at the event, whilst theirs and our friends would behold the spectacle with horror. That the mission itself would place both republics in a new dilemma, and from which they could not both well extricate themselves with honor; that something was due, in the opinion of the world, to the character of the mission, its success must be brilliant, or the public would be disappointed, and this might induce them to insist on terms they would not otherwise have thought of; and which would increase their mutual embarrassments; that as soon as the mission was known to foreign powers, they would commence their intrigues to make it the means of separating us; that all were interested in our separation, none in our union; and that our separation was an evil equally to be deprecated by both parties; that the success and terror of their arms might diminish the number of their active enemies, but as we had never confided in the friendship of any power, but in that of France, so I was satisfied they had no real friend except America; that republics could never count upon the friendship of monarchies; if they did count upon it, they would always be deceived. Peace there might be; but peace and friendship did not always mean the same thing.[274]

---

[274] By the time of this correspondence, the Jay Treaty, most accepted, had all but nullified American–French alliance. Still, technically, no treaty provision violated any part of the agreement with France, and, in fact, the Jay Treaty specifically stated that no part was to be so interpreted as to conflict with previous treaty obligations. Americans could argue that all French rights had been reserved. This argument not only failed to convince many Frenchmen but left many Americans, perhaps a majority, believing that the pro-British Federalists had been guilty of bad faith. The commercial treaty with France provided for the application of the principle of free ships make free goods. France held that this imposed the duty on the United States of upholding that principle against Great Britain. The Federalist controlled

---

I observed, further, that France had gained credit by her late conduct towards us: For whilst England had seized our vessels, and harassed our trade, she had pursued an opposite, and more magnanimous policy; and which had produced, and would continue to produce, a correspondent effect, by encreasing our resentment against England, and attachment to France. But as soon as the latter should attempt to assume a hostile and menacing deportment towards us, this motive diminishes, and the argument it furnished lose force. That by this, however, I did not mean to be understood, as advising that well founded complaints, if such existed, or were thought to exist, should be withheld: On the contrary, I was of opinion, they should always be brought forward; as well to obtain redress where it was wished, and could be given, as to make known, in a frank and friendly manner, the sentiments which each entertained of the conduct of the other, in case that were interesting to it. That on my own part, I was always ready to enter into such explanations, when required, and would do it in the present instance with pleasure; since by being possessed of our view of the subject, they would be better able to decide, whether com plaint was well or ill-founded, and of course how far it merited to be considered in that light. In short, I used every argument that occurred to divert the Government from the measure proposed, assuring him, in the most earnest manner, that I was satisfied, it would produce no good effect to France; on the contrary, that it would produce much ill, both to her, and to us.

The minister replied, that France had much cause of complaint against us, independently of any treaty with England; but that, by this Treaty, ours with them was annihilated: That he considered our conduct, in these respects, as absolutely unfriendly to them, under which impression, that it was their duty, so to represent it to us: That the mode which was proposed of making

---

executive branch held that the United States could not possibly impose the rule on England and was under no treaty obligation to do so. The French, quite understandably, viewed the surrender of the central principle of her treaty arrangements with the United States to the rulings of her mortal enemy as a barefaced betrayal.7 Republicans in the United States described it in just such terms. The Republicans had logic and the spirit of faithful treaty observance on their side. France responded to the final ratification of the Jay Treaty with a forthright announcement to James Monroe that the alliance with the United States was no longer in effect. The French foreign minister, Delacroix, said he would send a special envoy to the United States to deliver the message. The Directory favored a declaration of war. James Monroe mustered the best arguments he could to delay hostilities. A declaration of war, he warned, would push the United States directly into the arms of England. France, he urged, should take into account the fact that she had a host of friends in the United States. In desperation he held out the hope that the coming presidential election might bring a member of the pro-French party into office. Monroe believed that his arguments saved his nation from an immediate opening of hostilities. (Varg 1963, 120-121)

such representation had been deemed mild and respectful, and as such ought not to give offence. He admitted, however, that the objections I had stated against it were strong and weighty with him, and that he would immediately make them known to the Directory, and by whom, he doubted not, all suitable attention would be paid to them. Since this I have not seen him, but propose seeing him again, either to-day or to-morrow, on this subject; and after which I will immediately apprize you of the state in which it may be.

This affair has given me great concern, because it opens a new era upon us; and whose consequences, unless the measure itself be prevented, may be of a very serious kind. I shall do every thing in my power to prevent it, and in any event communicate to you, and with the utmost despatch, every incident that turns up connected with it.

So far, my object has been to break the measure in question; and after which, if effected, I shall most probably be called on for explanations of the treaty complained of; and in which case I shall of course avail myself, in the best manner possible, of those communications, which have been heretofore received from your Department.

I am, Sir, with great respect and esteem, y' most obt servant, Jas Monroe.

To James Madison, Paris, February 27, 1796

This will accompany your china which is addressed to Mr. Yard. I enclose also the charge by wh. you will be able to pay the duty.

About a fortnight past I was informed by *the minister of foreign affairs that the government had at length resolved* how to act *with us in respect to our treaty with England.*[275] That *they considered it* as having *violated* or rather *annulled our treaty of alliance with them and taken part with the coalised powers. That they had rather have an open enemy than a perfidious friend.* That it was *resolved to send an envoy extra. to the United States to discuss this business with us* and whose *powers would expire with the execution of the trust. I was astonished with the communication and alarmed with its probable consequences.* I told him *it might probably lead to war* and *thereby seperate us which was what our enemies wished.* That *it hazarded much and without a probable gain.* That from the moment *a person of that character arrived their friends would seem to act under his banner* and which circumstance would *injure their character and lessen their efforts. In truth I did everything in my power to prevent this measure* and in which I am now told by *the minister that I have succeeded* the *Directoire having resolved to continue the ordinary course*

---

[275] Italicized text in this letter was originally in cipher. Decoded text provided by the National Archives. (Mason and Sisson 2020)

of representation only. But thro' this *I hear strong sentiments will be conveyed. The whole of this is made known to the executive by me.*[276]

Mr. Adet has sent in his resignation & pressed earnestly the acceptance of it. Of course a successor will be sent in his place.[277]

I am astonished that I have heard nothing from you, it is now I think 9 months, altho' I have written you so often & communicated so freely. From me too there is some hasard in communicating & for reasons that will occur & wh. has been encreased by the multiplication of duplicate dispatches & wh. were forwarded merely because the originals if recd were not acknowledged. To me the motive for this reserve is impenetrable & therefore I repeat agn my astonishmt. at it.

The state of things has varied little since the organization of the new govt; great preparations are making for carrying on the campaign with vigor on both sides. It is said the army of the Rhine & Moselle will amt. together to 300,000 men, & that in Italy to 150,000. On the opposite side too great preparations are making, so that unless peace shod. close the scene, a greater carnage may be expected this than in any preceding campaign, and at present there is but little prospect of peace, at least I see none.[278]

The forced loan was less productive than was expected and the embarrassment in the finance extreme. Some think another movement at hand but I see no evidence of it at present. In all calculations on this subject it ought to be recollected that the executive are sound and having the government in their hands are strong.

There are strong symptoms of an actual rupture between us and this country. The minister of the gove' preferred to have us as open rather than

---

[276] Early in 1796 the French government hoped to arouse pro-French sentiment in America and force a repudiation of United States policy toward Great Britain. To do so, the Directory appointed Citizen Charles Humbert Marie Vincent, director of fortifications in Saint-Domingue, as envoy extraordinary to the U.S to facilitate the plan and present their case directly to the American people. Monroe learned of the plans in a conversation with Charles Delacroix, minister of foreign affairs, on February 15, 1796. At a meeting with Delacroix the next day and in a private letter to him on the February 17, Monroe argued that the proposed special mission could well bring about an outright breach between the two countries and, further, that it might lead to war. (Bowman 1974, 239; Mason and Sisson 2020)

[277] Pierre Auguste Adet's recall was announced in Paris along with the appointment of Vincent, but the minister, in fact, had not requested it and was annoyed when the report reached Philadelphia. (Turner 1904, 896-898).

[278] In a decree on January 6, 1796, Lazare Carnot [then Director of the French Directory] gave Germany priority over Italy as a theater of war. Jean Baptiste Jourdan commanding the Army of Sambre et Meuse was instructed to besiege Mainz and cross the Rhine into Franconia. Farther south, Jean Victor Marie Moreau leading the Army of Rhin et Moselle was ordered to mask Mannheim and invade Swabia. On the secondary front, Napoleon Bonaparte was to invade Italy, neutralize the Kingdom of Sardinia and seize Lombardy from the Austrians. (Chandler 1966, 46-47)

perfidious friends. Other proofs occur to shew that this sentiment has gone deep into their councils.

Jas Monroe.

To the Secretary of State [Thomas Pickering] Paris, March 10, 1796

Sir,—I informed you in my two last, of the 16th, and 20th, ultimo, of a communication made me by the minister of foreign affairs, that the Directory had resolved to send an Envoy Extraordinary to the United States, to remonstrate against the late treaty with England, and of my efforts to prevent it; and I now the pleasure to add, that I have reason to believe those efforts have been successful; the minister having assured me in a late conference, that the Directory was disposed to accommodate in this respect, and to make its representations, on that subject, through the ordinary channel. He repeated, however, upon this occasion, in terms equally strong with those he had used before, the sense which he said the Directory entertained of the injury done to France, by that treaty, and upon which explanations were expected, and would be sought.

I asked him, what were his objections to the treaty; and to which he replied, as before, in general rather than in precise terms; urging that thereby we had violated our treaties with France, and greatly to her injury, in the present war. I replied, that it was not admitted by our government, that any, the slightest, deviation was made from our treaty with this republic; nor ought it to be presumed, until it was shewn, that such was the case, especially as I had before informed him, and now repeated my willingness to discuss that point, whenever he thought fit. He intimated, that I should certainly hear from him on the subject, and in time to receive a reply, and attend to any observations I chose to make on it; but being now before the Directory, he could not well enter on it, in the manner I proposed, until he had the further orders of that body, in that respect. Thus therefore the matter now stands; and I have only to repeat to you, my assurance, that I shall continue to pay to it all the attention it deservedly merits.[279]

The state of affairs here has not varied essentially of late, either in the internal, or in the external relations of the republic. The forced loan was less productive, than it was expected to be, and of course the relief it gives must be considered as partial, and temporary only. Nor is any system yet adopted to supply what will be necessary, after the amount thus raised is exhausted; though as the subject is still under consideration, it is possible

---

[279] Italicized text in this letter was originally in cipher. Decoded text provided by Hamilton. (Hamilton 1899, 464)

this may yet be done.[280] On the other hand, the Directory, by means of the organization and police seems to gain strength; and to which a late measure has essentially contributed. At the Pantheon, and other quarters, there were nightly meetings of people, not inconsiderable in point of numbers; and who complained of various grievances, proceeding as they said, from the actual government, and which ought therefore to be changed. The Directory had its eye upon those assemblages, and, as I hear, gained full proof, that they were put in motion by foreign influence; and, under the mask of patriotism, more effectually to promote the purpose of disorganization, and in consequence shut the doors of the houses where they resorted. As many of those who were at the head of those meetings were active and ferocious agents in the popular societies, during the reign of terror, and were probably then moved by the same cause, this discovery, if to be relied on, tends to throw great light upon the source to which the atrocities that were then practised ought to be ascribed. Time, perhaps, and especially if the revolution weathers the storms it has yet to encounter, will doubtless more fully unfold the real authors of those scenes, which were so frightful to humanity, and disgraceful to man; and that they may be discovered must be the wish of all those who are the friends of truth, wherever they reside.

Russia has in the course of the winter increased her force, 40, or 50,000 men; and, it is said, exhibits a menacing aspect towards Holland; though her minister continues here, and is apparently well received. Spain too continues her military establishment, as before the peace, and whose minister, Del Campo, is daily expected from England, where he has long resided.[281] The probable conjecture, with respect to Spain, is, that as she feared an attack from England, when she made her peace with France, so she finds it necessary to guard herself against it, by suitable precautions, till the war ends. Russia, it is believed, contemplates a blow against the Turks; in the hope, now that Poland is annihilated; France otherwise sufficiently occupied, and the other powers in amity with the Empress, to wrest Constantinople from the Porte, which has long been the object of her inordinate ambition. On the

---

[280] The "forced loan" was a December 10, 1795, effort where, in order to buttress the dwindling treasury, the Directory had implemented a mandatory open-market initiative wherein wealthy taxpayers were required to turn over a specific quantity of funds in exchange for interest-bearing coupons admissible in payment of future tax liabilities. The funds were accepted at a 100:1 ratio, and the government expected to collect 600 million livres within ten weeks. However, the Directory's inability to collect taxes efficiently doomed the plan: it took five months to collect 50 million livres. (Sargent and Velde 1995, 509)

[281] Bernardo del Campo y Perez de la Ser, the Marquis del Campo, had been the Spanish ambassador to England. He was known to be a diplomat of pleasing manners who spoke English fluently and entertained with great elegance. In February 1796, he was appointed Ambassador to the French Republic. (De Bellaigue 1984, 326)

other hand, France seems to be collecting her forces together, and to exert every nerve her system admits of, in preparations for the war; exhibiting to her enemies a countenance, firm and independent, and announcing to the beholding nations her resolution to conquer, or to perish.

With due respect, I am, Sir, your most obedient and very humble servant, Jas Monroe.

To the Minister of Foreign Affairs, Paris, March 15, 1796 [25 Ventose l'an 4] and 20th, of the Independence of the United States of America

Citizen Minister,—I was lately honoured with your note of the 19th Ventose (March 9th) objecting to several measures of our government, that have occurred in the course of the present war, and to which, I presume I shall herein render you a satisfactory answer. For this purpose I shall pursue in reply the order you have observed, in stating those objections; and, according to the light I have on the subject, give to each the answer it requires.[282·283]

These objections are comprized under three distinct heads, a summary of which I will first expose, that my reply to each may be better understood. First. Your first complaint is, that we have failed to execute our treaties with you, and in the following respects.[284]

---

[282] Charles Delacroix would serve as the French minister for foreign affairs until June 1797. (Woods 2011, 194)

[283] In the face of increasing bellicosity on the part of France towards the United States, Monroe became correspondingly more defensive. By the time of this letter, he was largely convinced that the French had no justifiable right to complain, saying that "although we have not ameliorated the law of nations in that respect, yet certainly we have not changed it for the worse; and which alone could give you just cause of complaint." Monroe wrote that "These principles [of the League of Armed Neutrality] are extremely dear to us; because they are just in themselves, and in many respects very important to our welfare: We insert them in every treaty we make with those powers who are willing to adopt them; and our hope is, that they will soon become universal. But even in the war of which you speak, and when the combination against England was most formidable, all the maritime powers being arranged against her, you well know that she never acceded to them. How compel her then, upon the present occasion, when that combination was not only broken, but many of the powers, then parties to it and against England, were now enlisted on her side, in support of her principles? You must be sensible, that under these circumstances, it was impossible for us to obtain from that power the recognition of those principles; and that , of course, we are not culpable for having failed to accomplish that object."(Oosterveld 2016, 222)

[284] As background, while Jay was in England in 1794 negotiating the Anglo–American treaty, Monroe was instructed to "remove all jealousy with respect to Mr. Jay's mission to London" and to assure the French that the American envoy was "forbidden to weaken the engagements between this country and France. "In this respect, therefore, Monroe replied in this March 1796 letter to the French complaints. He stated that the Franco–American treaty of 1778 did not forbid the enemies of France to enter American ports unless they entered with prizes (captured vessels and cargoes). Most important of all,

1. By submitting to our tribunals the cognizance of prizes brought into our ports by your privateers. 2. By admitting English vessels of war into our ports, against the stipulation of the 17th article of our treaty of commerce, even after such vessels had taken prizes from you, and in some cases with their prizes. 3. By omitting to execute the consular convention in two of its most important clauses; having failed to provide, as you suggest, suitable means for carrying those clauses into effect; the first of which secures to your consuls within the United States the exclusive jurisdiction of all controversies between French citizens; and the second, the right to pursue, and recover, all mariners who desert from your vessels. 4. By suffering in the port of Philadelphia, the arrestation of the captain of the Corvette Cassius, for an act committed by him on the high sea, and which you say is contrary to the 19th article of the treaty of commerce, which stipulates, that the commandants of public and private vessels shall not be detained in any manner; ' and the rights of nations, which put such officers under the protection of their respective flags: And by likewise suffering the arrestation of that Corvette, though armed at the Cape,[285] upon the pretext, that she was armed in the United States.

Second. Your second complaint states, that an outrage, which was made to this republic, in the person of its minister, the citizen Fauchet, by an English vessel (the Africa) in concert with an English consul, in arresting, within the jurisdiction of the United States, the packet-boat in which he had embarked, searching his trunks, and afterwards remaining within the waters of those States for near a month, to watch the movements of the vessel in which he finally sailed, was left unpunished; since you urge, that the measures which were taken by our government, in regard to that vessel, and the Consul, were not taken in a suitable time to remedy the evil, and were produced by a subsequent outrage, and of a very different kind.

Third. Your third and last complaint applies to our late treaty with England and which you say, not only sacrifices, in favor of that power, our treaty with France, but departs from that line of impartiality, which, as a neutral nation, we were bound to observe. Particular exemplifications are given of this charge in your note, and which I shall particularly notice when I come to reply to it.

Jay's Treaty was a necessity from an economic point of view because of the specific character of American trade and the need to enlarge the freedom of commerce and diminish the list of contraband. Essentially, it was a point by point answer which did not, however, satisfy the French part, although they did not show their intentions immediately after the reply. (Loizos 2003)

[285] Cape François. (Hamilton 1899, 468)

This is a summary of your complaints, and to each of which I will now give a precise, and I flatter myself, a satisfactory answer.

First. Of the inexecution of our treaties with this Republic, and of the first example given of it: 'The submission to our tribunals of the cognizance of prizes brought into our ports by your privateers.'

Permit me, in reply to this charge, to ask whether you insist, as a general principle, that our tribunals are inhibited the right of taking cognizance of the validity of your prizes, in all cases; or are there exceptions to it? As a general principle, without exception, I think it cannot be insisted on; because examples may be given, under it, of possible cases, which prove it cannot be so construed and executed, without an encroachment upon the inherent and unalienable rights of sovereignty in both nations, which neither intended to make, nor does the treaty warrant. Suppose, for instance, a prize was taken within our jurisdiction; not upon the high seas, nor even at the entrance or mouths of those great rivers and bays, which penetrate and fertilize our country; but actually in the interior, and at the wharf of some one of our cities. Is this a case over which our tribunals, or some other branch of our government, have no right to take cognizance? Do you conceive, that the true import of the treaty imposes upon us, and likewise upon you in turn, the obligation thus to abandon, as a theatre of warfare, in which you bear no part, the interior police of your country? Can it be done consistently with the dignity or the rights of sovereignty? Or, suppose the privateer which took the prize and led it into port was fitted out within the United States, the act being unauthorized by treaty; could we tolerate this, and refuse the like liberty to the other nation at war, without departing from that line of neutrality we ought to observe? You well know that those rights which are secured by treaties, form the only preference in a neutral port, which a neutral nation can give to either of the parties at war; and if these are transcended, that the nation so acting makes itself a party to the war; and in consequence merits to be considered and treated as such. These examples prove that there are some exceptions to the general principle; and perhaps there are others which do not occur to me at present. Are then the cases in question, and which form the basis of your complaint, within the scale of these exceptions? If they are, and I presume they are, I am persuaded you will concur with me in opinion, that the complaint is unfounded; and that we have only done our duty; a duty we were bound to perform, as well from a respect to our rights as a sovereign and free People, as to the integrity of our character; being a neutral party in the present war.

You will observe, that I admit the principle, if a prize was taken upon the high sea by a privateer fitted out within the Republic, or its dominions; that in such case our courts have no right to take cognizance of its validity. But is any case of this kind alleged? I presume none is or can be shewn.

2. The second article in this charge, of failing to execute our treaties with this Republic, states, that in contravention with the 17th article of the treaty of commerce, we have admitted British vessels of war into our ports; even such as have taken prizes, and in some cases with their prizes. The article referred to stipulates the right for your vessels of war and privateers to enter our ports with their prizes; and inhibits that right to your enemies. It does not stipulate that the vessels of war belonging to your enemies shall not enter; but simply that they shall not enter with their prizes. This latter act, therefore, is, I presume, the subject of your complaint. Here too, it only stipulates, that in case such vessels enter yours or our ports, proper measures shall be taken to compel them to retire as soon as possible. Whether you were rightly informed with respect to the fact, is a point upon which I cannot decide, as I know nothing about it. Our coast is extensive; our harbours numerous, and the distress of the weather may have forced them in: Or they may have entered wantonly and in contempt of the authority of our government. Many outrages have been committed on us by that nation in the course of the present war, and this may likewise be in the catalogue. But I will venture to affirm, that no countenance was given by our government to those vessels, whilst they were there; and that all suitable means were taken to compel them to retire, and without delay. You know we have no fleet, and how difficult it is, without one, to execute a stipulation of this kind, with that promptitude which your agents in our country, ardent in your cause, and faithful to your interest, might expect.

3. The third article under this head, states, that we have omitted to execute the consular convention in two of its most important clauses; the first of which secures to the consuls of each nation, in the ports of the other, the exclusive jurisdiction of controversies between their own citizens, and the second of which gives to the Consuls a right to recover such mariners as desert from the vessels of their respective nations.

Upon the first point, the supposed incompetency of the law provided on our part, to execute the judgements of your consuls within our jurisdiction, I can only say, that as no particular defect is stated, so no precise answer can be given to the objection. And upon the second, which states, that the judges charged by our law to issue warrants for arresting such of your mariners, as desert from their vessels, have latterly required, and against the spirit of the treaty, the presentation of the original registers of the vessels to which they originally belonged, as the ground whereon to issue these warrants, I have to observe; that by the clause in question (the 9th article) the originals seem to be required; and that the copies spoken of in another part of the treaty (the 5th article) obviously apply to other objects, and not to this. More fully, however, to explain to you the conduct of our government upon this subject, permit me here to add an extract from our law, passed on the 9th of April, 1792, expressly to carry into effect the convention in question, and which applies to both cases.

"The district judges of the United States shall, within their respective districts, be the competent judges for the purposes expressed in the 9th article of the said convention; and it shall be incumbent on them to give aid to the Consuls and vice-Consuls of France, in arresting and securing deserters from the vessels of the French nation, according to the tenor of the said article. And where, by any article of the said convention, the Consuls and vice-Consuls of France are entitled to the aid of the competent executive officers of the country, in the execution of any precept, the Marshals of the United States, and their deputies, shall within their respective districts be the competent officers, and shall give their aid, according to the tenor of the stipulations." By this extract you will clearly perceive, that it was not the intention of our government to frustrate or embarrass the execution of this treaty: On the contrary, that it was its intention to carry it into full effect, according to its true intent and meaning; and that it has done so, so far as could be done by suitable legal provisions.

It may hereafter be deemed a subject worthy consideration, whether the first of these clauses in that convention had not better be expunged from it. The principle of a foreign court established within any country, with jurisdiction independent of that country, cannot well be reconciled with any correct idea of its sovereignty: Nor can it exercise its functions without frequent interference with the authorities of the country; and which naturally occasions strife and discontent between the two governments. These, however, are not the only objections to the measure, though with me they are unanswerable. Under circumstances the most favorable, it were difficult for these consular tribunals to serve their process and execute their judgments. A limited jurisdiction to a town or village only, admits of it. In the United States, therefore, and in France, where the territory is immense, and the number of citizens of each country in the other considerable, as is now the case, it becomes impossible. Many of these, in each country, dwell perhaps in the interior, and not within one hundred leagues of any Consul of their nation; how compel their attendance before him? How execute the judgment afterwards? For the tribunals of one country to call in the aid of the officers of another, to execute its decrees or judgments, is an institution at best objectionable; but to send those officers round the country, through the range of one hundred leagues is more so.

Permit me then to ask, what are the motives on yours or our part for such an institution? In what respect are you or we interested, that yours or our consuls should have the exclusive jurisdiction of controversies between yours and our citizens, in each other's country? Why not submit those controversies, in common with all others, to the tribunals of each nation? Some considerations in favor of the institution, it is true, occur; but yet they are light and trifling, when compared with the numerous and strong objections that oppose it. So much, however, by way of digression.

4. Your fourth and last example, under this head, states, that the Captain of the Corvette Cassius was arrested in Philadelphia, for an act committed on the high sea; contrary, as you suggest, to the 19th article of the treaty of commerce, which stipulates, 'that the commandants of vessels, public and private, shall not be detained in any manner whatever;" and of the well known rights of nations, which put the officers of public vessels under the safeguard of their respective flags; and that the said Corvette was likewise seized, though armed at the Cape, upon the pretext that she was armed some time before in Philadelphia.

As you have not stated what the act was with the Commission whereof the Captain was charged, I can of course give no explanation on that head. Satisfied, however, I am, that if the crime was of a nature to authorise our courts to take cognizance of it, he would not be exempted from their jurisdiction by the article of the treaty in question; since that article, as you perceive, was intended to establish a general principle in the intercourse between the two countries; to give a privilege to the ships of war of each, to enter and retire from the ports of the other; and not to secure in favor of any particular delinquent, an immunity from crimes: Nor, in my opinion, does the law of nations admit of a different construction, or give any other protection. I am happy, however, to hear that he is released, since it furnishes an additional proof that the whole transaction was a judicial one; regular, according to the course of our law, and mingling nothing in it in any view that ought to give offence here.

With respect to the seizure of the Corvette, upon the pretext that she was armed in Philadelphia, I have only to say; that if she was armed there, it was the duty of our government to seize her; the right to arm not being stipulated by treaty: And if that was alleged upon sufficient testimony, as I presume was the case, there was no other way of determining the question than by an examination into it, and in the interim, preventing her sailing. It would be no satisfaction to the other party to the war, for us to ex amine into the case after she was gone, provided the decision was against her. On the contrary, such con duct would not only expose us to the charge of committing a breach of neutrality, but of likewise doing it collusively.

Second. Your second complaint states an outrage which was committed by a British frigate, upon your Minister, the Citizen Fauchet, in concert with a British consul; in boarding the Packet in which he embarked, opening his trunks, &c. within the waters of the United States, and remaining there after wards to watch the movements of the frigate in which he sailed; and which you say was not resented as it ought to have been by our government; since you add, the measures which were taken by it in regard to that vessel, and the consul, were the effect of another and subsequent outrage.

The punishment which was inflicted by our government upon the parties who committed that outrage, by revoking the exequatur of the Consul, and ordering that all supplies should be withheld from the Frigate; as likewise that she should forthwith depart without the waters of the United States, was, I think you will admit, an adequate one for the offence. Certain it is, that as we have no fleet, it was the only one in our power to inflict; and that this punishment was inflicted in consequence of that outrage, you will, I presume, likewise admit, after you have perused the act of the President upon that subject; a copy of which I herewith transmit to you; and by which you will perceive, that there was no distinct outrage offered to the United States, upon that occasion, by the parties in question; but that both the one and the other act (the attempt made upon the packet boat in which your minister had embarked, by the Captain of a British Frigate, and which constituted the first; and the writing of an insolent letter, by the same Captain, to the governor of the State of Rhode Island, in concert with the British consul there, and which constituted the second) were only several incidents to the same transaction, forming together a single offence; and for which that punishment was inflicted on those parties.

I think proper here to add, as a further proof that the President was neither inattentive to what was due to your rights upon that occasion, nor to the character of the United States; that he gave orders to our minister at London, to complain formally to that government of that outrage; and to demand of it such satisfaction upon the parties, as the nature of the insult required; and which has, doubtless, either been given, or is still expected.

Third. Your third, and last complaint applies to our late treaty with England; and which, you say, has sacrificed, in favor of that power, our connection with France, and the rights of neutrality the most common.

1. In support of this charge you observe, that we have not only departed from the principles of the armed neutrality adopted in the course of the late

war; but have abandoned, in favor of England, the limits which the rights of nations and our own treaties with all other powers, and even England in her treaties with many other powers, have given to contra band.

2. That we have also consented that provisions should be deemed contra-band, not when destined to a blockaded port only, as should be the case; but in all cases, by tacitly acknowledging the pretensions of England, to place at pleasure and by proclamation, not only your Islands, but even France herself in that dilemma.

The principles of the armed neutrality set on foot by the Empress of Russia, in harmony with the other neutral powers, at the time you mention, and acceded to by all the powers then at war against England, are extremely dear to us; because they are just in themselves, and in many respects very important to our welfare: We insert them in every treaty we make with those powers who are willing to adopt them; and our hope is, that they will soon become universal. But even in the war of which you speak, and when the combination against England was most formidable, all the maritime powers being arranged against her, you well know that she never acceded to them. How compel her then, upon the present occasion, when that combination was not only broken, but many of the powers, then parties to it and against England, were now enlisted on her side, in support of her principles? You must be sensible, that under these circumstances, it was impossible for us to obtain from that power the recognition of those principles; and that, of course, we are not culpable for having failed to accomplish that object.

I regret also, that we did not succeed in obtaining from that power, a more liberal scale of contraband, than was obtained: For as our articles of exportation are chiefly articles of the first necessity, and always in great demand here, and every where else, it was equally an object of importance to us to enlarge the freedom of commerce in that respect, by diminishing the list of contraband. Perhaps no nation on the Globe is more interested in this object, than we are. But here too, the same difficulty occurred, that had in the preceding case; and it was in consequence deemed expedient, for the time, to relinquish a point we could not obtain; suffering the ancient law of nations to remain unchanged in any respect. Is it urged, that we have made any article contraband that was not so before, by the known and well established law of nations; which England had not a right to seize by that law, and did not daily seize, when they fell in her way? This cannot be urged; because the fact is otherwise: For although we have not ameliorated the law of nations in that respect, yet certainly we have not changed it for the worse; and which alone could give you just cause of complaint.

With respect to the objection stated to a clause in the 18th article of the treaty with England, which presumes we are thereby prohibited bringing pro visions from the United States to France, I have only to add; that no such prohibition is to be found in it, or other stipulation which changes the law of nations in that respect: On the contrary, that article leaves the law of nations where it was before; authorizing the seizure in those cases only, where such provisions are contraband, by the existing law of nations,' and according to our construction, when carrying to a blockaded port; and in which case payment is stipulated; but in no respect is the law of nations changed, or any right given to the British to seize other than they had before; and such, I presume, you will agree, is the true import of that article.

You will observe, by the article in question, that when our provisions destined for a blockaded port are seized, though by the law of nations subject to confiscation, they are nevertheless exempted from it; and the owners of such provisions entitled to the payment of their value. Surely this stipulation cannot tend to discourage my countrymen from adventuring with provisions into the ports of this Republic; nor in any other respect prevent their enterprises here: On the contrary, was it not probable, that it would produce the opposite effect; since thereby the only penalty which could deter them, that of confiscation, in the case above mentioned, was completely done away?

Thus, Citizen Minister, I have answered, according to the views of our government, and the light I have upon the subject, the objections you have stated against several of its measures adopted in the course of the present war; and I hope to your satisfaction. That any occurrence should take place in the annals of the Republics, which gave cause for suspicion, that you doubted, in any degree, our sincere and affectionate attachment to your welfare, is a circumstance that cannot otherwise than give pain to our government and our people. That these, however, should be removed by a fair and candid examination of your complaints, on both sides, is the best consolation that such an occurrence can admit of. If by my feeble efforts, I contribute in any degree to promote that end, and preserve the harmony and affection which have so long subsisted between us, and I trust, will always subsist, be assured that I accomplish an object the most grateful to my feelings, that I can possibly accomplish.[286]

---

[286] As can be seen, in this reply to numerous French concerns, Monroe sought to address each complaint in order. The cognizance of French prizes by American courts he considered a violation of the treaty only when they had been taken on the high seas. He practically admitted that British privateers had been allowed to enter American ports, claiming as justification that, since the United States had no fleet, this could not be prevented, and that such vessels could not be denied admission in stress of weather. The consular cognizance of offenses committed by French citizens, he declared, was a most difficult matter to manage in so large a country, but the federal courts had always aided the consuls in the

Permit me in concluding this letter to assure you of the respect and esteem with which I am, Sir, your very humble servant.

James Monroe

To the Secretary of State [Timothy Pickering], Paris, March 25, 1796

Sir,—Finding from the communication of the minister of foreign affairs, that the character of the mission about to be despatched to the United States, and its objects, were still before the Directoire, and fearing that the

apprehension of deserters. As to the corvette *Cassius*, he claimed that the courts should determine whether or not she had been fitted out in Philadelphia contrary to law. This answer of Monroe was in accordance with the facts. Of the four charges, Monroe did not wholly deny the first and the fourth, merely resting his refutation upon the construction to be placed on the law by the American courts. The second and third charges were practically admitted, but with extenuating circumstances. The weakness of the American navy and the difficulty of communication were excellent excuses and pointed to unintentional violations of the treaty in these two instances. Monroe's defense of these alleged violations of the treaty between the United States and France was, therefore, as strong as the circumstances warranted, though it would seem that the administration had interpreted the treaty with as little latitude in favor of France as possible. While Monroe had given as strong an answer as he could to the first count in the French indictment, he did not attempt to deny the truth of the charge that Fauchet had been seized by a British ship in American waters. In extenuation he explained that the President had taken ample measures to avenge the outrage, having revoked the exequatur of the consul who had been responsible for the seizure. Moreover, the minister to England had been instructed to bring formal complaint. The weakest point of the defense is in answer to the third cause of complaint, the Jay treaty. England, Monroe showed, had never acceded to the principle of armed neutrality. Conditions had at least not changed for the worse. Where before there had been no regulations at all, an exact definition of rights had been secured, though better terms might have been desired. The Jay treaty, Monroe pointed out, did not prevent provisions from being carried to France, except where they had already been classed as contraband. As a sop to the French indignation at this stipulation, he called attention to the compensation guaranteed to the owner where provisions destined for a blockaded port were seized. He concluded with the hope that by candid explanations all such suspicions might be removed. The feebleness of this last defense is obvious. Monroe had evaded any direct answer to the specific complaints, and for an excellent reason. The stipulations of the Jay treaty which classed as contraband materials for ship building, and allowed provisions to be seized merely by proclamation, constituted in fact an infringement upon the previous treaty with France. Such a matter was not to be mended by a more exact definition of contraband. The charge of favoring Great Britain and so of surrendering the former friendship for France, Monroe ignored. He had already been informed, in the defense of the United States by Randolph, that an attempt to negotiate a commercial treaty with France had failed owing to the inordinate demands of the French government. This fact he should have mentioned as meeting the charge that the United States had favored Great Britain in contracting a commercial treaty, though it could not have justified the clauses that violated the treaty with France. With this exception Monroe's defense, while weak, was as strong as the facts warranted. Possibly he could have effectively met the bill of complaint with a similar list of instances in which France had violated her treaty obligations with the United States. Still, evidence suggests that Monroe answered the French concerns charges in accordance with the information that had been furnished him by his superiors in Washington. (Bond 1897, 59-61)

ulterior communication promised me by the minister, would be made at such a time, as to render it impossible for me to produce any effect on the measure itself (if, indeed, in any case it were so) I deemed it my duty, and accordingly demanded an audience of the Directoire on that subject, stating the information already received from the Minister thereon, as the basis or motive of that demand. An audience was granted, and in consequence I attended the Directoire on the 8th instant, in full council, assisted by the minister of foreign affairs, and the minister of marine.[287] As I had demanded the audience, it became necessary for me to open the subject; and I did by stating what the Minister had informed me of their dissatisfaction with our treaty with England, and some other measures that had occurred during the present war; and respecting which it was contemplated to make some representation to our government by their Minister, who was about to depart for the United States. I told them, that unless I knew distinctly what their complaints were, it was impossible for me to refute, or even answer them: That I did not come there to ask from that body such exposition, for the purpose of discussing the subject with it, because I knew it was against rule: That I wished, however, the Directoire would cause the minister of foreign affairs to lay open those complaints to me; receive my answer, and enter into a full discussion of them; and in the interim, that it would suspend any decision, in regard to the merit of those complaints, or of the mission spoken of, until the result of that discussion was before it: That the discussion itself could not otherwise than throw light on the subject, and in the degree promote the interest of both countries, so far as that might be affected by their decision in the case in question. The Directoire replied that nothing was more reasonable than my demand, and that it should be complied with. Some general observations were then made by that body, upon the subject of its complaints; and to which I made the answers that occurred at the time; dissipating its doubts in one or two instances at once, and particularly with respect to the countenance it heared was given in the United States to their emigrants; by stating, that we received all Frenchmen who visited

[287] This note concludes the series of letters (November 5, December 6 and 22, 1795, January 26, February 16 and 20, and March 10 and 25, 1796) that Pickering acknowledged so severely in his reply of June 13, wherein [although admitting that the reasons by which Monroe had dissuaded France from her contemplated course "were certainly very cogent"] he conveyed to the Minister Plenipotentiary the Administration's censure on his line of conduct in regard to the Jay Treaty, alleging that he had withheld documents [seemingly a reference to Randolph's letter of July 14, 1795, received by Monroe about the first of October, and Pickering's letter of September 12, received about the first of December] illustrative of the American government's views on that treaty. Monroe had received Pickering's letter of June 13, in September, answering it on the 10th of that month. His recall, dated August 22, 1796, would not be received until November. (Hamilton 1899, 484)

us, as friends: That we did not, nor could we, discriminate between them generally, on account of their political principles; because we did not know what their principles were: That we saw in them all, the people of a nation to which we were much attached for services rendered us by it in the day of our difficulties, and treated them accordingly: And with respect to the President, that he had given orders, that certain distinguished Emigrants, otherwise in some respect entitled to attention, but known to be obnoxious here, should on that account be excluded his public Hall, which was open to all other persons. Several of the members of the Directoire reciprocated with great earnestness, professions of friendship for us; assuring meat the same time, that no step should be taken in the business in question, but upon due deliberation, and after the discussion I had asked should be finished, and my arguments fully weighed; and thus I left them.

I shall transmit to you, as soon as it is closed, the result of any communication which may pass between the minister and myself; and I doubt not the discussion will produce a favorable effect. I shall certainly avail myself of all the lights within my reach, to do justice to a cause of so much importance to my country.

Upon some misunderstanding with the Directoire, Pichegru has sent in his resignation, and obtained his dismission; an event that must be deemed unfortunate to the Republic, as he is, doubtless, a man of great talents, and integrity. Clairfait has done the same thing with the Emperor; so that each army is deprived of a great chief.

The finances here continue in derangement; and which is not likely to be remedied by a late act, calling in the assignats, and issuing in their stead a species of paper, called mandats, founded on the national domains, with the right in the holder of that paper to take property for it, where he likes and where he pleases, at the ancient value. This project resembles a bank whose stock consists of, and whose credit of course depends on, land; and which, as it never succeeded well in the lands of individuals, will most probably never succeed well in the lands of the public.

I herewith transmit you extracts of two letters lately received from Mr. Barlow; and which I do with a view of giving you every information that comes to my knowledge upon the interesting topic on which they treat.[288]

---

[288] Joel Barlow had promised to write Monroe from time to time such details as might be interesting. Barlow's frigate sailed on January 23, 1796, from Marseilles for Alicante, the half-way point to the port of Algiers, but heavy seas forced it to seek refuge in the Bay of Roses. Impatient with the delay, Barlow took the arduous but picturesque overland route to Alicante, where he had to wait nearly a month for his ship, which had been hindered by contrary winds, and for final instructions from Humphreys. In the interim he learned that Donaldson actually had negotiated a peace treaty and that it included a financial pledge of $640,000 to be paid by the United States within three months. He

With great respect I am, Sir, your most obedient humble servant, Jas Monroe.

To the Secretary of State [Timothy Pickering], Paris, May 2, 1796

Sir,—I informed you in my last of the 25th of March, that I was promised by the Directoire in an audience I had obtained of that body, that the minister of foreign affairs should state to me such objections, as were entertained by this government, to certain measures of our own; and, in the interim, that no step should be taken, under the existing impression, nor until my reply was received and fully weighed; and I now have the pleasure to transmit the result of the communication which afterwards took place between the minister and myself, on that subject.

I do not know what effect my reply has had upon the mind of the Directoire; because it was only sent in a few days since. I shall endeavour to ascertain this, if possible, and in case I do, will immediately afterwards apprize you of it.

I think proper to communicate to you an incident which took place between the minister and myself, after I had obtained from the Directoire a promise that he should state the objections above referred to and discuss their merits with me, and which was as heretofore intimated to you on the 8th of March last. Soon after that period I received from the minister the communication promised in a note of the same date but different in some other respects from the present one, and particularly in the number of complaints, two of the catalogue being now given up by him and to which I replied as soon as I could prepare my reply in a note bearing likewise the same date with that which I now enclose you. After he had perused my reply he was sensible he had insisted on some points that were not tenable, and in consequence asked that I would permit him to retake his note re turning mine, that he might correct himself, and of course that I would consider the discussion as yet to be commenced. I told him immediately that I would do so with pleasure, because I did not consider myself in the light of a solictor

also learned that Donaldson had dispatched Philip Sloan, a captive sailor, to Lisbon with an urgent appeal for funds. Barlow could not know, however, that David Humphreys, United States Minister to Portugal, had been unable to raise the money in Lisbon and had sent another former captive, Captain Richard O'Brien of the brig *Sophia*, to London, where the financial house of Baring & Company, the official American brokers in the British capital, held United States certificates in the amount of $800,000, a sum that Congress had specifically set aside for the purpose of settling with Algiers. Meanwhile, a general European war had created a scarcity of gold and silver, and the Barings were unable to supply O'Brien with the $640,000 which he had been instructed to carry to Lisbon. (Cantor 1963, 175; Hamilton 1899, 487)

bound to catch at and take advantage of little errors: that I wished upon all occasions, and with every one, and especially upon the present occasion with him to act with candour and in consequence I soon afterwards restored him his note and took back my own.[289]

At the time when I made the minister this promise, I thought it in my power fully to comply with it. I had it is true, according to custom, written and enclosed you a copy of both papers but yet I thought Dr. Brockenbrough to whom I had entrusted my letter to you was in France within my reach, so that I might recover it.[290] Upon enquiry however I found he had departed by way of Dunkirk for London, a route I knew he intended to take, and in which state of things all that I could do was to write and request him to return me that letter and which I immediately did. I have not yet heard from him and of course cannot tell whether I shall recover it or not. As soon however as I knew that he had gone I apprised the Minister of it, as likewise of the above circumstances, satisfying him that I had acted with good faith so far as depended on me, in fulfilling in every respect the promise I had made; and in communicating the above to you. I do it as well to explain this transaction, and which will require explanation in case you receive that letter, as to make known to you as far as depends on me, the condition in which you receive it.

The Minister thought proper to give his second communication the same date with the former one, although more than a fortnight had intervened between the one and the other: and in consequence I followed his example giving my latter reply the same date with the former one. His motive I did not enquire into: mine was that the Directoire might see that the delay which took place did not proceed from me.

In some respects I was pleased that the minister requested this accommodation from me because the yielding it could not be otherwise than grateful to him and produce in consequence a suitable correspondent impression in his mind towards: and because I knew that time would thereby be gained for reflexion, always necessary upon great questions, and often favourable to wise and temperate councils; and lastly because I knew that no possible injury could arise from the delay, the Directoire having promised me that no step should be taken until after my answer was received and fully weighed, and in none of these respects have I according to appearances been disappointed.

---

[289] Hamilton notes that this [and the paragraphs immediately following] were omitted by Monroe in the state papers. (Hamilton 1899, 490)

[290] Dr. John Brockenbrough, of Essex county, Virginia, had served as a surgeon in the Virginia navy during the American Revolution. Long a justice of Essex, he served as president of the Bank of Virginia. (Virginia Historical Society 1898, 448)

The campaign was lately opened on the side of Italy, by a suite of three brilliant victories obtained in the space of a few days, by the French under Buonaparte, over the Austrians, commanded by Beaulieu; and in which the latter lost, in slain, about five thousand men, and in prisoners, between 8 and 10, 000! The road is now open to Turin, where it is thought the French are pressing and perhaps by this time arrived. On the Rhine, however, the armies are still inactive; and from which circumstance some persons conjecture, that a negotiation is still depending with the Emperor, and will doubtless, if such is the case, be essentially aided, on the part of France, by these late victories. The Vendee war was lately greatly checked, to say no more, by the total dispersion of the troops gathered there, in opposition to the government, and the apprehension and execution of Charette and Stofflet, the two principal chiefs who heretofore headed it.[291] And subsequent circumstances favor the idea, that rebellion there is laid more prostrate than it was at any preceding period, since it began. But such has been the varied fortune of that extraordinary war, and so often has it revived after it was supposed to be totally extinguished, that appearances, however strong, are not to be too implicitly confided in; nor can it well be pronounced at an end, until the revolution itself is closed.

I send you herewith an extract of a letter from Mr. Barlow, from Algiers, just received; and which will, perhaps, give you the latest intelligence from that quarter.

With great respect and esteem, I am, Sir, your very humble serv, Jas Monroe.

P.S. Mr. John Gregorie, late of Petersburg, in Virginia (a naturalized citizen of the United States) originally established at Dunkirk, and now residing there, has been recommended to me, by respectable authority, as a fit person to fill the Consulate in that city; I add therefore his name to the list heretofore sent you, of competitors for that office.[292] [LAYOUT – Fn 292]

---

[291] The Directory had succeeded in ending the civil war in La Vendee, a result attributable to the firmness and moderation of General Louis Lazare Hoche. He defeated insurgent leader François Athanase de Charette and took him prisoner. Jean Nicolas Stofflet, another principal, was betrayed into the hands of the republicans. Stofflet was shot at Angers, the old capital of Anjou, on February 15, 1796. Charette suffered the same fate at Nantes on March 19, 1796. The Count d'Autichamp and the other Vendean generals signed a treaty of peace with General Hoche. George Cadoudal, the leader of the Chouans, and other Vendean chiefs briefly renewed the war in Brittany but were also soon defeated by General Hoche and either submitted to the Directory or fled to England. The Directory announced to the legislative councils the end of the civil war in La Vendee on July 17, 1796, this ending the resistance of the Vendean royalists to the Republic. (Clifford 1914, 3407)

[292] In connection with this letter, the last from Monroe immediately preceding his recall, Pickering privately wrote to President Washington the following account of the reception of the letter, with the French government's complaints, from John Churchman, the

To the Secretary of State [Timothy Pickering], Paris, May 25, 1796

Sir,—Since my last of the third [second] instant, I have heard nothing from this government upon the subject communicated to you in that and several of my preceding letters; and which had been discussed by the Minister of foreign affairs and myself, as was shewn by the papers trans-mitted in my last. Nor have I understood, through any other channel, that any decision is taken on the subject. I flatter myself, therefore, that I shall hear nothing further on it. As yet, however, no successor is appointed to Mr. Adet, according to his own request; and who remains, of course, the locum tenens until one is appointed. I mention this circumstance, because as such an appointment was contemplated, when that discussion commenced, and was probably delayed by it, so nothing can be satisfactorily inferred, at least for the present, of the final decision of the Directoire, upon the topic in discussion, until that of the appointment is likewise resumed and settled.

I was lately favored with yours of the 7th of January, communicating the correspondence which took place between the President and the Minister of France, when the latter presented the flag which was voted by the conven-

Maryland scientist: "Department of State, July 29, 1796. Sir, about noon today Mr. John Churchman who has been these two or three years in Europe on account of his supposed discoveries relative to the variation of the magnetic needle, called at the office. He came last from Bordeaux, and was the bearer of Mr. Monroe's letter of the 2nd May. I told him it had been broken open; & after a few questions, asked him to give me a certificate of the circumstances which attended his receipt of it; and offered him pen, ink and paper to write it; unless he chose to do it at home. He said he would go home, and call himself at five in the afternoon (if that hour was convenient to me) as the matter required some consideration. He called at five accordingly; and then told me (with some emotion) that he thought it best to be candid; for he could not think of giving a certificate that might excite suspicions of innocent people He had himself broken the seal, tho' by mere acci-dent; and as soon as he discovered his mistake, closed the letter again, without reading it. He handed me a letter from his friend in London, (a quaker) inclosing the copy of a diploma, in Latin, given him by order of the Empress of Russia, declaring him a member of the Russian Academy of Sciences. This letter he recd thro' Mr. Monroe; and by the same channel expected to receive the Diploma itself. When therefore at the point of embarcation at Bordeaux for America, he received a letter from Mr. Monroe, addressed to him, and within the cover another of a size likely to contain the Diploma, without looking at the superscription, he broke the seal. He had hoped this inadvertence would be excused; and especially as he was careful to deliver the letter with his own hand; it was he who called and delivered it in the evening, as mentioned in my former letter. This account, having all the marks of truth and candour I begged him give himself no further uneasiness about it; promising to communicate the explanation to you. I then entered into conversation with him about his travels in France, and the sentiments of the French people towards America & particularly the government; and as he had been so long in France, whether he had observed any material change of sentiment, especially on account of the Treaty with Great Britain. He answered that he had observed no material change; that very little was said by Frenchmen about the treat, tho' much was said against it by the American Citizens in Paris." (Hamilton 1899, 494)

tion; as likewise the resolutions of both Houses of Congress on the same subject, with the letter of the President to the Directoire, in consequence thereof, which letter you desired me to deliver without delay. Accordingly, the day after I received it I waited on the Minister of foreign affairs, and presented the letter to him, with a request that he would deliver it to the Directoire as soon as possible; and to which communication I have since received the reply, of which I herewith inclose you a copy.

There was lately announced by the Directoire to the Council of five hundred, the discovery of a conspiracy against the government; whose avowed object was to overthrow the present constitution, and establish that of 1793 in its stead.[293] The details furnished exhibit a project, which sought to marshal one description of patriots against another; the leaders of the innovating party differing from the established order, by the greater fervor of their zeal; and offering as an allurement to the poor, and in support of their interests, the free pillage of the wealthy. Fortunately, however, the project was discovered in good time, by the Directoire and crushed in embrio. What its object was, who were its real authors, and how many were comprized in it, time will doubtless disclose. Perhaps the trial of Drouet, a member of the five hundred, lately a prisoner in Austria, and who is accused of being a principal in it, will throw light on the subject in both views.[294] The discovery of this plot excited anew the jealousy of this government against foreigners, some of whom were suspected of having an agency in it, and which subjected our countrymen, in common with those of other powers, to some trouble. The foreign ministers were, in consequence, called on for a list of their countrymen here, with the business of each respectively; which I have given, and by which, I presume, permission to remain will be obtained for all those who are American citizens.

The success of the French troops in Italy, whereby the Austrian and Sardinian armies were completely routed, in several severe conflicts, and with great loss to the Austrians, has already obtained for the Republic a very advantageous peace with Sardinia; by which the king has not only abandoned the coalition, but ceded forever to France Savoy and Nice; and even put himself in effect, for the residue of the war, under the protection of the French Republic. The papers forwarded will give you the details of this event, as likewise of the provisional treaty which ensued with Parma.

---

[293] A reference to Conspiracy of the Equals of May 1796, a failed coup d'état led by François Noël Babeuf, who wanted to overthrow the Directory and replace it with an egalitarian and proto-socialist republic, inspired by Jacobin ideals. (Harkins 1990, 427-428)

[294] Jean Baptiste Drouet (1763-1824), French Revolutionist, is chiefly noted for the part he played in the arrest of Louis XVI. Drouet was implicated in the conspiracy of Babeuf, and was imprisoned; but made his escape into Switzerland. (Chisholm 1911, 592)

It is generally admitted, that the road to Rome is opened; and said, that the Pope is so sensible of this, that he has offered to the Directoire, among other inducements, to use his apostolic authority to appease the discontents in the Vendu, and reconcile the disaffected there to the Republic, in case they will spare him, for the present, the honor of a visit. A minister or ministers are reported to be on their way from Naples, so that 't is probable some adjust-ment will likewise soon be made with that power. Beaulieu, with the residue of the Austrian army, has retreated beyond Milan, to the heights between the lake DeGarda and Mantua, a strong position, and noted as being formerly occupied by Prince Eugene; whither too he was pursued by Buonaparte, who now keeps him in check, or rather invests him there. Efforts are making by both governments, to send to both their armies reinforcements; so that, perhaps, until they arrive, the final fate of those armies will not be settled.

I inclose you some letters just received from Mr. Barlow, at Algiers, and am, with great respect and esteem, your most obed' servant, Jas Monroe.

To the Secretary of State [Timothy Pickering], Paris, June 12, 1796

Sir,—I have the pleasure to inform you that in a late informal conference with one of the members of the Directoire I was advised by him, that the Directoire had done nothing in regard to us, upon the subject communicated to you in several of my preceding letters; and that he presumed they would do nothing upon that subject I trust therefore that their councils are thus settled upon this interesting topic, and that I shall hear nothing farther from them on it. But should they take a different turn, of which at present there is no particular symptom (for the probability of such a course was greatest in the commencement, and whilst the first impressions were at their height) I shall not fail to apprize you of it, and without delay. As yet no successor has been appointed to Mr. Adet; nor can I say what the intention of his government is in that respect. I presume, however, upon the authority of the above communication, that in case one is appointed, it will be merely in consequence of Mr. Adet's request; and be of course only an ordinary official measure, of no particular importance to us.

As yet none of our countrymen have been compelled to leave Paris, under the late decree, respecting foreigners, and which was occasioned by the late conspiracy. Whether they will or not is uncertain; for the Directoire, in executing the power granted it by the decree, have authorized none to stay of any nation, for whose good conduct their respective ministers have not made themselves personally responsible. I could not discriminate between my countrymen, by admitting some, and rejecting others; but did everything in my power to obtain an exemption for all. I send you copies of my letters upon that subject to the minister of foreign affairs, and to which I have yet received no official or other definite answer.

The truce was lately terminated by the Emperor, in the manner prescribed by the convention which formed it, which stipulated, that it should cease after the expiration of 10 days, upon notice given by either party; and immediately afterwards the campaign was opened by the French, and with the same success, at least to a certain degree, as attended their efforts in Italy.[295] In two encounters between considerable divisions of the army of the Sambre et Meuse and the Austrians, on the right of the Rhine, the former have gained complete victories; taken in the first (excluding the killed and wounded) about 2400 prisoners, and in the second about 3000, exclusive of the killed and wounded. In Italy, two new victories have been gained, and by which Beaulieu was forced to retreat through the Venitian territory to the Tyrol, leaving the French masters of that country. I send you the papers which give you the details, and am, with great respect and esteem your most obedient and humble servant, Jas Monroe.

To Doctor George Logan, Paris, June 24, 1796

Dear Sir,—I give you within a short sketch of the actual state of things here, a copy of which I like-wise send to one or two other friends of whom Mr. Beckley is one.[296] If you and Mr. Beckley, if in Philadelphia, deem it worthy the attention, I have no objection to your inserting it in Baches paper, the first paragraph excepted. And if you likewise approve, I will hereafter keep you regularly apprized of the course of events, whereby the community at large may be more correctly informed of the progress of the revolution than they heretofore have been or can be from the English prints. The character will be from a gentleman in Paris to his friend in Philadelphia, occasionally varied as from some other quarter, as Bordeaux, that it may not appear to be

---

[295] At the end of the Rhine Campaign of 1795 the two sides had called a truce, but both sides continued to plan for war. In a decree on January 6, 1796, Lazare Carnot, one of the five French Directors, gave Germany priority over Italy as a theater of war. The French First Republic's finances were in poor shape so its armies would be expected to invade new territories and then live off the conquered lands. Knowing that the French planned to invade Germany, on May 20, 1796, the Austrians announced that the truce would end on the last day of May and prepared for invasion. (Dodge 2011, 286-287; Chandler 1966, 46-47)

[296] The paper enclosed by Monroe in his letter to Dr. Logan gave a very long detail about French affairs. On the last page he touched on the British Treaty, concerning which he says, that the report of a new connection thereby formed between the U.S. and Great Britain, "operated like a stroke of thunder, and produced in all France amazement." (Hamilton 1900, 7)

a regular thing; tho in that respect act as you please, for as truths only will be communicated and with temperance, it is immaterial what the conjecture is, provided it be only conjecture.

You promised me a visit: Cannot you make it, as we shall be very happy to see you and Mrs. Logan, and will certainly make your time as comfortable as possible.297 In your absence Mr. Beckley can attend to the little object of my communications, for I wish you and him to act in concert whilst he is in the neighborhood, and indeed if you were both absent you will arrange matters confidentially with Mr. B. himself, who likewise possesses mine.[298]

I beg you to present my respects to Drs. Rittenhouse and Rush, and that you believe me sincerely your friend and servant, Jas Monroe.

To the Secretary of State [Timothy Pickering], Paris, June 28, 1796

Sir,—After my last of the 12th instant, I flattered myself that I should hear nothing further from this Government on the subject of our late treaty with England; but find that in this respect I was disappointed; having since received from the minister of foreign affairs, a letter upon that subject, and of which I herewith forward you a copy[299], as likewise of the answer I made

---

[297] George Logan was an American physician, farmer, legislator and politician from Philadelphia County, Pennsylvania. An associate of Thomas Jefferson, he would travel to France in 1798 to treat unofficially for a better understanding between the two governments, which action was subsequently responsible for the passage of the Logan Act in 1799, prohibiting a private citizen from undertaking diplomatic negotiations; appointed and subsequently elected as a Democratic Republican to the United States Senate to fill the vacancy caused by the resignation of John Peter G. Muhlenberg. (Biographical Directory 2020)

[298] "Mr. B" is a reference to Benjamin Franklin Bache, a Philadelphia newspaper editor and the grandson of Benjamin Franklin. The grandfather had financed and directed Bache's education in Europe and America with a strong emphasis on inculcating republican principles. Bache, like most Jeffersonian Republican editors, championed the democratic ideals of the French Revolution and cheered France's military victories in the 1790s. (Ibid; Smith 1999, 81)

[299] Delacroix had written to Monroe. "Our last intelligence informs us that the House of Representatives of the Congress has consented by the majority of fifty-one against forty-eight votes, to carry into execution the treaty concluded at London between the United States and Great Britain in November, 1794. As this advice is derived only from the gazettes I desire, Citizen, that you will be pleased to inform me what official information you have upon this subject. After the chamber of representatives have given its consent to this treaty, we ought, without doubt, to consider it in full force. And as the state of things which results from it merits our profound attention, I wish to learn from you in what light we are to consider the event, which the public papers announce, before I call the attention of the Directory to those consequences which ought specially to interest this Republic." (Hamilton 1900, 9)

to it.[300] It is probable that this act of the Minister proceeds from himself, and not from the Directoire, since it is presumable from the intimation heretofore given me by a very respectable authority and which I communicated to you in my last, that that body had already determined not to trouble us further on that subject, and in which case less inconvenience is to be apprehended from it. But let it proceed from whatever source it may, I shall not fail to use my utmost efforts to prevent its further progress. I shall see the Directoire today at a general audience, being a day (the first Decadi of every month) on which they receive all the foreign Ministers, and as I propose then to speak with some of the Members upon the subject, I shall doubtless be able to give you further, and, I hope, more satisfactory information on that head in my next, I have notwithstanding thought proper to forward to you immediately the above, and am, with great respect and esteem, Sir, your most obedt. humb. Serv, Jas Monroe.

To James Madison, Paris, July 5, 1796

Dear Sir,301— *Yesterday the Fourth of July was celebrated here by the Americans. I intended to have done it but having given them an entertainment last year they returned the compliment this. You will observe by the copy sent in that to the American government the term executive is used and not president. The course of the business was as follows.* The project began *first with the friends of the British treaty and fell through and was then taken up by its enemies and after wh. the others came in. But the first party had appointed a committee (or rather the second in order) and who conducted the business the majority of whom were for giving the Congress only or drinking no toasts. I told them if they wod. give the executive I supposed all would be satisfied and I would attend & wh. I could not otherwise well do. The first party however in order were not consulted or disliked what was done and when the toasts [were] gone thro one of them rose & proposed a volunteer in favor of G. Washington &c and which was opposed by some of the others. This made a noise here and perhaps will with you and as some slander may in consequence be leveled at me I therefore give you the facts. The ministers of France and the foreign ministers were present.*

I trouble you with another incident of the same kind. *Paine having* resolved to continue *in Europe* sometime longer & knowing it was inconvenient *for me to keep him* longer *in my family* & wishing also *to treat on our politicks & which he* could not well *do in my house left me* sometime since. He thinks *the president winked at his*

[300] This paper (found later among the Monroe papers) in the handwriting of his Monroe's secretary appears to be a memorandum of arguments used by Monroe in his efforts to counteract the partisans of war in the Councils of France and to reconcile that Government to the final action of the United States in carrying the treaty with England into effect. (Ibid, 11)

[301] Italicized text in this letter was originally in cipher. Decoded text provided by the National Archives. (Mason and Sisson 2020)

imprisonment and even wished he might *die in goal and bears him resentment for it. He thinks* also he is *shaping an attack* upon *him of* the most *virulent* kind. Thro' *a third person I have endeavoured to divert him from* it without effect. It may be said *I have instigated him but the above is the truth.*

But to come now to a subject of more importance. I think myself ill treated here by the administration and doubt how to act in consequence of it so as to advance the publick interest without injuring my own character. The following is a literal extract from my instructions after many professions of the president's attachment to the French revolution. "And to remove all jealousy with respect to Mr. Jay's mission to London you may say that he is positively forbidden to weaken the engagements between this country and France it is not improbable that you will be obliged to encounter on this head suspicions of various kinds but you may declare the motives of that mission to be to obtain immediate compensation for our plundered property and restitution of the posts." With much more in the same spirit, an equivocation may be taken on the word motives but the true sense is a declaration that he had no other business there and which was otherwise.

The *object I presume was to lay a good basis here by means of my mission and taking advantage of which and of the success of France which would procure us the respect of the English court make a barter for commercial stipulations of our faith and alliance with France and which probably would have succeeded had I not blown them up by discourse in the convention and by their own documents by means whereof that court lost all confidence in them thinking their professions insincere and of course that what it gave was given for nothing or had the negotiator possessed as capable a head as he did a corrupt heart.*[302]

Since the ratification of the treaty by the president I have received but three letters from the Department of State and which were from Timothy Pickering and the last now six months old and these were not of a very conciliatory kind; after denying that this government had any right to complain of the treaty he adds that the article respecting contraband inserted the old list only by way of admonition to our people to avoid danger. *That the provision article was useful to us as it paid us for contraband* and in respect to other *seizures that we were the* only judges *whether we would go to war for cause or otherwise* accommodate the difficulty & would never consult *another power* on that head, and without *any profession of regard for this country or* explanation of *future views breaks off* the subject & thus ends it.

This tone may proceed either from a desire *to court a rupture with this country* or be the effect of wounded pride: and it would be natural to ascribe it *to the last cause if the president* had not owned *that the ratification of the treaty hazarded a war here and if* policy did not dictate as the way to *avoid it a more conciliating* one: or if *he* was not *conciliating thro G. Morris at the same moment the court of England: or if*

---

[302] As intimated in Monroe's September 2, 1794, letter to James Madison, this appears to be a reference to Monroe's initial address to the National Convention where he presented a letter from Secretary of State Edmund Randolph and resolutions on Franco–American relations from the American congress.

*the gasconade business of the flag*303 had not been a desultory *movement calculated to deceive the people of America while it gave disgust here or if a different tone* had not been assumed *in my instructions before the issue of the treaty with England was known* and whilst appearances here were *necessary to obtain a favorable issue.* These considerations make the *motive of this conduct more doubtful than* it otherwise wod. be.

It is however the interest of America to avoid a rupture here and I have in consequence done all in my power to prevent it and I think *and without vanity with some effect. If* things stand as they do here & *our administration changes everything will come right. A new treaty may be formed here* of a different *stamp from that with England &* which will *not only tie the two republicks closer together than they were* ever before *and by ties of interest but by contrasting its credit and advantage with that of the other by reviving the friendship and harmony with this country which was nearly gone and which is desired by our citizens completely relieve us our present dangers and difficulties and ruin the aristocrat faction.* But if *you do not change the administration odium lies with the Republican party who will always be branded as anarchists and the present administration continuing and the interest of the two nations requiring it and surmounting all obstacles a new treaty will be* formed here *under its auspices and which tho less favorable than* might otherwise be obtained will serve *as a colouring* whereby *to deceive posterity as to the nature of the crisis we have passed as well as many of the present day with respect to the merits of the contending parties, still however I consider it as the effect of passion only for Washington is an honest man.*

I have suffered much personal mortification here and for reasons that are obvious and should demand my recall did I not think that my continuance for some time longer was somewhat necessary in the views above suggested. *And did I not wish rather to be recalled than to demand it, for in the last case I am to defend my character to my country and which I would do by a publication of my whole correspondence instructions &* the like, *and which I could not otherwise well do; how long I shall be able to bear my situation I can't say. I will bear it* however till *I hear from you in reply to this or until the ensuing elections shall confirm in office the present tenants.*

I should like much to make a new treaty with this government after things are settled on both sides because I think a good one might be made *for both countries: and in my opinion here is the place to make it; let the trust be committed to a minister in Phil-*

303 On January 1, 1796, the new French minister to America, Pierre Auguste Adet, publicly presented George Washington a flag which celebrated the triumphs of the French Republic and "the American people as her most faithful allies." So that the friendship between the two republics would not be forgotten, the National Convention requested that the French banner be placed in the hall of the people's representatives. With cheers from the crowd ringing in his ears, Washington accepted the tricolor. However, having no desire to display a standard depicting France's military victories, Washington sent the flag and Adet's message to Congress for review and then deposited it in the "archives of the United States." (Conlin 2000, 499)

adelphia and his own credit is the object. *But appeal to the government itself and a* different spirit may be found. And *having borne the storm* whilst *my efforts were employed only to prevent disunion I should like to have an opportunity to promote union.* However *this is of no consequence.*

I most earnestly hope that Mr. Jefferson will be elected and that he will serve; if he is elected every thing will most probably be right *here from that moment and afterwards* on the other side *of the channel. And in my opinion* there never was such *an opportunity offered for the acquisition of great fame in the restoration of national credit abroad and* at *home* as is now presented, independant of the gratification an honest mind will always feel in rendering useful service to his country. He will be able at the same time that he secures *the preponderance of republican councils and gives stability to republican government to conciliate the* well meaning of the other *party and thus give peace to his country.*

In a few words I give you the state of the war. All Italy is in truth subjugated, & peace made with all the powers (either by definitive treaties or provisional agreements) Naples excepted, & who has an Envoy now on the road to treat also. They have all paid or agreed to pay considerable sums, given up pictures, the most celebrated pieces of art, and in truth accepted their authorities from this govt. The representative of St. Peter has agreed to pay 21 millions of livres for the provisional suspension of arms, to give up 100 pictures & 300 manuscripts: to exclude the British from his ports &ca &ca.[304] The French have entered the territory of the Gd. Duke & put a garrison in Leghorn, upon the principle that the Englh. held it, & had violated agnst France the neutrality of Tuscany. In entering they laid hold of ⬜all the english⬜ p⬜rope⬜rty they cod. find wh. they say was worth 7 or 8 millions of livres. And upon the Rhine the same good fortune has attended the French arms. In several engagments the French have prevailed, & seem now to have gained a complete preponderance.[305] In short their success seems to be complete, so much so however as to threaten ruin to the Emperor if he does not make peace, & which is therefore in all probability now at hand. Engld. will be reserved for the last, & agnst whom the resentment of this country if not encreased by its tyde of good fortune is certainly not diminished. Projects are spoken of in regard to that country, wh. never seemed to merit attention before, but wh. now & especially if a peace is made with the Emperor, assume a more serious aspect.[306] You will conjecture these & therefore I will not mention them.

[304] A reference to Pope Pius VI. The Papacy concluded the Armistice at Bologna with Napoleon on 23 June 1796. (Woolf, 1991, 252)

[305] French armies in the summer of 1796 crossed the Rhine, occupied the Palatinate, and penetrated as far as Munich. (Lefebvre 1964, 320)

[306] Monroe was seemingly alluding to French plans for an invasion of Ireland in conjunction with Theobaid Wolfe Tone's uprising. (Ibid.)

July 31.

This is the third copy I have sent you of the above, or rather this is the original of the two already forwarded. Since the above the scene has varied but little in any respect. The French continue to hold their superiority on the Rhine, but press forward with great circumspection, the Austrians retiring to strong positions, protecting their retreat by the strong fortifications wh. line the rivers which empty into the Rhine, on its right bank; & protecting in turn those fortifications. Frankfort is taken by the French, & upon wh. city an imposition was laid of 35 millions of florins, but wh. it is thought cannot be paid.

This will be committed to Dr Edwards & who will hasten home as fast as circumstances will permit.[307] He is possessed of very extensive and correct information of affrs. here, as well in regard to those wh. concern this republick & the war in general, as our own affrs., & to him therefore I refer you for such details as are not here communicated.

From what I learn from the bearer of this and notwithstanding my efforts to prevent it Paine will probably compromit me by publishing some things which he picked up while in my house. It was natural unaided as *I have been here or rather harassed from every quarter that I talk with this man but it was not so to expect that he would commit such a breach of confidence as well as of ingratitude; perhaps it may appear to proceed from other sources if so my name will note involved* and that is greatly to be wished: *but otherwise the above is the state of facts.*

Upon no point but in my relations with either government am I personally uneasy let what may happen and this is a thing *of personal delicacy* more than anything else.

To George Clinton, Paris, July 25, 1796

Dear Sir,—I have been fav'd with yours of 15 of April by Major Fulton by which I was much gratified to hear that you were upon the recovery of yr. health, & wh. I sincerely hope will be completely reestablished soon, for I promise myself much pleasure in yr. compy. upon my return to my country.308

In truth you ought to have good health for twenty years more & I hope you will not be deprived of what you have so just a title to. I think the events on this side of the Atlantick are calculated to chear yr. spirits, and restore

---

[307] Enoch Edwards was an American physician and a leading Patriot during the American Revolution. A close friend of Thomas Jefferson, and he was closely associated with, and trusted by, Monroe during Monroe's tenure in France. (Higginson 1886, 281; Ford 1895, 495-495)

[308] George Clinton was an American soldier and statesman. A prominent Democratic-Republican, Clinton would serve as vice president in the presidential administrations of both Thomas Jefferson and James Madison. (Purcell, 2010, 34-44)

you to health, even were you ever so much reduc'd, for never was the cause of republican gov't more triumphant than it now is here. The armies of France are victorious in every quarter: Italy may be considered as subdued, for the Austrian army after being defeated in several actions has finally fled the field: Sardinia has accepted the terms prescribed by France ceding Savoy & Nice; the Pope does the same, paying money, giving up pictures, &c. Naples now has an envoy on the road to make proposals favorable to France & whereby all that quarter will enjoy peace & upon the terms prescribed by France. The French have also entered Leghorn because the Engl'h held it as a kind of deposit for supplies for Corsica & other parts of the Medeteranean sea & because also the Engl'h had violated the neutrality of Tuscany agnst the

French. Upon the Rhine too their armies are equally successful having defeated the Austrians likewise in several actions : The French are now on the right of the Rhine and are pressing into the interior of the country. Frankfort is taken: indeed they seem to have gained a decided preponderance in that quarter also.

In the interior too the prospect is good: great harmony exists between the two councils & the Directoire & the people, even those heretofore deemed unchangeably hostile to republican govt, begin to relax their enmity & to think it better to rest where they are, which they find good, than hazard everything by new experiments. The general idea is, it is better to remain in the port where they are, than embark again upon a sea, whose storms they still remember with horror.

I think it probable peace will be made soon with the Emperor, tho' it is to be observed that that court is proud and not easily subdued. I hope however France will shew moderation &close with that power now that she stands on such favorable ground to command suitable terms. With Engld the war will still be continued. I beg you to remember me to Mr. M. Smith, Mr. Gelston whose son has been ill but is recoverd & to other friends & that you will believe me affecy, yours Jas Monroe.

I write in haste & therefore can not go into further details. Inform Mr. G his sisters are well.

To Thomas Jefferson, Paris, July 30, 1796

Dear Sir,—I have lately received your favors of the 2d. and 21. of March last and by which I find, to my surprise, that only two letters from me and those of the last year had reached you, tho' I had written one more of the last year and two of the present one.

Frouillé as I informed you in one of these was one of the victims of the reign of terror; Dr. Jemm is living and much gratified to find he has a place in your memory. The old Gentleman was somewhat afflicted with the hypocondria on my arrival, and which proceeded from the horrible abuses that were practic'd rather before that period; but he is now well, having breakfasted with me today, walking a league to do it, and desires to be affectionately remembered to you. I will procure for you the books you mention, but to execute that of the Encyclopedie it will be well for you to send me an account of what you have already received, as otherwise it may be difficult from the confusion which took place, even in those things, here at a certain time; I will also thank you to procure for me a like note of what I have, as I wish to send them at the same time for us both. I believe the work is now complete.

On this side of the water the scene has greatly changed for the better, in favor of republican government: for since the adoption of the New constitution liberty has as it were been rescued from the dust, where she was trampled under foot by the mob of Paris, whose leaders were perhaps in foreign pay, and restored to the elevated station she ought to hold, and where she is becoming as she ought to be, the idol of the country. France never bore, at any period of her history so commanding a position as she now bears, towards all the powers of Europe, nor did she ever approach it. Since the opening of the Campaign all Italy has in a great measure been subjugated. The Austrian army combined with the Sardinian and which protected Italy (by which I mean those powers in the coalition) was vanquished in the very opening of the campaign, in several severe actions, and finally driven thro' the Tyrol country out of Italy. After this, or rather after two or three defeats, Sardinia obtained peace, upon terms you have doubtless seen, and since all the other powers have done the same Naples excepted and who has now an Envoy here to obtain it.[309] They have all paid money, yielded pictures, and in the instance of the pope, manuscripts of great value, and shut the Englh. from their ports.[310] The French have likewise entered Leghorn, on the principle the Engh. held it as a deposit for supplies for Corsica &ca., and had likewise violated the neutrality of Tuscany against the French; and in pursuit of the Austrians who fled that way, they entered after them the Venetian territory. Thus you see the state of affairs in that quarter. Upon the Rhine

---

[309] In a treaty signed with France on 15 May 1796, Sardinia obtained peace by renouncing all ties to the Coalition and allying itself with France. Sardinia maintained existing civil government while allowing free access by the French military. (Stewart 1951, 675)

[310] Beauvais suggests that the French government was so impressed by the pictures, statuary, and antiquities Napoleon Bonaparte sent to France from northern Italy [particularly items from the Papal collection] that the Directory instructed other commanding generals to follow his example. (Beauvais 1876, 516)

too the French have been victorious, in several actions against the Imperial forces, driving them all on the other side, on which side, and some distance in the interior, the French armies now likewise are. They seem indeed to have gained a decided preponderance over their enemies here, tho' by no means in the degree they have in the other quarter; for the Austrian armies tho several times defeated, and seeking apparently to shun for the present a general action are nevertheless strong and united, protecting the country by their positions as well as by the forts which line the rivers emptying into the Rhine. It is often rumoured that negotiations are depending with the Emperor and in Paris, and which I think more than probable but yet know nothing certain on the subject. If the French should not be discomfited by some sudden reverse of fortune, and of which there is at present but little prospect, it cannot well be otherwise than that peace should be made soon with the Emperor, since he must now abandon all hope of recovering the Belgic &c. and since it is to be presumed the French will insist on nothing beyond what they claimed in the commencement of the campaign. It is to be observed they have entered Frankfort and upon which city they have laid an imposition of 35. Millions of florins, a sum I presume beyond the ability of the place to pay it.

The general sentiment is to have no peace with Engld. for the present, and to which they are inclined as well in gratification of the resentment they bear that country for the trouble it has brought on this, as in the policy of keeping some employment for the immense force that will be on foot after the war on the Continent is closed. It seems to be the fixed determination of this government to inflict some great and rigorous punishment upon that nation if in its power, and with this view, and for the purpose of striking at the source of its prosperity all its treaties with the Italian powers are formed, and whereby Engld. will scarcely find admittance into any of their ports. This however is a delicate subject for me to write on, considering this letter passes thro' Engld., the bearer Dr. Edwards prefering that rout to the necessity of making a visit to Halifax or Bermuda, and which he would probably be forcd to do in case he sailed directly from a port of France. To him therefore I refer you for whatever is interesting in this or any other topic omitted here, and relating to French affairs and with which he is perfectly well acquainted.

In the interior relations the aspect is equally flattering as in the exterior. The financial system it is true, is bad, but yet not worse than it has been ever since my arrival. Their national domains is the great fund, and two or three times they have passed laws for throwing this away,[311] but upon an

---

[311] Laws passed on 21 November 21, 1795, and April 25, 1796, had suspended sales of the French domaines nationaux, then restored them as a means of backing the new currency,

idea the plan adopted was solid and would be productive: soon however it was discovered that these plans were visionary, and answered no end but to cede their property and 1 give discontent to the whole nation, a few land jobbers in each district excepted and some foreigners of the same respectable description, and whereupon they came back upon what they had done and remodified it. They seem to consider the ill success of the plan as a kind of breach of contract on the part of the purchasers, and therefore making it void ab initio. One thing however is to be observed that they never do the purchasers any real injustice, so far as to enable them to say they are made to pay even so much as a third of the value of the property: they only give them cause to make a great noise about publick faith &c and which you know none are so apt to make as those who have no faith at all. This government seems to have a horror of banks funding systems &c and therefore attempts every other resource in preference to those.

In other views the prospect is excellent. The party of discontented among those who were marshalled on the side of the revolution, diminishes daily and seems to be gradually reducing to those who dishonored it in the days of Robertspre. and his associates; men who were probably in the pay of foreign powers and employed to perpetrate those atrocities merely to make the revolution odious and thus oppose it, and who in consequence expect punishment from any established order of things. There are it is true some exceptions to this, and among men of principle who seem to fear the government will incline too much into the other scale, but at present I see no cause for such a suspicion. And on the side of royalty, its adherents likewise seem daily to diminish in number, and to be likewise declining to those, who are inflicted with a bias for that kind of government, which nothing can eradicate: upon whose minds no proof can work conviction. But the ranks of this corps throughout France has lessened, since this government was established, comparatively to nothing. Before this event the people of this country estimated the merits of republican government by those of the revolution, and therefore it is not surprising that many, and even among those who were ardent and active agents in putting it in motion, should have shrunk from it. Europe presented no example of republican government or of any other kind of free government, upon which they could dwell with pleasure, and therefore the revolution was their only standard. But since this government was established a new and more impressive example is before them, and which be assured has produc'd already a wonderful effect in reconciling the bulk of

---

the mandats territoriaux. In addition, a proposal by prominent bankers in February 1796 to issue a circulating currency supported by large cessions of national property met approval in the Directory but was stopped by the Five Hundred. (Mason and Sisson, 2020)

the people to it. I have this from many quarters and therefore confide in what I communicate.

This is a short sketch of the actual state of things here, according to the view I have of it, and which may be durable or fluctuating according as events yet depending may unfold themselves: for yet the scene of this great movment is not closed, nor can any one pronounce what its issue will be untill it is closed.

I rejoice that you pay attention to the improvement of my farm near you, since we look to it as to a place of comfort from the unquiet theatre on which we now stand: for to me and in more views than one it has been a very unquiet one indeed. But I think you can readily perceive why it is so, when you contemplate all the circumstances that apply to me, in regard to publick events since my arrival in the country: tis therefore unnecessary and unsafe to enter into them upon the present occasion. We never meant a long continuance here, and probably the term we had in view may yet be shortened. I wish therefore I could form a commencment of the house you suggested this fall or as soon as possible, and upon which head one of my letters was very minute: upon this I shall write you soon again.

I have done every thing in my power in favor of Mr. DeRieux but without effect. We have a small house next his aunt, and which we took to supervise the education of our child at St. Germains, as likewise that of Mr. Jones and a son of John Rutledge's who are at school there, in the hope too of seeing the old Lady and entreating her to assist him. But she shuns me, as she would an officer of the peace from whom she expected a process of the revolutionary kind: and a visit which Mrs. M. made her sometime since in the hope of appeasing her fears, of importunate solicitation, was render'd very disagreeable, by her abruptly opening the subject, as soon as she entered and speaking of nothing else whilst she staid, but the impossibility of rendering any service to her nephew. Under these circumstances it will I fear be impossible to obtain any thing for him. I will however if possible. The order some time since enclosd for his uncle I still have, being unwilling to forward it, lest it should be paid in assignats or mandats, but I will attend to this object also in suitable time.

We are well and desire to be affectionately remembered to Mr. and Mrs. Randolph, Maria, and all our good neighbours. I thank you for information that my brother is well, and the more so because I never hear from him. With great and sincere esteem believe me sincerely your friend & servant Jas Monroe.

I have just heard that I am charged with having become a speculator here, with other things still more exceptionable, and god knows what. I send therefore by this opportunity to Mr. Madison an ample refutation of these charges, advising that they be published if my friends think fit. He will probably see you on the occasion. I think I can ride any storm if I get safe to port from the sea upon which I am now embarked. Surely no man was ever in the hands of such a corps as I am at present. Augt. 6. 96.

To the Secretary of State [Timothy Pickering], Paris, August 4, 1796

Sir,—Within a few days past, Mr. Mangourit, formerly consul at Charleston, now secretary of embassy in Spain, was appointed with the rank of charge d'affaires, to succeed, with us, Mr. Adet.[312] This event, as well in respect to the gentleman employed, as the grade chosen, gave me great concern; and, therefore, merited my immediate attention. Accordingly I visited the Minister of foreign affairs this morning, and remonstrated earnestly against the mission of Mr. Mangourit to the United States; as a person who, having given offence to our government upon a former occasion, could not be well received by it, upon the present one. To the grade, however, I thought proper to make no explicit objection; because I had no reason to conclude that it was chosen with any unfriendly view towards us; and because I presumed, if the measure was broken in one part, it would probably be so in the other. The Minister replied to me in terms sufficiently respectful; but nevertheless, in such as induced me to believe, that in case any change was accorded in the measure, it would not be with his consent. He observed, however, that if I would write him a short note on the subject, he would lay it before the Directoire; and which I promised I would do.

Within a few days past, too, I heard that the Directoire had passed an arrete, authorising the seizure of neutral vessels destined for England; to take effect when the English likewise seize them. This arrete was not announced officially; but by the copy of a letter from the minister to Barthelemi, the French ambassador at Basle, published in the gazettes, I saw that the report was true. In consequence, I likewise spoke to the Minister on this subject;

---

[312] Michel Ange Bernard Mangourit, France's consul to South Carolina, was named to replace Adet, but not as minister. His title would be chargé d'affaires. To Monroe, this was a double snub; Mangourit had been another pest to Washington during Genet's tenure, and this lower title for his duties was another French insult to Washington. This was bad enough, but when Monroe read in a Swiss newspaper that the Directory had already authorized the seizure of American merchantmen carrying British goods in their holds, he paid an immediate visit to Delacroix, who merely assured him Mangourit's appointment had been rescinded. (McGrath 2020, 162)

---

and received from him, in reply to my remonstrance against it, a general answer, corresponding much in sentiment with his letter above mentioned, a copy of which I herewith inclose you.[313]

It is said, that a treaty of alliance, offensive and defensive, between France and Spain, is in great forwardness, whereby the latter cedes to the former Louisiana, and, perhaps the Floridas. I have no authentic information of this; but the source from whence it came is of a nature to merit attention.

I have the pleasure to transmit to you herewith, some communications respecting our affairs at Algiers, by which it appears, that Mr. Barlow had the good fortune to succeed with the Dey, in prolonging the term allotted for the payment of the sum due him, concluded by our late treaty for the ransom of our prisoners, and for peace; and finally, and although the money was not received, that he had obtained the discharge of our prisoners, and who were fortunately arrived safe at Marseilles. Upon this event, therefore, which not only liberates from a long and painful captivity so many of our country-men, but in all probability secures the peace which was endangered by the delay of the money stipulated to be paid, I beg leave to congratulate you; since it is an event, not only important in respect to the consolation which it yields to humanity; but equally so in regard to the extension and security of our commerce, in a region of the world heretofore unexplored by it, and where it promises to be very productive.

I commit this letter, with other communications for you, to the care of Doctor Edwards, who will deliver them in person; and to whom I beg to refer you for other details upon the subject of our affairs here, upon which you may wish information. He has been more than a year in Europe, and the greater part of that time here; has had opportunities of correct information, and which he has improved to advantage. To him, therefore, I beg to refer you, as to an authority well informed, and very deserving of confidence.

I am, with respect and esteem, your most obt. Servt, Jas Monroe.

To James Madison Paris, September 1, 1796

Dear Sir,[314]—Within a few This government has at last and against my utmost efforts to prevent it sent an order to their minister to withdraw giving for reason our treaty with England and declaring that the customary relations between the two nations shall cease. I have no official communication and can't be more particular. After deliberating about seven months they resolved that the honour of their country would be tarnished in their hands

---

[313] Ibid.

[314] Italicized text originally in cipher. Decoded text provided by Hamilton. (Hamilton 1900, 52-54)

if they acted otherwise. They say I have detained them seven months from doing what they ought to have done at once. It is impossible to foresee the consequences of this measure which I sincerely regret but here no change can be expected and of course if the same councils prevail in America the alliance is at an end not to count the other injuries we shall receive from the loss of this nation so preponderant as it is; with such valuable posses-sions in our seas. I do not know whether my functions are suspended; in any event I must wait the orders of our government. At this moment I receive a letter from Timothy315 in reply to my first on this subject addressed as from an overseer to the foreman of his gang ascribing (if not absolutely the existence of any complaint to me) yet that it is altogether owing to my misconduct that it broke out since I had acknowledged a [letter]316 from him three months before which he says proved they had no right [to] complain; hence he concludes that I suppressed that luminous work. To this I have yet given no answer nor do I at present propose. It will occur to you that I could not defend the treaty till there was a charge brought against it and to prevent which was always the object of my efforts. Delay therefore was always favorable. This letter corresponds so much with the publication in the New York paper317 that it tends to create a suspicion they were written by the same hand but these little Connecticut jockey tricks were too easily seen thro' now a days to produce any effect. Poor Washington into what hands has he fallen!

To the Secretary of State [Timothy Pickering], Paris, September 10, 1796

Sir,—I have been just favored with yours of the 13th of June; the only one received from the Department of State, since that of the 7th of January last, a note from Mr. Taylor, of the 13th of May excepted.318

---

315 Timothy Pickering (Ibid 53)

316 Ibid.

317 The newspaper, the "Minerva" of New York, announced, with an affected emphasis, that a letter from Paris to New York, intimating that influential persons in the U.S. were urging measures on France which might force America to choose to be against England as the only alternative for war against France. It is probable that categorical steps on the part of France towards America are anticipated as the consequence of what had been effected by the British party in the United States, and that much artifice would be prac-ticed by it to cast them in some unpopular form on its Republican opponents. (Ibid.)

318 This letter speaks for itself and, for all intents and purposes, is Monroe's forth-right response to Pickering's grievances. In September, Monroe received a Pickering letter dated June 13, 1796. In it, Pickering categorically detailed a litany of criticisms of Monroe's actions in Paris, concluding his observations with abject distain. "It is painful to dwell on this subject." Monroe read both Pickering's lines and what was between them. Obviously, the letter was not painful at all to Pickering. Monroe

You charge me in this letter with a neglect of duty, in omitting, as you state, to dissipate by a timely and suitable application of the lights in my possession the discontents of this government, on account of our late treaty with England; and you support this charge by a reference to certain passages in my own correspondence, which state that this discontent broke out in February last, four months after I had received a letter from yourself and Mr. Randolph, upon the subject of that treaty; and whence you infer, and on account of the delay or interval which took place between the one and the other event, that I was inattentive to that important concern of my country, and urge the previous and strong symptoms of discontent which I witnessed and communicated, as an additional proof of my neglect.

Permit me to remark that this charge is not more unjust and unexpected, than the testimony by which you support it is inapplicable and inconclusive. Indeed it were easy to shew, that the circumstances on which you rely, if they prove anything, prove directly the reverse of what you deduce from them.

If such discontent existed and the formal declaration of it, or commencement of measures in consequence of it was delayed (and the greater the discontent, and the longer the delay, the stronger the argument) and any inference applicable to me was drawn from the circumstance, I should suppose it would be precisely the opposite one from that which you draw. Where a discontent exists, it is natural and usual for the party feeling it, to endeavour to remove it, or express its sense of it; but the pursuit of an opposite conduct for a great length of time, and especially a time of revolution, and when a different and more peremptory one was observed to all the other powers, is no proof, without other documents of negligence in me.

But why did this discontent not break out before these letters were received? You saw by my communications, as early as December 1794, and which were frequently repeated afterwards, that it existed, was felt upon our affairs here, and was likely to produce the most serious ill consequences, if the cause continued to exist. If these accounts were correct, why did this government take no steps under its first impressions, and particularly in August 1795, when Paris was starving, and our vessels destined for the ports

---

was furious, and here, throws caution to the wind as he reveals his most candid thoughts. "You charge me in this letter with a neglect of duty....This charge is not more unjust and unexpected, than the testimony by which you support it." In truth, at this juncture, Monroe was doubtless as tired of being Washington's minister as Washington was of him. He believed he had been set up, not just by Washington's Federalist cabinet but by the man himself. As a diplomat, Monroe had succeeded with the French public, if not their government. Perhaps no American could have prevented the Directory's reaction to the Jay Treaty. Delacroix tactfully pointed out to Monroe that he had not failed; his government had. (McGrath 2020, 162-163)

of France were seized and carried into England? Was not this a crisis difficult for me to sustain here; when the eyes of France were fixed upon me, as
the representative of the nation upon whose friendship they had counted;
as the man who had just before been the organ of declarations the most
friendly? Why leave us afterwards, and until the last stage, to our unbiased
deliberations upon that subject, and without an effort to impede their free
course? Do difficulties like these, with the result which followed, give cause
to suspect that I was idle or negligent at my post? That I was at any time a
calm or indifferent spectator of a storm which was known to be rising, and
which threatened injury to my country? Or that I withheld any light which
came to my aid, and which might be useful in dissipating it?

I do not wish to be understood as assuming to myself the merit of this
delay; because I know, thinking and feeling as the government did on this
subject, that the strong bias of affection which this nation entertained for us,
was the true cause of it. But I well know, that I have done everything in my
power, and from the moment of my arrival to the present time, to promote
harmony between the two republics, and to prevent this from taking any
step which might possibly disturb it, and which I have done as well from a
sincere attachment to both, as from a persuasion, let the merit of the points
in discussion be what they might, that a continual, temperate, and friendly
conduct towards us was the wisest policy which this government could
adopt, and would › produce the best effect upon that union, which it is. I
presume, equally its wish and its interest to preserve, and of course leave to
its councils less cause hereafter for self reproach. It is from the sincerity of
these motives and the knowledge this government has of it, that I have incessantly made efforts to preserve that harmony, and been heard in friendly
communication, and often in remonstrance upon the topics connected with
it, in a manner I could not otherwise have expected.

But you urge, that as I knew this discontent existed, I ought to have
encountered and removed it. I do not distinctly comprehend the extent of
this position, or what it was your wish, under existing circumstances, I
should have done. Till the 15th of February, no complaint was made to me by
this government against that treaty; nor did I know before that period that
any would be, for from the moment of its organization till then, the utmost
reserve was observed to me by it on that subject. The intimations which I
witnessed, were written before the establishment of the present government,
and drawn of course from circumstances which preceded it. Of the probable
views therefore of the present government in that respect, I spoke only by
conjecture. Was it then your wish, that because I suspected this government
would be or was discontented with that treaty, that I should step forward,

invite the discussion, and provoke the attack? Would it have been politic or safe for me to do it; and especially upon a subject so delicate, and important as that was! And had I done it, would I not have been justly censured for my rashness and indiscretion? And might not even different motives have been assigned for my conduct? To me, I own, it always appeared most suitable, as well as most wise, to stand on the defensive; and to answer objections only when they were made; upon the fair and reasonable presumption, till they were made, that none would be; and upon the principle, if none were made, that our object was obtained; and if there were, that then there would be sufficient time to answer them, and in a regular and official manner. By this however I do not wish to be understood, as having declined at any time informal friendly communications, on this or other subjects, when suitable occasions occurred; for the contrary was the case, as is already observed.

What the circumstances were, upon which I founded my opinion of the probable ill consequences of that treaty, in case it were ratified, were in general communicated, as they occurred. There was however one other, and which was particularly impressive at the time, omitted then, but which I now think proper to add, because it was that upon which I founded the intimation given you, in my letter of the 20th of October on that head. Calling one day, upon the subject of our Algerine affairs, informally, upon Jean de Brie, who had, in the committee of public safety, the American branch under his care, I found him engaged upon that treaty, with a copy of it before him, and other papers on the same subject. I began with the object of my visit, and from which he soon digressed upon the other topic, and with great asperity; adding that he was preparing a letter for me on that subject, to be submitted to the committee. I answered his charges in the manner which appeared to me most suitable, and finally asked him, if he had received the correspondence which took place on that subject between Mr. Adet and Mr. Randolph; and to which he replied that he had not. I then informed him I had that correspondence, which was an interesting one; and requested he would permit me to give him a copy of it; and further that he would delay his report to the committee, until after he had perused and fully weighed it, which he promised; and in consequence I immediately afterwards gave him a copy of that correspondence. This incident took place just before the movement of Vendemiaire, by which the execution of the project contemplated was probably prevented. I omitted this before, because I hoped it would never be revived; and because I did not wish to give more pain on this subject, and especially as I soon afterwards found that the treaty was ratified, than could be avoided. And I now mention it, as well to shew the strong ground upon which that intimation was given; as to prove that none of the lights furnished me, in that respect, were withheld.

So much I have thought proper to say in reply to your favor of the 13th of June; and now it remains for me to proceed with a detail of the further progress of this business here, since my last; at least so far as I am acquainted with it.

I sought immediately after my last was written, and obtained as soon as I possibly could obtain it, an informal conference with some members of the Directoire, upon the subject of my last; beginning by expressing my concern to hear they were still dissatisfied with us, and proposed taking some step in consequence thereof; and which I sincerely regretted because I had concluded the contrary was the case, after the explanation I had given to their several complaints; and because I thought any measure which had an unfriendly aspect towards us, would be equally detrimental to theirs and our interest. They severally replied, they were dissatisfied with us, on account of our treaty with England, and thought that the honor of their country would be sullied in their hands, if they did not say so. I endeavoured to lead them into conversation upon the points to which they objected; but soon found they were averse to it, and were of the opinion that too much time had already been bestowed on that subject. One of the members however observed, that the abandonment of the principle that free ships made free goods, in favor of England, was an injury of a very serious kind to France; and which could not be passed by unnoticed. I told him, that in this nothing was abandoned, since by the law of nations, such was the case before; and of course that this article only delineated what the existing law was, as I had fully proved in my note to the minister of foreign affairs; that we were not bound to impose the new principle on other nations. He replied, if we could not carry that principle with England, nor protect our flag against her outrages, that that was always a reason why France should not complain; that they never asked us to go to war, nor intended so to do; but that the abandonment of that principle formally by treaty, at the time and under the circumstances we did it, in favor of that power, was quite a different thing. Finding that a further pressure at the time might produce an ill effect, and would certainly not produce a good one, I proceeded next to the other points, and to hint what I had heard of their intention with respect to Canada and Louisiana, and to which it was replied, that in regard to Canada, they had no object for themselves; and in regard to Louisiana, none which ought to disquiet us; that they sincerely wished us well, and hoped matters might be amicably adjusted, since they were disposed to meet suitable propositions to that effect with pleasure; adding in the close, that the minister of foreign affairs was instructed to communicate to me the arrete they had passed; but in a manner to impress me with a belief it was done rather for the purpose of enabling me to transmit it to you, than address them at present further on the subject. Through other channels I have since heard, that this arrete is withheld from me, and will be, until the dispatch is gone; and with a view of securing themselves against further interruption from me, in the present stage, upon the measure adopted.

From what information I can collect of the contents of this arrete from other sources (for from the above none was collected) it is to suspend Adet's functions; instructing him to declare the motive of it; and which, I presume, will correspond with what was declared here, leaving him there for the present : But what he is farther to do is not suggested, nor can I form a conjecture of it, until I receive the communication promised by the minister of foreign affairs; and which I shall endeavour to procure, as soon as possible.

I herewith enclose you a copy of a communication from the minister of foreign affairs, with my reply to it; and by which it appears that a truce is obtained by our agent from the Regencies of Tunis and Tripoli, and with the aid of France.

I have the honor to be, Sir, your most obt humble servt, Jas Monroe.[319]

---

[319] This is the final item in the source material, *The Writings of James Monroe 1794–1796*, vol.3, edited by Stanislaus Murray Hamilton, published in 1900 by G.P. Putnam and sons, the volume that concludes Monroe's Paris correspondence.

Afterword

Monroe received a letter from the Secretary of State of the August 22, 1796, announcing his recall, with the appointment of General Charles C. Pinckney of South Carolina as his successor. And on December 6, 1796, General Pinckney arrived in Paris and requested that Monroe set a time when they might meet so as to present Monroe with the relevant documents. Although Monroe also requested a meeting with the French in order to introduce Pinckney, on the December 11, he received as note which informed him that the Directory had determined that it would not recognize or receive any Minister from the United States until reparation had been made for their grievances.[320]

Having received his recall in the winter, and there being no American vessel in France which could afford suitable accommodations for his family had he been willing to encounter a passage at that season, her ports being generally blockaded, Monroe was compelled to delay his departure till the spring. During this period be began to perceive, and later wrote "that his recall by his own government had removed from the most jealous and prejudiced in that of France all doubt of the good faith with which he had promoted a good understanding between the two republics, and labored to prevent the French government from adopting any unfriendly measure towards the United States in consequence of their treaty with England, but had excited a generous feeling towards him under the sense of the injury they had done him by that suspicion, he was very anxious to show, so far as he might be able, every expression on its part of that sentiment in his favor." He saw distinctly that every indication of kindness towards him by the government of France, especially after the rejection of General Pinckney, would be

---

[320] Brown, Baker and Ferraro 2017, 193-196.

323

considered by his political opponents as proof of connivance between him and that government, and of the charges alleged against him by the Secretary of State; further that the stronger the expressions of support by the French, the more complete would be the proof of his guilt. He resolved, therefore, to leave France and to proceed to Holland, to remain there during the winter, which he accordingly did. In the spring he returned and passed hastily through Paris to Bordeaux, from where he sailed on April 20, 1797, arriving in Philadelphia at the end of June.[321]

But the administration's conduct had enraged Monroe. Upon his return to the United States, he published an account of his ministry, A View of the Conduct of the Executive, in the Foreign Affairs of the United States, Connected with the Mission to the French Republic, during the years 1794, 1795, 1796, in which he criticized the conduct of the Washington administration. In it, Monroe laid out his entire three-year ministry, complete with accompanying correspondence. In his private letters he lashed out at Washington, acerbically deriding the tone of his famous farewell address as akin to historical monarchs who "practiced ingratitude in their transactions with other great powers." He continued with a typical anti-Federalist tirade, asserting that "where these men will plunge our affairs God only knows, but such a collection of vain, superficial blunderers, to say no worse of them, were never I think before placed at the head of any respectable State." According to Monroe, America had enjoyed a standing with France "so advantageous...so easy to preserve! And yet all these advantages have been thrown away." The administration instead sought to "plunge us into a war with our ancient ally, and on the side of the kings of Europe contending against her for the subversion of liberty!" The Federalists, Monroe claimed, hoped to bring the United States in line with England and had in the process thrown "our national honor ... in the dust." All this might easily have been avoided. If the administration had simply "stood well with France...we might have preserved our ancient renown...and even appeared as a defender of liberty" without the necessity of reverting to arms. This last is a critical point. Monroe primarily wanted to lend moral support for republicanism in France. He did not advocate U.S. military intervention in the French Revolution, but he wanted the government to provide unequivocal ideological support for the cause. By failing to do so the United States had squandered an opportunity that would haunt the nation for ages to come, "nor will centuries suffice to raise us to the high ground from which we have fallen."[322]

---

[321] Ibid.
[322] Poston 2016, 294-295.

Due to the potential inflammatory nature of the scathing critique of his administration, George Washington, unsurprisingly, swiftly obtained a copy and read it with interest, responding extensively in the margins. The tone of Washington's response is obvious from Monroe's very first sentence.[323] Monroe writes, "In the month of May, 1794, I was invited by the President of the United States, through the Secretary of State, to accept the office of minister plenipotentiary to the French Republic." Washington ripostes, "After several attempts had failed to obtain a more eligible character."[324] It is a fascinating document that offers considerable insight into "the times."

After Monroe left Paris in 1797, his political career soared while republicanism in France collapsed. Monroe was elected governor of Virginia in 1799 and helped Jefferson win the presidency in 1800. He went on to serve as Secretary of War and Secretary of State under his friend James Madison, before being elected in his own right as the fifth President of the United States in 1816 where he served two terms. James Monroe died in New York City on July 4, 1831, at 73 years of age.

[323] Wolfe 2012.
[324] Monroe 1797, iii.

Works Cited

Adams, Randolph Greenfield. *A History of the Foreign Policy of the United States.* New York: Macmillan, 1924.

Alger, John Goldworth. *Englishmen in the French Revolution.* London: Sampson Low, Marston, Searle & Rivington, 1889.

American Philhellenes Society. "George Jarvis," 2020.

Ammon, Harry. *James Monroe: The Quest for National Identity.* Charlottesville: University of Virginia Press, 2001.

Archontology.org. "Jean Antoine Joseph de Bry," 2020.

Ashton, John. *Old Times: A Picture of Social Life at the End of the Eighteenth Century.* London: John C. Nimmo, 1885.

Atkin, Nicholas, Michael Biddiss, and Frank Tallett, *The Wiley-Blackwell Dictionary of Modern European History since 1789.* Malden, MA: Wiley-Blackwell, 2011.

Aulard, F. A. *The French Revolution: A Political History 1789–1804*, trans. Bernard Miall. Vol. 3. London: T. Fisher Unwin, 1910.

Banning, Lance. *The Sacred Fire of Liberty: James Madison and the Founding of the Federal Republic.* Ithaca, NY: Cornell University Press, 1995.

Barrow, Robert G. "Editors Page." *Journal of the Early Republic.* Vol. 5, No. 2, (1985).

Beach, Vincent, et al. in *Historical Dictionary of France from the 1815 Restoration to the Second Empire*, ed. Edgar Leon Newman and Robert Lawrence Simpson. New York: Greenwood Press, 1987.

Beauvais de Preau, Charles Théodore, ed. Victoires, Conquêtes, Désastres. Vol. 3. Paris: *1876.*

Bickman, Troy. *The Weight of Vengeance: The United States, the British Empire, and the War of 1812.* New York NY: Oxford University Press, 2012.

Biographical Directory of the United States Congress, "Biography of George Logan." Washington, D.C.: U.S. Congress, 2020.

Blumenthal, Henry. *France and the United States: Their Diplomatic Relations, 1789–1914.* Chapel Hill, NC: University of North Carolina Press, 1970.

Bond, Beverly W. *The Monroe Mission to France 1794=1796.* Baltimore: John Hopkins Press, 1897.

Bowman, Albert Hall. *The Struggle for Neutrality: Franco–American Diplomacy During the Federalist Era.* Knoxville: The University of Tennessee Press, 1974.

Brace, Richard Munthe. "The Problem of Bread and the French Revolution at Bordeaux." *The American Historical Review* 51, No. 4 (1946).

Brant, Irving. *The Fourth President: A Life of James Madison.* Indianapolis: Bobbs-Merrill, 1970.

Broadwater, Jeff. *James Madison: A Son of Virginia & a Founder of the Nation.* Chapel Hill, NC: University of North Carolina Press, 2012.

Brown, Gordon S. *Toussaint's Clause: The Founding Fathers and the Haitian Revolution.* Jackson, MS: University of Mississippi Press, 2005.

Brown, Stuart Gerry. *The First Republicans: Political Philosophy and Public Policy in the Party of Jefferson and Madison.* Syracuse. NY: Syracuse University Press, 1954.

Brown, Stuart, Donald G. Baker and William M. Ferraro. *The Autobiography of James Monroe.* Syracuse, NY: Syracuse University Press. Kindle Edition, 2017.

Buel, Richard, Jr. *Joel Barlow: American Citizen in a Revolutionary World.* Baltimore, MD: Johns Hopkins Press, 2011.

Burstein, Andrew. "Jefferson's Madison versus Jefferson's Monroe." *Presidential Studies Quarterly,* 28 No. 2 (1998).

Burton, Richard D. E., *Blood in the City: Violence and Revelation in Paris, 1789–1945.* Ithaca, NY: Cornell University Press, 2001.

Campbell, Heather (ed.) "Constitution of 1795, Year II." *Britannica.* Chicago: Britannica Group, 2020.

_____. "Chouan" *Britannica.* Chicago: Britannica Group, 2020.

Campbell, Wesley J. "The French Intrigue of James Cole Mountflorence." *The William and Mary Quarterly,* 62, (2008).

Cantor, Milton. "Joel Barlow's Mission to Algiers." *The Historian,* 25 No. 2 (1963).

Carrière, Joseph Médard. "Early Examples of the Expressions 'American Language' and 'Langue Américaine'." *Modern Language Notes* 75, No. 6 (1960).

Chandler, David G. *The Campaigns of Napoleon.* New York, NY: Macmillan, 1966.

Charles, Joseph. "The Jay Treaty: The Origins of the American Party System." *The William and Mary Quarterly,* 12 No. 4 (1955).

Chesney, Robert M. "Democratic-Republican Societies, Subversion, and the Limits of Legitimate Political Dissent in the Early Republic." *North Carolina Law Review* 82, No. 5 (2004).

Chisholm, Hugh, ed. "Drouet, Jean Baptiste." *Encyclopædia Britannica. Vol. 8.* Cambridge: Cambridge University Press, 1911.

Clercq, Alexandre Jehan Henry, ed. *Treaty Series of France: 1713–1802.* Paris: A. Durand and Pedone-Laurie, 1864.

Clifford, John Garry. "A Muddy Middle of the Road. The Politics of Edmund Randolph, 1790⊡1795." *The Virginia Magazine of History and Biography* 80, No. 3 (1972).

Clifford, John H. *Standard History of the World.* New York: The University Society Inc, 1914.

Cobban, Alfred. *A History of Modern France.* Vol. 1. Baltimore, MD: Penguin Books, 1961.

Cobbett, William. *Parliamentary History of England.* Vol. 32. London: Bagshaw, 1818.

Conlin, Michael F. "The American Mission of Citizen Pierre-Auguste Adet: Revolutionary Chemistry and Diplomacy in the Early Republic." *The Pennsylvania Magazine of History and Biography* 124, No. 4 (2000).

Connelly, Owen and Fred Hembree, *The French Revolution.* Arlington Heights, IL: Harlan Davidson, 1993.

Cooper, Jules. *Recollections of the Private Life of General Lafayette.* London: Baldwin and Cradock, 1835.

Corvisier, André and John Childs. *A Dictionary of Military History and the Art of War.* Hoboken, NJ: Wiley-Blackwell, 1994.

Craiutu, Aurelian. *A Virtue for Courageous Minds: Moderation in French Political Thought, 1748–1830.* Princeton, NJ: Princeton University Press, 2012.

Crook, Malcolm, ed., *Revolutionary France: 1788–1880.* New York: Oxford University Press, 2002.

Dallas, Alexander James. "The Children of George Meade." *The American Catholic Historical Researches* 5, No. 1 (1888).

Davis, Curtis Carroll. "An American Courtier in Europe: Lewis Littlepage." *Proceedings of the American Philosophical Society* 101, No. 3 (1957).

Davis, William Stearns, *A History of France from the Earliest Times to the Treaty of Versailles.* Boston: Houghton Mifflin, 1919.

Dawson, Matthew Q. *Partisanship and the Birth of America's Second Party, 1796–1800: Stop the Wheels of Government.* Westport, CT: Greenwood Press, 2000.

De Bellaigue, Geoffrey. "Huzza the King Is Well!" *The Burlington Magazine* 126, No. 975 (1984).

_____. *The Life and Letters of John Paul Jones.* Vol. 1. New York: C. Scribner's Sons, 1913.

DeConde, Alexander. *A History of American Foreign Policy.* New York: Charles Scribner's Sons, 1963.

Dekker, Rudolf M. and Judith A. Vega, "Women and the Dutch Revolutions of the Late Eighteenth Century." *Political and Historical Encyclopedia of Women,* ed. Christine Fauré. New York: Routledge, 2003.

Desan, Suzanne. *The Family on Trial in Revolutionary France.* Berkeley CA: University of California Press, 2004.

Dodge, Theodore Ayrault. *Warfare in the Age of Napoleon: The Revolutionary Wars Against the First Coalition in Northern Europe and the Italian Campaign, 1789–1797.* United Kingdom: Leonaur Ltd, 2011.

Doyle, William Doyle. *The Oxford History of the French Revolution.* Oxford: Oxford University Press, 1990.

_____. *The Oxford History of the French Revolution.* Oxford: Oxford University Press, 1989.

Duruy, George, ed., *Memoirs of Barras, Member of the Directorate.* Vol. 2. New York: Harper and Brothers, 1895.

Dusenbury, Jonathan E. "Motives of Humanity: Saint-Domingan Refugees and the Limits of Sympathetic Ideology in Philadelphia." Amherst MA: University of Massachusetts Press, 2014.

Farnham, Thomas J. "The Virginia Amendments of 1795: An Episode in the Opposition to Jay's Treaty." *The Virginia Magazine of History and Biography* 75, No. 1 (1967).

Fennell, Christopher. "Speculative Holdings in Kentucky and Elsewhere" in *The Ash Lawn-Highland Plantation and History of James Monroe's Land Holdings.* Urbana, IL: University of Illinois, Department of Anthropology, 2012.

Ferling, John E. *Apostles of Revolution: Jefferson, Paine, Monroe and the Struggle against the Old Order in America and Europe.* New York NY : Bloomsbury, 2018.

_____. *A Leap in the Dark: The Struggle to Create the American Republic.* New York NY: Oxford University Press, 2003.

_____. *Adams vs. Jefferson: The Tumultuous Election of 1800.* New York NY: Oxford University Press, 2004.

Fischer, David Hackett. *Paul Revere's Ride.* New York: Oxford University Press, 1994

Fischer, Hartwig. "Monneron Brothers." *The British Museum.* London: UK, 2020.

Fish, Hamilton. *Treaties and Conventions Concluded between the United States of America and Other Powers Since July 4, 1776.* Washington, D.C.: Government Printing Office, 1873.

Ford, Guy Stanton. *Hannover and Prussia 1795–1803: A Study in Neutrality.* New York NY: Columbia University Press, 1903.

Ford, Paul Leicester, ed. *The Writings of Thomas Jefferson: 1792–1794.* New York: G. P. Putnam's Sons, 1895.

Formisano, Ronald P. *For the People: American Populist Movements from the Revolution to the 1850s.* Chapel Hill, NC: University of North Carolina Press, 2008.

Forsdick, Charles. "Postcolonializing the Bagne." *French Studies.* Vol. 72, No. 2 (April 2018).

Fremont-Barnes *The Encyclopedia of the French Revolutionary and Napoleonic Wars,* Santa Barbara CA: ABC-Clio, 2006.

_____. *The Royal Navy 1793–1815.* Colchester UK: Osprey Publishing, 2007.

Frey, Linda S. and Marsha L. Frey. *The French Revolution.* Westport, CT: Greenwood Press, 2004.

Gardner, Hall. "NATO Enlargement and Geostrategic History: Alliances and the Question of War or Peace." *NATO for a New Century: Atlanticism and European Security.* ed. Carl C. Hodge. Westport, CT: Praeger, 2002.

Gilje, Paul A. *Free Trade and Sailors' Rights in the War of 1812.* New York NY: Cambridge University Press, 2013.

Green, Thomas Marshall. *The Spanish Conspiracy A Review of Early Spanish Movements in the Southwest.* Cincinnati OH: R. Clarke & Co, 1891.

Greenstein, Fred I. "The Political Professionalism of James Monroe." *Presidential Studies Quarterly* 39, No. 2 (2009).

Hamilton, Alexander, and Harold C. Syrett. *The Papers of Alexander Hamilton.* Vol. 20. New York: Columbia NY: Columbia University Press, 1974.

Hamilton, Stanislaus Murray. *The Writings of James Monroe 1794–1796.* Vol. 1. London UK: G. P. Putnam's Sons, 1898.

_____. *The Writings of James Monroe 1778–1794*. Vol. 2. London UK: G. P. Putnam's Sons, 1899.

_____. *The Writings of James Monroe 1794–1796*. Vol. 3. London UK: G. P. Putnam's Sons, 1900.

Hanson, Paul R. *Contesting the French Revolution*. New York NY: Wiley, 2009.

Harkins, James. "The Socialism of Gracchus Babeuf on the Eve of the French Revolution." *Science & Society* 54, No. 4 (1990).

Harper, John Lamberton. *American Machiavelli: Alexander Hamilton and the Origins of U.S. Foreign Policy*. New York: Cambridge University Press, 2004.

Hart, Albert Bushnell, ed. "National Expansion, 1783–1845." *American History told by Contemporaries*. New York NY: The McMillian Company, 1901.

Hayes, Carlton J. H. *A Political and Social History of Modern Europe*. Vol. 1. New York NY: Macmillan, 1916.

Hayes, Kevin J. *The Road to Monticello: The Life and Mind of Thomas Jefferson*. New York NY: Oxford University Press, 2008.

Hazen, Charles Downer. *Contemporary American Opinion of the French Revolution*. Baltimore, MD: John Hopkins Press, 1897.

Headley, J.T. *Washington and His Generals*. Vol. 2. New York NY: Baker & Scribner, 1848.

Heath, John Morgan and William Barnes. *The Foreign Service of the United States: Origins, Development, and Functions*. Washington, DC: Washington Historical Office, Bureau of Public Affairs, Department of State, 1961.

Higginson, Thomas Wentworth. *A Larger History of the United States of America to the Close of President Jackson's Administration*. New York NY: Harper & Brothers, 1886.

Homan, Gerlof D. *Jean-Francois Reubell: French Revolutionary, Patriot, and Director (1747–1807)*. The Hague NL: Nijhoff, 1972.

Hume, Edgar Erskine. "A Proposed Alliance Between the Order of Malta and the United States, 1794: Suggestions Made to James Monroe as American Minister in Paris." *The William and Mary Quarterly*, 16 No. 2 (1936).

Hunter, Brooke. "Wheat, War, and the American Economy during the Age of Revolution." *The William and Mary Quarterly*, Third Series, 62, No. 3 (2005).

Ingram, Augustus E. "Early American Consular Service Notes." *The American Foreign Service Journal*. Vol. 6, No. 4 (1929).

Israel, Jonathan. *The Dutch Republic: Its Rise, Greatness, and Fall, 1477–1806*. Oxford UK: Clarendon Press, 1995.

Jacobs, James Ripley. *Tarnished Warrior: Major-General James Wilkinson.* New York NY: Macmillan, 1938.

Jefferson, Thomas. "Two Unpublished Letters of Thomas Jefferson." *The William and Mary Quarterly,* 17, No. 1 (1908).

_____. *Papers,* ed. Barbara B. Oberg. Vol. 38. Princeton, NJ: Princeton University Press, 1950.

Johnston, R.M. *The French Revolution: A Short History* New York NY: Henry Holt, 1909.

Jordan, John Woolf. *Colonial and Revolutionary Families of Pennsylvania.* Vol. 1. New York NY: Clearfield, 1911.

Kaplan, Lawrence S. *Jefferson and France: An Essay on Politics and Political Ideas.* New Haven, CT: Yale University Press, 1967.

Keitner, Chimene. "The Forgotten History of Foreign Official Immunity," 87. *New York University Law Review* (2012).

Kennedy, Paul M. *The Rise and Fall of the Great Powers: Economic Change and Military Conflict from 1500 to 2000.* New York NY: Vintage Books, 1989.

Kurtz, John W. *John Frederick Oberlin.* New York NY: Routledge, 2018

Langguth, A.J. *Patriots: The Men Who Started the American Revolution.* New York NY: Simon and Schuster, 1988.

Lardner, Dionysius, and Mary Shelley. *Lives of the Most Eminent Literary and Scientific Minds of France.* Vol. 2. London UK: Longman, Orme, Brown, Green and Longmans, 1839.

Lee, William. *A Yankee Jeffersonian: Selections from the Diary and Letters of William Lee of Massachusetts, Written from 1796 to 1840.* ed. Mary Lee Mann. Cambridge UK: Belknap Press of Harvard University Press, 1958.

Lefebvre, Georges. *Thermidorians and The Directory.* New York NY: Random House, 1964.

Leo Gershoy, *The Era of the French Revolution, 1789–1799: Ten Years That Shook the World.* New York NY: D. Van Nostrand, 1957.

Levy, Darline Gay. *The Journal of Modern History* 72, No. 3 (2000).

Loizos, Demetris I. "Franco–American Relations and the Elections of 1792 in the U.S.A." *Anistoriton,* 32, June 2003.

Lucchesini, Girolamo. *Causes and Effects of the Confederation of the Rhine.* London UK: John Warren, 1821.

Lynch, Joseph M. *Negotiating the Constitution: The Earliest Debates over Original Intent.* Ithaca, NY: Cornell University Press, 1999.

Mansel, Philip. *Paris Between Empires 1814–1852.* London UK: John Murray, 2001.

Markham, F. M. H. *Napoleon and the Awakening of Europe.* London UK: English Universities Press, 1954.

Markoff, John. *The Abolition of Feudalism: Peasants, Lords, and Legislators in the French Revolution.* University Park, PA: Pennsylvania State University Press, 1996.

Marzagalli, Silvia. "Establishing Transatlantic Trade Networks in Time of War: Bordeaux and the United States, 1793–1815." *The Business History Review* 79, No. 4 (2005).

Mason, Thomas A. and Jeanne K. Sisson (eds). "To James Madison from James Monroe, 8 September 1795," *Founders Online* Washington, DC: National Archives and Records Administration, 2020.

Mason, Laura. *Singing the French Revolution: Popular Culture and Politics, 1787–1799.* Ithaca, NY: Cornell University Press, 1996.

Mayer, Arno J. *The Furies: Violence and Terror in the French and Russian Revolutions.* Princeton, NJ: Princeton University Press, 2000.

McGrath, Tim. *James Monroe: A Life.* New York: Dutton, 2020.

McPhee, Peter. *The French Revolution, 1789–1799.* New York NY: Oxford University Press, 2002.

Mitchell, Broadus. *Heritage from Hamilton.* New York NY: Columbia University Press, 1957.

Mitchell, Julia Post. *St. Jean De Crevecoe.* New York NY: Columbia University Press, 1916. 222.

Monroe, James. *A View of the Conduct of the Executive in the Foreign Affairs of the United States: Connected with the Mission to the French Republic, During the Years 1794, 5, & 6.* Philadelphia: Benjamin Franklin Bache, 1797.

Moore, John Bassett. *The Principles of American Diplomacy.* New York NY: Harper and Brothers, 1918.

Morris, Richard J. "Redefining the Economic Elite in Salem, Massachusetts, 1759–1799: A Tale of Evolution, Not Revolution." *The New England Quarterly* 73, No. 4 (2000).

Office of the Historian. "Edmund Jennings Randolph." Washington, D.C.: U.S. Department of State, 2020.

_____. "John Quincy Adams, Chiefs of Mission for Netherlands." Washington, D.C.: U.S. Department of State, 2020.

_____. "Timothy Pickering." Washington, D.C.: U.S. Department of State, 2020.

Oosterveld, Willem Theo. *The Law of Nations in Early American Foreign Policy: Theory and Practice from the Revolution to the Monroe Doctrine.* Boston MA: Brill Nijhoff, 2016.

Owen Connelly and Fred Hembree, *The French Revolution.* Arlington Heights, IL: Harlan Davidson, 1993.

Palmer, R. R. "Much in Little: The Dutch Revolution of 1795." *The Journal of Modern History,* 26 No. 1 (1954).

Parmet, Herbert S. and Marie B. Hecht, *Aaron Burr: Portrait of an Ambitious Man.* New York: Macmillan, 1967.

Perkins, Bradford. *The First Rapprochement: England and the United States, 1795–1805.* Philadelphia PA: University of Pennsylvania Press, 1955.

Perkins, Dexter. *A History of the Monroe Doctrine.* Boston MA: Little, Brown, 1955.

Popkin, Jeremy D. *A New World Begins: The History of the French Revolution.* New York NY: Basic Books, 2020.

Poston, Brook Carl. *James Monroe and Historical Legacy.* Ft. Worth, TX: Texas Christian University, 2012.

_____. "Bolder Attitude: James Monroe, the French Revolution, and the Making of the Monroe Doctrine." *The Virginia Magazine of History and Biography* 124, No. 4 (2016).

Preston, Daniel. *A Comprehensive Catalogue of the Correspondence and Papers of James Monroe.* Vol. 1. Westport, CT: Greenwood, 2001.

Preston, James. *James Monroe: Life Before the Presidency.* University of Virginia, Miller Center: Charlottesville, VA, 2020.

Public Affairs, *A Little History of the U.S. Consulate General Hamburg.* Hamburg, Germany: U.S. Consulate General, 2019.

Purcell, L Edward. "George Clinton." *Vice Presidents.* New York NY: Facts on File, 2010.

Purviance Family Papers, Archives and Manuscripts. "Biography of John Henry Purviance." Durham, NC: Duke University, 2020.

Rice, Howard C. "James Swan: Agent of the French Republic 1794–1796." *The New England Quarterly* 10, No. 3 (1937).

Richards, Sylvie L. F. "Alexander Hamilton, Trusts and Estates." New York, NY: Law Offices, 2016.

Riley, James C. "Foreign Credit and Fiscal Stability: Dutch Investment in the United States, 1781–1794." *The Journal of American History* 65, No. 3 (1978).

Rives, G. L. "Spain and the United States in 1795." *The American Historical Review* 4, No. 1 (1898).

Rives, John C.(ed). *The Congressional Globe Containing the Debates and Proceedings of the Thirty-Fifth Congress*. Princeton, N.J.: Princeton Microfilm Corporation, 1858.

Robertson, William Spence. "Documents Concerning the Consular Service of the United States in Latin America." *The Mississippi Valley Historical Review* 2, No. 4 (1916).

Rothenberg, Gunther E. "Soldiers and the Revolution: The French Army, Society, and the State, 1788–99" *The Historical Journal* 32, No. 4 (1989).

Rudé, George E. "Prices, Wages and Popular Movements in Paris during the French Revolution." *The Economic History Review* 6, No. 3 (1954).

Sargent, Thomas J., and François R. Velde. "Macroeconomic Features of the French Revolution." *Journal of Political Economy* 103, No. 3 (1995).

Scherr, Arthur. *John Adams, Slavery, and Race: Ideas, Politics, and Diplomacy in an Age of Crisis*. Santa Barbara, CA: ABC-CLIO, 2018.

Scott, Samuel F. and Barry Rothaus, eds., *Historical Dictionary of the French Revolution 1789–1799*. Vol. 1. Westport, CT: Greenwood Press, 1985.

Scott, Samuel F. *Historical Dictionary of the French Revolution 1789–1799*. Vol. 2. Westport, CT: Greenwood Press, 1985.

Seaburg, Carl, and Stanley Paterson. *Merchant Prince of Boston: Colonel T. H. Perkins, 1764–1854*. Cambridge MA: Harvard University Press, 1971.

Short, John Cleves. "William Short, The Second President of Phi Beta Kappa." *The Phi Beta Kappa Key* 4, No. 5 (1920).

Smith, Digby. *The Napoleonic Wars Data Book*. London UK: Greenhill, 1998.

Smith, Jeffery A. *War & Press Freedom: The Problem of Prerogative Power*. New York NY: Oxford University Press, 1999.

Smith, Walter Burges. "America's Diplomats and Consuls of 1776–1865." Washington, D.C.: Foreign Service Institute, U.S. Dept. of State, 1987.

Southwick, Leslie. *Presidential Also-Rans and Running Mates, 1788 through 1996*. Jefferson, NC: McFarland, 1998.

Sparks, Jared. *The Writings of George Washington: Being His Correspondence, Addresses, Messages, and Other Papers, Official and Private, with a Life of the Author*. Vol. 11. Boston MA: Little, Brown and Company, 1858.

Stephens, H. Morse. *A History of the French Revolution*. Vol. 1. New York NY: Charles Scribner's Sons, 1911.

Stewart, John A. *A Documentary Survey of the French Revolution*, New York NY: Macmillan Company, 1951.

Teclaff, Ludwik A. "United States River Treaties." *Fordham Law Review* 31, No. 4 (1963).

Thomas Jefferson Foundation. "James Monroe." *Monticello, Home of Thomas Jefferson.* 2019.

Thompson, J.M. *The French Revolution.* New York NY: Oxford University Press, 1945.

Tilly, Charles. "The Analysis of a Counter-Revolution." *History and Theory* 3, No. 1 (1963).

Tomokiyo, Satoshi. "Thomas Jefferson's Codes and Ciphers., *Cryptiana,* 2014.

Tracy, Uriah. "Monroe's View of the Conduct of the Executive Connected with a Mission to the French Republic in the Years, 1794–1796. *The Magazine of History, with Notes and Queries.* Tarrytown, NY: William Abbatt, 1915.

Turner, Frederick Jackson. "Jean Baptiste Ternant, Edmond Charles Genet, Pierre-Auguste Adet, Létombe, and Joseph Fauchet. *Correspondence of the French Ministers to the United States, 1791–1797.* Washington D.C.: Government Printing Office, 1904.

Tyler, Lyon G. "Terrill Family." *William and Mary College Quarterly Historical Magazine.* Vol. 13. (1905).

Unger, Harlow Giles. *The Last Founding Father.* Boston MA: Da Capo Books, 2011.

United States Court of Claims. *French Spoliation Cases: Opinions of the Court, with Findings of Fact.* Washington D.C. Government Printing Office, 1886.

United States House of Representatives. "Biography of John Fowler." Washington, D.C.: U.S. Congress, 2020.

_____. "Biography of Alexander Dalrymple Orr." Washington, D.C.: U.S. Congress, 2020.

United States Senate. "Biography of Aaron Burr." Washington, D.C.: U.S. Congress, 2020.

_____. "Biography of James Ross." Washington, D.C.: U.S. Congress, 2020.

_____. "Biography of John Langdon." Washington, D.C.: U.S. Congress, 2020.

_____. "Biography of Pierce Butler." Washington, D.C.: U.S. Congress, 2020.

Valentine, Alan. *Lord George Germain.* Oxford, UK: Clarendon Press, 1962.

Varg, Paul A. *Foreign Policies of the Founding Fathers.* East Lansing, MI: Michigan State University Press, 1963.

Vincent, Bernard. *The Transatlantic Republican: Thomas Paine and the Age of Revolutions*. Amsterdam NL: Rodopi, 2005.

Vincent, John Martin. *International and Colonial History*. Vol. 25. Baltimore, MD: Johns Hopkins Press, 1907

Virginia Historical Society. "The Brockenbrough Family." *The Virginia Magazine of History and Biography* 5, No. 4 (1898).

Walt, Stephen M. *Revolution and War*. Ithaca, NY: Cornell University Press, 1996.

Watkins, William J. "We Have Not a Government: The Articles of Confederation and the Road to the Constitution." *Independent Review* 24, No. 2 (2019).

Watson, Robert P. *The Presidents' Wives: Reassessing the Office of First Lady*. Boulder, CO: L. Rienner, 2000.

White, Andrew Dickson. *Fiat Money Inflation in France: How It Came, What It Brought, and How It Ended*. New York NY: D. Appleton &company, 1933.

Williams, Greg H. *The French Assault on American Shipping, 1793–1813: A History and Comprehensive Record of Merchant Marine Losses*. London UK: McFarland and Company, 2009.

Wolfe, Brendan. "Read and Then Riposte." *George Washington, Virginia History*. Charlottesville, VA: Project Blog, *Encyclopedia Virginia*, 2012.

Wood, Gordon S. *Empire of Liberty: A History of the Early Republic, 1789–1815*. New York NY: Oxford University Press, 2009.

Woods, C. J. "Samuel Turner's Information on the United Irishmen, 1797–1798." *Analecta Hibernica*, 42 (2011).

Woolf, Stuart. *Napoleon's Integration of Europe*. New York NY: Routledge, 1991.

Ziesche, Philipp. *Cosmopolitan Patriots: Americans in Paris in the Age of Revolution*. Charlottesville VA: University of Virginia Press, 2010.

Index

Printed in the United States
by Baker & Taylor Publisher Services